LEEDS 1
FIASCO[1]

The story of the 2013/2014 season

[1] Definition, Oxford English Dictionary:
"A complete failure, especially a ludicrous or humiliating one"

If you get the chance, and if you are not offended by the odd rude word or six, click the link below and have a listen to @BigDaveLUFC s witty little number going by the same title, "Leeds United Fiasco"[2] sung to the tune of Ronnie Hilton's 1964 release, "Leeds United Calypso"

[2] *http://BigDLUFC sings Leeds United Fiasco*

By the same author:
All books available from Amazon.co.uk

**LEEDS UNITED,
IN PURSUIT OF
THE PREMIERSHIP**
The 2010/2011 season

**LEEDS UNITED,
LIGHT AT THE END OF
THE TUNNEL**
The 2011/2012 season

**LEEDS UNITED,
Déjà vu**
The 2012/2013 season

Click link for David's Amazon page: www.amazon.co.uk

LEEDS UNITED, FIASCO

The story of the 2013/2014 season

The author recounts his own story of following Leeds United home and away as they continue their quest to return to the Premiership.

David Watkins

Front cover photograph: David Watkins with his collection of programmes from the 2013/2014 season.

First published 2014
This paperback edition published 2014

Copyright © 2014 by David Watkins

No part of this book may be reproduced, stored in a retrieval system, or transmitted by any means without the prior written permission of the author

ISBN 9781849144636
ISBN10 184914463X

Self-Published using CompletelyNovel.Com

Websites: http://dlw10.wix.com/inpursuitofthepremiership

http://t.co/4WbqA9Rdb5

http://www.completelynovel.com/search?query=david+watkins+leeds+united&commit=Go

ACKNOWLEDGEMENTS

Once again this is my opportunity to thank everyone who has helped to bring this latest episode in Leeds United's pursuit of the Premiership to life.

I am indebted to my good friend Brian for once again agreeing to do the proof reading – though of course I take full responsibility for any errors or omissions contained in the text.

I am sure that my other life, at home with the family, must suffer to some degree from my addiction to Leeds United, and so to Karen, Mark and Adam, I once again apologise for my regular absences and for decimating the family budget on match tickets, fuel, train fares, and, ahem, burgers and beer!

To the many fans who I now share my match-days with, I also say thank you; very many of you will be mentioned within these pages, albeit no doubt with aliases or nicknames...you will know who you are! Part of the joy I get from following Leeds is meeting you folks every week all over the country and I know we are all going to have one hell of a celebration when this enforced absence from the Premiership finally comes to an end as it must surely do soon.

Finally, assuming Massimo Cellino is allowed to continue to drive the Leeds United bus, I thank him in advance for his passion and determination to help us.

DW

A note on the Author

David Watkins worked as a Finance Director for over 33 years before he 'retired' in March, 2011. He promised himself he would then spend time indulging his passion for Leeds United, a passion that he'd never been able to fully pursue in the past due to work and family commitments. He's followed Leeds since the 1960s although he readily confesses that most seasons he would only get to see a handful of games. He has now missed just three games in the last four seasons and by his own admission is completely 'addicted'. The original intention was to write just one book, the one documenting the return of Leeds United to the Premiership; this is book four and he says he will now have one more go... next season!

"Summer Days Drifting Away"[1]

A car door slammed shut somewhere outside the bedroom window and I woke with a start; I had one of those momentary panics as I wondered why I didn't recognise my surroundings. Then I remembered I wasn't at home and I leant over and grabbed my watch. It was almost eight o'clock in the morning on 19th June, the day the fixtures come out, and I was on my own in the spare bedroom of the in-laws home in Edinburgh. I could hear the father-in-law mooching about downstairs; there was no one else in the house. Mrs W was still enjoying her spa break at Stobo Castle down in the Borders, with the mother-in-law; they were due back later this afternoon. This is a special day in the life of a football fan, the day when the new season begins to take on some shape and meaning, and I wasn't the only Leeds fan getting excited at the thought of seeing the fixtures for the new season. A "ping" from my mobile signalled a Facebook post from Simon, he of the Surrey Whites: "Good morning and happy fixtures day all ...." he wrote. I guessed there were thousands of us all over the country, maybe all over the world, firing up our smartphones or computers, eager to begin our first tentative travel plans for the new season.

It was one of very few moments of excitement Leeds fans had experienced so far this close season. The previous campaign had come to an end with that surprising but very enjoyable victory at Watford, back on May 4th, more than six weeks ago, bringing to an end a mostly forgettable season. Some cup successes against Everton, Southampton and Spurs, being the only oases in a desert of mediocrity and frustration. Since then I had religiously logged into the official club website every day, hoping to see news of a new signing, or less expectantly, news of a further injection of funds into the club. One signing had been announced; the giant striker Matt Smith, all six feet six inches of him, had joined us from Oldham on a free transfer, to a mixed reception from the fans. But that was it so far. The only other Leeds news we had seen in the press was

---

[1] *Summer Nights, from Grease the musical, written by Jim Jacobs and Warren Casey, Single by John Travolta & Olivia Newton-John, 1978, RSO*

an incident reported from Senegal, where El-Hadji Diouf had allegedly been "beaten up" by some locals in the loos of a nightclub[1]. Dioufy seems to get into bother every time he gets his todger out. There had also been a few mentions for our international stars in the sporting press; Tom Lees, Sam Byram, Paul Green and Rudy Austin. Tom played in the third of three games the England Under-21s lost in the European Championships, in Israel; the England youngsters cost Stuart Pearce his job for failing to progress beyond the group stages. Byram was named in the England squad to go to the FIFA Under-20 World Cup, in Turkey, but then immediately pulled out with a recurrence of the hip-injury that caused him to miss the final two games of last season. It would blight much of his coming season too. Paul Green similarly pulled out of the Irish squad for a friendly against England at Wembley; while Rudy did feature for Jamaica in their fast fading World Cup campaign.

Slightly unsavoury news was that a club director, Salah Nooruddin, who'd only been appointed as recently as 20th May, was already trying to use his influence to get the son of a business contact into the Leeds United academy! The Yorkshire Post reported that Idris Tahar had been given a trial and was rejected but Nooruddin allegedly put pressure on the academy staff to still give the youngster a place. Eventually GFH upheld the decision not to accept him but it was an embarrassing episode nonetheless.[2]

That was pretty much it so far this summer and hence the publication of the fixtures had been seized on by Leeds fans with even more gusto than usual. But when I dialled into the official site just after 9:00am, I was somewhat underwhelmed. I don't know what I was expecting, but the names of the teams all looked very, err, very familiar. The first game, on August 3rd, would see Brighton and Hove Albion at Elland Road, in a repeat of the final home game of last season; I couldn't

---
[1] *http://www.thesun.co.uk/sol/homepage/news/4935773/El-Hadji-Diouf-beaten-up-in-Senegal.html*

[2] *http://www.yorkshirepost.co.uk/news/main-topics/general-news/leeds-boardroom-row-after-director-tries-to-get-academy-place-for-friend-s-son-1-5738957*

remember that ever happening before. Rudy Austin and Dioufy would miss that as they would still be suspended following their red cards in that game at the end of April of course. Maybe Diouf was now regretting grabbing his dick through his shorts and waving it proudly towards the Brighton fans. The game everyone was searching for in the list was no doubt the first game against Wigan. They were already installed as one of the favourites to climb straight back to the Premiership, despite losing their long-time manager Roberto Martinez to Everton; Owen Coyle had taken over the reins. Wigan would be at Elland Road in early December. The other two teams down from the Premiership, QPR and Reading, were less attractive fixtures as they'd both been in the Championship as recently as the season before last, and had both managed just a single campaign at the top table of English football. I quickly got bored looking through all the games and so just checked where we'd be on Boxing Day (Blackpool), New Year's Day (home to Blackburn), and the last day of the season (home to Derby County). I had a quick look on Twitter to see what the fans had to say and noted just one tweet of interest. Ever eager to spot a good omen, one fan with the handle @micklufchall wrote: "Last time we started with a home game and end [sic] with a home game we went up that season lets home [sic] it happens again for Leeds United....MOT". He was quite right too. In 2009/2010 we began our League One campaign with a 2 – 1 win at Elland Road against Exeter City and then secured promotion against all the odds with that amazing last day victory against Bristol Rovers, coming from a man, and a goal down. Something along those lines this season would do nicely if the old ticker can stand it.

All went quiet again on planet Leeds for the next couple of weeks, with the only fierce debate taking place on my favourite Leeds United forum, LUFCtalk, being whether the club was right to use space on the official website to report that their under-11 side had won a tournament in Krakow. Some suggested, like the official site proclaimed, that: "the future's bright", as some of these lads would one day be plying their trade for the first team. Others suggested most would fall by the wayside in the coming years. Heady stuff, excuse me while I stifle a yawn!

The lack of any news, and in particular the lack of any new signings, began to get Leeds fans irritated and Twitter became a veritable morass of despair. Almost every tweet was negative. GFH took the brunt, with most suggesting they were as good as broke. Brian McDermott was interviewed towards the end of June and his comments did nothing to allay the fans' fears as he seemed to be suggesting that he may well have to, "wheel and deal"; sell some players to release enough funds to buy the new ones he wanted. He was asked if he felt let down by the owners but refused to answer the question, preferring instead to say how he was still impressed with the club's supporters and the goodwill they were showing towards him. There were a few voices of moderation of course, and none-other than regular Twitter correspondent Ross McCormack was eager to point out that it was still very early days. He tweeted: "For every1 moaning about lack of transfers to me, remember we ain't even in July yet!!You can judge when the window's closed". Perhaps Ross was trying to deflect attention too when he tweeted on 28th June: "Leeds should have a separate tv deal from everyone else…#onskyloads" in reference to the fact that Sky had already chosen three of our first five Championship games to screen live on TV, with the inevitable consequence that kick-off times had been changed. Perhaps Sky knew something the rest of us didn't; maybe they thought we would be the early season pace-setters!

Those summer nights were already drifting away, well, a bit anyway, with still no news coming out of Elland Road. In fact the only thing coming out of Elland Road was Steve Morison. It was announced, surprisingly, that he'd be joining Millwall for a season long loan. This is the same Steve Morison who Neil Warnock had suggested would become a legend at the club, when the striker was struggling at the end of last season. But no one was prepared for the avalanche of news that would come on 1st July, or the sheer fanatical optimism that would begin to build in the next few weeks.

Most on Twitter had remembered that Ken Bates would be stepping down as Chairman at the end of June, and so many had celebrated this auspicious occasion on Sunday evening, the last day of June. Then, the following day, the club announced formally that Bates was no longer Chairman and instead our friend the honourable Mr Nooruddin was to take over that role, with David Haigh becoming Managing Director and Shaun Harvey stepping down from MD to plain old Director. That was great news for most fans as it was another big step in having all trace of Ken Bates expunged from the club; Harvey having been seen as something of a Bates' puppet in recent years. Just as we were all absorbing, not to say savouring that news, we then heard that Leeds had shelled out £1 million to bring Luke Murphy to the club. Twitter was in a pickle…there was suddenly bugger all for Leeds fans to moan about! The Twittersphere went quiet for only the briefest of moments though before we began to see tweets complaining that Bates was still there (he was of course now taking up his 'role' of president), while others questioned the ambition of the club in 'only' being able to afford £1 million for a Crewe Alexandra midfielder, and questioned if that was sufficient to turn us into a Championship winning side. A few moderate voices did point out it was the first time in almost eight years that Leeds had spent £1 million on anybody. (Richard Cresswell in August 2005). I checked out Mr Murphy on Google and concluded that a six foot two inch, 23 year-old midfielder, who scored 21 goals in 161 appearances for Crewe, many as their captain, was a pretty good acquisition. Brian McDermott thought so too, claiming the player was, "the best player in his division last year", and that he was, "young, hungry, wants to work hard and very obviously talented".[1] I wondered if he would turn out to be our Bremner, Strachan, or McAllister.

Two days later, Noel Hunt joined Leeds from Reading, linking up with his former boss, to complete McDermott's first hat-trick of acquisitions. If squad numbers were anything to go by then Murphy and Hunt looked likely candidates for regular

---

[1] *http://www.bbc.co.uk/sport/0/football/23127898*

starts, as they were handed the shirt numbers '6' and '10' respectively, while Matt Smith would wear '20', despite the fact that the coveted number '9' shirt was still vacant.

Off the pitch, GFHC, the outfit that bought the club from Bates, continued to move in mysterious ways, and was not being helped by various scurrilous headlines from fringe publications. On 4th July, Sportsdirectnews.com carried the headline: "Leeds try to pull veil over club ownership", with an article second guessing why GFH had surreptitiously moved the ownership of the club from GFHC to another of their companies, Brendale Holdings Limited, on 20th June. The reason, the news outfit argued, could be so that further chunks of the football club could be disposed of away from the prying eyes of the fans and the media (due to less stringent disclosure rules applying to Brendale than GFHC) while GFH continued to claim publicly that they were, "in it for the long haul"[1]. I really couldn't give a hoot. It would be nice if GFH had pots of money to invest, but they didn't. I just hoped that Brian McDermott felt he was getting enough support to at least give the Championship a bit of a go this season.

The first indication we had of how our slightly modified squad would perform in the coming months, was the first pre-season friendly, on 6th July, at Farsley. We'd gone there in pre-season last year under Neil Warnock and beat them 5 – 2. Sadly, I couldn't be there in person to see if we could improve on that this year as I was baking in the first weekend of the heat wave that had appeared from nowhere all across the UK. I was at the Aussie Pink Floyd concert at Jodrell Bank and by the time that closed I was "Comfortably Numb" from a combination of the searing heat and more than a few pints of the excellent Robinsons' ale 'Dizzy Blonde', that was on offer from the real ale marquee. Twitter reported that we had safely negotiated our game at Farsley by an encouraging 5 – 0, with goals from Dom Poleon, Matt Smith (2), Noel Hunt, and Aidan White.

Other news from the game was that McDermott had played all of his available players with only Sam Byram, El-Hadji Diouf,

---

[1] http://www.sportsdirectnews.com/sports-business/27610-leeds-try-to-pull-veil-over-club-ownership.php

and goalkeeper Jamie Ashdown missing, all currently sidelined with injury, and Ryan Hall missing....well, just missing really. No one seemed to know what was happening with him or where he was.

The following Monday, the Leeds squad flew out to Slovenia for a ten–day training tour and three more games. Yet again I was unable to join them and the 1,500 or so fans that had made the trip. I would have loved to be there. Last year, I went down to Devon to be at the Torquay pre-season game and I so enjoyed the atmosphere that I decided there and then that I'd do the full tour next time, wherever it happened to be. Unfortunately, my sister-in-law decided to have her 25th Wedding Anniversary party in Italy the week Leeds were in Slovenia, and despite my protestations that, "I bet Gary Edwards wouldn't miss a pre-season tour for his sister-in-law's anniversary", my wife was unmoved and insisted I be in a hotel on the shores of Lake Iseo, while the team were just three hundred and thirty three kilometres away across the Italian/Slovenian border. I did research into the availability of flights from Milan to Ljubljana and back, but ultimately decided that the cost of a divorce would probably spell the end of my Leeds season ticket for about a thousand years, so discounted the idea. I consoled myself with a trip to Maranello to the Museo Ferrari and then to Modena to the Museo Casa Enzo Ferrari. Ferrari is another great love of my life and I'd always wanted to visit the factory and the museum. Sadly, the factory tour was sold out but I spent several hours drooling over the exhibits in the museums. Funnily enough, later this season, Leeds United would be likened to a Ferrari.

The 1,500 Leeds fans that *were* able to make the Slovenia trip seemed to be having a whale of a time. There were many photos posted on Twitter showing dozens of Leeds flags hung all around the towns where the three matches were played, and frequent tweets from the lads and lasses enjoying the Slovenian hospitality. The only disappointment was that our performances and results were not very good. It started well enough with a 3 – 1 victory against a Slovenian Representative XI, with goals from Smith, Hunt, and Poleon. But then two defeats, to F C Domzale 2 – 1 (Poleon again), and then 1 - 0 to the Hungarian giants Ferencvaros, rather took the gloss off it all. The feeling of many who were there was that the quality of our play was not quite what it ought to be and the games were, not to put too fine a point on it, boring. The one moment that cheered the travelling fans was when Brian McDermott handed a fifty euro note to LUSC White Rose member Dan Lambert, to help, "Get the beers in for the lads." "It was all I had on me", McDermott told reporters later.

I was still in Italy on July 20th, while the Leeds team and their most fervent supporters had returned to the UK and were now heading for the 30-degree temperatures of balmy Walsall, as the longest heat wave in recent memory continued to scorch the UK. Once again Leeds came up short, and the Saddlers beat us by a single goal. This time it was not just the fans complaining; Brian McDermott was vocal too. Interviewed on the OS on the Monday after the game, McDermott said:

"I didn't see that one coming; I was really disappointed on Saturday...There wasn't enough energy in the team, when you play football you have to run; you have to go beyond defenders. The players have to do the right things when they haven't got the ball so they have to make sure that they get the details right.

"You are always concerned after a performance like on Saturday but you cannot get carried away. I never get carried away with a great victory and I never get carried away with a bad performance like Saturday but we don't want to see too many of them."

Sadly, we'd see a few similar statements this season.

One man who possibly had other things on his mind for the Walsall game was striker Ross McCormack. 'The Mirror' reported that he'd been fined £200 and had to pay costs of over £900 for dumping his Christmas packaging in a layby on the A58, near his home in Bardsey. He'd left address labels on the packaging which led the Leeds City Council fly-tipping police directly to him! I suspect he fully intended to put his litter in the bins nearby… but as he does most Saturday afternoons, he dragged it well wide.[1]

[1] http://www.mirror.co.uk/news/uk-news/leeds-united-star-ross-mccormack-2063588

The Hunt for a shirt

On Monday, July 22nd, there were a couple of new arrivals. In London's St. Mary's Hospital, The Duchess of Cambridge gave birth to the now third in line to the throne, later named George Alexander Louis. (Won't he get teased being called a gal?) In Leeds, Paul Hunt was named as the club's new 'acting' CEO, having recently been deputy CEO at Blackburn Rovers, and prior to that, Commercial Director at Wigan Athletic. Hunt replaced Shaun Harvey, who'd stepped down earlier in the month. Football anoraks will remember it was Paul Hunt who was sacked by Blackburn Rovers when a letter he wrote to the owners, the infamous Venky's Indian chicken farmers, was leaked to the press. In the letter Hunt had called for the sacking of Rovers' then manager, Steve Kean. [1]

When Leeds had announced their pre-season schedule and I had failed to negotiate a trip to Slovenia with her that wears the trousers, I knew that the first pre-season game I would get to see would be at Stevenage Borough, on 23rd July. As soon as I got home from Italy on the Monday I was straight on to footballgroundguide.com to check out the Lamex Stadium, or Broadhall Way as most Stevenage fans still call it. It looked a tidy little stadium, with a capacity of 6,546, according to the website. It would be my first visit to the Lamex although it would not be the first time I'd watched 'The Boro' live. I'd seen them win the FA Trophy at the brand new Wembley Stadium, in 2007, when they beat Kidderminster Harriers 3 – 2 in the first ever competitive club game to be held there. Kidderminster was one of my local sides when I lived in Worcestershire in a former life and although Worcester City is my main love down there, I also have a soft spot for 'Kiddi'. Ironically, now that City have had to vacate St George's Lane in the centre of Worcester for financial reasons, they will now be ground sharing at Kidderminster for the next couple of seasons. But I digress.

---

[1] *http://www.bbc.co.uk/sport/0/football/18005433*

We were now well into the fourth week of the heat-wave in the UK and I had to enter a new round of negotiations with Mrs W; this time to get the use of her brand new Peugeot 208, complete with functioning air conditioning. The AC in my old Pug had packed up some weeks ago under the strain. It was good to get back in the saddle, despite facing a three hour, 137 mile trip to deepest Hertfordshire; during the journey I mused that former Stevenage resident Lewis Hamilton would do the trip in less than half that time in his F1 Mercedes, although the vast number of roundabouts I encountered in and around his birthplace might have slowed him just as it did me. Unscathed, I arrived in the handy car park opposite the Lamex at just after 5:30pm. As footballgroundguide.com had accurately documented, the car park was free! I was already in love with this place. No sooner had I stepped out of the ice-cool Pug into the sub-tropical heat of Broadhall Way, than I was hailed by Marc and Shaun from the Norwich Whites, who I've frequently bumped into all over the country in recent seasons. Marc is just completing a biography of former Leeds striker Ian Baird, due to be published later this year. The three of us bobbed and weaved in the traffic that was playing a dangerous game of motor dodgeball with us as we crossed the busy dual carriageway separating the stadium from the car park. We were headed for 'Our Mutual Friend', a real ale hostelry just a few minutes' walk from the ground. Pavements didn't seem to feature very highly on the local council's list of priorities and there seemed to be more than one aspiring Lewis Hamilton on the roads this evening. As with Lewis, none of these buggers would give way.

In the beer garden outside the pub, I bumped into many familiar faces. I knew Conor and Adam would be there as they'd texted me earlier, but I was soon greeted by Andy, Wayne, big Cliff and Simon, from the Surrey Whites, and then spotted Mike and Paula from the Sussex contingent too. Steve and Stu the twins were there and countless others, too many to mention. It was a typical Leeds away day. It was impossible to stay inside the pub for long; the public bar had developed a micro-climate more suited to cannabis growing than ale-supping, so there was a constant stream of folk dashing in to refill glasses before returning to the relative cool of the shaded beer garden. The chatter was full of optimism; the optimism all football fans gorge themselves on in those last few days before the new season. If I had a pound for the number of times I heard, "I think this could be our year you know", I would have been able to buy that central defender I felt we needed to complete McDermott's modestly rejigged side. As if to confirm my point, Conor announced the starting eleven for the game, just received on his phone as: "**Kenny, Thompson, Lees, Pugh, Drury, Green, Brown, Norris, White, Varney, and Poleon.**" The subs were: Cairns, Warnock, Peltier, Tonge, Lenighan, Austin, Murphy, McCormack, and Hunt. Danny Pugh was starting at centre back tonight; not something that filled anyone with great confidence. There were eight changes from the side that lost at the weekend so woefully to Walsall, but whether that was always planned or whether it was McDermott's response to the poor display we'd never know.

As it happened, for 45 minutes, the changes appeared to have made no improvement at all, as Stevenage, doing a passable impression of Walsall, made all the running, looking sharp and decisive every time they attacked. Several times the ball flew into Leeds' six-yard box and more often than not the Boro strikers were first to it. The names in our defence were different, but the malaise of last season was still evident. We were failing to stop crosses coming in and then failing to win the ball in our box. We need that central defender desperately; a commanding presence to lead by example and dominate in our own box. Thankfully their ability to hit the target was on a par with our ability to defend. The huge Leeds contingent filling the South Stand mostly ignored our lack of prowess on the field and instead worked their way cheerfully through their repertoire of chants, perhaps to make sure that any new followers among the ranks were up to speed by the time the first competitive game arrives. But all of the lads and lasses near me could see that this particular line up was unlikely to set the Championship alight. By pure coincidence, my ticket had placed me next to Mike, Paula, and 'Welsh' Andy, (he's not Welsh but it's a long story!) and just in front of big Wardy, another of the Surry Whites' lads. Young Kentley from Stoke was also stood nearby. We all tutted and shook our heads each time our back-line failed to clear the ball but thankfully a new slim-line Paddy Kenny looked secure enough behind them. I conservatively estimated that Paddy had lost at least a stone during the summer…and that was just off his backside. Leeds did have the ball in the net in the first few minutes, when Luke Varney drilled a shot into the corner, but that was disallowed. The only other highlight of a frustrating first half was when a stuttering announcement came over the PA about a blue Ford Focus that was blocking in six cars somewhere in the vicinity. The Leeds songsters immediately broke into a chant of, "We park where we want, we park where we want, we're Leeds United, we park where we want". There were plenty of the now familiar "If Varney scores we're on the pitch" too. Oooh, it felt good to be back!

The second half wasn't much better, at least not until McDermott made a few changes in the 59th minute, with Austin and McCormack replacing Green and Norris. Almost immediately we had more options going forward. It took Austin just ten minutes to make his mark, with an inch perfect cross that Luke Varney steered into the corner of the net. Five minutes later it was Varney again, this time latching onto a ball over the static home defence to rifle a shot that the keeper couldn't get enough on to stop it ricocheting into the net. "It's yer keeper's fault 2 – 0", rang out from the 1,400 travelling Leeds fans, and the unfortunate Boro keeper, Chris Day, had a face on him the colour of his vivid pink strip. Varney completed his hat-trick just four minutes later, when he won, and then converted, a penalty. Each time he scored, Varney playfully gestured to the Leeds fans to get, "on the pitch".

At the end of the game the Leeds players trooped towards us applauding our efforts as we did theirs. Noel Hunt stripped off his shirt and threw it into the crowd just below us and I could see 'Welsh' Andy was the lucky recipient. As we all walked back to the car park, Andy modelled his Hunt shirt for us, disproving the general consensus that, "He'll never fit into that", though it was more than a tad tight! In the hunt for a shirt in the starting line-up against Brighton in ten days' time, I didn't think many had improved their chances tonight.

Looking for a Hero

Browsing on the official website on the Friday before the F C Nurnberg game, the last of the seven main pre-season friendlies, I came across an LUTV video reporting that Flamingo Land Resort, the official sponsor of the Leeds United Academy, had launched a new ride. The £8 million flying rollercoaster was named 'Hero' and several Leeds heroes were present at the launch, including Peter Lorimer, Dom Matteo, and Eddie Gray. Even Brian McDermott was there, although it may still be a bit early to put him in our hero category. One man that achieved hero status among the Leeds fans overnight though, was Managing Director David Haigh. The reason? He announced on the official site:

"Ken Bates has ceased to be President of Leeds United Football Club. Mr Bates will now no longer have any role within the football club".

This simple statement appeared late on Friday night, with no further comment from anyone at the club or from Bates himself. It appeared to be confirmation of what thousands of Leeds fans had been waiting to hear for more than eight years. A few folk on Twitter expressed curiosity as to what had brought about this sudden expulsion of the former owner, as the statement had all the hall marks of a less than amicable parting of the ways, and Bates was of course only 25 days into his new role as president, a role we'd been told was good for at least three years if not for life. Most though just revelled in the fact that he was gone and there was an air of celebration about most tweets I saw. It would be a few days before details began to surface and we would be told by Bates himself in an interview on Talksport[1] that he'd been sacked for an alleged breach of contract. He had apparently signed a renewal of a deal to supply a private jet for the next three years to ferry him back and forth between his home in Monaco and Elland Road.

---

[1] *https://soundcloud.com/cas707/ken-bates-interview-on-talk*

There were rumours that the contract was worth £500,000! Bates was adamant that GFHC were fully aware he'd been using this company for years, as he argued it must have been spotted during the due diligence process. Hence he saw no problem in signing a renewal as a director of the club just prior to the end of his period as Chairman. GFHC clearly felt he had gone behind their backs, acting without their permission and committing the club to a major future cost at a time when the club was apparently struggling to make ends meet. Bates made it clear he was likely to seek legal redress for his 'unfair' dismissal!

The sad thing for me was that for just a few minutes on Friday night it looked as though the distraction of Bates had finally been removed from the club and I'd really looked forward to not hearing those, "Bates out", chants every five minutes at future games. I thought maybe we could look forward to a period of unity, with everyone behind the team and the club. Now it looked as though we'd continue to hear Bates' name for some time to come as a potentially lengthy legal process seemed inevitable. It was a typical Leeds United moment...a few seconds of joy ...and then it's snatched away from us. A bit like that goal Diouf scored against Brighton last season, when just seconds later he spoiled it all by waving his manhood about. Or that cracking goal at Hillsborough that Michael Tonge scored only for that idiot to immediately run on the pitch and fell Kirkland. Yes, this was typical Leeds United alright.

Whatever the legal position, all I knew was that it was completely unacceptable for the club to be asked to foot a bill of £500,000 just to ensure he got to and from Leeds games in comfort. I could only imagine the fans reaction if he ever turned up for a game again. I have in the past applauded some of the changes Bates has made at Elland Road – the upgrading of facilities in particular – but this latest episode really did show that he has little concern for the future success of Leeds United. In the Talksport interview, he also suggested that GFH continued to operate on a knife edge financially, and indeed he suggested this private jet episode was actually leaked by GFH as a diversionary tactic to hide their real problems. Watch this space.

None of this was uppermost in my mind as I journeyed up to Elland Road on Saturday morning. Instead, all I wanted to see was a much improved performance from what I assumed would be Brian McDermott's most likely first choice eleven for the first competitive game the following Saturday, at home to Brighton.

Everything at Elland Road was refreshingly familiar. The same chap was on duty at the entrance to the car park, as he has been for the last few years, and the price remained £6. Stevenage take note, you could be making a fortune! I called into the club shop to make my usual first game purchase of the new away shirt, although in the end I plumped for the training top in the same mustard colour. It was rumoured the team would be playing in the new mustard (the club calls it gold) and dark blue kit this afternoon. Many fans had already voiced their disappointment over the new away kit, and the new home kit for that matter, which is predominantly white but has a wide royal blue stripe down the front. Some fans had likened the home shirt to the packet design for Embassy Lights cigarettes! However, there seemed no shortage of customers in the shop who were snapping up both the home and away tops.

As I wandered into the Pavilion, it was clear they were not expecting a huge crowd; only half of it was open. The rest was curtained off similar to what they did last season when the East Stand was being redeveloped and East Stand guests took over one half of the Pavilion. All the usual folk were in there though and first to greet me was Wolfie, who'd just made his first 250 mile trek of the season from darkest Milford Haven. As we chatted, I calculated in my head that by the end of the season he would have clocked up 11,500 miles travelling up and down to Elland Road. I resisted the temptation to tell him that his fuel alone would cost something in the region of £1,700. Sadly, this would all become apparent to Wolfie himself as the season progressed and eventually he had to give up his season ticket and ration his visits to the occasional game every now and again. I would miss his cheery face. Martin and the boys rolled in later, as did Liz and Bogdan, and then Jo aka 'clown' introduced herself to me. Jo was one of a quartet of fans stood in front of me at Watford, in fancy dress, at the end of last season. I resisted the obvious temptation to say something like, "Jo! I didn't recognise you in your clothes!"

As at the Stevenage game, everyone was very positive. Yes, there was a certain caution that perhaps only three new faces were not quite enough to transform last year's team, but no one seemed quite as troubled by this as me. When the team was announced it lined up as follows:

Kenny
Peltier Lees Pearce Warnock
Green Murphy McCormack White
Varney Poleon

The substitutes were named as: Cairns, Pugh, Drury, Tonge, Brown, Norris, Hunt, Smith, Thompson, Hall, and Lenighan.

The surprises to me were that there was no starting place for Matt Smith and that Ryan Hall had suddenly materialised into the squad having been seemingly lost in space for so long. The obvious weakness was that defence, which was basically the one we used at the end of last season when Byram was injured. No one can tell me that a defence with those names in it, or even with Byram in there for that matter, is good enough to have a shot at promotion. There was still no Diouf and no Austin, both of whom couldn't play in the Brighton game next week due to suspension, so were unlikely to play until at least the Leicester game on August 11th.

As the game kicked off, in front of a disappointingly tiny crowd of just 9,455, it was immediately obvious that McDermott had ditched his thus far favoured diamond formation and was instead playing a fairly narrow 4 – 4 – 2. Whether this was a possibility next week or whether McDermott was just fitting the formation around the players available today, was hard to judge. The Kop looked pretty full to me and the other section that was well populated was the far end of the West Stand, where the German fans looked magnificent in their red shirts and they were making plenty of noise. All credit to them, and they didn't really deserve the derisory chant of, "Who the f****** hell are you", that blasted out from the Kop in the third minute, as Nurnberg scored.

It was a goal I saw us concede more than 20 times last season. A free kick delivered with pace and accuracy from the right wing to land on the right foot of the unmarked Daniel Ginczek at the back post. His volley was met by the forehead of Luke Varney, but for reasons known only to Luke, he was stood a good yard behind the goal line. The linesman signalled straight away that it was in and there was little protest from Leeds or the Kop. It looked well over to me.

Urged on by their fanatical following, F C Nurnberg looked every bit the accomplished Bundesliga side they are, full of German strength and efficiency, silky smooth like a new Audi, full of vorsprung durch technik. In stark contrast, Leeds resembled a yellow-ochre Morris Marina, built on a Monday morning in the 1970s! Well, actually no, it was nowhere near that bad. But for long periods the game did resemble many we saw last season in the Championship. Yes, the opposition was more polished than we were and they passed the ball better and retained possession better than we did. But we had plenty of energy and we hustled and bustled and now and again Aidy White or Luke Varney would suddenly burst through and try their luck without ever really threatening the visitors' net. But all the time I was concerned that, just as we usually did in close games last season more often than not, we would give away a soft goal. In contrast, looking along the back line of six-footers in red shirts, I couldn't see them offering us anything in the way of gifts. It was still only 0 - 1 at half time though.

The second half followed the same pattern. Leeds' passing was never fluent and our control was never instant. When we did get a sight of goal our shots were tame or wayward. In contrast the Germans' passing was crisp and assured and their shooting mostly accurate. The huge following the Germans had brought was possibly the reason there was no let up from their team and they really did seem to be taking it seriously. Not that Leeds were holding back either. At one point in the second half, McCormack squared up to his marker and it looked for a moment as if the two of them would trade punches. They didn't, but then moments later all 22 players converged in a brawl after another crunching tackle. It looked like a war zone out there for a few seconds. That got both sets of fans on their feet and inevitably the England-Germany rivalry came to the fore. The Kop began it with a rousing chant of "In-ger-land, In-ger-land, In-ger-land", while the Germans responded with…well, I'm not entirely sure as it was in German, but I'd guess it wasn't complimentary! Then the Kop took things a stage further with, "Shall we win a war for you?" which raised the already boiling temperature another notch. Just after the hour mark, McDermott made a triple substitution, bringing on Drury, Tonge and Hunt, for Warnock, Green and Varney. My guess was this was more about protecting the latter three than winning the game, now that things were getting a bit tasty out there. The Kop then launched into a rousing rendition of:

There were ten German bombers in the air
There were ten German bombers in the air
There were ten German bombers, ten German bombers,
There were ten German bombers in the air

And the RAF from England shot one down
And the RAF from England shot one down
And the RAF from England, the RAF from England,
The RAF from England shot one down.[1]

The RAF shot down one German bomber after another, much the same way the ten green bottles fell off the wall!
Out on the pitch there was still a game of football going on and unlike two World Wars and the '66 World Cup Final, Germany was winning. In the 69th minute, a right wing corner flashed across the box in front of the empty South Stand; it took a touch at the near post before that man Ginczek met it at the back post to find the top corner. 2 – 0. Matt Smith, the giant Leeds striker, replaced Dom Poleon in the 75th minute, and I got my first look at him. He is clearly a threat in the air,

[1] http://fanchants.co.uk/football-songs/england-chants/10-german-bombers-in-the-air/

particularly to low flying aircraft, but he doesn't look to be the most mobile player I've ever seen; more of a Beaufort Bomber than a Spitfire! In many ways he bears a striking resemblance to former Leeds striker John Charles, having that same broad forehead, huge backside and immense thighs. I never saw big John play for Leeds in the flesh, but I saw him many times late in his career playing both centre forward and centre half (not at the same time obviously) for Hereford United. The Bulls were in the same division as my beloved Worcester City, the old Southern League, and I saw JC bury many a header in the City net. If Smith turns out anything like JC then we really have found a gem. It remains to be seen how much McDermott uses him in the coming months. My guess was that Poleon would get the nod next Saturday alongside Varney.

And that was pre-season done and dusted; three wins and four defeats in the seven match programme. After the game McDermott seemed happy with the effort his players had given and was quick to acknowledge the quality of the Nurnberg side. He did say he was not happy to have given away two soft goals. "Disappointing to lose two goals from set plays, need to make sure we get that right", he told Eddie Gray in that soft clipped English he often uses, and when asked about his team selection for the Brighton game he replied: "I know the formation and I know the 18 players for Brighton".

One further friendly was arranged against Shelbourne in Ireland, on the Monday of the week before the Brighton game and McDermott took a strong squad including Austin, Hall, Smith, Hunt and Drury. Leeds won the game 4 – 0, with Hall scoring two and Ross Killock and Noel Hunt bagging one each. I wondered if anyone had caught McDermott's eye sufficiently to change his mind on his 18 for Saturday. Since he told no one who the 18 were, he could easily make a switch or two!

My guess for the starting eleven on Saturday was: Kenny, Peltier, Lees, Pearce, Warnock, Green, Murphy, McCormack, Tonge, Varney, and Poleon.

Top: The sizeable Nurnberg support greets the players' arrival.
Bottom: Another Leeds header goes wide.

Murphy's Law

The excitement built all week leading up to the Brighton game. Hero Haigh was at it again, announcing that Yorkshire Radio was to close with almost immediate effect, at 6pm on Tuesday 30th July. The reason given, in another of those very short and to the point statements on the official site, was so the club could focus on LUTV and the soon to be launched new website for all of its digital output. But it was an open secret that the radio station had been losing significant amounts of money for many months so its closure came as no real surprise and fitted in with the business-like approach GFH were taking on most issues. Mind you, I'm not convinced that is necessarily a good thing. I'm currently reading the book 'Soccernomics' by Simon Kuper and Stefan Szymanski in which they conclude: "Nobody runs a football club in order to turn a tidy annual profit". They argue that football clubs are not, and cannot be, run on normal business lines if they actually want to satisfy their fans and employees' desire to play decent football and actually win trophies. "The business of football is football", they claim, and clubs are more like, "the British Museum: public-spirited organisations that aim to serve the community while remaining reasonably solvent", though they acknowledge that, "few of them achieve even that". The whole book is a worthwhile read if you are interested in the wacky economics of football. [1]

Eddie Gray and Thom Kirwin were reprieved when they were told the following day they would now run the match commentaries on LUTV, having been the mainstays of Yorkshire Radio's match coverage in recent times.

On Wednesday, Brian McDermott issued his message for the new season. He wanted everyone to, "stand together", for the whole season. The message further fuelled the gathering momentum and ticket sales for the Brighton game soared. Almost 30,000 tickets had been snapped up with several days still to go. All sections of the ground were opened and even

---

[1] *Soccernomics, Kuper & Szymanski, Harper Sport, 2009*

the upper tier of the East Stand was filling up. Hero Haigh and new CEO Paul Hunt then had a, "burger in Billy's Bar", together with Gary Cooper and Paul Keat from LUST (Leeds United Supporters Trust) in the spirit of keeping in touch with the fans. Haigh explained: "One of our priorities when we first came into the club was to re-engage with the fans and the different fan groups that support the club." GFH had met with the LUSC (Leeds United Supporters Club) in recent weeks as well. Salah Nooruddin, the recently appointed Chairman of the Board, then appeared on LUTV with the message that it would be a slow and sure progression with no instant quick fixes to take Leeds into a new era. He spoke of getting the business model right and stabilising the club financially and how the fans must get behind the team and again how we must all work together. More tickets sold with every utterance from the new owners. The players then did their bit to stoke up even more interest with some of them appearing at the site of the new temporary 'pop-up' club shop in Trinity Leeds, ahead of its formal opening on Thursday; while Ross McCormack and Luke Varney answered phones in the ticket office talking with fans. It was all part of the new, "re-engagement with the fans", policy which seemed to have caught the supporters' imagination in spades. On Twitter, the fans themselves joined the crusade, urging each other to get to the game. Someone going by the handle @BatesOut tweeted: "If you haven't yet bought a ticket for Saturday, do it now. Let's make a big statement to the rest of the league that we're back. #BatesisOut". Yet more tickets sold and more season ticket sales were reported. At the end of most articles on the website there was a handy "click here" link to the ticket office. It seemed a new initiative was coming along every few minutes; it was hard to keep up with it all.

On Thursday, Twitter was carrying rumours of an imminent new investment in the club. @bbcleeds tweeted, "@bbcleeds understands #lufc owners GFH Capital are near to securing multi-million pound investment which includes the purchase of Elland Road". Many thought this could be the recently rumoured investment by Red Bull, who were said to be interested in buying Elland Road and renaming it the Red Bull

Stadium, similar to what they did with Salzburg in Austria. Other tweets claimed it was another party and not Red Bull at all that was preparing to buy the ground. Either way, most fans were further encouraged by the thought of more money coming into the club. I hoped that any potential investor was not browsing Amazon's list of football titles and picking out 'Soccernomics", lest they find out there is actually no money to be made from a football investment!

Still the changes kept coming; the new official website was formally launched, proclaiming that the Brighton game was already set to record the highest opening day attendance at Elland Road in ten years. And all this was announced on 'Yorkshire Day', 1st August. Each summer, the Yorkshire Ridings Society aims to celebrate the heritage of 'God's Own Country' with a public reading of the Yorkshire Declaration of Integrity – an assertion that Yorkshire is, "Three Ridings and the City of York" and ending with the cry, "Yorkshire forever, God save the Queen"[1] Rousing stuff for Leeds' fans already stoked up to fever pitch by recent events!

I did worry that we were not yet a strong enough side to put a performance together on Saturday that would satisfy the new appetite for success, and that thousands of the returning fans would go away once more, disappointed and vowing not to, "watch that sh*** again". If the famous Leeds United rollercoaster comes off the tracks this weekend it will be a spectacular catastrophe indeed, and we were all well used to seeing Murphy's Law operate at Leeds; "If it can go wrong, it usually does". But at the same time the excitement was infectious; how fantastic will Elland Road look, full to the brim in the sunshine on opening day. I was drooling like the proverbial Pavlov's dog, all down the front of my new mustard training top.

The trip up the M6 on Saturday morning was a pain in the proverbial. For whatever reason the traffic was horrendous and it was stop-start all the way. Maybe it was football traffic; I spotted several car loads of Leicester fans heading for their

---

[1] http://www.gazettelive.co.uk/news/teesside-news/yorkshire-day-yorkshire-declaration-integrity-5397105

opener at Middlesbrough, and a few Blackpool fans on their way to Doncaster. At one point I noticed the cars in front of me all swerving to avoid something in the road and I was astonished to recognise it as a huge polythene bag stuffed full of empty beer cans! I wondered which football coach had jettisoned that on the move and hoped it wasn't one of ours!

I still arrived in the car park by 12:15pm, and was amazed at how busy it was. It was the same in the Pavilion. This early before kick-off I normally have the choice of any table I want but today most were already full! I met Wolfie at the door and we found a couple of places as we tucked into our first beers of the afternoon. It seemed like everyone wanted to be at Elland Road today; it was being seen as the start of a new era, a post Bates era. Many fans were returning for the first time in several years, having made self-imposed resolutions not to attend until, "That Chelsea b*****d, was out of our club". Consequently, there were many new faces among our number today. 'NottinghamWhite', aka Phil, I'd met before on a couple of occasions, but he was just one of a number of LUFCtalk forum members to arrive at our table this afternoon. 'WiganWhite', aka Alan, and '18longleeds', aka Max, all rolled in, as well as regulars Kev, Zack, Bogdan, Liz, 'RamseyWhite', Martin and the boys, Nigel, Adam and Conor and many, many more. The queues at the bar built up quickly and were soon five or six deep at every pump, while my quest for a decent pie went unfulfilled, as only cheese and onion was left by the time I tried to get one at 1:45pm. Conor proudly informed me he'd nabbed the last meat and potato just seconds earlier.

On the big screen we watched as Burnley and Bolton, two of the original 12 founder members of the Football League, fought out a 1 – 1 draw in the early kick-off. It was one of six fixtures this weekend specially arranged to celebrate 125 years of the League.[1] Last night Sheffield United beat another founder club, Notts County, 2 – 1, while two other fixtures paired four more of the original dozen clubs; Preston v Wolves and Derby v Blackburn. Rochdale would play Hartlepool this

---

[1] *http://www.theguardian.com/football/2013/aug/01/football-league-125th-anniversary-fixture*

afternoon in what is apparently the most frequently played fixture between any two clubs in the history of the FL, and Newport play Accrington, with Newport's Rodney Parade, being the newest of the 72 current grounds. I have to confess that few in the Pavilion were taking much notice of the game on the screen, or of Lorimer, Ormsby and Mick Jones, when they took to the stage to discuss our own fixture. All everyone wanted to know was what the starting eleven would be. Just after 2pm, Daniel was able to reveal all, as he spotted the first tweet listing the team as:

Kenny

Peltier   Lees   Pearce   Warnock

Green

Tonge   Murphy

McCormack

Varney   Hunt

Subs: Ashdown, Drury, Smith, Brown, White, Norris, Poleon.

My guess was just the one out – I had Dom Poleon in there instead of Noel Hunt. Maybe it was Hunt who'd taken the eye at Shelbourne on Monday night, in that hastily arranged additional friendly. I was OK with the side in terms of it being about the strongest we could field, but that defence was still a concern for me. I was taught that, "If you always do what you always did, you will always get what you always got". That defence has been proved time and time again to be susceptible at this level, so I just could not conceive that it wouldn't let us down today.

Nigel, who sits next to me on the Kop, walked with me over to the stadium at 2:45pm; we were among the last to leave the Pavilion today, but I still had time to buy a copy of The Square Ball, the Leeds fanzine, from a seller outside the ground. The main feature in this issue was a double page spread under the heading: "KEN BATES, A TRIBUTE FROM THE WORLD OF FOOTBALL"…Both pages were intentionally left completely blank! A fitting tribute I thought.

As I took my place in row GG on the Kop, I was in awe. Elland Road looked stunning. I glanced behind me and saw not a single seat empty anywhere in the North Stand. In front of me the pitch looked immaculate, like a freshly ironed Subbuteo cloth. The South Stand end of the ground and the lower tier of the mammoth structure of the East Stand to my left, were packed with tens of thousands of expectant faces, while the upper tier was full except for the corporate section in the centre. The West Stand to my right was full except for an area surrounding the 1,500 visiting Brighton fans at the far end. We'd heard in the Pavilion that the game had officially sold out around 2pm.

As the teams emerged from the bright yellow plastic tunnel at the far end of the West Stand, the crowd erupted in a spontaneous and deafening roar of approval and as the PA began the first playing of 'Marching On Together' all 30,000 odd Leeds fans stood and belted out the anthem, everyone with arms aloft and then one fist pumping the air three times in time with the final chorus of, "Leeds, Leeds, Leeds!" I could imagine the same folk shouting that Yorkshire Day refrain, "Yorkshire forever, God save the Queen!" Murphy's Law was never far from my mind though; the Leeds United rollercoaster has a habit of derailing just when things are on the up, just when expectancy peaks.

Within seconds of the kick-off, a chant rose from the back of the Kop that quickly spread right around the ground: "He's out of our club, he's out of our club, that Chelsea b*****d, he's out of our club", echoed around the old stadium, to be followed by a very traditional round of applause. I looked up to the directors' box, high up to my left, in the centre of the East Stand, miles above the half way line, and I swear I could see David Haigh lean across to someone up there as if he was muttering, "Best thing we ever did was to sack Bates..."...and then Murphy's Law struck.

We'd already winced in union, all 30,000 of us, as the Leeds defence allowed Andrea Orlandi the freedom of Elland Road to shoot from 20-yards after only five minutes of the game. On that occasion the new streamlined Paddy Kenny had flown gracefully through the Elland Road sky to palm the ball away to safety. But in the 13th minute we were at it again. You would have thought the Seagulls were a protected species and the Leeds defence had all signed up to the **RSPB** over the summer as Bruno Saltor was allowed to roll the ball through a line of four of our defenders unchallenged. Leonardo Ulloa was onto the ball in a flash to smash it past Kenny from six yards, while Tom Lees was still looking for his binoculars. We all began to twitch. It was a blow, no doubt, and for all of thirty seconds the Leeds crowd was silenced. But then we found our voices again and we seemed to have decided that, come what may, nothing was going to spoil our day in the sunshine.

Although it seemed like an age at the time, just five minutes after gifting Brighton the lead, we had levelled it up again. Michael Tonge twisted and turned in the south west corner, right in front of the Seagulls' fans, who were still celebrating their early goal. Suddenly Tonge whipped in a cross with his right foot and found Varney challenging for the ball with Gordon Greer at the near post. The ball merely skimmed off Varney's head, but fell perfectly at McCormack's feet at the back post. A quick shimmy from McCormack was too sharp for Bruno Saltor, and Ross slotted a left foot shot across keeper Kuszczak and into the corner of the net. It was a finish that must have impressed Gordon Strachan, the Scotland manager, who was watching from the stands, and it may well have been enough to put Ross back into the reckoning for an international recall. Everything was back on course!

There was little between the sides in the last twenty five minutes of the first half and it looked as if, like many games last season, this one might be settled by the odd goal.

A new half time penalty competition saw one very accomplished fan test his skills against Leeds' under-18 keeper Brad Dixon, including one audacious attempt at 'the dink' which sadly cleared the bar. He got two out of four though, to win himself a free £50 bet with SkyBet.

The second half was a feisty affair between two sides who obviously wanted all three points. The one factor in Leeds' favour was Luke Murphy; slowly but surely, as the game wore on, Murphy got stronger and more influential. It was almost as if he needed to acclimatise himself to the pace of the Championship compared with his time at Crewe, in League

One. He started to orchestrate Leeds' play, and most attacks began with the ball at his feet. As Murphy improved, so did Leeds' general play, although gaps were still appearing at the back. With an hour gone, Paddy Kenny pulled off a stunning double save; first parrying a shot from Andrew Crofts, low to his right, and then recovering quickly to block the follow up from Calderon. On 67 minutes, McDermott made his first change, bringing on the pace of Dom Poleon to replace Noel Hunt. This was now the side I'd expected to start. Poleon was immediately a handful for the Seagulls' defence, literally. He almost had the shirt torn from his back as he broke in the inside left channel. The referee played a good advantage though as Poleon got himself free, but his shot was wayward. With ten minutes left, McDermott made his final changes, first replacing an injured Warnock with Adam Drury, and then adding the height and weight of Matt Smith, who replaced Luke Varney. Varney made his way off the pitch to a rousing "Varney's Army", a fitting reward for a tireless display. The attendance went up on the big screen at the far end from the Kop as 33,432, and there was another huge roar of approval followed by another rendition of, "he's out of our club...", and another energetic round of applause. At that point every Leeds fan present would have settled for the draw and would have moved on to 20,000 parties around the UK.

Matt Smith is a huge unit. Not only is he six feet six inches tall, and head and shoulders, literally, above any other player on the pitch, but he is also very strong and he looks very heavy. As the Brighton defence began to tire, the last thing they needed was to be battered by our own Beaufort Bomber. A couple of high balls were lofted in towards Smith that he completely missed, but I swear I felt the ground shake as he landed each time. Leeds were now well on top, with Murphy calling all the shots in the middle and Poleon pillaging on the left hand side. But once more that Achilles heel of ours almost cost us the game. On a rare sortie into the Leeds' half, Brighton suddenly whipped the ball into the Leeds six-yard box from wide on the left wing. Inexplicably, Will Buckley was left completely unmarked, five yards out doing the protected Seagull thing again. His powerful header looked destined to win the game and there was a groan from the Kop as we watched in horror as the ball rocketed towards goal. But Paddy Kenny looks in inspired form, almost a different player to last season, and he somehow got both hands to the ball to knock it away to safety. We were still chanting the, "Paddy Kenny's having a party", song as another high looping ball was sent up towards the giant figure of Matt Smith, lurking just outside the box in front of the Kop. Smith rises like the Saturn 5 rocket used to appear to, almost in slow motion, and then nods the ball down and into the path of Luke Murphy, racing towards goal like a man possessed. The ball bounces up and for a split second it looks like Murphy just nudges the ball past his marker with his right arm down by his side. But he carries on anyway and with just Kuszczak to beat he opens his body and side-foots the ball to the keeper's left. We are all up on our toes at this point and then we sink just a few millimetres as Kuszczak gets his left arm in the way of the ball. But incredibly it still finds its way into the top corner. The referee is running back to the middle, seemingly unaware of the Brighton handball protests and suddenly all hell breaks out. The whole of Elland Road is on its feet and the roar must have been heard in Huddersfield as Luke Murphy wheeled away to the touchline and then danced his way towards the dug-out. The rest of the Leeds players did well to catch him and in fact his progress was only stopped as Luke Varney and Noel Hunt appeared from the bench to wrap their arms around the youngster. This was a new experience for Leeds fans, a new form of Murphy's Law. How many times in recent seasons have we been on the wrong end of game-winning goals in injury time. It was unbelievable. There was just enough time for James Adcock, the referee who'd sent Tom Lees off at Ipswich last season, to blow his whistle to get the game restarted and for Leeds to immediately win the ball back and launch it towards Poleon. The noise was so incredible that no one could hear the referee's final whistle, but as Poleon controlled the ball and prepared to shoot, suddenly Leeds' players were cavorting around the pitch with their arms aloft and the Brighton players had stopped, shoulders slouched, hands on knees. Poleon took aim anyway and blasted the ball into the side netting, before running off to celebrate with his team-mates. In Brighton this afternoon, the 40th annual Gay Pride celebrations were taking place...at Elland Road our visitors from Brighton were neither gay nor proud. This was Leeds' day, Leeds' party, and we'd cry if we want to... and I could see many that were.

I stopped in my seat for ages after the players had left the pitch, just savouring the moment. There is no better feeling than coming from behind to win a big game, and to do it with just seconds to go. As I looked around at the now almost empty stadium, it looked somehow serene, at peace with itself, satisfied with a job well done. As the last few spectators went up the steps past me, we exchanged smiles and nods and a few clenched fists. Football was back! Maybe even Leeds United is back! I had to remind myself of course that we could so easily have lost this game; the three saves from Paddy Kenny were probably the difference between the sides today. On this evidence we should be able to mix it with the best in the Championship, but I would still expect us to lose as many games as we might win; today the breaks went for us but on another day...

When I got home I watched a recording of Brian McDermott's post-match interview on LUTV, and he acknowledged that the game could easily have gone the other way. "Both sides could have won no doubt, but in the Championship if you try and win and keep going you get the breaks". For now that was all we could do, keep going; keep going and try to win every game in the knowledge that we still have Byram, Diouf and Austin to come back and further strengthen the side. I will not feel confident though until we have at least one new name in that back four.

At the end of the first round of games, Leeds were officially 4th in the table. Ten teams had picked up first-day wins including Wigan, who thrashed Barnsley 4 – 0 at Oakwell, confirming their favourites tag. Only the Wigan game and Blackpool's 3 – 1 win at newly promoted Doncaster were won by more than a single goal though. It is going to be tight again this season. One down, 45 to go!

Nice distraction

On the Monday following the Brighton game, Mrs W and I flew out to Nice, on the Cote D'azur; the French Riviera. We'd had the offer of a few days in a holiday home in Villecroze, Provence, owned by a former work colleague of my good lady; we joined him and his wife there for four nights from Monday, returning on Friday. It meant I'd have to miss the first round of the Capital One Cup, in which Leeds had been drawn at home to League Two Chesterfield. It would be only the second game I'd missed, home or away, in three seasons. I considered it a worthwhile sacrifice though to benefit from the 'free' accommodation in one of the most picturesque spots in Europe. There was also the not insignificant factor that Mrs W might consider this a sacrifice of sufficient proportions to allow me to attend the remainder of the games this season!

It just so happened that on the Wednesday Leeds were playing the Spireites (their name derives from the crooked tower on the church in the centre of the town), our hosts in France were celebrating their wedding anniversary. So, I learned the outcome of the game whilst sat outside a beautiful little restaurant in the village, enjoying a meal and a couple of carafes of the local rose wine. The Leeds website described a game in which we'd apparently dominated, yet only just managed to win by the odd goal in three; having come from a goal down. The BBC Football website showed that possession was split exactly 50 – 50 and seemed to suggest Chesterfield were unlucky, even hitting the post late in the game.

I wouldn't get to see the goals until I arrived home late on Friday night, courtesy of Monarch Airlines flight ZB467 being SIX BLOODY HOURS DELAYED! Having spent an entire day in Nice airport, and then having to wait over half an hour in Birmingham International Airport's baggage reclaim area, praying for our suitcase to appear, I was in no mood to then watch a video of the Chesterfield goal, which came from the head of Eoin Doyle. Unbelievably, Doyle was completely unmarked at the back post, as he rose to meet a right-wing cross and power it past Paddy Kenny, who was making his 600th career appearance. When will we learn? Why can we not defend balls into our six-yard area? We seem to have more trouble with crosses than ever Dracula did. Surely this weakness has been spotted by McDermott? While browsing the internet looking for info on the game I spotted an article posted on dailymail.co.uk suggesting that Brian McDermott was trying to sign a young centre-back from Manchester United by the name of Scott Wootton. McDermott was apparently at the County Ground, Leyland, last night, watching the 21 year-old Wootton playing for Manchester United reserves as they beat Manchester City reserves 2 – 1 in the final of the Lancashire Senior Cup.[1] Was Wootton to be the man to sort our defensive problems out? At this stage it was just press speculation of course, as was news in the same article that Leeds had rejected a £1 million offer from Middlesbrough for Ross McCormack. There would be a few more offers for him as the season progressed.

My mood improved marginally when I saw the nature of our goals; a tremendous shot from distance by Michael Brown and a solo effort from the rapidly improving Dom Poleon. I chuckled as I watched the replay of Poleon's goal celebration; a sort of slow motion fire-walk! I learned later that the crowd was 17,466, with over 2,000 from Chesterfield. That was encouraging; far and away the biggest crowd of all of the first round matches. It really did look like the Leeds fans were coming back in their droves.

The team that defeated Chesterfield gave few insights into Brian McDermott's long term plans. I was surprised to see Paddy Kenny in there; Ashdown played in all of the cup games last season apart from the first one against Shrewsbury. It may have just been to get that 600th appearance out of the way. The back line of Drury, Lees, Pearce and Zac Thompson, looked like it was just providing a rest for Peltier and Warnock and since there were no other centre backs available (Ross Killock was currently injured) Lees and Pearce had to play I guess. The midfield four were our tricolour trio, Green, White

---
[1] http://www.dailymail.co.uk/sport/football/article-2386516/Leeds-target-Scott-Wootton-Manchester-United.html

and Brown, together with David Norris, while the two late subs from Saturday, Smith and Poleon, started up front. McCormack and Murphy, the two goal scorers from Saturday, got half an hour at the end of the game, replacing White and Norris. So, my guess was McDermott was resting those he could, while not being prepared to play anyone out of position if no cover was available. Whatever, it just about did the trick. I tried to get a first-hand report by asking on Twitter and got just one response, from @msh9369, aka Mike from the Sussex Whites. He Tweeted: "…wasn't a great show mate, commonly described as an ugly win…" Not a great endorsement really. I think I chose a good game to miss and perhaps it was just a nice distraction from the pressure of the new league campaign for the players. Incidentally, talking of Nice distractions, if you ever get the opportunity to explore the area of Provence, make sure you get to see the Gorge of Verdon; I had never even heard of it before this trip but it is rightly claimed to be the most beautiful canyon anywhere in Europe. It is simply stunning.[1] The draw for the second round of the cup ensured I would be heading for another lakeside venue; the Keepmoat Stadium in Doncaster.

Stunning scenery; Lake Sainte Croix

1   http://www.lesgorgesduverdon.fr/en/index.html

Leeds fan Chris is an avid reader!

More Flare than Flair

I'd arranged to fly home from Nice on Friday, to ensure I was back in time for the Leicester game, originally scheduled for Saturday afternoon. That was before Sky got involved. In the event, this was the first of several Leeds games to be moved for TV and it was now a 4:30pm kick-off on Sunday, presumably so as not to conflict with the Community Shield game between Man U and Wigan, at Wembley at 2pm.

My elder son Mark was with me for this one, his first game of the season. His work commitments mean it's not always possible for him to be free at weekends these days but for once the ridiculous kick-off time worked in his favour. We made for the car park we used last season, a huge expanse of rough ground just off Filbert Street, near to where the old Leicester City ground used to stand. It wasn't open! Not only that but judging by the height of the grass and weeds growing through the gravel, it hadn't been used for some time. We asked the two lads at the entrance of the adjoining private car park where we could park; they said we couldn't use their area...and they had, "no idea mate". What's wrong with the world today? Thousands of Leeds fans arriving for the game, many by car, an opportunity to pull in £5 or £6 a time...and no one seems interested! If they don't want the money why on earth not just leave the gate open and let us fend for ourselves. It was a Sunday afternoon of course so there were a few roadside spots available but we opted to support the local rowing club, just back over the river where we parked a couple of years ago. As we got out of the car a very irate lady went dashing past us to try to catch the occupants of another car that had just sneaked in; they were now legging it up the road having not waited around to pay their £5. "Tight-fisted bas****s", she shouted after them, shaking her fist in their direction. We paid up meekly and informed Irate Lady that we were sure the miscreants were not Leeds fans! I did wonder if there might be a car in the river when we got back; it would only need a bit of a shove and I'm sure there were plenty of burly rowers on hand if required!

We wandered off towards the Counting House Pub, where we'd sampled pre-match beers before each of the last three games here. It's a perfect pub for a pre-match pint and usually has a few Leicester fans as well as the inevitable throng of Leeds'. It's about half a mile from the King Power Stadium, on Almond Road, just on the edge of the Freemen's Common retail park, opposite Morrisons. As we rounded the corner and made our way up the pedestrian walk-way, we could see there were already hundreds of Leeds fans stood outside enjoying the sunshine or sat with their beers at the few tables by the front door. Another feature of this pub is that there is usually a makeshift game of football being played on the pedestrian area by some of the youngsters while mums and dads enjoy their pints. Today it was just the same. They were playing with a bright yellow leather football and it was rolling down the walk-way towards us after a wayward shot down the hill eluded the keeper; a sort of Ross McCormack free-kick effort that passed well over the imaginary crossbar. Unable to resist the temptation, Mark traps the ball expertly, flicks it up in the air a couple of times, and then launches it back up the hill with his left foot. It was reminiscent of that John Smith's TV advert where Peter Kay hoofs the ball off the playing field onto the roof of a nearby house, before admiring his handy-work with that immortal phrase, "Have it, oh yes!"[1] Mark is a decent footballer I have to admit, but this time the ball begins to veer off towards the many Leeds fans gathered outside the pub and those wooden tables loaded with foaming pints. Had it been a golf shot he would have been obliged to give a shout of, "Fore left!" One or two folk spot the bright yellow missile hurtling towards them and they take evasive action, whipping their pint pots out of the way. A shout of, "Heads!" is heard and that alerts a few more to the impending danger. Alas, one woman spots it too late; just catching sight of the ball out of the corner of her eye she instinctively throws out a hand to try to deflect it. She made contact, but only served to parry it, Rachubka like

---

[1] *http://www.youtube.com/watch?v=JOQcCviNi5Q*

towards a pint glass sat on the edge of her table. It bit the dust, instantly smashing into a thousand pieces and showering innocent bystanders with ale. In the inevitable commotion that followed, Mark and I ducked unseen into the pub. It was not a good start to Mark's new season.

Inside the pub it was already rocking. We spotted from the TV screens on the walls of the pub that the Community Shield game had just kicked-off and sadly Wigan were already a goal down. They must have conceded in the first minute or so of the game. We bumped into Adam and Conor and then Marc and Shaun. Lily, fresh from her family holiday visiting Kruger Park in South Africa, said hello, and was obviously gushing about the trip, and later on RamseyWhite and Nigel bowled up. The Leeds choir was in great voice, and put absolutely everything into one rendition of, "shoes off, if you hate Man U", presumably in the hope of it being heard as far away as Wembley. Annoyingly, Wigan conceded again and lost 2 – 0. There were a couple of Leeds flags on display in the pub; Leicester Whites had theirs tied up between two pillars while the lads from Nottingham Whites held theirs aloft between beers. I asked the Nottingham Whites if they knew Phil from the LUFCtalk forum which they did. "He's our leader!" they cried. Rich and Andy explained that Phil had been instrumental in establishing the branch and his daughter Sarah was still the branch treasurer, as she has been since its formation.

Another great initiative in Leicester is that a programme seller visits the city's pubs before the game and when he arrived I bought my copy of the very formal looking magazine. The front cover was a photo of club Chairman, Vichai Srivaddhanaprabha (I have checked it!) and I wondered if he'd ever requested his name on the back of a shirt and what that would cost. On the back cover were the squads, and Conor pointed out that, as with Brighton last week, our squad was bigger than Leicester's. As with Brighton's though, a quick look through the names of these two outfits told me that the opposition probably had more quality if not quantity. Among the Leicester names were Kasper Schmeichel, Paul Konchesky, Wes Morgan, Andy King, Neil Danns, David

Nugent, and Chris Wood; all were named in the 18 for today's match. When the Leeds team was announced on Twitter, there were no surprises. It was the team that started against Brighton with the exception that Rudy Austin came straight back into the side after his three match ban. He replaced Michael Tonge who was now a sub, knocking David Norris off the bench altogether. Rudy was also named captain, thus relieving Lee Peltier of that duty.

A disappointing crowd of just 22,725 was in the King Power Stadium, (it has a capacity of 32,500 according to footballgroundguide.com), meaning that there were plenty of blue plastic seats visible on three sides of the ground as we looked out from the inventively named 'Away Stand' at the north end of the ground. Leeds had a tremendous following of 2,851, maintaining our reputation as the best supported team away from home in the whole of the Football League. As the teams came out, with the Beatles' 'Hey Jude' blasting out over the PA and the Leeds fans all joining in with the, "La, La, La, La-La-La-La", I noted that Leeds once again wore training tops over their shirts, reminiscent of the Don Revie days; they were dark blue today but had been white for the Brighton game. Quite what the reason for the tops is, I'm not sure; it was not cold by any means, so I assumed it was a marketing gimmick to get us all to buy one!

In the first half, neither side was able to impose any kind of superiority on the other, and with just two shots on target, both easily saved, the teams went in at half time all square at 0 – 0. The Leeds fans on the other hand had been totally dominant. Many of them had warmed up in the Counting House earlier, and were now as vocal as I could remember in many a long day. When I watched the game back on Sky+ on Monday, I was amazed that the TV techies had not turned down the volume from our end. Very early in the game there was the inevitable, "He's out of our club", chant including a very loud, "Chelsea bas****", closely followed by a clearly audible, "If you're watching on the telly you're a c***!" For much of the first half we used the infamous Leicester drummer as our rhythm section and then perversely every now and again would remind the Leicester faithful that, "We're Leeds United, we don't need a drum". In contrast I wondered if the Foxes were sponsored by 'Silentnight' and not 'King Power'.

Simon Thomas was presenting the TV show with Ipswich boss Mick McCarthy who said he was pleased to get the opportunity to be watching Leeds as his side plays us in a couple of weeks' time. He referred to the new optimism that was sweeping Leeds along at the moment and he commented, "I'm glad there's a bit of optimism there, it was my club as a kid". He also commented that the last time his side played at Leicester, "We got 'dicked' by six here!" Can he say that on live TV before the 9pm watershed?

Mick was not surprised it had been a tight first half with few if any chances and he commented that most games at this level were the same, often with just one break deciding the outcome. Mick reckoned, "Leeds just shaded it". Bill Leslie, the commentator, also mentioned that both sides had one hundred per cent records so far this season, having each won both of their games 2 – 1. It did have a look of 0 - 0 about it.

The second half continued in the same vein and once again there was only really one decent chance at either end. Leicester brought on the lively Chris Wood and he smacked a shot against a post, while Leeds brought on Poleon and Smith late in the game, with Smith having a header well saved by Schmeichel. It finished 0 – 0 and both sides would be happy with that, although perhaps ruing a lack of flair in most areas of the pitch. In fact the only flare we saw all day came hurtling out of the Leeds section towards the pitch, landing just a few yards in front of Mark and me. It was a stupid act that could have had far more serious consequences had it struck the ball boy sitting just a yard or so from where it landed. We'd seen earlier just how much damage a badly aimed missile can cause! It wasn't the only black mark for our fans either. At one point in the second half we became aware of a scuffle somewhere up behind us and very quickly a number of police were despatched to restore order. I presumed it was an attempt to find the bloke who threw the flare. The whole subject of flares would ...ahem, flare up again later in the season.

The one positive for Leeds, apart from the obvious one of getting a point away from home and keeping a much sought after clean sheet, was the storming performance of Rudy Austin. He was immense and clearly 'The Beast' is back. It looked a great decision to make him skipper. On Radio Leeds after the game, McDermott told us that Rudy, "is a leader", leading by example, and a, "special person". Whether he goes on to be as influential in getting us out of this division as Gordon Strachan once was, remains to be seen. But he could do. Leicester manager Nigel Pearson told reporters after the game, "You credit Leeds for how they went about the game and that's how games are in the Championship - very tight and there for the taking." It was something we would get used to hearing throughout the season; there wasn't much to choose between most of the Championship teams.

Four points from the first two games, against two of the so called fancied teams at this level, is OK in my book. At the end of the second round of games in the Championship, Leeds held 8th spot, with an identical record to Leicester. Only three sides had managed to win both opening games; Watford, who thrashed newly-promoted Bournemouth 6 – 1 yesterday, Blackpool, and Nottingham Forest. Wigan had only played one league game of course because of that Community Shield encounter earlier today, but I fully expected them to be up there eventually. It was all shaping up nicely and I was already looking forward to next week and the home game with Dave Jones' struggling Sheffield Wednesday who so far had 'nil points'. As every Leeds fan knows though, it's the games against sides we are expected to beat that more often than not trip us up.

"Ross McCormack is not for sale"

In the week between the Leicester and Sheffield Wednesday games, details of more manoeuvrings in the ownership of Leeds United were published in a report on 'theguardian.com' under the headline: "Leeds Utd owner quietly sells off more than half stake"[1]. Quoting data originally published by Reuters, taken directly from the second quarter financial results for GFH Capital, the article explained that the shareholding in the club was now divided between IIB (10%), which GFH had disclosed publicly several months ago; GFH Capital: and Envest Limited, a company owned by Chairman Salah Nooruddin and his wife. I checked the club's website, under the 'club' tab and sure enough the revised ownership of the shares is actually documented on there as follows:[2]

The club's ownership statement...

Leeds United Football Club Limited ('LUFC') the company that holds the share in the Football League, is a member of the West Riding County Football Association and a Full Member of the Football Association.

LUFC is a wholly owned subsidiary of Leeds City Holdings Limited ('LCH').
LCH is wholly owned by LUFC Holding Limited ('LUH') a company based in Grand Cayman.
LUH is managed by GFH Capital ('GFHC') on behalf of its investors.
The shareholders in LUH that hold over 10% are: -
i. GFHC
ii. International Investment Bank
iii. Envest Limited

GFHC is a wholly owned subsidiary of Gulf Finance House, BSC.
Envest Limited is owned by Mr and Mrs Salah Nooruddin.

---

[1] *http://www.theguardian.com/football/feedarticle/10931358*

[2] *http://www.leedsunited.com/club-ownership*

So, that's all that cleared up then. It sort of fell in line with what GFH told us many moons ago when they first got involved; that they were merely the management vehicle buying the club on behalf of several other investors. The change in ownership didn't seem to have given the club access to any additional funds though, as it still appeared we would have to sell a player or players before we could bring in anyone new. The rumours were rife that the three most likely candidates to leave were Aidy White and Ross McCormack, both linked with Middlesbrough and Blackpool, and El-Hadji Diouf. The website dailymail.co.uk, suggested that all three could be on their way, while Boro manager Tony Mowbray confirmed he'd spoken with Brian McDermott. Leeds confirmed they'd received and rejected two offers for McCormack. I couldn't help thinking that any attempt to sell McCormack would be met with outrage from the majority of the fan base and I wondered if the Kop would be vocalising their annoyance at the game this weekend.

By a strange quirk of the fixtures, our first two home games this season were two of the last three home games of the last campaign. Brighton was the final home game last season while Sheffield Wednesday had been the third last, and Brian McDermott's first in charge. We went a goal down in that one, before an inspired change by McDermott, moving Luke Varney into the middle in attack, turned the game. Two Varney headers, both from McCormack crosses, won it, and gave McDermott the perfect start. I hoped this one would be a little less stressful; I checked the BBC Football website on Friday, noting that Wednesday had lost all three of their competitive games so far, while we were unbeaten. I was also pleasantly surprised to read that only two teams out of the last 22 to visit Elland Road in all competitions had managed to stop us scoring. In fact, in the last 34 games at Elland Road we had only failed to score on two occasions; two 1 – 0 defeats, to Birmingham City and Cardiff. I would no doubt find an opportune moment during the game to show off with that stat!

I picked up Bogdan in Warrington, on the way through to Leeds and we both wandered into the Pavilion not long after 10am; it was another TV game, live on Sky, this time with a

12:15pm kick-off. It seemed busy at the bars considering there were said to be only 22,000 tickets sold as of last night; those who were here were obviously very thirsty, despite the fact that the sun wasn't anywhere near over the yardarm yet! The inability of the Pavilion staff to pour pints quick enough was perplexing, as they now had those 'ten second pint' pumps installed for the Fosters, which seemed to be the lager of choice for most, even at the exorbitant price of £3-60. Another disappointment today was the food. At 10:30 in the morning, I just didn't fancy my usual pie, mushy peas, and gravy, so I opted for a sausage bap. Fortunately, I'd spooned plenty of brown sauce on it, but even so, as I got the first bite into my mouth I discovered the bread was as dry as the proverbial funeral drum! It was a case of washing down each mouthful with a swig of Fosters and then hoping it wouldn't get stuck on its journey through the digestive system. I eyed Bogdan's pie and peas enviously.

Lorimer's guest in the Pavilion today was Mel Sterland, Leeds' right back from 1989 to 1994. I saw many of the 16 goals he scored for us in that period, but I will never forget the one he got at Roker Park in December 1990. It was a screamer from outside the box and it won the game 1 – 0. It was two days before Christmas and Mrs W was there, seven months pregnant with Mark. We smuggled a little stool into the ground for her to sit on! Those were the days. Mel is a tad bigger these days than he was then, no doubt a result of his self-proclaimed drinking exploits since he packed up the game. Sterland also had a long spell with Wednesday at the start of his career and he clearly had divided loyalties. Pressed by Lorimer to give a score prediction for the game, he eventually came up with a 2 – 2 draw. Any sort of a draw today would be a big disappointment I thought, and my betting slip went in with my usual 4 – 0 Leeds prediction, a 44/1 shot. I know, I should know better after all these years.

Inside the ground I was pleasantly surprised at how full it looked in most areas. The upper tier of the East Stand was all but empty and there were plenty of spare seats over in the West Stand in the visitors' section, but the rest of the ground looked almost full. Wednesday brought just 900, with many missing Owls said to be boycotting the game because of the £36 price tag and the appalling location of our away section. When the attendance was displayed on the big screen during the second half, it read 23,766; only 172 less than we got for McDermott's debut game against the Wendies on that Saturday lunchtime last April. Still, it was a shame we couldn't fill the place again like we did for Brighton, as it would have looked and sounded great for the TV coverage.

As it was, it still sounded pretty good to me. We gave Dave Jones a very early greeting with a rendition of, "We are Leeds, we are vile, David Jones is a paedophile". Happy 57th birthday Mr Jones! I'm only reporting this stuff…not condoning it!

It was a typical Yorkshire derby, with a few tasty tackles and played at a rip-roaring pace from the off. Leeds made one change from the side that drew at Leicester last Sunday; Dom Poleon getting a first league start in place of Noel Hunt, who was relegated to the bench. El-Hadji Diouf was also deemed fit enough to take his place in the dug-out with Aidy White the latest player to slip off the bench altogether. Wednesday had a few enormous players in their ranks, none bigger than Atdhe Nuhiu, wearing '34' in the Owls' attack. He dwarfed the Leeds defence and was the inevitable target for several early corners and crosses in front of the Kop. Paddy Kenny did well to stop one of his towering headers right on the goal line. Everyone near me on the Kop was expressing concern that our vertically challenged and notoriously porous rear guard would concede at some point today. We got through the first 36 minutes unscathed though, and indeed Dom Poleon was probably the most dangerous looking player on the pitch, ruffling the Owls' feathers with several barnstorming runs. Ross McCormack tested Kirkland too, with a clever left-foot chip that the keeper touched over the bar.

In the 37th minute though, it was situation normal at the back for Leeds. A right wing corner found Antonio free as a bird, an Owl in fact, at the back post. He intelligently headed it back across goal where Kamil Zayatte easily out jumped Tom Lees to lob a header over Paddy Kenny and into the corner of the net, right in the spot Stephen Warnock vacated just a second earlier. In the statistics, it will be recorded as yet another header conceded from within six yards. How many more must we concede before someone sorts out this mess?

The half time score was 1 – 0 to the Owls, just as in April, and Leeds looked in need of another masterstroke from McDermott. I suddenly remembered my stat of the day and was able to tell Mike, sitting behind me, that all was not lost; Leeds had only failed to score in two of the last 34 home games…Mike pondered who the two were.

The change McDermott made was to bring on Michael Tonge for Paul Green; we assumed due to an injury to Green who we'd seen feeling his hamstring in the final few minutes of the first half. Tonge did appear to inject more bite into Leeds' midfield although a lot of the good work there was then wasted by a poor final ball further up the pitch. Then, in the 57th minute, a moment of pure genius lit up Elland Road. Austin clipped the ball down the line in front of the East Stand. Varney cushioned the ball on his chest directing it inside to McCormack, running onto it at pace from just inside the Owls' half. He kept going; outpacing two defenders and then pushing the ball to the right of Zayatte while sprinting past him on the left. He collected the ball again on the edge of the box before sliding it under the diving body of Chris Kirkland. It was a goal out of nothing; typical McCormack. Ross ran across towards the centre of the East Stand and cupped his hands behind his ears as he stared up towards the directors' box. Then he spread his arms wide as if to say, "Now, do you really want to sell me?" The Kop by now was chanting, "Ross McCormack, Ross McCormack", with everything it had, and then, spotting him gesturing to the directors, we burst into, "Ross McCormack's not for sale".

"Mmmn, it will be even more difficult to sell him now surely?" I thought to myself. Ross was another birthday boy this weekend; he'd be celebrating his 27th birthday on Sunday.

The rest of the game saw Leeds make most of the running; Smith and Diouf were introduced for Varney and Poleon but neither of the subs was able to work any magic. Indeed it was Wednesday who went closest to sewing up the three points as a scramble in the Leeds area saw Warnock and Pearce throwing themselves in the way of the ball. It struck Pearce on the arm in the ensuing melee but referee Roger East either didn't see it or deemed it accidental, which undoubtedly it was.

The game ended all square and we gave the Leeds players a standing ovation despite the disappointment; three points would have put us on top of the table, at least for a couple of hours until everyone else had played. I couldn't remember the last time we'd been in that position. In the centre circle, Ross McCormack and Wednesday skipper Anthony Gardner were being interviewed for the live TV broadcast with a sound track provided by the Kop. "Ross McCormack's not for sale", we belted out again and again. We couldn't hear what was being said on TV at the time but when I watched the recording later that night Ross was very cagey as he responded to the questions: "What does the future hold for you, you know that Middlesbrough have made another bid for you this week? Do you want to stay at Leeds?" He told the reporter, "Listen, I'm happy to do my talking on the pitch, it's up to the guys above, and they'll probably decide my future. As I've always said I'm happy at Leeds and it's always nice for clubs to show interest in you". He then collected his Man of the Match champagne from Gardner and left the pitch applauding the Kop. I rewound the interview again and again, but try as I might I couldn't read between the lines and I was none the wiser as to whether he'd still be with us come September 3rd, the day after the current transfer window slams shut. A flick through the many Leeds fans' blogs later that night showed that the movement was already underway to keep him. Keith Ingham, who I exchange tweets with periodically, wrote an article on the excellent 'weallloveleeds.co.uk' under the heading: "Please don't take our Ross away" that summed up most fans' feelings.[1] On the BBC, Brian McDermott, when asked to comment was quoted as saying: "We've turned down two or three bids and you know my view, that's not changed. I've spoken to Ross and you saw the quality that he brings, you saw his celebration as well. He loves this football club and I

---

[1] http://www.weallloveleeds.co.uk/20/post/2013/08/please-dont-take-our-ross-away.html

like working with him and want him to be here". On whether the owners *would* sell him, McDermott said, "That's their prerogative to do what they like."

On Twitter on Saturday night, some fans were tweeting that they would boycott Elland Road if Mac was sold, yet still we all knew that unless *someone* went, it was unlikely anyone would be coming in, and we all knew we needed that centre-half!

By coincidence, I also spotted a link on Twitter to a new interview with Salah Nooruddin on the UAE website 'The National'. He was saying all the right things as far as I was concerned. In an article titled: "Leading Leeds United are the sleeping giants with Arabic spice"[1] (No, I didn't really understand the title either, but that is right honestly!) Nooruddin told 'The National', "Any investment made in football cannot be made solely on financial merit. It has to also be driven by passion and that is what I found at Leeds. This club is more about passion than finances." It sounded like he'd also been reading *Soccernomics*! He again stressed it was his aim to stabilise the club, to get the finances in order whilst acknowledging, "...while stability may not offer instant gratification, it will pay off in the long-run". I tended to agree with that but was much more sceptical of the statement by the interviewer that Nooruddin, "...has spoken with Leeds supporters and found them accepting of a three-year plan to gain Premier League promotion." I could think of more than a few who would baulk at the idea of having three more years in the Championship...and I was one of them!

It was a wide-ranging interview in which Nooruddin spoke about everything from increasing shirt sales by improving the Leeds brand in places like China; to strengthening the current playing staff. Encouragingly, he was said to be ready to sign off on two new signings; "We need a centre-back and a right winger...Brian is looking and we are supporting him." Hoo-bloody-rah! At last confirmation that someone knows we need

---

[1] http://www.thenational.ae/sport/football/leading-leeds-united-are-the-sleeping-giants-with-arabic-spice

a new centre-back! I will sleep more soundly tonight knowing that. He also spoke about the possibility of bringing Arabic players to Elland Road. "We have been thinking about players from Egypt and Algeria, but there is not enough time in this [transfer] window," he said, "it is something we will likely explore in the January window or next summer. And why not? We should give Leeds some Arab flavour." I saw at least one tweet that suggested unkindly that we already had more than enough camels in the squad!

One other interesting utterance this weekend came from none other than Dave Jones. In his comments to the BBC after the game he confirmed that Wednesday were in just the same situation as Leeds were in respect of having to jettison a few players before they could contemplate adding any new ones. "I've still gotta get people out, still gotta move people at this moment in time if I'm gonna generate the money to bring people in". It was at least some comfort that it wasn't just us.

Leeds prepare to kick-off against Sheffield Wednesday

Chinese Whispers

Twitter continued to debate ad nauseam the pros and cons of the rumoured sale of Ross McCormack. Some recognised that if money was not available for further transfers then if we really did need players to come in someone had to leave; McCormack seemed to be the only player anyone wanted. McDermott had said for weeks this was the case; "one out, one in", he'd told us. Others though felt that retaining McCormack was more important as a sort of signal of intent by GFH, a signal that no longer would we be selling our best players. The losses of Gradel, Howson, Snodgrass and Becchio were still raw memories. As usual it was hard to know what to believe, if anything, that was being touted about as 'knowledge" either by those claiming to be 'In The Know' (ITK) on Twitter, or indeed in the pages of the daily papers. Some papers reported that El-Hadji Diouf was ready to move on, but then suddenly a piece appeared on the Leeds website with the man himself saying how happy he was at Leeds and McDermott was said to consider him central to his plans for the season. We were all playing a giant internet game of Chinese Whispers. Incidentally, on the same theme, I chuckled when I read about the winning entry for the Edinburgh Festival Joke of the Year. The joke, performed by Yorkshire comedian Rob Auton, went:

"I heard a rumour that Cadbury is bringing out an oriental chocolate bar. Could be a Chinese Wispa."[1] He has certainly raised the bar with that one...

On the evening of Tuesday 20th August, the Chinese whispers about Leeds signing Scott Wootton surfaced again. At one point a Twitter account under the name of @scottwootton doubled its follower count in a matter of minutes as Leeds fans hooked into it believing it was Scott Wootton's actual Twitter account; then it was revealed to be a fake. The dailymail.co.uk website then carried an article under the headline: "From Red to White: Manchester United defender Wotton [sic] heads to

---

[1] http://www.independent.co.uk/arts-entertainment/comedy/news/edinburgh-2013-former-salesman-rob-auton-raises-bar-with-cadbury-gag-to-win-funniest-joke-of-the-year-award-8774567.html

)und it hard to believe that one either,
1 got his name wrong! I tweeted to ask if
ot and someone with the handle
ponded, "Jesus, hope they've got the fee
resumably not believing Wootton to be
ely, someone else then tweeted that the
ow confirmed that Wootton had indeed
ee year contract, although not mentioning
any fee. It was... a universally popular signing of course because inevitably there were those who'd prefer we never signed anyone who'd worn that particular hue, but others were quick to point out that Giles and Strachan had made that journey too, and they became Leeds' legends!

So, another one had come in, but still no news that anyone had gone out. Salah Nooruddin had said in that interview the other day that he'd given the green light for *two* signings and that McDermott wanted a central defender *and* a right winger. One down, one to go! Even better news was that according to a tweet from Phil Hay, reporter for the Yorkshire Evening Post, Leeds had tonight rejected a third bid from Middlesbrough for Ross McCormack.

While Leeds fans were celebrating the arrival of Wootton, Doncaster Rovers were playing Wigan at the DW stadium, eventually coming away with a point and a 2 – 2 draw. At one point they'd led 2 – 0 and I was beginning to think my tip for the Championship title, Wigan, was perhaps a long way off the mark. Wigan had lost at newly promoted Bournemouth on Saturday in another surprise result. With all sides now having played three games, the table was headed by Nottingham Forest, the only side with a one hundred per cent record. Five teams had seven points; Bournemouth had six, and then came Reading and Leeds with five. Leeds held 9th spot, one of just eight teams so far undefeated.

"Have you seen they're thinking about stopping beer sales at Elland Road, Dad?" My son Adam doesn't say much, he's a typical teenager, very much an impact social creature. So when he does speak, I tend to sit up and take note. He turned his laptop around so I could see the article on the screen. It was another one from dailymail.co.uk. Above a rather unflattering picture of Leeds director Salem Patel, that made him look like the lovechild of Basil Brush and Alan Carr (Chatty Man), was the headline: "Leeds director in bid to ban alcohol at Elland Road on religious grounds"[1]. This was not the first time it had been mentioned that GFH, a Muslim organisation, might want to impose Islamic beliefs at Elland Road, but neither was it the first time dailmail.co.uk had printed complete boll****! I have to confess, I considered it unlikely that the Daily Mail, or even its internet stable mate, would print an article with absolutely no element of truth to it, but the general consensus seemed to be that is exactly what they'd done on this occasion. At least that was the gist of what the Leeds United Twitter correspondents believed. I would have preferred myself to see Salem Patel come out and totally refute the article, which said he'd raised the matter at board meetings at the club, but this he hadn't yet done. The YEP did carry an article refuting the whole affair though, quoting David Haigh saying: "The board has never discussed banning alcohol and has no plans to change the current licensing arrangements at Elland Road"[2]. That's alright then; breathe easy lads! It was only days if not weeks ago that Leeds had signed a deal with Heineken for "pouring rights" at ER.

Meanwhile, Ross McCormack was now said to be in discussions with the club about extending his current contract, though the doomsayers were still adamant that that nasty Mr Mowbray was going to drag him off to Teesside, kicking and screaming, "I am Leeeeeeeeds!" I was getting desperate for some more football.

As I trundled down the M6 on the first part of my journey to Ipswich, I spotted many cars and coaches sporting the red and white colours of Wigan Warriors, and a few less in the black and white colours of Hull. They were all on their way to Wembley for the Rugby League Challenge Cup Final; it was August Bank Holiday weekend of course. On the Danny Baker show coming through the car radio, another Lancashire v

---

[1] *http://www.dailymail.co.uk/sport/article-2399365/Leeds-director-wants-ban-alcohol-Elland-Road--Charles-Sale.html*

[2] http://www.yorkshireeveningpost.co.uk/news/latest-news/top-stories/leeds-united-quash-talk-of-booze-ban-for-elland-road-bars-1-5976988

Yorkshire contest was taking place in his regular 'sausage sandwich' competition. Today, the two contestants were representing Manchester United and Leeds United, in one of those lovely coincidences I'm always looking out for. A win for the lad supporting Leeds would be a great omen for the game at Ipswich later, I mused. Then, when the Manchester United bloke won it 2 – 1 on a tie break, I dismissed the notion as bunkum! I was annoyed with Danny Baker though, as I reckoned he'd cheated Leeds of victory. Mike Gatting was the celebrity answering the questions about himself, presumably chosen because the fifth and final Ashes Test was taking place at the Oval. The tie break question for 'Gatts' was: "Have you ever varnished your nails?" Gatting started to say, "No", the answer the Leeds lad gave, but then added that he did once have his nails coated with stuff to stop him biting them. Danny Baker only seized on this to say that counted, and gave the win to the Manchester lad! Unbelievable! They even cheat at the sausage sandwich quiz! If you've never heard Danny Baker's sausage sandwich quiz…oh, it's too complicated to explain.

It all served to pass the time on the 200 mile trip to the home of the Tractor Boys. I was meeting my Southend United supporting friend Andy again this year; he'd tempted me with the promise of a visit to the 31st Annual Ipswich Beer Festival, down on Orwell Quay. I'd never been down to the Waterfront before, despite having been to Portman Road many times; I should've though because it's a lovely spot. Today, the whole of the Waterfront was lined with stalls selling all sorts of crafts and advertising everything from maritime curiosities to ballroom dancing; as Andy and his son Jim and I walked through, we actually had to side-step couples gyrating around their makeshift dance floor! And all of this was just yards away from hundreds of little boats and yachts bobbing about in the waters of the River Orwell. It was a fantastic atmosphere, despite the heavy clouds threatening to soak us at any moment and it was all part of the Celebrate Ipswich Festival, 2013.

The beer festival itself was also buzzing with activity and despite the police request that no football shirts were to be allowed in (presumably in the hope of keeping Leeds fans away); I spotted many Leeds tops of various vintages and hues poking out from under jumpers and jackets. *"We're Leeds United, we drink where we want!"* Both Andy and Jim were actually sporting Southend United logos on their jackets too but the Shrimpers don't fall into the category of 'football' anymore! Keith, who actually lives in Southend, and who I've met a few times at various games, was in there, and we all chatted together while sampling the ale.[1] Adam and Conor disappointed me enormously by refusing to change the habits of a lifetime. They sought out the few lagers on offer! "I can't drink that real ale crap", Adam complained. "Southern heathen", I lambasted him.

With an hour to go 'til kick-off, Conor, Adam and I said cheerio to Andy and Jim and made our way to the ground, regretting not going a couple of minutes earlier as the heavens opened. A very soggy Nigel met me in the ground and we squelched our way up to our seats in the upper tier. The away fans at Portman Road are housed along the touchline at one end of the Cobbold stand, similar to how we now do it at Elland Road. The difference being that 1,950 Leeds fans, fully watered either at the beer festival or one of the many local boozers, make far more noise than the home fans, regardless where they put us!

Brian McDermott reverted to the side that got that impressive goalless draw at Leicester, meaning Dom Poleon dropped back to the bench with Noel Hunt recalled. Ipswich had not had the best of starts to the season having only won one game, and that win over Millwall was closer than the 3 – 0 score line suggested, according to their very honest manager, Mick McCarthy. Leeds had the weight of recent history against them though, having not won here since a Premier League fixture in 2001, and having suffered a horrendous run of red cards in this fixture in recent years. For me, I felt that avoiding defeat here would signal a continuation of the momentum we were building, while a defeat might just stop us in our tracks and bring out all the doubters and doom mongers again. After just

---

[1] *For the record I sampled Nettlethrasher (Elland Brewery, 4.4%); Pale Ale (Pheasantry Brewery, 4.0%); Blonde (York Brewery, 3.9%); and Nutty Black (Thwaites, 3.3%).*

12 minutes of the game the second scenario looked far more likely.

Ipswich came out of the traps like jet-propelled greyhounds and tore into Leeds like their lives depended on securing the win. With seven minutes on the clock the ball was in the Leeds net, Jay Tabb turning the ball in after a left wing cross from Aaron Cresswell and a mishit McGoldrick shot left the Leeds defence embarrassed. This time the linesman on the touchline opposite flagged for offside, but it looked to me as if Peltier was playing everyone on. Maybe this was karma for that run of bad luck we'd had here in recent years. Not that luck played much of a part in the 12th minute, when the ball was buried in our net again; this time it would stay in the record books.

David McGoldrick scored twice in the 3 – 0 defeat we suffered here just last March, so you would have thought we'd pay close attention to him. But when Daryl Murphy rose above Pearce to head the ball onto him, right in the middle of the pitch, about 30 yards out, Tom Lees gave him far too much room and merely watched the striker as he moved first to the left and then to the right before smashing the ball past Kenny from 20 yards. By this time, Lees was so bamboozled he was left sat on his backside, watching as McGoldrick struck the ball home. Dozens of previous goals we'd conceded where one or more of our defenders had ended up on their arses came flooding into my mind and for the umpteenth time I wondered why we were persisting with this defence. I cast a weary eye over to the bench to see if I could spot Scott Wootton. In the 23rd minute yet another Ipswich attack down the Leeds left ended with a lovely curling shot by Cresswell crashing back off the Leeds crossbar with Kenny clawing at the sky. "F****** hell, we could've been three down already", says the bloke next to me to no one in particular. Always looking for a positive sign, I recalled the game here two seasons ago when Leeds completely dominated the first half but could only score one goal; and then Aidy White got himself sent off and Ipswich won the game with two late strikes. Maybe this was our turn to "steal" one. Suddenly, that looked a real possibility, as Ross McCormack hit a speculative long range shot that cannoned off a defender straight to the unmarked Luke

Varney, 12 yards out. Varney, hardly believing his good fortune, drilled the ball high past Loach in the home goal. All square at half time, and we'd come back from a goal down for the fourth time in five matches!

The second half was a far more even affair after McDermott had subtly changed the Leeds formation, if not the names, on the pitch. Hunt, McCormack and Varney all pushed up in a 4 – 3 – 3 formation, presumably relying on the, "attack is the best form of defence", principle. It seemed to work, as Leeds spent far more time in possession and within minutes of the restart had grabbed the lead. Varney weaved his way down the right wing before whipping the ball across to McCormack in the far corner of the area. His stretching header merely tipped the ball up and behind him but he was onto it in a flash and Ipswich were good enough to allow him to turn and move the ball onto his right foot some 20 yards out. His luck was in again as his shot caught the boot of a defender on the way through and then somehow went right through the keeper as well! Mac looked almost embarrassed as he jogged over towards us to celebrate. "Ross McCormack is not for sale", we all sang, but there was no sign of reaction to that from the Scot.

Both teams had a few near misses and in the final five minutes Leeds fought a rear-guard action as Ipswich threw corner after corner under our crossbar but on this occasion we saw it through. As referee Mike Dean brought the game to an end, the Leeds fans celebrated like we'd already won promotion. Out on the pitch the Leeds players all hugged each other, still all rooted in our six-yard box where they'd been for the last few minutes. It was a special feeling. I had that familiar lump in my throat as I turned around to see the mass of the Leeds support belting out 'MOT'. Several familiar faces made their way down the steps above me as I waited for the crush to wane. First to appear was Keith, I swear there was a tear in his eye as we high fived and then he clenched his fist in that universal sign that says, "Yes, we did it!" Simon was next, babbling something about a cock-up by the Millwall kit-man who'd apparently forgotten to take the kit to their game at Hillsborough today. While I was still trying to digest that piece of random news I spotted Jo (the lady dressed as a clown at Watford last season) and we embraced. Phil, aka RamseyWhite, was next to appear, a broad grin etched into his craggy face. Everyone I saw was dewy eyed. This was a huge win for Leeds United. In months to come it may even be seen as a defining win; at least that's what I was thinking.

I jogged back to the car through the rain; it was now a very unpleasant wet evening, and then listened to Sports Report on the radio as I made the usual slow progress out of Ipswich and back towards the A14. It was a horrendous journey home, the rain lashing down so hard at one point that the wipers couldn't cope and everyone slowed to a crawl, everyone apart from a few of those bas***** driving their Chelsea Tractors. When I got back on the M6, many of those Wigan fans were now on their way home again, flying their colours and celebrating their 16 – 0 victory at Wembley, but I doubt they were as satisfied as me. Once the worst of the storm was behind me, I was able to relax a bit and savour our own victory, a victory that left Leeds sixth in the table. The five above were Forest, Blackpool, Leicester, and QPR, all on ten points, and Watford with eight, as we had. Confirming how bad the weather had been in places today, the game at Charlton was abandoned at half time due to a waterlogged pitch with Doncaster leading 3 – 1; Leeds head for Doncaster on Tuesday in the League Cup.

All smiles as Ross McCormack puts Leeds ahead at Ipswich

Giants

In yet another article this week, this time on arabianbusiness.com, (look, research is everything in this writing lark!) Leeds' MD, David Haigh told us: "The term 'sleeping giant' is often bandied around, but I think in this case it really is true...Leeds is very special. It's got a phenomenal history and we want to bring back those glory days."[1] Well, the next opportunity was coming up fast. On Tuesday, Leeds were due at The Keepmoat Stadium, home of Doncaster Rovers, in the second round of the Capital One Cup. Victory there and we could well be drawn against one of the big boys again. Leeds had shown an uncanny knack of being drawn against the giants of the Premiership in recent seasons; either in the League Cup or the FA Cup. Arguably, the top seven Premiership sides of the current era, Man U, Man City, Chelsea, Arsenal, Liverpool, Spurs and Everton, had all come out of the velvet bag paired with Leeds in the last three seasons. I pondered who the next in line was in terms of the pick of the Premiership, and concluded it was probably Newcastle United. A trip to St James' Park with five or six thousand Leeds fans would be some night out on the Toon! But we are getting ahead of ourselves.

I set off for Doncaster just after 2pm; the AA route planner suggesting the 96 mile trip would end just before 4pm, which it did; still three-and-a-quarter hours before kick-off. In an attempt to cut down on my intake of pies and burgers, I decided to break new ground today; I took home-made sandwiches! The life of a football fan dictates that your diet is one long stream of beer, pies and burgers. You tend to meet up in a pub before a game, a pub that when Leeds are in town is usually bursting at the seams. The chance to eat in said pub is therefore limited. You may, if you're lucky, be able to grab a burger, but more likely you'll not be prepared to queue, or the pub may actually not be doing food because it's just too busy. More often than not, in my case, I'll grab something at the

---

[1] *http://www.arabianbusiness.com/why-i-bought-leeds-united-514786.html*

ground, usually from one of the inevitable burger vans. At Leeds, I eat in the Pavilion, and nine times out of ten I'll have pie, peas and gravy. But in the last few days I've also been doing a bit of mystery shopping, and in particular I've been allocated several McDonald's restaurants...six in the space of the last three days, i.e. six burgers in the space of 72 hours! Hence the radical sandwich step. I sat in the car on Lakeside Boulevard eating 'dinner', before setting off to the Keepmoat. It was a warm afternoon and there were a number of folk sunning themselves on the grass bank that separates the stadium from the 50-acre man-made lake that looked absolutely stunning today; as picturesque as any of your Italian lakes. Dozens of swans were gliding along its surface when I was there, causing tiny imperfections in the mirror–like reflections of the lakeside buildings. As the clock ticked on towards 5pm, I made for my usual pre-match watering hole here, the Lakeside Beefeater, just a few minutes' walk from the ground and opposite a big McDonald's restaurant; I cursed myself for not having checked online to see if there were any mystery shopping opportunities there. Even at this early hour, there were plenty of Leeds fans already in the pub, and a few Donny Rovers ones too. I bumped into Andy and Wayne whilst wading in the impromptu paddling pool otherwise known as the pub toilets. I think it was just the residue from an overzealous bout of cleaning ...but Andy and Wayne both eyed me suspiciously as I squelched past them zipping up my flies and they tip-toed carefully to the urinals. I muttered something about, "Bloody cleaners could've mopped up a bit", to further deflect any suspicion of guilt!

The first task for any visiting members' branch is to display their flag to the front of the pub. It's a bit like an astronaut landing on the moon, or a climber scaling Everest; it's a statement of occupation! *"We're Leeds and we are here, we sh*g your women and drink your beer!"* I know most of the Surrey and Sussex guys and gals now, and was soon enjoying a beer with them at one of the wooden tables outside the pub. We took photos of each other with their flags as our back drop, but then a couple of staff appeared to ask that they be taken down. Quite what the logic of this is I will never understand.

There were plenty of Rovers' fans sat outside with us, and the flags were no problem for them. But, with the staff holding all the cards (a refusal to take down the flags would inevitably be met with a refusal to serve us beer and probably eviction from the premises), down they came. It was a shame as a very colourful scene then became, well, less colourful. It seemed that the Beefeater was the pub of choice today as everyone was there. Paula, Mike, Simon, Wayne, Tim, and 'Welsh' Andy, all appeared to have driven up together, and another Andy took a group photo of us all; Bogdan and Nigel arrived separately; Nick and Karen spotted us and sat down with us; Ian appeared from nowhere as did Jo.

The general feeling was that the pressure was off for this game; we expected a tough match against a confident Donny side that had started the season well, while we expected quite a few changes to the Leeds side. We knew of one new name; McDermott had told the official website that Scott Wootton would definitely start. What we didn't know was who he would replace, although many assumed it would be the recently error prone Tom Lees.

Someone picked up the team from Twitter at about 7pm.

Kenny
Peltier   Wootton   Pearce   Drury
Austin   Mowatt   Tonge   McCormack
Smith   Poleon

Subs: Ashdown, White, Murphy, Brown, Hunt, Diouf, Hall.

The inclusion of young Alex Mowatt caught everyone by surprise. He'd been a prominent member of the Under-18 squad last season, featuring in 18 of their 22 games and scoring 10 goals. He then appeared on the bench for the Chesterfield League Cup tie earlier this season. Now, the 18 year-old central midfielder would make his full debut.

A familiar name on the Donny bench was Billy Paynter; Banjo Billy! Very early in the game Billy did a warm-up run down the touchline to our right, and the huge Leeds following of 3,770 fans greeted him with his signature tune: "If Paynter scores we're on the pitch". I hoped he wouldn't even get a game today...if he did I just knew those football gods up there would put us to the test.

In a crowd of only 10,890, Leeds had well over a third of the support, and we were packed into the North End of the ground. We goaded the few Donny fans over to our right with, "3 – 1 up and you still don't win", reminding them of their disappointment at the weekend. Then we told them, "You're just a town full of Leeds fans", just for good measure. On the pitch though, their lads were doing OK. Like so many Championship sides they are a big, powerful team, with pace to spare, and they rocked the new look Leeds back on their heels. Mowatt looked very much at home though, and quickly became a favourite of the fans, as did his fellow debutant, Scott Wootton. Indeed, Wootton's first contribution was to clear the ball off his own goal-line! Gradually Leeds settled to their task and the two new boys, together with Poleon, Smith, and Adam Drury, began to weld together with the 'regulars'. It looked as though the first half would end goalless, but with four minutes to go, Adam Drury and Mowatt broke down the Leeds left; Mowatt swung over a cross to the back post to find Matt Smith; and Smith's looping header found Scott Wootton racing in at the back post to bury a header that ricocheted in off the underside of the bar. For the first time this season we had scored the opening goal in a game.

Doncaster made one change at half time, bringing on Mark Duffy for James Coppinger, and he did give the home side some impetus, although they rarely looked like scoring. They then turned to Billy Paynter, exactly on the hour mark.

Billy Paynter played 23 times for Leeds in his first season and scored just one competitive goal, at the 17th time of asking. He would make just four more appearances the following season and score two more. It has to be remembered that many of his appearances came from the subs bench though and I always felt there must be a decent striker lurking underneath that number '9' shirt, despite his various nicknames of 'Barn Door', 'Banjo' and 'That Wan*** Paynter'. But as he strode purposely onto the pitch tonight I think we all knew exactly what was about to happen...

There is some question as to whether it was Paynter's first touch or not, some reports I've read suggested it was actually his third; I'm sorry but I wasn't counting. But there is no doubt as to the quality of his finish. We were still singing about what we would all do if he scored as the ball was flashed across from the Donny left wing, at the far end of the ground. Even at that distance it was plain for all to see that it was our mate Billy who was rising like a salmon with a jet pack to meet the ball about 12 yards out. His head swivelled in a blur and the ball went like a missile across the face of goal to bury itself in the far corner, with Paddy Kenny no more than an interested spectator. It was a class header, and it reminded me of several I saw scored by the great John Charles in the twilight of his career while playing for Hereford. It was a moment of great irony tonight of course, and we were all too well behaved, not to mention too shocked, to carry out our threat to get "on the pitch". Most of us just shook our heads, mumbling, "F****** typical is that".

Donny then had their best spell of the match, as they pressed to win the game, but we had our own modern day 'Gentle Giant' in the shape of big Matt Smith. By now, Alex Mowatt had taken his bow and he'd been replaced by Luke Murphy. Mowatt got a fantastic and very well deserved standing ovation from the Leeds fans and we all hoped we'd see him progress just as quickly as Sam Byram did last season. Murphy immediately stamped his authority on the game and soon picked out a pass to Lee Peltier, moving down the right wing. Pelts had wasted more than a few crosses today, but this time he found Matt Smith perfectly, and Smith's huge forehead crashed the ball past Ross Turnbull.

We were still celebrating that one when Dom Poleon weaved his way into the corner of the box right in front of us, only to be pulled down; more in hope than expectation we were all on our toes again shouting, "Penalty!" Referee Scott Mathieson thought for only a nanosecond before pointing at the spot. Poleon and McCormack had a bit of a debate about it, but there was never any doubt that McCormack was taking it. I don't mind admitting I was nervous. McCormack's shooting today had again been wayward, and the last time he was having a game like that he missed a penalty, against Millwall in March. But this time he was as efficient as the proverbial German Engineer, or even German penalty taker, sliding the ball inside the keeper's left hand post as he dived away to his right. "That's how you win 3 – 1, that's how you win 3 – 1", sang the Leeds faithful, further rubbing the Donny noses in the dirt as their fans headed for the exits.

In the last ten minutes, Leeds knocked the ball about with a freedom we haven't seen for a very long time. OK, Doncaster's hearts were already broken, but the confidence in Leeds' play was really encouraging to see. "Olé", we cried each time a pass was completed, and then we spotted the Rovers' fans leaving and we gave them the usual, "We can see you sneaking out", and, "Time to go, time to go, time to go, time to go, time to go, time to go-oh, time to go-oh-oh f*** off!" I know it's childish but I love the finality of that one! Six games played and no defeat in the record book yet. On Wednesday night, the draw for the third round of the Capital One Cup was made. I knew, I swear I knew; it would be Newcastle United away.

Paula, Mike, Tim, Wayne, Simon, Andy and me.

Back to the future?

On the eve of the QPR game, Ross McCormack signed a new four-year deal with Leeds, ending all speculation that he was about to join Tony Mowbray's Middlesbrough. The transfer window still had three days to go, but this would prove to be the last action affecting any Leeds player; there would be no more new additions and no one leaving, at least until the emergency loan window opens in a couple of weeks' time. Brian McDermott would report that he'd refused to continue discussions over one 29-year-old player when the player's current club disclosed they wanted £600,000 for him, even though his existing contract terminated in June; it was rumoured to be Chris Burke, a right winger with Birmingham City. McDermott also confirmed one Leeds player had refused a loan move to Barnsley, despite both clubs agreeing terms; it was assumed that was Aidy White.

The QPR game was a huge disappointment on so many levels. It was another Sky TV game, and another 12:15pm kick-off, so the first let down was a crowd of just 23,341. It was very similar to the attendance for the previous home game against Sheffield Wednesday (23,766), also screened in that same Saturday lunchtime slot. We all dreamed of another full house like we saw for the Brighton game on the opening day, but bearing in mind the cost of football these days, it's hardly surprising that many otherwise dedicated Leeds fans choose to watch the TV games from the comfort of their own homes, and spread their limited football budgets over a few less visits to the ground. The Burnley game at Elland Road in three weeks' time will tell us the real level of support post Bates; that one was not scheduled to be on the telly.

The QPR game itself would hardly have kept viewers' arses glued to their sofas. It was yet another typically close fought Championship game between two sides who largely cancelled each other out. McDermott went with the side most predicted; the side that started down at Ipswich, but with new recruit Wootton replacing Tom Lees, who was relegated to the bench. In fact, McDermott's' first eleven for league games was now more or less predictable. Now and again he would swap Poleon for Hunt (my preference was Poleon for his pace), and Wootton has pushed Lees out, but the rest were seemingly guaranteed a start. Hence we lined up: **Kenny, Peltier, Pearce, Wootton, Warnock, Austin, Murphy, Green, McCormack, Varney and Hunt,** with the last two up front. QPR came into the game unbeaten in the league just like ourselves and four other teams, but they'd dropped just two points, whereas we'd dropped four. Both sides had scored only five goals in their four games though, so it was never going to be a high scoring affair.

Before the game, just after the 'respect' handshakes had been completed, the entire Leeds team lined up in front of the West Stand and then all turned slowly, waving to each side of the ground. As they have done before most games this season, they still wore their white retro tracksuit tops with their names on the back. It was a little bit spooky actually; a sort of 'back to the future' moment, imitating what the great Revie side of the early 70s, the 'Super Leeds' team did. Was this a coincidence? Or is it an attempt to connect with those glory years? The wave, imitation sock tags, tracksuit tops, the pre-match huddle, it all seemed too much of a coincidence. The Square Ball website noticed it too and posted a photograph of the 'wave'.[1] A few days after the game, Brian McDermott explained why he'd introduced these various homages to the Revie era. He told BBC Radio Leeds he had tremendous "respect for the history of this club" and was interested in any little advantage he could gain on a match day by intimidating the opposition and getting the crowd behind the team. He explained: "I distinctly remember that years ago, I remember that team walking out on the pitch at Elland Road, and it was like a group of soldiers coming out, and it was bordering on a little bit scary...and I liked it". If only we could play like 'em.

QPR had the irrepressible Joey Barton in their midfield, and it was Barton who had the ball in the net in front of the Kop after only 8 minutes. The linesman flagged for offside to the great amusement of everyone around me, but when I watched the

---

[1] *http://www.thesquareball.net/2013/09/04/the-return-of-the-elland-road-wave-and-a-respect-for-the-past/*

recording of the game back some days later, it was clear the goal should have stood. It was another example of that worrying trend we saw a lot last season when our back four all have a hand in the air appealing for offside while one of them is actually playing the striker on. At least it got the crowd going, as they derided Barton with another rendition of, "Jo-ey Bar-ton, is a wa**er, is a wa**er!", and then roundly booed him every time he touched the ball for the rest of the game. It was a let off, but one that overall I felt we deserved. There were no goals in the first half; in fact there was only one shot on target, from QPR. Leeds had four attempts but three of them, from Green, Austin and McCormack, went into row 'Z' in the South Stand. We all expected Brian McDermott to raise the bar in terms of our quality of attacking play this season but our strikers seem to think the bar has *literally* been raised, about thirty feet! Surprisingly, Leeds dominated the corner count, with five in the first half compared with Rangers' none, but our delivery was appalling; another problem we've suffered for a couple of years. Noel Hunt had an abysmal first forty five minutes in which he could do nothing right.

Early in the second half, Dom Poleon and Matt Smith joined the fray replacing Varney and Hunt, the latter having arguably his weakest game in a Leeds shirt thus far. The changes seemed to add different options to our play, particularly with Poleon's pace down the inside left channel, but I couldn't claim I thought we would score. It had nil-nil written all over it for me.

In the 61st minute of the TV commentary, when I watched the game back the following week, Andy Hinchcliffe, predicts, "One mistake, one slip up, could prove very, very costly". At the ground around the same time, I was only thinking we hadn't yet made our defensive mistake for the day; perhaps I expected the addition of Wootton back there would ensure there wasn't one. If I did, I was wrong, and in the 74th minute we were behind. I should have seen it coming I suppose; Paddy Kenny had been superb so far this season, arguably responsible for the unbeaten start. So it should have surprised no one that when he tried to clutch a Joey Barton free kick from out on the left wing, he merely spilled it a la Rachubka.

Charlie Austin's boot flicked the loose ball to Clint Hill, and Hill smacked it into the net from point blank range. Yawn! What is it about our defence? Are they all involved in some sort of match fixing scandal? The type of errors we've been making could easily be seen as evidence of it. Either that, or maybe the curse that Don Revie tried to rid us of all those years ago has returned and we need another visit from Gypsy Rose. Maybe that's the next retro step we need to take. Come to think of it, maybe this was the reason all the beer in the Pavilion today was as flat as a witch's tit! It's all cursed!

Rudy Austin so nearly sent us all home happy when he hit a swerving shot from all of thirty yards, in the last couple of minutes. It had Robert Green (who we'd taunted with, "You let your country down"), beaten all ends up, but just nicked the outside of the top right angle. One day Rudy will hit one of those and it will win goal of the decade.

The statistics from the BBC website showed QPR having 57% of the possession and 16 shots to our 11, so there was a case for saying the score line did just about reflect the game. But equally, I couldn't argue with Brian McDermott's assessment as reported on the BBC: "Did we do enough to win? Probably not. Did we deserve to lose? Probably not. We got done at a set-play which is disappointing to say the least and we didn't do enough with the ball. Without possession we were diligent and solid. No-one could fault the players' effort…"[1]

It was a disappointing way to go into the next international break; it almost felt like our bubble of optimism had been spiked by that one slip by Kenny, by one long witch's fingernail that just nicked the ball out of Kenny's clutches. Anyway, I was off to North Wales for a couple of days to get rid of my football induced post-traumatic stress and I intended to put it completely out of my mind.

---

[1] *http://www.bbc.co.uk/sport/0/football/23822540*

Barcelona, buses, and Bolton

When Mrs W and I returned from Nefyn, we immediately had to get ourselves ready for our next trip; four days in Barcelona, as we continued to make the most of the international break. In Wales, we spent two days with friends in a lovely cottage on the coast, getting drunk and walking off our hangovers along the beach. In Barca, it was just Mrs W and me, and there would be absolutely no football. Well, when I say absolutely none, of course we couldn't resist a trip to the Camp Nou!

To get to the Camp Nou we decided to use the second day of a two day ticket we'd bought for the open top bus, but before we arrived I had a job to do. It was Wednesday, September 11th, and tickets for the Newcastle cup game went on sale to Gold Membership card holders at 10:30am UK time today; 11:30am Barcelona time. I'd waited until now to ensure Mark (who only has a Gold Membership) and I could sit together; I could have bought my ticket (as a season ticket holder) the previous week had we been prepared to sit separately.

The open top buses used for the two-hour hop-on, hop-off circular tours are very thoughtfully equipped with Wi-Fi, as well as a multi-lingual local history commentary fed to individual ear-phones. My plan was to ensure we were back on a bus just after 11:30am local time and I'd make the ticket purchase on my mobile before we then got off again at the Camp Nou. It had rained earlier, and I shivered as the damp air whistled through my hair when the bus got up to speed, but Mrs W was well wrapped up, and I'd promised her this wouldn't take long….

An hour and forty minutes later, the screen on my mobile was still telling me: "This site is currently very busy and you have been placed in a queue. Please do not close your browser". The yellow progress bar still appeared to be working and was inching its way across the tiny screen, albeit at the pace of an asthmatic snail. I was also slightly perturbed that the 'estimated time left' counter had been stuck on '8 minutes' for the last hour or so! But I assumed that heavy demand for tickets was causing the long delay and that I was actually still connected in a cyber-queue and would soon be invited to enter my membership number and password to carry out my purchase…

It never happened. Did I mention it was cold and damp up there on the top deck out in the open? Mrs W was by this time getting very annoyed and she pointed out that we had long since passed the Camp Nou stop and were in fact now almost back to where we started; not far from our hotel on Las Ramblas. "David, this is f****** ridiculous", Mrs W barked at me. "I'm cold, hungry, and that f****** connection is obviously not working". Mrs W doesn't swear much, so when she does you know you are in serious doo dah. And if there are two things you don't want Mrs W to be, cold and hungry are well up the list! I once read that red-heads, thin people, and women, feel the cold more than other people…and Mrs W scores highly on each of those attributes. But what to do? It might only be a few seconds more before I get to the front of the cyber-queue if I sit tight. If I close the browser now it might take me at least another hour and forty minutes to get to the same point…and I didn't have enough battery left for that! Not to mention absolutely no chance of keeping Mrs W on this bus for another hour and forty minutes in the cold without food! If it *was* due to heavy demand for tickets then I might also be running the risk of missing out altogether and not getting to see the game!

My only other option was to gamble that it was in fact my mobile connection that wasn't working; close it down, get off the bus, and head back to the hotel to use one of the laptops in the lobby. Again though, I might still face a long delay if it was a demand issue and there really was a huge queue of fans waiting online to buy tickets. Mrs W made the decision much easier for me. She stormed off the bus at the next stop.

I quickly gathered up my things and got up to follow her, still clutching my mobile and forgetting I still had my little red ear phones in! My feet carried on walking while my head was snapped back by the wire connecting my ear pieces to the bus causing not a little mirth among the few other passengers braving the elements with us. This was not going well. Not going well at all.

To try to help matters along, I told Mrs W I would jog on ahead to the hotel while she walked at a more leisurely pace, so that by the time she got there I'd hopefully be done and dusted. Thus, I reasoned, I could rescue the rest of our day, the holiday, and potentially our marriage of 29 years. It would also now require as a minimum a slap-up lunch for Mrs W, that piece of expensive jewellery she'd spotted yesterday on the market, and a trip on the metro to get us back to the Camp Nou before it closed for the day.

Have I ever mentioned that I'm useless at local geography? As I sped off along Las Ramblas, Mrs W calls after me, "You know where you're going do you?" "Ha-ha, very funny", I shout over my shoulder as I pick up speed, just managing to dodge round a big group of teenage Spanish girls wearing regulation frayed denim shorts with golden sun-tanned legs up to their arm-pits...not that I really noticed...

Twenty minutes later, having reached the other end of Las Ramblas, I concluded I was lost! I'd somehow managed to miss the hotel entrance as I sped along weaving around the crowds of tourists that constantly pack this particular pedestrian thoroughfare. I was totally convinced that the Husa Internacional Cool Local Hotel should have been on my left as I went north up Las Ramblas, heading inland from the harbour. I was wrong; it was in fact on my right! As I stood scratching my head in Plaza de Catalunya, I eventually worked this out. I began to retrace my steps, more slowly this time, and looking both sides of the street to spot either the hotel entrance, or the more prominent 'American Soda' café that I remembered was right opposite and where we had breakfast this morning. By the time I did spot the 'American Soda' sign I had broken out in a hot sweat, the inevitable result of my sprint along Las Ramblas; the sun breaking through and scorching my unprotected head; my state of panic at realising that I'd now wasted another half an hour during which thousands more Leeds fans would have been snapping up those Newcastle tickets; and not least the fear of facing the wrath and ridicule of Mrs W when I eventually got back to the hotel!

As I burst in through the hotel entrance, launching myself up the stairs three at a time towards the 1st floor lobby, I wracked my befuddled brain for an excuse to explain to Mrs W where the hell I'd been for the last half hour; any phrase that didn't include the words, "I got lost", or, "I was distracted by a crowd of Spanish girls in denim shorts", would have come in useful. Mrs W was already waiting, stood with arms folded across her chest, head to one side, and one foot tapping relentlessly on the floor, in that universal pose of a woman who has you caught bang to rights. "You got lost didn't you?" she says. It wasn't a question; it was a statement of fact. I muttered something about running so fast that I must have missed the hotel, and then slumped down in front of the lap top and began tapping "Leeds United" into Google.

The whole process of buying two tickets for Newcastle took just a couple of minutes on the laptop and it was clear I could've been sat on that bus 'til Christmas and it would not have let me get any further in the process. There weren't thousands of Leeds fans clogging the system; it was just that the mobile phone connection hadn't been working, as Mrs W had correctly surmised. "You've just wasted three hours of our holiday", Mrs W chided me, and I just knew it was going to cost me, big time.

For the record, I bought Mrs W a lovely lunch at a restaurant on Las Ramblas, and then we took the metro back to the Camp Nou where we spent a good couple of hours on the tour of the stadium and the excellent museum. I wore my Leeds top for a few pictures inside the stadium with those famous words: "Mes que un club", (More than a club), in the background. I marvelled at how small Messi's boots were; several pairs were on display in one of the exhibition cabinets. The scale of the trophy cabinet was unbelievable, and we watched with smug satisfaction as they re-ran highlights of the 2011 European Cup Final, when Barca beat Man U, 3 – 1. I can thoroughly recommend the tour, which is well worth the 23 Euro entrance fee. You could easily spend three hours or more in there.

There was added interest today, September 11th, as it was also La Diada, Catalan National Day, when the region commemorates the defeat of its troops in the Spanish War of Succession in 1714. These days the celebration is more of a political rally, a call to the Spanish authorities to grant Catalonia its freedom from Spanish rule, and today several hundred thousand Catalonians would join hands to form a human chain, 400 kilometres long, running from the French border to Valencia, publicising their demand. Everywhere we went today the city was awash with the red and yellow stripes of the Catalan flag, 'La Senyera', which is of course also the colour scheme of this season's Barca away strip. We got the tube back to the Plaza de Catalunya and we sang and cheered with thousands of Spanish revellers in front of a huge TV screen that was beaming live pictures from all over the region. Afterwards, as we made our way slowly back to our hotel once more, the ticket buying fiasco was almost forgotten.

We flew back from Barcelona on Friday afternoon, touching down at Liverpool's John Lennon Airport just after 3:15pm, bang on time, imagine! They played that very annoying trumpet fanfare that Ryanair flights insist on playing every time they land a flight on time. Remembering our recent six hour delay on a Monarch flight out of Nice, I wondered if maybe Monarch should do the same…and if they did, would it ever get played? The latest international break was thus over, and domestic football was back on the agenda this weekend. England managed a 4 – 0 victory over Moldova last Friday and then a nil-nil bore-draw with Ukraine on Tuesday, described by the Daily Telegraph as, "a hideously ugly performance". It left England top of their group but still needing decent results in their final two qualifiers at home to Montenegro and Poland next month to ensure they will be going to Brazil for the 2014 World Cup. Leeds had three players on international duty during this break – McCormack, Green and Rudy Austin, although only Paul Green played for any length of time. McCormack got only five minutes for Scotland while Rudy was suspended for Jamaica's game this week. It was a near full strength squad therefore that Brian

McDermott had for the Trotters trip this weekend. Only Sam Byram continued to convalesce with the reserves.

I had my wingman Mark back for this game; it was only his second appearance of the season due to his work commitments, but he'd arranged his schedule to give himself a full day off for this one. I met him and his girlfriend Jess at their flat in Altrincham, just before 10:00am. Typical of Mark, he wasn't even out of bed when I arrived, and he wasn't sure of the tram or train times either. The journey to Bolton was therefore a bit of an adventure! We got a lift to Altrincham tram station with Jess and then I watched in dismay as a tram to Piccadilly pulled in, and then out, with Mark still trying to coax a couple of tickets out of the machine on the platform! We got on the next one that pulled into Piccadilly at 10:45am, and then had to sprint, first to collect tickets for the train to Horwich Parkway, and then again to platform 14 to try to get the 10:54am train. Platform 14 was about half a mile away, or so it seemed to me. We both arrived puffing and panting, seconds before the train did! It was a gentle ride then across north Manchester and out towards Bolton.

Horwich Parkway is just yards from the Reebok, but we walked on past, heading instead for the Beehive, where we went last season. Once again it was a designated pub for away fans. It was more of a wasps' nest than a beehive today, but I reduced their population by regularly swatting them with a rolled up newspaper, much to the amusement of the Leeds fans. They cheered loudly each time they heard the thwack of the paper on the window or wall. It was more entertaining than watching Man U v Palace on the big screen in the pub anyway. On the rare occasions my eyes strayed to the screen, all I could see was Ashley Young trying to con the ref with a series of outrageous dives – one of which got him a yellow card and one which got a penalty which Van Persie converted. Wally Rooney, with a thick black headband covering a head wound, also scored from a free-kick, to complete a 2 – 0 win for the Salford Divers. One lad wearing a fake Man U top was the centre of some playful banter from the Leeds fans, until he was persuaded by the door staff to take it off in case it caused us vile animals to riot! He had some cohonas though!

I finally got to meet Chris and a few of his mates today. Chris is the scaffolding manager who caused great amusement on Facebook recently by posting a photo of himself reading 'Déjà vu' while perched in a harness on scaffolding high above Regent Street in London! (See page 34) He's surprisingly normal! All the usual travelling army of Leeds fans were in today; I got to chat with Nick and Karen (who'd been so early they even managed breakfast!), Andy and Lily were there as always, Kevin and Zack, Nigel, they were all there.

Karen was first to get the team news and the screen on her Samsung mobile listed just one change from the side that succumbed to QPR a fortnight ago. Tonge was in for Paul Green, presumably recognising Green's efforts in playing a full game for The Republic of Ireland in Austria on Tuesday (lost 1 - 0). More interesting was the inclusion on the bench of young Alex Mowatt. The side thus lined up as follows in the usual diamond formation.

Kenny

Peltier Wootton   Pearce Warnock

Austin

Tonge Murphy

McCormack

Hunt Varney

Subs: Cairns, Lees, Mowatt, Green, Diouf, Smith, Poleon.

As I've said before, I was less than enamoured that we were persisting with Hunt but other than that it was hard to criticise. Bolton were not in good shape, going into this game bottom of the table; tellingly there was no table even printed in today's programme. On the bench for the Trotters was former Leeds hero, Jermaine Beckford.

The game itself was hardly memorable; fitting the template of games so far this season perfectly. There were plenty of efforts at goal, 27 in all, but only three hit the target. One, in the sixth minute of the game, went in. You might describe it as a 'Lukey' break. Luke Murphy swung in a corner from the left wing, and Luke Varney met it perfectly in the six-yard box, glancing a header across Adam Bogdan inside the back post. If

Leeds had conceded such a goal it would have been no surprise, merely one more in the ever growing total of such goals against us in recent seasons. But for us to score such a goal, from a set piece, well, that was a thing of beauty! It was only the second time this season Leeds opened the scoring.

The rest of the game was fought out in midfield, with those other two attempts on target both saved; one by Kenny (Bolton's only shot on target, from Beckford) and one by Adam Bogdan. Beckford had come on for the last half hour, getting a great reception from us and responding with a Leeds salute; he's another bloke with huge cohonas, doing that in front of his own fans! For Leeds, Pelts went off in the 54th minute, but was seamlessly replaced by Lees, no stranger to our right back berth of course. A sell-out Leeds following of 4,800 enjoyed toying with the paltry Bolton support in the September sun and even offered some paternal advice to the red haired Bogdan with: "Get out of the sun, get out of the sun, you ginger bas**** get out of the sun"!

This was a great example of how to win games in this very tight division. The key is to make no mistakes. We didn't; Bolton did. Leeds ended the day 6th, amazingly boasting the division's third best defensive record. Only the top two, QPR and Blackpool, had conceded fewer. Bolton actually went up one place due to Millwall getting another walloping, 5 – 1 at home to Derby, but I doubt Bolton will bother to print the table in their programme for some little while yet!

The Shrimper's tale

We were now into a crucial spell of seven games in three weeks, with league games against Reading, Burnley, Millwall, Bournemouth and Derby following the Bolton game, and the Newcastle cup game sandwiched in the middle. The Reading game was a logistical puzzle for me, as I had a rare business meeting in central London on the morning following the game. It would go like this: travel by train to Euston on Wednesday morning and then the tube to Blackfriars to drop my bag at the Hotel. Then tube to Paddington and a train to Reading. Rendezvous this time was the World Turned Upside Down pub on Basingstoke Road, 15 minutes from the Madejski Stadium. Then, after the game, Adam had agreed to give me a lift to Hanger Lane tube station to make the trip back to the hotel; meeting in Blackfriars Thursday morning, tube back to Euston, train back to Stafford, simples! Now if that's not dedication to the cause I don't know what is – I bet Gary Edwards might blanch at that schedule! I was due to meet up with my Shrimper (Southend United) friend from Ipswich, somewhere along the line, as he was joining me at the game as an honorary Leeds fan. Andy is in the process of 'doing the 92', that is, visiting all 92 current English Football League and Premiership grounds. The Madejski was number 83 for him.

The train down to Euston was uneventful. I did cast an eye towards Wembley Stadium as we trundled past, wondering if we might conceivably be visiting in May; whether my old heart is strong enough to withstand a play-off final, I'm not sure. A couple of hours later and I was on the 16:18 Paddington to Bedwyn service on my way to Reading, sat by two lovely pensioner ladies, sisters-in-law, who live there. In conversation I mentioned I was going to the football and then had a meeting back in London the next day. They gave me some excellent directions to the World Turned Upside Down and then the one old dear, assuming obviously that I still worked, told me, "You keep working for as long as you can love, this retirement lark is not all it's cracked on to be!".

While suffering the total tedium of my meeting the next day, her words came back to me...and I was confident she was so very wrong! The retired lady also told me the WTUD did a fantastic carvery for only £4.19.

Just as I arrived at Reading station, my mobile beeped. A text from the Shrimper began: "After a lot of huff n puff am not that far behind u – vaulted the barrier 2 just get the 16:45 out of Pad". Andy vaulting a barrier I would love to see! (You don't know him!). I decided to wait at the station for him but then cocked an ear as I heard, "Marching on Together", wafting into the station. It was coming from the Three Guineas pub next door. I quickly texted the Shrimper back to tell him I'd meet him outside the Three Guineas, and then nipped in for a swift pint of Greene King IPA. It was manic in there and many of the lads looked well lubricated already; it was only 5pm.

Andy arrived at 5:15pm and we set off on the walk to the pub; it was a lot further than I remembered and we were both gasping after the half-hour march. Once again though we were in good company and gradually the WTUD filled with the sounds of the Leeds travelling choir. The Surrey lads were there in force as you might expect down here, and Adam and Conor were taking advantage of that £4.19, 'as much as you can eat', carvery; they later emerged to tell us they'd managed six Yorkshire puddings between them! My only gripe with the WTUD was their queuing system for the bar; they had four or five staff serving but the queue stretched out into the front beer garden, and once the sun disappeared it got flipping cold standing out there. Big Cliff and 'Welsh' Andy from the Surrey Whites rescued me on one occasion, by adding my round into theirs (for a small commission!) since they were already at the bar. Even my old mate Nigel was forced to get a double round in for himself when he spent half an hour waiting.

Arriving at the ground, the Shrimper and I got burgers from a van outside the away end. Six bloody quid for a 'Deluxe Burger'! Adam and Conor thought this hilarious and were well chuffed now with their £4.19 carvery experience...and they reminded us many more times during the evening! It had been another excellent pre-match session though all in all, and everyone agreed that a draw tonight would cap a decent away day just nicely. And that's how it should have ended.

Brian McDermott, returning to his former employer for the first time since his sacking last season, made just the one enforced change; leaving Tom Lees at right back continuing to deputise for the injured Lee Peltier. Reading had been steady so far in the Championship; they had nine points from their opening six games and had lost just the once, to Blackpool, by a single goal. The last time we came to the Madejski, Adam Le Fondre, a 69th minute replacement for Noel Hunt (then at Reading), punished us late in the game with two goals. He was on the Reading bench again tonight, while Hunt was now in the Leeds starting eleven of course. That game two seasons ago also saw young Zac Thompson sent off early in the game and Reading's Jem Karacan go off with a broken ankle following a Michael Brown tackle. I recalled seeing on the BBC website yesterday that Leeds had the best disciplinary record in the Championship this season with just 5 yellows and no reds. I should have been afraid, very afraid.

The game followed the usual Championship template we've witnessed all season. It was tight, there was nothing between the sides, and from very early on it looked like a single goal would settle it; either a mistake or a flash of brilliance. Leeds looked solid, and urged on by 3,268 well watered followers, were every bit as effective as Reading. The Madejski was nowhere near full, with only 21,167 inside the 24,200 capacity arena and there were plenty of empty seats visible around the other three sides of the ground. The most vocal Reading fans were over to our right, in the south east corner. They gave it a good go, but there were nowhere near enough of them to compete with us.

After just eight minutes, history once again began to repeat itself, as the unfortunate Jem Karacan was stretchered off again, this time after a tussle with Ross McCormack. He was carried off the last time these sides met of course albeit he was five minutes earlier this time! It took 15 minutes for either side to get a shot on target, and when it came it was our own Paddy Kenny coming to the rescue. Leeds first (and only as it turned out) shot on target was saved by former Leeds loanee Alex McCarthy, in the 26th minute from Luke Varney. At half time there was unsurprisingly no score. There'd been plenty of shots but most of them flew harmlessly over the bar or wide of the posts. I continue to be amazed at the paucity of strikes on target in this division. The only other significant moments of that first half saw three bookings; two for Reading, and Stephen Warnock for 'unsporting behaviour'. One shot on target for Leeds in 45 minutes' football is just not good enough albeit this was a statistic we would repeat many times this season.

On the hour, Noel Hunt was substituted – nine minutes earlier than Le Fondre replaced him in that game two years ago. Dom Poleon was the Leeds man to take his place this time; how I wished we had someone of the calibre of Le Fondre to throw on. Instead, Adam Le Fondre was on the pitch for Reading just six minutes later, replacing Robson-Kanu. We should have known what was coming shouldn't we? In the 83rd minute, Matt Smith came on for the tiring Varney, but you know, Matt Smith won less in the air than Varney had done.

"It was a nil-nil game", McDermott would tell us after the match, and it really should have been. But it wasn't. After 90 minutes the board went up telling us there would be four minutes of added time. We looked comfortable. In fact we had probably been the better team during the last 20 minutes. As the last of the four extra minutes ticked by, Ross McCormack sent over a free kick from the Leeds right wing. Jason Pearce met it perfectly at the back post and the ball flashed towards the corner of the net. For a split second 3,268 Leeds fans were on their toes, arms aloft, ready to celebrate. But then we heard the tell-tale, "Ha-Ha-Haaaaah!", coming from the Royals' fans on our right, as they realised before us the ball had gone wide, not in. "Ah well, not to worry, a point down here is a good point, not many teams will get anything down here", says a wise old sage in the row in front of me.

The game is still going on; we are now into the fifth minute of added time and that man Le Fondre is racing down the right wing, at the far end of the ground. Stephen Warnock clatters into him; free kick. Everyone is waiting for the final whistle;

we think it may have gone as Stephen Warnock is walking off the pitch towards the dug-out. But he's going on his own and applauding us...where's the substitute then? No one comes on. We're into the sixth minute of added time. Reading whip the ball into the Leeds penalty area and suddenly I'm reminded of a moment on Nefyn beach when Mrs W and I were skimming stones. The flat low cross takes a first skip off one Reading head, then a second, then nestles in the corner of our net. Suddenly there are Reading fans all around the ground going mental; those that hadn't already left at any rate. Our world was suddenly turned upside down and it was that man Le Fondre who got the final touch. Un-frickin-believable!

Sat in traffic after the game, in Adam's car, Adam, the Shrimper and I, listen mournfully as Conor reads the details off the BBC football website. Stephen Warnock had been sent off for a second bookable offence; his reckless tackle on Le Fondre. Brian McDermott was, "gutted", but not prepared to lay the blame with anyone in particular. He said that Warnock had already held his hand up to acknowledge that he'd made a mistake in making the challenge. But equally McDermott stressed we ought to have been able to defend the free-kick. It was of course another of those headers in the six-yard box that we seem unable to stop. We are not learning that mistakes in this division will cost us games. Elsewhere tonight, QPR and Brighton drew nil-nil – neither of those sides making any costly mistakes. Reading and Brighton had drawn nil-nil at the weekend. Yet again Leeds had been on the very cusp of a place in the top four had we been able to win this game. But tonight we slipped back down to 11th, with it all to do again. Leeds just specialise in frustration! QPR went clear at the top with 17 points tonight, six ahead of Leeds.

The traffic outside the Madejski was a nightmare. We crawled along for miles before reaching the M4 and then we inched along the M4 which was down to a single lane at one point for some of those invisible road works – you know the sort, loads of cones but not a single blemish on any part of the road. It was gone midnight when Adam dropped the Shrimper and I at Park Royal tube station as an alternative to Hanger Lane, which we couldn't find. Inside Park Royal station was a little sign pointing back outside: "Hanger Lane 730 yards ->" It was 12:10am...In the car the Shrimper and I had casually considered what time the tubes stopped running...

Andy and I jogged the 730 yards (that's 41% of a mile by the way) arriving at the ticket barriers at Hanger Lane sweaty and exhausted. I slid my Travelcard into the slot and swept it up again as I rushed through the barrier. The Shrimper pushed his ticket into the slot and...nothing. The barrier remained firmly closed. A couple of other people dashed through another lane and ran down to the platform. The Shrimper tried again, and then again. Still nothing! Would I see him vault the ticket barrier after all? Well, as good as! A well-to-do bespectacled fellow approached the barrier to leave the station. The Shrimper was like a coiled spring, a cat down on his haunches stalking his prey. Well-to-do slips his ticket into the slot and the barrier opens but before he can move to go through, the Shrimper has launched himself at the opening from the other side. Well-to-do is tossed aside like a rag doll being thrown from a toddler's pram and the Shrimper is off, galloping away down to the platform. I am creased up with laughter as I try to keep pace with him, not daring to look back to see what carnage was left in our wake and still wondering if all this effort was to be in vain if we'd already missed the last tube! A guard on the platform informs us that the last tube on the Central line will be arriving in less than a minute!

After a mind-numbing meeting in plush offices just off Fleet Street, on Thursday morning, and another dash for a tube, I arrived hot and sweaty once more on Euston's platform 17, (it was to become a recurring theme this season), at 14:45....for the 14:46 to Stafford. I wouldn't live in London for a million pounds...well, maybe.

Reflecting on the match as I watched Wembley flashing past again, I couldn't help but think how incredibly similar it had been to our last trip to the Madejski. More than that though, I just wondered what the outcome might have been had Le Fondre come on for us and not the Royals. We will never know of course. One player we would not now be seeing in a Leeds shirt any time soon was Ryan Hall; he'd joined Sheffield United on a one month loan.

Vintage Clarets

In response to a question posed after the Reading game, Brian McDermott refused to rule out the possibility of Sam Byram returning for the visit of Burnley. He also intrigued us all by saying that Aidy White could well, "be the man", to come in for the suspended Stephen Warnock. It really is a funny old game isn't it? We'd lost both regular full-backs in the space of two games, with Peltier still carrying a knock and Warnock suspended. So, the sight of the names Byram and White in the team list on Pecky's mobile were no surprise as we crowded round her in the Pavilion. The fact that Diouf's name was on there too was a surprise, albeit a pleasant one for me as the other name missing was Noel Hunt. The full side was:

Kenny
Byram Wootton   Pearce White
Austin Murphy Tonge
McCormack   Varney   Diouf

Subs: Cairns, Green, Smith, Poleon, Brown, Mowatt, Hunt.

It looked like a 4 – 3 – 3 formation this time, but it was hard to discuss the team selection in the Pavilion as we could barely hear each other speak over the din being made by the Rhodes Brothers, a two-piece acoustic band playing on the Pavilion stage. This was the first act of another new initiative, this time at the behest of Heineken, the clubs Official Beer Partner, (a post I actually felt I was more than qualified for myself incidentally). Pecky suggested this was a clever move by the big brewer, as since we couldn't talk we would probably drink more! It was a pain in the arse to be honest and I hope this particular initiative is short-lived. The band was decent enough but folk don't want music in there, they want to chat about the upcoming game and watch the TV match, (Charlton 0 Millwall 1).

The match-day programme, 'We Are Leeds', explained that goalkeeper Jamie Ashdown had been involved with the first get together of the Leeds United rowing team (I kid you not) during the recent international break, and I assumed at the time that was the reason Cairns was chosen again as back-up for Kenny. In fact, I subsequently learned that Ashdown had an injured foot...and there will be no jokes from me about him putting a toe in the water! Apparently the rowing team (which also boasts first team Physio, Harvey Sharman, and Managing Director, David Haigh) is aiming to row across the Channel from Dunkirk to Ramsgate, next June, to raise money for the Myfanwy Townsend Melanoma Research Fund in memory of former Leeds United fitness coach Bruce Craven who died in 2005 from melanoma.

The programme also featured a two page article on yours truly, the latest in the '#IamLeeds' series. I joked with Pecky and Bogdan that when Mrs W handed me the phone the other day to tell me, "It's Leeds United for you", my first thought was, *"Where the f*** have I put my boots!"*...

As I took my place on the Kop, the sun was burning my face and arms. Elland Road looked good; there were 26,465 inside the old ground today and expectations were high for the rejigged United side. There was lots of razzmatazz out on the pitch as the teams emerged with dozens of school kids holding a giant Leeds shirt as part of the Grass Roots Ticketing publicity, whereby the club hopes to connect with local football clubs, schools and youth organisations. It was a colourful scene and I had no problem with this particular initiative. The team went through the ritual of the handshakes with the opposition and then Leeds lined up again to do the 'Revie Wave', still with their white tracksuit tops on, each with the player's name emblazoned on the back. It was very reminiscent of the Don's era...but then the game started and all similarity with that great team evaporated quicker than the moisture on the pitch in the hot sun. What we saw was vintage Clarets and not classic Whites.

Let's start by saying that Burnley are a decent side this season. Sitting fourth in the table, they had the best goal difference in the division. They'd only lost one league game, at Brighton, 2 – 0, about a month ago. True, they'd lost the services of the prolific Charlie Austin, he was plying his trade against us a couple of weeks ago for QPR of course; instead they now rely on Danny Ings and, yet another former Leeds loanee, Sam (I was almost as bad as Billy Paynter) Vokes. But even so, no one expected them to come at us quite the way they did. They also did that despicable thing of winning the toss and making us play towards the Kop in the first half.

McDermott would later describe the first half as us being, "beaten up", and he was pretty much spot on. In the first five minutes Paddy Kenny was called upon three times to thwart decent efforts. El-Hadji Diouf was the only Leeds player to shine in this period, one of very few able to hold the ball for more than the blink of an eye. Leeds fell behind in the 17th minute. Kieran Trippier scuffed a low ball diagonally into the Leeds box from the right; Sam Vokes did what we remember him for most, fluffing a swinging right foot shot that cannoned off Scott Wootton. It rebounded to Scott Arfield at the back post and his initial left foot shot was well blocked by Byram, sliding in. But Arfield was then able to turn a full 360 degrees to bang the ball right-footed low past Kenny just inside his near post. Kenny shouldn't have been beaten there.

A few minutes before half time things got worse. The sprightly Michael Kightly crossed from the Burnley right wing to find Sam Vokes all on his lonesome eight yards from goal. Vokes' header is well saved by Kenny, down to his left, but it's only pushed out a couple of yards; Vokes was quickest to react, pouncing on the loose ball and rifling it across Kenny into the opposite corner. If I'm honest, Kenny should have done better, or a Leeds defender should have been on hand to clear the loose ball. A former Leeds player had done us again..

It was by no means all Burnley in that first half, Leeds actually had numerous chances. Varney in particular had a great opportunity with a back-post header, but nodded it tamely over the bar. McCormack had probably the best chance, also with a header from close range, but the Scot nodded his wide of the post. We had a couple of good shouts for a penalty too, when a Byram shot was blocked with an elbow and when Aidy White was bundled over on the angle of the six-yard box. Referee Lee Probert was unimpressed with both claims. In fact Probert was having a bit of a nightmare himself; at one point he waited for a signal from the linesman over on the east touchline who eventually signalled a Leeds' corner. Then Probert inexplicably awarded a goal kick instead! The Kop predictably went mad and we were reminded that, "We always get sh** refs"! In truth though we couldn't blame the ref for our predicament; it wasn't him smashing the ball over the bar or wide of the post, and it wasn't his fault that our final pass missed its intended recipient more often than not. Austin and Murphy were having appalling games, while nothing would go right for McCormack either. The best we had on show were Byram and White strangely, and Diouf.

In the second half, McDermott left it ten minutes before giving both Byram and Murphy the hook and replacing them with Green and Poleon. We presumed that the move recognised that Sam was not yet match fit and that Murphy had been, well, crap. Green immediately did well filling in at full back while Poleon was his usual barnstorming self, albeit usually trying to beat one man too many and losing the ball before delivering a cross. Leeds were probably now the better of two poor teams, but still we blasted every chance we got into the South Stand. By the end of the game we would have registered 22 attempts at goal but only five hit the area between the sticks. A couple were magnificently saved by the Clarets' keeper, Tom Heaton, including one world class effort from a Diouf header that even Paddy Kenny applauded. The excellent Heaton had also stopped a point blank rocket from Varney in the first half. With 15 minutes to go, McDermott switched to route one football by bringing on Matt Smith for Luke Varney. The arrival of the giant striker immediately caused panic amongst the Burnley defenders and it took him only four minutes to get on the score sheet, rising at the back post to head in a Diouf free kick. He won most everything he challenged for after that but the ball just wouldn't go in for us. Once again, a draw would probably have been the 'fair' result, but then again, if we can't hit the target and we can't defend why should we be rewarded? The game ended in a 2 – 1 win for the visitors and Leeds slumped to 13th in the table.

Toon and Out

Mark woke me up with his call at 7:30am; I was still in bed. "Sorry old man, I'm not gonna make it tonight; four of my staff have rung in sick with the sh**s." Mrs W and I were supposed to be picking him up later this morning, on our way to the North East and he was supposed to be my wingman again for the Capital One Cup game at St. James' Park. Clearly that wasn't going to happen. I felt like reminding him about all the trouble I had in Barcelona trying to order the bloody tickets, but I knew he would be devastated at missing the game so I just wished him well in trying to get his store up and running with four staff missing and told him to check the loos in his shop had plenty of bog-rolls. He's on a graduate training scheme with a well-known supermarket group, and is currently running a sizeable store in South Manchester. If he sorts this out he will certainly get plenty of kudos with his bosses for not taking any sh** from his staff.

Mrs W made a quick phone call to our friends Brian and Sheila in Darlington, where we were stopping tonight, and informed Brian he would be going to a game! I've mentioned Brian before many times in these books; he and Sheila have been good friends of ours since we met them on our honeymoon in the then Yugoslavia way back in 1984. They were disappointed that they would not be getting to see their God-child, but Brian is a huge football fan and I sensed he was looking forward to the game even though his teams are Chelsea and Darlington. He's held a Chelsea season ticket for many seasons despite living and working in the North East for more years than he cares to remember. Brian is also my proof-reader…so you know who to blame!

We arrived in Darlington just short of two o'clock and as usual Sheila produced a meal fit for a banquet which we demolished whilst catching up with their latest news. Then Brian and I set out for the Toon.

I went to St. James' Park with Brian during a previous visit, back in 1992. On that trip to Darlington, Brian and I, ever on the look-out for a match, any match, made the trip up to Newcastle to see them host Swindon Town in a Second Division game, while Sheila and Mrs W entertained the then one year-old Mark. I can remember precisely nothing about that game, although I have the programme and I have looked it up on the internet while researching this chapter. The Magpies won the game 3 – 1, easing their relegation fears at that time; it was only Kevin Keegan's seventh game in management. Newcastle would go on to secure promotion to the Premier League the following season as runaway Champions, breaking all sorts of goal-scoring records as they did. 1992 was also the Toon's centenary year; they've played at St. James' Park all of that time. The stadium though has been transformed in the last twenty years, culminating with the completion of the massive Milburn and Leazes Stands in the year 2000. The stadium now has a capacity of just over 52,000 and boasts the largest cantilevered structure in Europe, an honour I believe it took from our own East Stand which itself was the largest when completed in 1993.

We parked not far from Central Station, on a meter; it was just 5:30pm so we only had to pay for an hour as it was free after 6:30pm. Brian is good with this sort of thing...we actually arrived three minutes too early but he spotted the problem and spent the necessary three minutes ensuring I was parked inch perfect as a warden looked on! Back a touch....forward a bit....straighten up! We were heading for the Mile Castle, a Wetherspoon Lloyds No. 1 bar, which was one of three pubs mentioned on footballgroundguide.com as 'away fan friendly'. We sat with Liz and Bogdan, who'd made the trip up from Leeds by car, and Stokie Kentley joined us later on; his mate Jim, who we met near the ground, failed to gain access to the pub without his ID. All three floors of the Mile Castle were buzzing with anticipation of the game – a game that Kentley and his mate almost didn't get to see! At one point, just before the Stokie found us, a lady in a Leeds jacket was circulating around the tables asking if anyone had lost their match tickets; she'd found some. It was only as we were leaving the pub that

Kentley discovered that his tickets were 'lost'! He retraced his steps and the bar staff eventually pointed him in the direction of the lady we'd seen earlier. It was a lucky escape for our Stokie friend! He told us he'd emptied his jacket pocket so he could store his second bottle of beer while drinking the first...he obviously forgot to put his tickets back in his pocket!
It was just gone 7:00pm when we stepped outside the pub into the gathering gloom of a misty early autumn evening and began the fifteen minute walk to the ground. The first sight of it we got was through the Chinese arch on St. Andrews Street, on the edge of Chinatown. The arch is eleven metres high, but it was still not big enough to frame the entire stadium in the distance. St. James' Park is just massive, a veritable Colossus of a stadium, a steel and concrete behemoth. Our tickets were for row 'Y' in the Leazes Stand; row 'Y' we discovered, is the very top row.
Brian and I climbed fourteen flights of concrete stairs just to reach the concourse outside the third tier of the Leazes Stand. In the concourse there were dozens of our 'more mature' fans bent double, gasping for breath; I wasn't sure if it was the climb or the rarefied atmosphere up there! We then had to climb countless more steps to reach the very top of the stand and row 'Y', seats 277 and 278. But when I turned around and looked out over the pitch I was awestruck. The pitch looked a magnificent fresh green, but it was about the size of a postage stamp! The roof of our stand appeared to stretch out from above our heads for miles into the distance, over the edge of the pitch, while above the roofline of the stand opposite I could see the flickering lights of the city twinkling like a million stars in the murky sky. It was an incredible sight. I have been to the Bernabeu, the Camp Nou only a couple of weeks ago, the new Wembley, the Stadio Olimpico in Rome, even the Telstra Stadium in Sydney, but I have never been blown away by a stadium like I was up there in row 'Y' of the Leazes Stand. Not all of our fans were in row 'Y' of course, but there were over 6,000 that had climbed this particular stairway to Heaven...or hell. *"Which would it be?"* I wondered as the game kicked off down below us.

Leeds made a few changes from the side that lost at home to Burnley at the weekend; Warnock was back following suspension, and he slotted in at left back replacing Aidy White. Young Alex Mowatt was given another chance to show us what he's got, with Luke Murphy making way for him; and Matt Smith and Dom Poleon started in place of Luke Varney and Diouf. Newcastle fielded a strong side, confounding the local papers' predictions that had suggested many more changes than Alan Pardew actually made from the side that lost to Hull on Saturday.

The Leeds support was magnificent but the Leeds team never quite matched us. In the first five minutes, roared on by the fans at their backs, Leeds looked good, and with a modicum of luck we'd have taken the lead. Ross McCormack collected the ball from Michael Tonge, just outside the centre circle and made progress towards the goal at the far end of the ground. About 30 yards out, Ross glanced up and spotted the home keeper, Tim Krul, just off his line. As we've seen him do a few times before from this distance, Ross launched a delicate chip shot that looked for most of its journey as if it was going to find the top corner. Sadly, it didn't dip quite enough and instead it bounced down off the bar and a defender beat Matt Smith to the ball to hook it away. An inch lower would have been totally different. Mrs W often tells me what a difference an inch would make!

In terms of goal opportunities for Leeds, that was just about it. The Leeds fans kept themselves amused though, all through the game. In the 11th minute we began our latest tribute to Gary Speed, and once again it was maintained for a full 11 minutes. Many Newcastle fans joined in, at least for the first few verses and for a generous round of applause at the end. Brian was impressed by our stamina. The Leeds fans took great pleasure in reminding the home crowd that they'd never won the league with a rendition of, "Stand up if you've won the league", and then, "Sit down if you've won f*** all", with the Leeds fans of course stood all through the game and the home crowd sitting. A rendition of, "Shearer took you down", was also designed to embarrass the Toon army and there were many, many more besides those. It was great fun.

As early as the 31st minute though, Newcastle had the lead, and they never really looked like losing it from that point on. The goal was yet another example of Leeds failing to stop a cross coming in and then failing to deal with it as it arrived in the general area of our six-yard box. Paul Dummett beat Sam Byram to the ball just inside his own half and immediately slotted a long ball down the line to Sammy Ameobi, younger brother of the far more famous Shola. Dom Poleon was in pursuit of the young Ameobi but Sammy just let the ball run outside him and past him a yard before whipping a first time cross into the Leeds box with his left foot. Meanwhile, in that box, the deadly Papiss Cissé was steaming in between our centre back partnership of Pearce and Wootton. In truth neither of them was in the same bloody parish as the Toon raider and Cissé met the cross perfectly and thumped a header past Kenny. It was a brilliantly executed move but it was one we've seen Leeds concede far too often and usually by lesser teams than this Newcastle outfit. It visibly took the wind out of our sails and all of the faults we witnessed at the weekend were suddenly apparent again; they probably never went away. We had trouble just controlling the ball, we often pushed it too far in front and allowed the opposition to get between us and the ball; Austin did this numerous times. Our passing was often dire, perhaps being the reason we frequently failed to control the ball when it arrived with one of our players. Our movement was poor, some would say non-existent, too often we left the man with the ball isolated, inviting the home side to challenge; in short, we just didn't do the basic things very well. It was an affliction affecting all our players, even the normally dependable Rudy Austin just seemed out of sorts. The one positive I took from this game was that Alex Mowatt didn't look out of place at all in this company. He didn't see an awful lot of the ball but what he did do was usually solid enough.

At half time we were all amazed to see a bloke on the pitch with a full size fridge strapped to his back. Apparently he runs marathons for charity like that! One lad near me muttered, "Why the f*** would you run with a fridge on your back?" to his mate stood next to him. "How else would he keep his beers cool?" was the reply.

Diouf replaced Tonge in the 63rd minute to try to rescue the situation for Leeds but he'd hardly got his eye in before Newcastle struck again. Sammy Ameobi touched a short ball to Yoan Gouffran who had Scott Wootton doing a passable impression of that fridge we'd just seen; Wootton was as tight to Gouffran as it was possible to be without committing a sexual offence. But it was Gouffran who kept his cool, managed to turn his man, and fired an unstoppable rising shot into the top corner of the net. It was game over; we all knew that.

At the end of the game we all cheered our players with genuine pride, there was no question we'd given our best; it was merely the case that our best today was well below what was needed to overturn this well organised and experienced Newcastle team. There was no shame in this defeat. But we do have to become much better at those basic ball skills if we are to make any impression on the Championship this season. That was for another day though, Saturday to be precise, down at Millwall.

Brian and I slowly made our way down those steps again, and then into the first of the fourteen stairwells. There we stopped for some reason; presumably the police were controlling the flow of fans on the lower levels. A chant came up from the level below, "Upstairs, upstairs, give us a song", so we belted out a rendition of, "We are Leeds", and then we demanded of those below us, "Downstairs, downstairs, give us a song", and they responded with 'MOT'. And so it continued until we were allowed to move once again. We were all determined to savour every last moment of this visit to one of the top grounds in English football. It's the sort of place we want to be going every other week; it was a reminder to us of what we have been missing these last ten years.

Leeds mauled at the Den

Match five of this little run of seven in three weeks was against the Lions of Millwall, another team that had found a bit of form just in time for our visit. They hadn't won a league game until the 17th September, but then they beat the Championship pacesetters Blackpool 3 – 1. They followed that with a 1 – 0 victory at Charlton last Saturday. In fact their season so far was almost a mirror image of our own; we'd started well but had now lost three out of our last four league games.

I was flying solo again for this one and so enjoyed a leisurely train journey from Stafford to Euston courtesy of the good folk of London Midland. I thought I'd booked a London Transport Travelcard for my return to the capital, but at the ticket barrier in Euston I had a Shrimper moment. Three times I put my ticket through the machine at the barrier and three times the gates refused to open. I did think about rushing the barrier behind someone else…but there were loads of people about and I was sure I'd be subject to a citizen's arrest! So I dutifully went to the ticket booth and asked them to check my ticket and they confirmed that, "No, that ticket won't work down here mate". Armed with a new ticket and seven quid lighter, I was on my way to Charing Cross tube station and thence on to the Lord Moon of the Mall, the usual watering hole for Simon and many of the Surrey Whites for games down this way. I felt comfortably at home in this one, it being my fourth or fifth visit in the last four seasons. They had my favourite ale, Old Speckled Hen, on draught at £3.29 a pint. Gradually the pub filled up and I was introduced to many new folk by Simon including his brother John, Dave, Alex and his brother whose name escapes me, while many of the regulars were there too; Mike and Paula, Big Wardy, Wayne, Paul, Adam, Conor, and the rest. I worked my way through five or six pints (well, I can't remember exactly and who's counting anyway?) of the excellent Morland brew and a very tasty burger, in the two and a half hours I was in there. Adam, Conor, Wardy and I, then headed back to Charing Cross for the train to London Bridge and then on to South Bermondsey. It was in the intimate confines of the second train, thankfully only a short four minute hop from London Bridge to South Bermondsey that I learned of the Leeds team for the game, from a mobile phone thrust up my left nostril in the crush. McDermott had tweaked his side again; Peltier was back in, with Byram on the bench; Smith and Poleon also went back to the bench, with Varney and Luke Murphy returning to the starting eleven. It also looked like yet another different formation, as BM went in search of a winning formula; this seemed set up as 4 – 5 – 1.

Kenny
Peltier Pearce Wootton Warnock
Austin Murphy Mowatt Tonge McCormack
Varney

Subs: Cairns, Byram, Green, Diouf, Smith, Hunt, Poleon.

Maybe I'm getting a bit cynical in my old age, but it smacked of deck-chairs on the Titanic to me. It's not the formation that needs to change; it's the quality of our play on the ball that needs to improve. And with goals in such short supply how on earth was having a 'lone' striker going to help? It's a 'loan' striker we need, and quick.
As always the Leeds fans had turned out in force, once again completely selling out our allocation of just over 2,000 tickets. A pathetic 13,063 would be reported as the total attendance and the only vocal section of the home crowd appeared to be just to our left, the other side of the big screen, and early doors there were the usual disgusting Istanbul chants that we always suffer at this Den of Iniquity. Jimmy Savile got a mention from them too, with, "He's Jimmy Savile, he's one of your own", but quick as a flash the Leeds lads responded with, "He's probably your dad, he's probably your dad, he's Jimmy Savile, and he's probably your dad"! Again, don't shoot the messenger!
The first half was another of those eminently forgettable halves of football that are becoming all too familiar to Leeds fans. There was nothing between the sides and it already looked like it could end nil-nil; neither side looked capable of

hitting the target, let alone getting the ball past the respective keepers. I was stood with Nigel, having bumped into him coming out of the bogs when I was going in; he reckoned the opening of his coffee flask was the most exciting event of the afternoon so far. I thought that a tad harsh on Millwall's Martyn Waghorn who whacked a shot against the post with half an hour gone. But from a Leeds perspective it was hard to argue with Nigel's assessment, although once again I felt Alex Mowatt was perhaps the least poor of our ten outfield players. The other positive was that we hadn't been quite as wasteful with the ball as in recent games, actually passing it about reasonably well. All that changed in the second half though.

It began really positively; only three minutes had passed since Nigel put his flask away, when young Alex Mowatt created some magic down the inside left channel, culminating with a sublime curling ball low behind the Lions' back line. He'd spotted Ross McCormack running in and it looked harder for Ross to miss than to score. But the way things are going for Mac these days, for some reason he decided to open his body shape and try to side-foot the ball, glancing it across David Forde. He managed that, but sadly he also managed to glance it inches wide of the post as well. Quite why he didn't just put his laces through it I will never know. The ball from Mowatt deserved better and it was another encouraging sign that this lad might just be the real deal. But almost immediately Millwall took charge of the match; it was as though Mac's miss had convinced them this was to be their day while for their part Leeds went to pieces. Suddenly we were over-running the ball; getting caught in possession; and almost as if in panic mode, we'd resort to clipping the ball forward to Varney all the time. Invariably he wouldn't get to the ball before Millwall did. Then on 65 minutes the Lions came up with a rare drop of quality in this cesspit of a game. Lee Martin played a short one-two midway in the Leeds half before slotting the ball diagonally through to Martyn Woolford. Woolford had Peltier close, but not close enough, not fridge-on-the-back close anyway, and he was able to take a touch before curling a low right-footed shot around Paddy Kenny into the far corner. The Den exploded in an instant;

suddenly the place was filled with noise from three sides of the ground, while we momentarily lost our voices as we choked back the anger at seeing our side opened up like a tin-can; it could be a can of worms I was thinking, if it stayed like this. It didn't stay like this though, it got worse.

McDermott threw on Byram and Matt Smith for Tonge and Varney, in the 69th minute, but seven minutes after that Millwall doubled their lead and there was no way back. It was another superb move that the Lions could take pride in (sorry!), the sort of move we long to see from our boys. Scott Malone and Liam Trotter played three one-two wall-passes in short order, completely bamboozling the shell-shocked Leeds defence before Malone took aim and fired the ball into the top corner, giving Paddy absolutely no chance. More roars from the Lions, more disgruntled shaking of heads all around me. To be fair to the Whites they refused to give up, and they battled vainly towards the end of the game to try to salvage something from the wreckage. The ball struck a Millwall post in the dying moments but it's probably telling that it was the knee of a Millwall defender knocking the ball past his own keeper; he then hooked the rebound to safety. At the other end another mix up amongst the Leeds back-line gave a free ball to that man Woolford again but his cool lob over Kenny also struck metalwork.

Towards the end of the game the Millwall fans sang, "You're sh** and you know you are", and a small group of Leeds lads over to my right applauded them and joined in with their own version: "We're sh** and we know we are". The last time I heard that ditty coming from our own ranks was that miserable game at Oakwell last winter, as the Warnock reign first began to unravel.

When Chris Foy blew his whistle for the final time, there were boos from a few of the Leeds fans. Not many, but enough to make sure the players knew this was not good enough; not good enough by a long stretch. Brian McDermott marched purposely from the dug-out straight towards us, and when he got to the edge of the area he held both arms aloft and applauded us genuinely for several seconds. Then he turned and headed straight down the tunnel, not waiting for his players, not even glancing at them. It told me he was angry; it was precisely the right thing to do, the brave thing to do after such a performance. I just hoped the players could now respond next week to the reality check I am sure McDermott gave them in the dressing room. On the BBC football website later McDermott was quoted as saying:

"The second half went wrong. We didn't turn up; we didn't do the ugly stuff well enough. It's the first time that's happened with me. The second half came as a shock. I'm bitterly disappointed with the players we've got who are decent but are not at the level at this moment. If the fans see another second-half performance like we did then we're going to have a problem. We need to keep the fans with us." Sadly, we would see many more performances like this as the season unfolded.

If there was any doubt how bad this performance was, as I was leaving the ground I heard several lads talking about it in the same breath as that horrible defeat at Hereford a few years ago in the FA Cup. The second half today was a truly ugly example of the art of the beautiful game. Next Tuesday's home game with newly promoted Bournemouth was now a massive, massive game. Aren't they all?

After an interminable wait in the compound outside the away end while the police ensured the Millwall fans were well away, we all piled onto the train and headed back into London Bridge station. We were some very miserable sardines indeed to begin with but by the time the doors opened at the other end of the four minute run, the Leeds fans had already recharged their batteries. "We are Leeds", belted out as we jostled along the crowded platform, the incredible sight of the London Shard soaring skywards above our heads. There was an announcement over the station PA: "Will all passengers on platform 14 please remain where they are and wait for a short while". Then, somewhere up ahead of us, we could hear Leeds fans 'interacting' with the police with shouts of, "Come on then", and then the Leeds lads broke out into, "If you hate Leeds United have a go", and, "We're Leeds United we don't give a f***". Some lads behind me were eager to get to the 'action' and began pushing folk out of the way and making angry gestures to the unseen enemy ahead. There were dozens of British Transport Police running from all directions to get to the epicentre of the fracas ahead, several of them hanging on to the leads of some very hungry looking dogs. It was a tad worrying! The rumour filtering back was that the Leeds lads at the front had suddenly chanced upon a group of Millwall fans while the police had them "kettled" trying to steer them en masse down the steps to the underground. I kept a circumspect distance behind the main throng of the crowd hoping it would sort itself out before I arrived on the platform for the tube up to Euston, which it did. I eventually learned that there were no Millwall fans around and that the police had just been rather over-zealous in their attempts to maintain calm. But the best part about it all was that one of the hungry dogs had taken a bite out of one of the coppers! A mobile phone video appeared on Twitter a couple of days later showing a lady police dog-handler trying in vain to pull back her straining beast that in turn had its vicious looking jaw locked onto a male colleague's wrist! Leeds were not the only ones mauled in South London today.

Leeds fans try to get pictures of the trouble at London Bridge.

Mac's Groundhog Day

On Tuesday evening I sat listening to Lorimer and Reaney discussing our current lack of form and was struck how perilously close we were to reliving the closing weeks and months of the Grayson and Warnock regimes. The run of five defeats in six games was bad enough but it was the manner of our capitulation in that second half on Saturday that had struck a chord with most of the Pavilion patrons. It reminded me of the way we'd collapsed against the likes of Blackpool, Barnsley and Birmingham, in the final weeks of Grayson's tenure, and then that awful game last January at Oakwell, when the fans booed Warnock's team off the pitch, signalling that his end was nigh too; there were boos emanating from one section of fans at The Den. Reaney is an astute follower of all things Leeds United, even if he often hides his insight behind a constant stream of witty and pithy retorts. He quite correctly forecast that another defeat for Leeds tonight, a sixth in seven outings, would plunge the club right back to where we set out with both Warnock and McDermott; having to start all over yet again. It would be the equivalent of a footballing Groundhog Day! Reaney told Lorimer he was disappointed with the standard of our defending and he acted out the positioning for that 97th minute Reading goal, as an example of what not to do. He concluded that far from needing a striker to score goals, the first requirement was still to strengthen the defence on the basis that if we don't concede, we don't lose! Hard to argue with that! Someone from the audience did then point out that had Jason Pearce got his header on target down at Reading we would probably have won, suggesting that an ability to finish is a handy attribute to have too. I felt that was harsh on JP and a remark that really needed making to our strikers. I was sure Pearce would get one soon; he's had enough near misses! Lorimer and Reaney went on to criticise some of McDermott's tinkering with formations which seemed less than sensible in this particular forum to me; it must be difficult enough for McDermott without folk so close to the club openly criticising him!. Reaney did still think Leeds would win tonight though, as he reckoned the Cherries were, "rubbish"; he went for a 3 – 1 victory. I felt that my favoured 4 – 0 was more a possibility tonight than most times, simply because the stakes were so high; so I stuck two quid on it at 40/1…

I was a tad less confident of my £80 profit when I heard the team. Part of me wondered if McDermott would keep the same side that produced that dire second half performance at The Den, to sort of give them a chance to redeem themselves; show they were better than that. But then again I felt that was also a risk in case we got the same again! In the event McDermott didn't actually change very much. He recalled Noel Hunt, Paul Green, and most surprisingly, Tom Lees, with Lukes Varney and Murphy, and Scott Wootton losing out. Alex Mowatt deservedly kept his place for a home league debut. Perhaps McDermott was unsure which way to go so he went half way? The glaring omission for me was that there was still no place for El-Hadji Diouf who I felt would add more than Hunt. An alternative I wouldn't have argued with was to have Dom Poleon instead of Hunt…or even my late Grandmother or Lucas Kop Cat, anyone with boots really!

Leeds and Bournemouth had met only nine times before, and we'd won seven of those with the other two games drawn. That little stat filled me with no confidence at all and nor did the knowledge that ex-Leeds hero Ian Harte now plied his trade for the Cherries as did a former loanee at Elland Road, substitute goalkeeper Darryl Flahavan. I couldn't make up my mind whether to include Flahavan in the category of dangerous returnee or not, as he never actually played for Leeds during his time with us in 2009 and was unlikely to feature tonight. But having witnessed Billy Paynter and Sam Vokes already punishing us this season I was sure one of these Cherries might pop up in the match report later.

Leeds began the game as if their careers depended upon getting a positive result; they probably did of course. Alex Mowatt was directing the Leeds engine room expertly while Ross McCormack looked much more at home roaming up front alongside Noel Hunt. Chances were still being squandered but we were creating far more than the visitors.

Then on the half-hour we got the big break we needed. A hopeful punt up-field eluded Ross McCormack on the first bounce but then landed perfectly for Noel Hunt as he ran through the Bournemouth defence. It was a race between Hunt and Ryan Allsop in the Cherries goal; Hunt stretched every sinew to just get a toe-end to the ball. The keeper was committed though and he crashed into Hunt sending the Leeds number '10' sprawling in the six-yard area. 13,000 heads on the Kop swivelled as one to seek out the referee David Coote. Coote was bold enough to point at the spot after pondering the incident for a second or two. We were on our feet celebrating in an instant and then redoubled our celebratory efforts as Coote showed a red card to Allsop. We watched as Hunt and McCormack high-fived each other at the prospect of going one up against ten men.

As we waited for the inevitable Bournemouth substitution, sacrificing their nippy winger Ryan Fraser for the substitute keeper Flahavan, I began to think about the penalty kick. I hadn't given any thought to it before that moment but suddenly I came out in a cold sweat. It was Ross McCormack who was holding the match-ball and that former Leeds loanee Flahavan would get his chance against us after all.

On March $2^{nd,}$ earlier this year, Leeds won a penalty kick at the Kop end in the home game against Millwall. I remember it like it was yesterday; it was Mark's 22nd birthday. Ross McCormack had been going through a torrid time in the matches leading up to that game, with a series of glaring misses in front of goal. He'd been subject to all sorts of criticism from the fans on Twitter and he must have been really low on confidence. I was horrified then by the sight of Ross with the ball in his hands and I said to Mark at the time he was likely to miss it. He did of course. That day he struck a tame effort to the keeper's left and David Forde pushed it onto the post before a defender hooked it to safety. Here we were again, Groundhog Day. I was horrified once more to see Ross with the ball tucked under his arm. Stephen Warnock had his arm around Ross's shoulders talking earnestly to him; was he telling him he had confidence in him? Or was he asking Ross if he really wanted to take it? We will probably never know. I knew what was going to happen (well, OK, as I said last year, I couldn't possibly have 'known'); I was convinced he would miss it though. I told anyone willing to listen that he was going to miss it and I reminded them all about that Millwall game. I pointed out that Ross's body language was all wrong. Mike, Nigel, Jo and Lynn, all told me to "shut up", "be positive man", and, "get a grip"; I felt helpless and I felt this was all going to be my fault! How ridiculous is that? After several minutes, Ross was able to spot the ball and then we waited for the referee's whistle. The next few seconds seemed to pass by in slow motion as Ross jogged up to the ball and tamely hit it low to the keeper's left…just as he did on March 2nd. Flahavan was down to it in a flash pushing it away with a strong left hand and a defender lashed it to safety. It was a replica of that Millwall penalty. Jo clipped me around the ear and told me it was all my fault.

There was still an hour to go and Bournemouth only had ten men on the pitch, so all was certainly not lost. But looking around the pitch there were a few Leeds players with haunted expressions on their faces, none more so than Ross of course. And once again a player with Leeds history had 'done' us on his return! Amazingly though, Leeds soon shrugged off the disappointment and laid siege to the goal just yards in front of me. It brought back memories of the Southampton game a couple of years ago when Leeds bombarded the same goal for forty five minutes without breaching it. Surely it wouldn't happen again would it? The ball was flying in from all angles but a combination of the new keeper, defenders legs and bodies, and the continuing failure of Leeds to find their shooting boots, meant it was still nil-nil as the half time whistle went. As Nigel poured his half time coffee he mumbled, "We know how this is going to end, they'll score in the 97th minute!"

In fact that isn't the way it ended at all. But it was a nervy second half performance by Leeds in which we were put through every emotion going. The second half was only seven minutes old when Stephen Warnock went rampaging down the left wing. Then he whipped over a perfect cross to the near post where Ross McCormack was sliding in to touch the ball past Flahavan. It was the finish Ross needed on Saturday when he touched Alex Mowatt's similar cross wide of the post. Today he made no mistake. 1 – 0 up against ten men and we were coasting; who am I kidding?

With 72 minutes on the clock, McDermott made his first change, sending on Dom Poleon to add some pace to further stretch the overworked Cherries; Noel Hunt was the man to make way after another less than encouraging display from the ex-Reading striker. Just one minute later and the unthinkable happened as Bournemouth grabbed an equaliser. It started with the second of those ex-Leeds players, Ian Harte. He launched a free kick into the Leeds area from well inside his own half and Tom Lees goes up for it with a Bournemouth striker. The man in red and black jumps higher and nods the ball forward again. This time it's Jason Pearce who rises in the aerial challenge and again the Cherry comes out on top. Finally the ball falls to Lewis Grabban behind the last of the Leeds defence, seven yards out, and he makes no mistake. We all fear the worst now; Nigel is going on and on about how he told us what was going to happen and I'm beginning to think he might be right. All credit to the Leeds fans, they cranked up the volume in support of the team on the pitch; we knew how important this game was. For their part the players were clearly also giving their all, but there was inevitably a degree of panic about their play as they began to contemplate the fall-out of failing to beat ten men. With ten minutes to go, Diouf and Byram could be seen stripping off their track-suits over by the dug-outs, it was to have been our last throw of the dice but they never did get on. Instead, Alex Mowatt made his own gamble. He clipped a half-volley to the back post where Jason Pearce leapt to head the ball back across goal. It fell perfectly on Poleon's right foot and he blasted it into the corner of the net. The relief around Elland Road was palpable but it was also tainted with fear; fear that we'd still find a way to let Bournemouth back into the game. Tom Lees went down with an injury and a few minutes passed; Leeds began running the ball into the corners at every opportunity. It didn't look pretty but desperate times call for desperate measures; the board went up showing five minutes of added time and in our minds it seemed like a lifetime. Finally the referee decided we'd been put through enough and he blew that final whistle. McDermott was as honest as ever after the game saying: "The only thing that mattered tonight was the result, nothing else, and we deserved to win. We could have gone under when they scored as they had nothing to lose, but we showed a lot of guts and created a lot of chances." The match stats confirmed that Leeds had 17 attempts on goal of which seven hit the target; Bournemouth managed only five shots of any description. Leeds also had the bulk of the possession. The Kop warmly applauded the players and manager as you would expect but on the walk up Lowfields Road the mood was still one of grave concern. We'd got away with it tonight, but we all knew nothing much had changed; this performance was no better than any of the recent defeats. There were some bright spots again in this display – most agreed that Mowatt, Green and Warnock, all had excellent games for example - but our general play was still disjointed and we were prone to sloppy looking errors in all areas of the pitch. We had scraped through against a team that had conceded more goals away from home than any other side in the division, a team that had to play with ten men for the last hour of the game with a substitute goalkeeper. On the big screen at the far end of the ground the rest of the night's Championship results went up and prominent amongst them was Derby County 4 Ipswich Town 4, a game that Ipswich had led 4 – 1 at half time. Derby had sacked their manager of four and a half years, Nigel Clough, at the weekend and had now appointed 'The Wally with the Brolly", Steve McClaren, to take over at their helm. Sods Law meant they were our next opponents, on Saturday at Pride Park. I knew we'd have to play better than we did tonight to get even a point down there. I hoped McDermott would come up with a different line up too, perhaps a line up with a little less Hunt in it! Well, no Hunt at all preferably!

After ten games, Leeds sat 11th in the table with 14 points, nine points behind the top three of Burnley, QPR and Leicester, and already five points outside the top six. But, we had won a must-win game and we had avoided making a crisis out of a drama…for the time being.

It never rains but it pours

"Every failure brings its own crop of excuses but the simple reality is that Leeds do not have enough high quality players...without substantial investment, Leeds are never going to hit the big time...What is the priority...? Is it profit or success on the pitch?
"You began by giving us one of the best managers in the game. Now get the players."[1]

I didn't write that, it was written in March 1998, more than 15 years ago, by then sports editor-in-chief of the YEP, Stephen White. I read it again recently in Peter Ridsdale's bio', 'United We Fall'. The article was an open letter to the then board of Leeds Sporting plc, at the time the holding company of Leeds United, and was an attempt to put pressure on the owners to spend big money on the team. George Graham was the manager referred to. We all know what happened next; Leeds did get plenty of money spent on the team as they chased, and initially at least, lived the dream under the next manager, David O'Leary. Then, after four glorious years of competing at the very top of European football, it all began to unravel and failure on the pitch led to falling revenues, rising debt, and ultimately relegation and administration. We've not yet recovered.

I've reproduced the piece again because it seems to me to be so relevant to the situation we again find ourselves in now. We are still in the first year of the ownership of GFH and we have a recently appointed manager who came with the tag of being one of the best. We are quite clearly short of quality in the team and many fans are calling for more money to be spent on a squad which recent results seem to show is not good enough to mix it in the Championship promotion race; speculate to accumulate is the mantra coming from many fans. In recent days club chairman Salah Nooruddin had been at pains to stress that his and GFH's involvement was a long term one and his objective was to maintain some financial stability at

[1] *p74, United We Fall, Peter Ridsdale, Macmillan, 2007*

the club; in other words, avoiding what happened in the early 2000s. In a wide-ranging interview with the Yorkshire Evening Post, on 3rd October[1], Nooruddin explained that the owners were ready to back Brian McDermott in bringing a striker and a winger to the club on loan, although McDermott separately stressed that he would not bring in players for the sake of it, he had to be sure anyone coming in would improve the squad. A Ridsdale style cash splash seems highly unlikely! Tellingly, the YEP summarised the current situation as: "Nooruddin's expectation of the squad this season is that they do better than last season. In other words, finish 12th or higher. He has not asked for promotion and does not intend to, mindful of United's results last month". Nooruddin spoke of on-going discussions with additional potential investors but there was no suggestion that any new investment would change the timescale. "Financially we're doing very well and as we've said, we're looking to bring investors with us – people who can add value to the club in terms of mobilising funds. All of that will fit into our medium to long-term objectives." I just hoped that this didn't mean we had to put up with watching the abysmal football of recent weeks for months and months to come. However, for the visit to Pride Park this weekend, I was fully prepared for more of the same, particularly when I saw the team McDermott had entrusted to the task of taking on Derby County, a team that had reeled off nine straight wins against Leeds in recent years.

I was sitting in the Pride Park Harvester with Paula and Mike, Andy, Wayne, Adam and Conor, and truth be told none of us was confident. Both Adam and I confessed to having posted defeats for Leeds in the LUFCtalk predictions league; I went for a 3 – 1 win for the Rams. Not that it should really worry anyone as my record so far this season was abysmal, getting just two of our 13 results so far correct. I explained to the others that my logic was based on McDermott playing the same team as on Tuesday and them all playing just as badly! But I really didn't think either of those events would transpire. How wrong was I?

[1] http://www.yorkshireeveningpost.co.uk/sport/leeds-united/latest-whites-news/leeds-united-nooruddin-defends-gfh-transfer-policy-1-6108892

Connor read out the team and then passed his mobile round for confirmation. Sure enough, it was the same starting eleven that just scraped through past ten-man Bournemouth four days ago. The consensus around the table, a table now stacked high with the empty plastic pint pots that had fuelled the discussion, was that the inclusion of Noel Hunt was likely to raise questions in the House of Commons when they reconvene next week and that Kop Cat must be wondering what more he has to do to claim that number '10' shirt. Having said that, I did spot an article on the Yorkshire Evening Post website that just made me think maybe we're all being a bit hasty in writing off Noel Hunt. The gist of the article was that Hunt had decided to take a break from all forms of social media, having unsurprisingly seen far too many negative comments about his performances. He came over as a bloke who really does care though, and one who knows that his performances have not been good enough. He said: "What I can't stand is the idea that I'm not trying or I don't care. That's nonsense, absolute nonsense. Ask any of the players here. Or better still, don't bother asking them. Go straight to their wives or their partners. They'll tell you what a nightmare we are to live with when we lose."

On a positive note, Hunt was confident that things will improve. "To score goals I have to be in the box and I've got my head around that. Perhaps I was too wide again on Tuesday but I can sense things coming together. …it's about adapting to players and fans, the training ground, the stadium. You want to feel at home and on Tuesday I did"[1]

Hunt also explained that he'd now finally set up home locally and his wife had moved up with him. This had taken a month longer than it should have done and he claimed it had all been a distraction. It sounded logical enough and we should all remember that these practical issues do affect people; footballers are only human after all. I was happy to accept this revelation at face value and see how he gets on today and in the next few games if he continues to be selected.

[1] *http://www.yorkshireeveningpost.co.uk/sport/leeds-united/latest-whites-news/leeds-united-hurt-hunt-can-see-better-times-ahead-1-6117007*

Derby were also unchanged, with Steve McClaren opting to stick with the side that battled so well on Tuesday night to come back from 4 – 1 down. It was a rallying call from Wally at half time in that game that was credited with turning around their fortunes. It wasn't raining as we walked down Pride Parkway towards the ground, so we were all resigned to not getting to see the famous McClaren brolly this afternoon, but all Leeds fans should have realised, 'It never rains but when it pours'.

As might have been expected, Pride Park was reasonably full to greet the new Rams' manager, (why do we always play teams right after they appoint a new manager?) and 26,204 were inside the ground, over 4,000 of them being Leeds fans. Our fans were, as always, an impressive sight, filling the South Stand, and we were, as usual, far more vocal than the locals. I was unsure who actually won the toss today, the main sections of vocal Derby fans appeared to be either side of us, so I guess both sides wanted to kick towards us in the second half; whoever did win it turned the teams around anyway, and Leeds kicked towards us. Predictably, the first real action was at the other end; Paddy Kenny was suddenly stranded miles away from goal as the peroxide blonde, Will Hughes, won the ball and tried to chip it in from the tightest of angles. Fortunately, his effort landed on the top of the netting and not in it but it was an early warning that this Derby side was quite able and willing to take advantage of any gifts on offer even though their match-day magazine reported they were yet to win a league game at home this season. It would not be the first time that Hughes, an 18 year-old, would show just what a player he was. But we had our own teenage sensation too in Alex Mowatt, and it was fascinating to compare them. Alex is just a couple of months older than Hughes and in the early stages of this game he again showed he was more than comfortable in this company. In fact, if I'm honest, Mowatt looked far and away the most accomplished player in the mustard yellow Leeds away strip. Several times he slotted the ball through the Derby defence with unerring accuracy and had his team-mates been more alert we could have profited. As it was, our finishing was still atrocious. Rudy Austin was the biggest culprit when, finding himself unmarked and just seven yards from goal, he skied his shot over the bar as we have seen him do countless times already this season. Minutes later and the true cost of that miss became apparent as Derby opened the scoring at the other end of the ground.

I hate to think what Gary Neville would have made of the Leeds defending had he been there with his interactive screen and Sky technology. Paul Green, the same Paul Green who I genuinely felt had been one of the two stars of an otherwise miserable performance on Tuesday (Mowatt being the other), inexplicably got caught in possession facing his own goal, just inside his own half. Straight away Derby's Chris Martin was on his way towards the Leeds box. On the edge of the area Derby were two against three, with Green already back to help out Pearce and Tom Lees, and Derby's Craig Bryson overlapping. What followed left all Leeds fans totally aghast. As Martin back-heeled the ball, all three Leeds players dashed towards Bryson, who by this time was about 12 yards out and to the left of goal. Bryson calmly flicked the ball straight back inside to the now completely unmarked Chris Martin and he simply lashed the ball past the helpless Paddy Kenny. Later that night, still pictures taken from the footage on the Football League Show would appear all over Twitter, showing Bryson with the three Leeds players all inches from him and to his right Martin all on his lonesome in front of goal. It was pathetic; no other word does it justice. Had it happened in an under-11 game in the park, little heads would surely roll! The home crowd were on their feet and the noise they made was impressive. There is still a great rivalry between these two clubs that dates from the days when Clough and Revie went head to head, so that was part of it, while the presence of Wally, sat up in the stand to our left was no doubt also being heralded. We were still trying to come to terms with what we'd just witnessed when it pretty much happened again. Leeds were sliced open with a through ball from the peroxide Hughes to Chris Martin and Martin yet again bamboozled the Leeds defence with a simple back heel inside to Johnny Russell. He took it in his stride and stroked it into the corner of the net, again giving Paddy no chance. 22 minutes gone and

Leeds were two goals down. It did cross my mind that I might not be far off with my 3 – 1 prediction, but at that precise moment it was no consolation whatsoever. My overriding feeling was one of being let down by the team. The pre-match session in the Harvester had been a very pleasant one, chatting with good mates over a few beers, but the team's appalling defending out on the pitch had somehow sullied the whole day, the whole trip. From that moment I don't believe many of our fans expected us to get back in this game. We continued to sing our hearts out of course and tried to persuade the Derby fans that, "We're Leeds United, we don't give a f***", but we did really, we'd all travelled from home at not insignificant cost, as we do every week, and we expected some entertainment and passion, not ineptitude.

The one, the only in fact, bright spot was the performance of Mowatt, who continued to bely his limited experience with a series of superb passes only to see his efforts usually wasted by sloppy work from his more experienced colleagues. I could only wonder what on earth he was making of it all.

Incredibly, a minute or two before half time, Leeds had a lifeline. It was so simple too. A diagonal ball into the box from Lee Peltier on the right had the Rams' keeper Lee Grant back-peddling furiously and flailing at the back post. He couldn't reach it and Paul Green was able to knock it back across goal for none other than Jason Pearce to nod it into the unguarded net! "Everything comes to him who waits", so the saying goes, and finally JP had his goal.

But it didn't seem to change the view of the majority of Leeds fans. In the bogs at half time most were still seething about the mistakes that led to the goals and most were convinced the Pearce goal would be no more than a consolation. Several were suggesting they'd seen enough of this particular Leeds regime and felt it was just a matter of time before it would be a case of all change again – GFH out, McDermott out, complete clear-out, start again. I climbed wearily back to my seat hoping for the best but fearing the worst. I was still on for my 3 – 1 prediction of course, worth seven points in the prediction league.

As has happened in many recent games, as bad as we were in the first half, our second half performance was even worse. Whatever was being said during McDermott's half time team talks seemed to be having the opposite effect to that desired. There was a marked contrast between the way Derby were going about their play, confidently and with a smile on their faces, and the way Leeds were approaching every foray forwards; seemingly frightened to death that they'd make another mistake if they were too ambitious. Consequently, if Mowatt wasn't involved in a move, then Leeds would just knock the ball back and forth in the middle third of the pitch until eventually, under pressure from the terrier-like Rams, we'd resort to hoofing the ball up-field, where inevitably the move would break down and Derby would begin their next sweeping assault. It was a depressing sight. The inevitable introduction of Matt Smith and Dom Poleon, just after the hour mark, for Green and Hunt, was greeted with cheers and then shouts of, "thank the f*** for that, f*** off Hunt you Reading tw**", and other similar calls that made it all too clear that Hunt had almost completely lost the support of the Leeds following. Clearly, they either hadn't read or maybe just didn't believe the content of that YEP article. Green too got his share of abuse for the several naïve errors he'd committed today. It's never pleasant being in the crowd when your own fans turns against particular players, but in the case of Hunt I started to think again he'd already had more than enough chances and this was now the inevitable consequence of the team management not acting earlier to keep him out of the firing line. Smith and Poleon made little impact to be honest and neither did Diouf when he came on for Tonge a few minutes later. Diouf did at least get involved though, and I would see one statistic on Twitter later from @LUFCDATA suggesting that, "El-Hadji Diouf had 15 touches after coming on in 14 minutes. 1 touch less than Noel Hunt made (16) in 62 minutes. Alarming! #lufc"

In the 78th minute, our peroxide friend had the last laugh as he capped a superb display with a sublime piece of skill earning me my seven points in the prediction league. He took possession of the ball outside our box and literally waltzed his way around Jason Pearce before shaping a delightful curling shot past Kenny. Our misery was complete, and part of me could only admire the way Derby had gone about their task. I still felt McClaren would not last long, but he has a confident, skilful side here to work with. It was a side put together over the last four years or so by Nigel Clough of course and I did idly wonder if 'son of Brian' would ever be accepted at Leeds if it doesn't work out for McDermott. As the game moved into the final five minutes, plenty of Leeds fans began to leave; something I don't ever remember seeing before, not even in our worst away days like Barnsley and Hull last season. The Derby fans taunted those of us who stayed to the bitter end with, "Leeds is a sh** hole, that's why you're still here", and, "How sh** must you be we're winning at home".

McDermott's post-match interview didn't do much to convince me his tenure in LS11 would be a lengthy one. He seemed to be distancing himself from blame for the current problems, suggesting our away form was already better than what went before. "In the last two games we have let ourselves down away from home but before I turned up here I think we had 21 games away from home and won one. We need to get a mentality away from home where we are very difficult to play against and we weren't today." Err, well, yes I suppose so, but the Bournemouth game was at home, and that wasn't all that pretty! I was more convinced than ever of a few things. Primarily, the next time I see Noel in print I want it to be on a Christmas card; Alex Mowatt is the only name that should already be on the team sheet for the Birmingham game in a fortnight's time; and we must bring in a couple of loan players of real quality before that game to freshen up the side. Longer term, GFH need to get those new investors on board and to support McDermott in building his own side, especially if he's disowned the present one. I'd now also accepted that promotion this season is already very, very unlikely. Oh, and Leeds fans really do know the meaning of the phrase "It never rains but it pours"!

If Carlsberg did Leeds games...

It was a tad depressing to see Andros Townsend smiling at me from the back page of the Daily Mail, arms aloft, celebrating a goal on his England debut last night. This was the man who, lest we forget, played six games for Leeds during the first few weeks of 2012 while on loan from Spurs. His performances with us had ranged from brilliant, in his debut against Burnley when he was Man of the Match, to plain awful. He'd joined under Simon Grayson, and then left not long after Neil Warnock was appointed. Now, like so many others who had briefly passed through the corridors of Elland Road, he was a world beater! Man of the Match and goal scorer in England's impressive 4 – 1 World Cup qualifier against Montenegro and then starring again a few days later as England ensured their qualification for Brazil 2014 by beating Poland 2 – 0. It's a funny old game!

The official Leeds United website was quiet over the two week break but now came news of a trial taking place for Lithuanian international Marius Zaliukas. Zaliukas is a 29 year-old central defender who made over 200 appearances for Hearts, many as captain. Hearts didn't renew the Lithuanian's contract in the summer and then trials with Rangers and Queens Park Rangers came to nought. If Ally and 'Arry didn't want him I wasn't sure I did! Other than that I was astonished to read McDermott's comment that the squad was given several days off following the Derby catastrophe and that they didn't actually report back for training until Thursday! I'd have had the buggers in at 7am on the bloody Sunday! Nevertheless McDermott promised us a much improved performance against Birmingham, once the league programme started up again. In his piece in today's programme he wrote somewhat obliquely, "We are trying to find a way to get the best from our squad, to play the best football we can, but most importantly, finding a way to win". I find that keeping a clean sheet and then banging a goal or two in at the other end usually does the trick Brian.

The first excitement on Sunday morning was meeting Lucas Radebe; The Chief. He was in the Pavilion signing copies of his book 'Lucas, from the streets of Soweto to soccer superstar'. What a nice bloke! He carefully printed a message in the books I handed him (Liz had given me hers to get signed as well) before finishing each with his unmistakeable signature and the number '5', his United shirt number. All the while he was chatting and smiling, recalling his days at Elland Road and how he was desperate to see us win today, before he flies home tonight. What a gentleman! What a player too! I joked with him, asking if he'd brought his boots (I know, I bet he'd hear that a thousand times today!), and then I suggested he have a word with some of our defenders, give them a few tips maybe. Quick as a flash he asked, "Which ones?" I decided not to mention any names but in my mind I was thinking *"All of 'em! They could all do with a coaching session from you, Chief."*

All the talk in the Pavilion was what side McDermott would come up with. Would he give his usual line-up one more chance to prove themselves after the Derby fiasco? Or would he ring the changes? What did he mean when he wrote about, "finding a way to play"? I was discussing this with Liz and Bogdan while cogitating what, if any bet to place on the game. I'd just about decided not to bother at all when Liz commented that she felt, "We'll either win this 4 – 0 or lose it 4 – 0!" I couldn't ignore that could I? My quid duly went on the 50/1 chance of Leeds beating Birmingham 4 – 0. We'd have to do it without El-Hadji Diouf though; he'd been given compassionate leave to return to Senegal to pay his respects to his one-time mentor and father figure, former Senegal coach Bruno Metsu, who'd just lost a year-long battle with cancer. At 12:15pm the official tweet appeared on Liz's mobile announcing the team. It was just a list of names on the screen but we eventually agreed it would probably line up like this:

Kenny
Byram Lees Wootton Pearce Warnock
Mowatt Murphy
Austin
Smith McCormack

Subs: Cairns, Pugh, Brown, Peltier, Varney, Poleon, Tonge.

Phew! That was a shock to the system. Four changes from the Derby game with no starting place for Peltier, Hunt, Green, or Tonge. Green and Hunt, who both had stinkers at Pride Park, were not even on the bench! It took us some time to come up with the fact that the only formation that could 'house' this line up would have to include three centre backs playing with two wing backs. I've cheated here by showing Austin playing behind the two strikers as that would only become obvious once the game started. At the time, we actually assumed he would play behind Mowatt and Murphy.

It was now clear to us all that McDermott was trying desperately to "find a way" of fitting these particular eleven players into a formation. It looked brave. It looked like sh** or bust in fact! If this bold move failed and we took a heavy beating, McDermott's job could be on the line! At the very least he'd be on trial. This game was to be broadcast live on Sky too; the whole of the Leeds United family all over the world would see it!

Nigel and I made our way over to the ground earlier than normal; The Chief was being presented to the crowd before kick-off. He got a fantastic reception and the Kop sang "Radebe, Radebe, Radebe, LUCAS!" and then, "Chief, Chief, Chief". We sing the same chants at most games anyway, but it was nice he was actually able to hear it for once. He would leave the pitch to make his way up to the stand, where he would sit with another Leeds legend, the one who, "scored a fu***** great goal in the San Siro", Dom Matteo. All we needed now was a sparkling performance on the pitch to complete a near 'perfect day' to borrow Lou Reed's famous song title.

Birmingham would be no pushovers though, or so we thought. They'd been just about as inconsistent as Leeds in the opening 11 games. Although they'd lost seven of their league games, they had recently thumped both Millwall and Sheffield Wednesday, scoring four on each occasion, and dumped Premiership Swansea out of the League Cup. It was 37 games ago since Leeds last scored four, at Huddersfield on December

1st 2012! We did score three up at Doncaster in the League Cup a few weeks ago, but other than that we had only managed a maximum of two goals in any game since that 4 – 2 demolition of the Terriers. Funnily enough, our next trip, on Saturday, is back to The John Smith's Stadium. The good news for Leeds was that the bean-pole striker, Nikola Zigic, he who famously scored all four of Blues' goals in their 4 – 1 win at Elland Road two years ago, was only on the bench. That game had been the final nail in Simon Grayson's proverbial coffin. The Blues did have Man United loanee Jesse Lingard in their number '9' shirt today though, and funnily enough he scored all four of those goals 'Brum' got against the Wendies on his Blues debut. Birmingham had also won their last five league games against Leeds. No, this wasn't going to be easy, but the number four keeps cropping up doesn't it?

A crowd of 21,301 were basking in the warm autumn sunshine in Elland Road for this one, a decent turn out I thought for a Sunday lunchtime game on TV, and the vast majority of them were well pleased with the way the home team went about their business. From the start Leeds were positive, their passing was sharp and accurate, our movement looked good, and our tackling was urgent and strong. Rudy Austin was leading by example, seemingly revelling in the freedom of his new role just in behind, or sometimes even ahead of, the new strike partnership of Smith 'n McCormack. That would make a great name for a Scottish firearms maker and they began the game with all guns blazing. The only thing wrong in the opening minutes was that our finishing was still wayward. McCormack had the best opportunity to open the scoring when he was left 'Scot free' (see what I did there?) on the edge of the Blues' box but he then fired straight at their keeper, Darren Randolph. But then in the 18th minute he made amends. Scott Wootton launched a long ball up-field towards the marauding Matt Smith. It went beyond the young striker, but he chased it towards the edge of the box anyway, with a Blues defender staying tight to him. For whatever reason, Randolph decided he was coming out for it as well, and all three players met right on the edge of the box. No one got a decisive touch, but the ball rebounded off the shins of the keeper back out to Rudy

Austin. Unfathomably, Randolph continued to chase out of his box after it! Rudy passed short to Ross McCormack who clipped it first time towards goal from all of 30 yards out. It found the perfect gap between two covering defenders and on the second bounce found the net. I'm not sure what was the funniest sight; the look of surprise on McCormack's impish face, or the sight of Darren Randolph doing bunny hops on the spot like a naughty child who'd just been told he couldn't have a lolly! This was only the fourth time in 16 games this season we'd taken the lead!

Leeds continued to press forward, and one of the regular lads in the row in front of me turned and suggested I could be on to a winner with my 4 – 0 bet for once; they all know I more often than not go for that one! In the 33rd minute we were ahead of schedule. Austin for once was deep in his own half as he aimed a long diagonal pass out towards Ross McCormack, hugging the left hand touchline in front of the East Stand. Rudy then charged straight down the centre of the pitch while Ross toyed with the Blues right back. Ross then spots the perfect moment to move the ball onto his right foot and to send in a cross that finds Rudy now unmarked, six yards out, in the centre of goal and he buries his header past Randolph! Typical of 'The Beast', his celebration included a full-bloodied punch of an innocent advertising hoarding that had done nothing other than be in the wrong place at the wrong time. Great as Ross's ball in was, and perfect as the finish was, it was defending reminiscent of our own back four earlier this season. Most agreed that Birmingham were far and away the worst team we'd seen.

12 minutes later, on the stroke of half time, we were in dream land, as Leeds made it three without reply. It was another long diagonal ball up towards Smith, this time launched by Tom Lees. Smith had a quick look behind him to spot that Ross was scurrying past his marker and he just touched the ball backwards off the top of his head to land it at the feet of the Scot. Ross lost no time in shifting the ball onto his left foot and hammering it at Randolph from a tight angle. The keeper blocked it well but it merely ricocheted back out to Smith. Instead of putting his laces through it, Smith cleverly clipped it

low towards the left side of goal, spotting that Randolph's momentum was taking him the other way. It glided ever so gently past the helpless keeper and into the net. Never slow to catch the mood of the moment, the Kop breaks into a very ironic chant of, "What the f*** is going on?", so foreign was this situation to us. 3 – 0 at half time! When did that last happen? Well, as far as I can tell, it was Scunthorpe United at home, in January 2011…Watt, Gradel, and Johnson, with a fourth scored by Davide Somma in the second half for a 4 – 0 win…

At half time, Nigel convinced me we were going to score at least another couple, so we started scratching our heads to think of the last time we got five in a game. (It was March 2011; Donny Rovers, 5 – 2 at Elland Road, since you ask!) A sign of just how nervous we'd all been before this game today was that some lads nearby were still cautioning that it wasn't that long ago we went in at half time 4 – 1 up against Preston…and we lost that one 6 – 4! The sight of Nikola Zigic stood on the touchline waiting to join the fray made a few more of us think we weren't safe yet.

Birmingham predictably made much more of a game of it in the second half, with Chris Burke, allegedly one of the targets McDermott has failed to land for Leeds, showing just why he is so valued. A chipped cross meant for Zigic was heading for the top corner until miraculously, Tom Lees got his head to it, while a shot on the turn from Zigic himself had Kenny soaring through the air like the proverbial flying pig, to again turn the ball over. David Murphy later struck a post from a free kick. A bit of luck or a bit more care and the Blues might have caused us more of a fright than they did, but equally Leeds had chances at the other end. Matt Smith and I both thought we were in the money when Alex Mowatt nudged the ball through to him and he powered a shot into the roof of the net, but that was ruled offside. My mobile beeped to signal a text from Mark that said simply, "Smith onside", suggesting it was a very close call. Smith also had a solid header clawed from under the bar by Randolph, imitating the Kenny dive of a few minutes earlier. But in the 74th minute, Smith finally got his second, and what a goal it was. I have since watched this goal over and over again and am still awestruck that a thing of such beauty could be crafted by this very ordinary team of ours. When I watched it back on the Sky+ recording, I noted down Bill Leslie's commentary. If you read the following script and gradually let your voice get louder and louder, you may well bring back the memory of the goal. It began with Alex Mowatt, inside his own half in the inside left channel. Mowatt fed Rudy on the wing racing to within a few yards of the byeline. Rudy touched it back and Mowatt clipped it first time with his left foot across to Smith.

"Mowatt… releasing Ru-dolph Austin…Mowatt…SMITH! This time he powers home a second, a fourth for Leeds United who are having big fun in the big sun. [Camera cuts to a shot of Matteo and Radebe smiling and applauding in the stand] Even The Chief approves! Leeds 4, Birmingham 0."

The last 15 minutes were a bit tense in our little section of the Kop. I tried to tell everyone, "It's only 50 quid, it doesn't matter that much", but apparently the sight and sound of me hopping up and down, urging our defence to keep a clean sheet at the one end while urging us to knock the ball into the corners at the other, suggested otherwise. Birmingham won a number of corners in the final minutes and each time the ball was lofted in towards Zigic I was sure he'd grab a consolation goal and mess up my day. But he didn't, and after three minutes of added time that seemed like a lifetime, referee Paul Tierney blew the final whistle.

I was giving Bogdan a lift back to Warrington today and we had plenty of time to dissect the game as we had to find an alternative route; an accident was blocking the West-bound M62 just before Junction 19. The Five Live commentary on the Aston Villa v Spurs game was on the radio. We concluded that we'd witnessed a near perfect display today and that somehow McDermott had at last found the right formation. In fact, if Carlsberg ever did games at Elland Road, we felt they would probably look pretty much like this one! In particular, the free role Rudy Austin had, roaming up front with Smith and McCormack, had enabled Rudy to play a blinder. He was fierce in the tackle, seemed able to run forever, and got his headed goal of course. He was named Sky's Man of the Match and we'd watched as Matt Smith handed him the trophy at the end of the game. But every single Leeds player had been magnificent today; it was a veritable feast of football after the tripe we'd been served up in recent weeks. Bogdan and I did chuckle at the few glaring misses that Ross had suffered early on, but we agreed he'd more than made up for that with his tireless running and movement later in the match. Leeds were up to ninth in the table tonight, with most teams having played 12 games. We had 17 points and were five adrift of the sixth and final play-off position. A quarter of the league season was now complete. Most Leeds fans had written off this season before kick-off today, now many, including me, were thinking, *"I wonder, I just wonder if there is still a chance after all."* I was snapped out of my dreamy thoughts by the radio commentary, informing me that that man Andros Townsend, he who could currently do no wrong, had just scored for Tottenham, with a cross ball that somehow eluded everyone and found its way into the Villa net!

The Chief and me in the Pavilion before the Blues game

John Smith's Bitter Taste

Ryan Hall has been the forgotten man this season; so forgotten that at one point Brian McDermott commented that he didn't have any wingers at the club! There had been various rumours that Hall wasn't fit but everyone assumed he was still trying his best to break into the team now he was back after a short loan spell with Sheffield United. But over the weekend Hall posted a tweet that made many Leeds fans very angry. It went: "Look on the bright side if your [sic] not getting played take the L out and get payed [sic]" Apart from his appalling grammar and spelling, which is a capital offence in itself, what really annoyed the fans was the intimation that as long as he was being paid he wasn't overly bothered about not playing. He hardly improved matters by then tweeting that many of those fans who'd complained were, "small minded people", and then, while we were in the Pavilion on Saturday, he tweeted again. This time he wrote: "football is such a short career and can end at anytime [sic] with an injury so do what ever [sic] you can to earn as much money as possible". It looked to me like a clumsy attempt to moderate his previous tweets. Whether it was linked to his tweeting exploits or not wasn't clear, but on Monday the club posted a very short statement on the official website: "Leeds United can confirm that Ryan Hall has been suspended from the club pending an investigation into a disciplinary issue."
Elsewhere in the Championship, this week the second managerial casualty of the season was announced as Middlesbrough parted company with Tony Mowbray, who until Monday was the longest serving Championship boss, with over three years under his belt. He'd replaced Nigel Clough at the top of that particular table when Clough was sacked the other week. Moving to the top now is Chris Powell at Charlton, with two years and 277 days in post as at 21st October, 2013. Powell must be shifting uncomfortably in that big leather chair at The Valley. Mowbray had been my tip for the next sacking along with Dave Jones at Wednesday, as Boro had been struggling for months. Going through the BBC

website I found an article dated 15 April 2013, at the end of last season, in which Mowbray told us: *"The boys are working hard but nothing is dropping and we can't score.*

"These defeats against Hull and Brighton, were they any better than us? No. But we are not winning football matches.

"I know the fans are angry and upset. They want us in the Premier League. So do I and so does the chairman."[1]

Other than the specific opposition teams mentioned, that could easily have been Brian McDermott speaking at any time during our recent poor run. That's why the Birmingham result was so important to all concerned. It crossed my mind that Boro would probably have a new manager in place just in time for their visit to Elland Road on 23rd November.

As if to confirm how difficult football management is, particularly on Planet Leeds, on Tuesday the Development Squad played a match at Thorp Arch against Sheffield Wednesday. In the Leeds side were Noel Hunt and Dom Poleon, as well as Aidy White and a couple of lads on trial; the Lithuanian central defender mentioned earlier and an ex-Arsenal schoolboy striker. Just when we all think we have the right pair up front in 'Smith n McCormack', and when everyone has decided that Noel Hunt is no more a striker than Ethel the tea-lady, guess who pops up with a hat-trick in the Development game? Then, on Thursday, the news breaks that Leeds have now taken Dexter Blackstock on loan from Forest, to give us even more options up front! Who'd be a manager eh? How do you keep them all happy? They can't all get in the side, and with the possible exception of Ryan Hall, they presumably want to.

I was absolutely certain Leeds would beat Huddersfield in the latest Yorkshire derby game on 26th October. In fact, I had this weird feeling we might even beat them 4 – 0. During some research into previous 4 – 0 victories, (it didn't take long), I'd noticed that four years ago, we'd won the last two games in October 4 – 0; at Bristol Rovers and home to Yeovil. It was even uncanny that we play Yeovil next week of course.

But history and omens apart, recent results suggested Leeds ought to win. We were coming off the back of that fabulous

---

[1] *http://www.bbc.co.uk/sport/0/football/22155481*

performance against Birmingham, while our Terrier hosts had gone six games without a win. So, acting on my hunch that we could once again win the final two games of October 4 – 0, I texted Mark to ask him to stick a quid on for me. Chris, (the mad scaffold manager I mentioned in a previous chapter), saw a tweet I posted about it and he then Facebooked me to tell me he'd done the same, presumably having heard I was successful last week. He got 60/1 against Leeds winning 4 – 0, with Ross McCormack to score at any time. (Mind you he also had a quid on Huddersfield to win 4 – 1 with Ross to score first and he got a massive 3,800/1 against that!) Now that someone else had money on it I was nervous! I promised Chris a pint if his bet went tits up!

I'd arranged to meet up with Nigel today, at the Old Mill, a Chef and Brewer pub on Wakefield Road, just outside Huddersfield. Nigel hails from nearby Dewsbury and he persuaded me he knew Huddersfield like the back of his hand. Over the course of the next hour or so I would conclude he must wear gloves! I arrived in the car park of the Old Mill at 10:30am as arranged and then waited another fifteen minutes before Nigel pulled up all smiles telling me he, "hadn't realised how bad the traffic was around here". Nigel's plan had been to have a drink in the Old Mill…but it wasn't yet open, so he suggested we drive a bit further into Huddersfield where there was a, "lovely little pub on Bradley Road that always has loads of real ale on". As I got into my car I shouted across to him, "What's it called?", "I can't remember", he shouts back. "Just follow me…"

We've all done it haven't we? Tried to stay in touch with another car on busy roads in an area you don't know. We were still at the exit of the car park when the problems began. Nigel spots a hole in the traffic and guns his little silver Honda Civic into the gap. In a split second I have to decide whether I can safely pull out behind him? I knew if I didn't I would lose him. I went for it. There was actually plenty of room, but there are some knobs on the road aren't there? The driver of the black 4 x 4 I pulled in front of had obviously decided he was only letting one car out of the car park; it wouldn't have crossed his tiny mind that we were together. 4 x 4 Man flashes his lights at me and pulls so close to my bumper it sets off my rear parking sensors. Presumably he thinks this will impress the blonde in his passenger seat as well as intimidating me. I hold up a hand in the time honoured, "Thank you", gesture, pretending I thought he'd let me out on purpose and then I nudge the rear view mirror so I can't see him anymore. Then, just for my own satisfaction, I make an exaggerated wan*** gesture to no one in particular. Meantime, we weren't going anywhere. The traffic was nose to tail and up ahead I could see at least two white Fourway coaches carrying Leeds fans to the ground. The army was on the move! Eventually we get going and we arrive outside The White Cross Inn, Bradley, where Nigel takes the only available parking space. I have to keep going up the hill another couple of hundred yards before parking up. My mobile beeps. A text from Nigel reads: "Wer've [sic] you gone...????" I ring him. "I'm just up the hill mate you nicked the only parking space, I'll walk down", I tell him, only for him to reply, "Don't bother, the pub's not open". This wasn't going well, not well at all. It was now gone 11:00am, the game was due to kick-off at 12:30pm and we still had to find Nigel's, "perfect parking spot near the ground", and then walk to the stadium. We decide to cut our losses and forget about trying to get a beer, but not before Nigel suggests we pull into the forecourt of the Marstons Chicken Shop, just around the corner from the White Cross Inn. It's a peculiar little place; a tiny restaurant and takeaway that Nigel reckons, "serves the best fried chicken in the universe. I kid you not!" There was only one problem though...that was shut as well! I've since googled the Chicken Shop and can confirm it does have an excellent reputation, although the Huddersfield Examiner article I found tells the story of how the shop was robbed in 2010 by a gang of men brandishing Samurai swords![1] "I kid you not", as Nigel would say.

We eventually pull into the car park of a sports complex on Leeds Road, Nigel's "perfect parking spot", and then set off

---

[1] *http://www.examiner.co.uk/news/west-yorkshire-news/two-huddersfield-shops-targeted-robbers-4996063*

on a route march to the ground. Nigel has a bit of a limp and doesn't walk too well, so why he chose this spot God only knows; it was still a good 20 or 25 minute walk to the ground. At one point we spot a big pub looming up in the distance on the left hand side of the road. As we get closer we can see it's called, 'The Peacock'. It must be an omen; Nigel suggests we call in for a quick beer. But as we get closer we can see that this one too is closed; well, not so much closed as totally boarded up! It was just not meant to be. In fact, it was a day reminiscent of the game here last season when Mark and I got tangled up in traffic and then had to park miles from the ground, once again failing to get a beer. We already knew there would be no John Smith's being served in the John Smith's, as the very helpful folk of West Yorkshire Police had tweeted about that earlier.

Finally, hot, sweaty and thirsty after the long walk in the warm sun, we find ourselves in the concourse of the Chadwick Lawrence Stand in the John Smith's Stadium; the designated away end where 4,000 Leeds fans would be cheering on the mighty Whites. I spotted RamseyWhite and chatted with him and then Martin and Ty and Martin's three lads all bowled in. Martin had very obviously had far more luck finding a beer today than we had!

Up in the stand, the guys and gals from down south were all there; Mike and Paula, Andy, Chris, all said hello. Chris showed me his 4 – 1 and 4 – 0 bets on his phone and reminded everyone I'd owe him a pint if they didn't come up! Just a few seats further along our row was young Coronation Street star Colson Smith, who plays Craig Tinker in the Manchester based soap. I only know this because @MOTForever tweeted me after the game asking if I'd seen the little Tinker. I had to confess that not only didn't I see him…I actually had no idea who he was anyway, not having watched the show since the days of Ena Sharples and Albert Tatlock, before young Tinker was even born.

Brian McDermott sent out exactly the same team that so convincingly saw off Birmingham last Sunday. That was no surprise to anyone who'd been at Elland Road. On the bench was one Dexter Blackstock who'd been given the prestigious number '9' shirt even though he was only on loan until January 25th. The other subs were ex-Huddersfield man Lee Peltier, goalkeeper Alex Cairns, Varney, Brown, Tonge and Dom Poleon. With the arrival of Blackstock I wondered if we would ever see Noel Hunt again, despite his recent hat-trick for the Development Squad.

Within two minutes of the start of the game, Leeds were ahead, and I was even more convinced that this was to be that second consecutive 4 – 0 I'd wagered my pension on. Matt Smith had been denied by the Terriers' keeper, Alex Smithies, just seconds earlier, but from the resulting corner, floated to the back post by Alex Mowatt, Smith rose to head firmly into the net with Smithies this time stranded in no man's land.

The Leeds fans celebrated with appropriate gusto while the other three sides of the ground were stunned into silence. I was choking...not with emotion, but from inhaling the fumes of a bright blue smoke canister that was fired just below us. My good friend Brian would have had a field day had he been here; he'd been in with the Chelsea fans at Elland Road for the League Cup game last season when they exploded a similar device. Brian wondered then how anyone could smuggle a, "big bang blue thing", into the ground when he even had to remove his cap when being searched at the turnstiles. There was no search today, needless to say. The whole thing about setting off smoke bombs and flares during games had been prominent in the media recently following a very colourful display of the art by Poland's fans at Wembley and an unfortunate incident at Villa Park last weekend when a linesman was hit on the head by one thrown from the Spurs section. My guess was that frisking at the turnstiles would soon become 'de rigueur' in an attempt to stamp out this potentially lethal activity.

Whether the smoke drifting onto the pitch was affecting the Leeds players more than the home side, I'm not sure. But something appeared to be upsetting our rhythm as the Terriers began to look more like top dogs than underdogs. It took them just eight minutes to level the game and destroy my latest battle with the bookies. It unfolded just yards in front of me as I looked on from behind the goal. Adam Hammill clipped a corner over from the Huddersfield left wing, my right as I watched from behind the goal. The ball arrived with Jamie Ward on the edge of the box and he had all the time in the world to trap the ball with his right foot and then hit an unstoppable shot into the corner of the net with his left. I was able to follow the trajectory of the ball as it curled away from Paddy Kenny and nestled in the net. It wasn't meant to happen like this; I really struggled to understand what was going on here. It was a poor goal to concede, no one was alert enough to spot the danger and to block Ward's shot. Why? We had the momentum in this game for all of a couple of minutes but now the stadium was rocking to the sound of Huddersfield fans going mental and our chant a few minutes ago of, "One – nil in yer cup final", now seemed a tad pre-emptory. This team that had not won in over six weeks suddenly looked pretty damn decent, while we looked, well, a lot more like the side that struggled so much before that last international break than the one that took Birmingham apart. It crossed my mind that maybe Brum had been way worse than I gave them credit for.

The rest of the first half passed by in a flash. It was a cracking game if you were a neutral or even a Terriers' fan, as they continued to look better than us. During the half time break Nigel and I watched bemused as a number of lads played football at the other end of the ground dressed in huge transparent plastic globes with just their legs sticking out at the bottom of their costumes. Not really sure what that was all about but it took our minds off the possibility that maybe that Birmingham victory was a one-off and not a turning point.

It could all have been so very different had Luke Murphy scored just on the hour mark. It came at the end of a superb spell of passing football that got Rudy Austin in behind the Terriers' back line. He squared the ball across goal to find Murphy totally unmarked at the back post. All he had to do was side-foot the ball into a space the size of a small bungalow. He dragged it wide. Right in front of us all, he dragged it wide. Within two minutes it was no longer Murphy's fault though; it was now Tom Lees' fault again, just as it was in Neil Warnock's last few games all those months ago. Adam Hammill swung in a cross from the left wing and

Tom Lees rose majestically at the near post to glance a header across the incredulous Paddy Kenny and into the far corner of his own net. From being within touching distance of victory we were now a goal down and facing defeat.

I didn't think we deserved to lose this game. We'd played OK most of the time, although we had begun to lump the ball forward to big Matt Smith more often than I would like and we were often being muscled off the ball by a very dogged and determined home side. We could all see Dexter Blackstock warming up on the touchline over to our left; he wore a very distinctive pair of sky-blue boots. I was desperate to see him on the pitch; sure the script was written for him to come on and save the day. The bloke next to me was bemoaning the fact we didn't have a game changer on the pitch and I told him I thought Blackstock could be that man. He scoffed and said something about, "Even Paul fu***** Daniels couldn't get us out of this mess". Rudy Austin chases a ball to the Leeds right wing and gets a shove in the back for his trouble. It's a free kick to Leeds, almost on the touchline and level with the edge of the area. There's now activity in the dug-outs though and the ref signals for a Leeds substitution. Dexter Blueboots waits while a weary Luke Murphy trots over to swap places. Blackstock makes straight for the six-yard area down below us shouting instructions to his team mates and pointing where he wanted everyone; clearly not short of self-confidence this lad. He then hovers near the front post. Alex Mowatt is standing over the ball. If we'd seen the events of the next few seconds play out in a movie we'd have laughed uncontrollably at the improbability of it all, but right in front of our eyes Mowatt swings across a perfect ball and Blackstock's forehead meets it just as perfectly to glance a header into the net. It was one of those, 'I was there moments'; the saviour had arrived. Blackstock wheeled away towards the corner flag to our left and was immediately mobbed by the entire team except Paddy Kenny who was leaping up and down at the other end of the ground. Within seconds of the ball hitting the net, a chant of, "Dexter Blackstock, Dexter Blackstock, Dexter Blackstock", blasted out to the tune normally reserved for Ross McCormack. I wondered if Ross was suddenly feeling a bit insecure. Far from thinking we'd rescued a point, most of the lads near me were clearly now expecting us to go on and win the game. Ross McCormack suddenly looked inspired; perhaps playing for his place in the side now. He forces his way into the box and goes down in a heap and 4,000 voices shout "Penalty!" We are still berating referee Neil Swarbrick for ignoring us as the ball is lofted down the Huddersfield right wing to Craig Scannell. He's got Jason Pearce in front of him but in an instant he's wrong-footed JP and is free in the inside right channel near the byeline. He sees John Stead lurking near the penalty spot and slides the ball into his feet. It's all down to Tom Lees now; he's behind Stead who is facing away from goal. But is Lees tight enough? Neil Warnock once said of Lees after a similar situation, "He has to hold on to the lad's shirt, they all do it, he has to learn". But Tom hasn't learnt, he's nowhere near close enough to grab Stead's shirt and Stead is able to turn and smack the ball past Kenny. Our joy over the Blackstock goal had lasted precisely four minutes. It was yet another example of our 'Ups and Downs', this time the 'Up' was even more short-lived than usual, while the 'Down' was likely to last at least a week until the next game, or longer, who knows? Yeovil will have a say in that.

It ended 3 – 2, although Blackstock also had a late penalty claim waved away by Swarbrick when it looked like he was pushed from behind. But all we were left with was a few 'ifs' and 'buts'. Brian McDermott got it pretty much spot on when he said after the game that it was, "One step forward, one back". It was a Halloween horror show come early for Leeds, one we hoped we could put right again before Guy Fawkes appears. We face Yeovil next Saturday in what suddenly becomes another must win game, a game in which we have to show we can get straight back on the winning trail. As I drove back down the M62, news came through that Yeovil had come up with the result of the day, beating high-flying Nottingham Forest 3 – 1! Oh great joy!

Funnily enough, and as so often happens, results elsewhere this weekend meant that Leeds didn't actually lose much more ground in the table. Six of the eleven games ended all square and so Leeds would finish this round of games in tenth spot, six points outside the top six. Burnley though were now three points clear at the top and a massive 15 points ahead of Leeds, having beaten previously undefeated QPR. It didn't mask the fact though that the John Smith's had left a bitter taste in the mouth.

So, 'perfect day' last week had turned to disaster this week. On Sunday came the news that Lou Reed had passed away…

The 'big bang blue thing' goes off to salute Leeds' opener

Yeovil

Brian McDermott stunned many Leeds fans on Monday evening with a revelation during his appearance on the Sky Sport's Footballers' Football Show. The theme of the show this week was 'scouting', with McDermott an obvious choice of guest being one of few current managers to graduate from the role of Chief Scout, a position he held at Reading for many years. McDermott was asked: "How do you use your chief scout? What instructions do you give them?" After a brief pause and looking somewhat embarrassed he answered:
"Well that's an interesting subject at Leeds, because we certainly need to improve what we've got. I wouldn't say we have a scouting structure per se. We are just in the process of getting a scout, a Chief Scout, who is going to put together a scouting programme, which I will do with him, but you know, for a club as big as Leeds, what is absolutely fundamental for me is scouting and recruitment, and it wasn't in place in my opinion." It was rumoured that it was Luke Dowling, formerly with Blackburn Rovers, whom McDermott had recruited.

It's not the only thing McDermott has discovered Leeds don't have either. In a press conference a couple of days later he disclosed that the club had not been using Prozone – the pioneering performance analysis tool used by many of the top teams in the UK. McDermott had reintroduced it at the Huddersfield game last Saturday. Phil Hay discussed this in an article in the YEP on the morning of the Yeovil game. It wasn't that Leeds hadn't been doing any analysis just that it had been done on a cut-price basis without the brand leading 'Prozone' software since our Premier League days. On the Sky programme on Monday, McDermott had commented that Leeds were still in the very early days of a new era and that there was still much rebuilding and lots of work to be done, but it was all reinforcing the impression that, as the Chairman keeps reminding us, this is a long term project and one that is geared towards making Leeds great again. The YEP article concluded with this cautiously optimistic note:

"Players and managers come and go from Leeds and when they come, they tell you the same thing – that everything here is in place for the Premier League. Actually, it isn't. No Prozone (until last Saturday) and no chief scout (though Dowling cometh); a stadium and training ground owned by other people. They amount to basic deficiencies at the level where clubs count their backroom staff in tens. But maybe, just maybe, the corner is being turned."[1]

My big Leeds branded quilted jacket came out for the Yeovil game as the temperature was down in single figures, a blustery wind was ripping the last of the leaves from the trees, and rain was in the air. I picked up Bogdan in Warrington as usual and we were the second car to arrive in the Hoxton Mount car park; it was 11:45am and the game today was one of those rare things, a 3pm kick-off. We were meeting Pecky in the Old Peacock Pub on Elland Road. I wanted to see what the newly refurbished pub was like inside, having not been in there for many years, not since my student days in the late 70s in fact, when a pint in the Old Peacock would always follow a visit to the fish and chip shop further along Elland Road.

There has been a Peacock pub in the area since Victorian times, although the present building and location only dates back to 1963. The fortunes of the pub and the football club across the road have tended to mirror each other – the opening of the new 'Old Peacock' in 1963 pretty much coinciding with the start of the great Don Revie era at Elland Road. The pub has been completely revamped this year at a reported cost of some £400,000 and it reopened on the eve of the new season. My whimsical mind mused how appropriate it would now be if the new-look pub would once again prosper, just as the club's fortunes begin to improve; this perhaps being seen in years to come as another turning point, the start of the great McDermott era. Oh, is that the coffee I can smell?

They've done a great job with this pub. It's now leased to the Ossett Brewery, a micro brewing and pub-company based in the West Yorkshire town of the same name and it's

---

[1] *http://www.yorkshireeveningpost.co.uk/sport/leeds-united/latest-whites-news/leeds-united-beginning-to-redress-the-balance-behind-the-scenes-hay-1-6208657*

consequently well stocked with real ale. I had a pint of the excellent '1919', a 4.0% ABV ale brewed specifically for the Old Peacock and celebrating the year the club was founded. I made a mental note that next time I'm here without the car I will sample the other eight or so pumps temptingly lined up along the bar. Ossett owner Jamie Lawson, son of founder Bob, is a Leeds fan, and that probably explains why they have even gone to the trouble of taking the red out of the Ossett logo wherever it's displayed here. Although it was still very early, there was already a sprinkling of customers enjoying the surroundings; we chatted with Rob Endeacott, the One Northern Soul author, who says he prefers the pub these days to the Pavilion, and I said hello to John and big Dave, who I frequently bump into at away games, while I debated the likely starting eleven today with Pecky and Bogdan.

The three of us wandered down to the Pavilion to continue the discussion and concluded that if any of us were in charge, Ross McCormack and Tom Lees would not be starting. Neither of them had played particularly well for a long while and we felt Ross would benefit from a break while Tom Lees just makes too many mistakes. In their places we'd have the two new men, Dexter Blackstock and Marius Zaliukas. But we don't choose the team (probably a good thing as the next couple of games would only serve to prove!) Thankfully, Brian McDermott still has that responsibility and in his wisdom Ross and Lees deserved another chance. In fact we reckoned the team would have been unchanged for a third successive time if everyone had been fit. There was one injury though; Sam Byram was still struggling with a thigh problem picked up at Huddersfield and so Lee Peltier got his first start since our defeat at Derby. Blackstock and Zaliukas were both amongst the substitutes. As far as we could tell at this stage, McDermott was going to continue with his $3 - 5 - 2$ formation using Lees, Wootton and Pearce as the three centre backs, Peltier and Warnock as attacking wing backs, Mowatt and Murphy in the middle, McCormack and Smith up front, and Rudy Austin marauding anywhere he fancied.

A surprisingly big crowd of over 25,000 turned up today, including about 500 from Somerset supporting Yeovil, presumably buoyed from seeing their side get an unexpected win last weekend over Forest that lifted them off the bottom of the table. When the teams arrived on the pitch we had to shield our eyes from the glare; not from the low autumn sun but from the Yeovil away kit of luminous lime green with black hoops. The match-ball was pretty bright too. This being the first game of November, we had an early viewing of the new hi-visibility winter match ball, though none of us could understand why there were red markings on the predominantly yellow Mitre ball. I heard several fans mutter words to the effect that, "There should be nowt red in Elland Road", and it crossed my mind that Mitre should maybe take a leaf out of Ossett Brewery's book of customer satisfaction. For the majority of the season, each side plays with a ball that includes its club colours but apparently the winter balls, used from November to the end of February, will all be the same colour – 'fluo yellow' with red and black markings. The Mitre advertising promises us: "The Delta V12 Fluo is the hi-visibility version of the most advanced FIFA approved quality match ball ever made. The fluo yellow colour is scientifically proven to deliver speedier player reaction times in poor visibility."

It was pleasant just to rest our eyes for a few moments as we paid tribute to the armed forces with the wonderful sound of a lone trumpeter playing 'The Last Post', the only sound during a quiet minute's reflection, this being the nearest home game to Remembrance Day.

This was not a memorable game. The BBC statistics reported that Yeovil had 58% of the possession, but I think the Prozone software must have been playing up, possibly due to the cameras being confused by that Yeovil kit. The Glovers certainly wove some pretty patterns on the Elland Road pitch when they did have the ball, but they created very few chances, just two shots on target in the entire game. For our part, our play was nowhere near as fluent as it was against Birmingham, but in the end we proved to have just about enough guile to see the game through. In the first half, Mowatt forced an acrobatic save from Wayne Hennessey in the Glovers' goal and Matt Smith added to the growing number of entries in the 'Leeds United Book of Horrendous Misses' by failing to make contact as the ball ran across him just a few yards from goal. Five minutes before the break, Stephen Warnock hobbled off with an injury, to be replaced by debutant Marius Zaliukas who I am told thus became the first ever player with a surname beginning with 'Z' to play for Leeds... It soon became apparent that Zaliukas had taken up one of the three centre back spots while Jason Pearce was given the left wing-back role vacated by Warnock. In his new role Pearce looked and played a bit like Norman Hunter did for that Revie side all those years ago and it was perhaps appropriate that Hunter was at the game today celebrating his 70th birthday. Pearce absolutely revelled in the freedom to raid down towards the Kop at every opportunity. In particular any high ball lofted over there in front of the West Stand was met by Pearce's head, while anyone stood in his way was cleared out without ceremony much as Norman 'Bites yer Legs' Hunter would have done. At one point he went in so hard that a Yeovil defender was literally pushed through an advertising board that was left sporting a huge hole! Zaliukas looks to be a decent player too, on the evidence of his second half performance, although at one point we all had our hearts in our mouths as he pushed the ball between the legs of a Yeovil forward on the edge of his own box before clearing it away. He's one cool customer! Either that or he's a clown!

Leeds opened the scoring just three minutes into the second half, when Rudy Austin threaded the ball through the inside right channel for Ross McCormack. Ross, confounding all those of us who had been calling for him to be left out, took one touch before rasping a shot past Hennessey. Hi-visibility ball notwithstanding, Hennessey didn't see it. Ross just has this habit of pulling something out of the bag just in time to save his skin. In fact, today it was his strike partner Smith who was not really impressing. Apart from his first half miss, he just looked a bit lethargic today and it was no surprise to me when Blackstock replaced him in the 58th minute. It was more of a surprise when in the 67th minute that man McCormack scored a second. It was set up by Rudy once again. This time he stretched to just toe-end the ball into the box where Ross was onto it in a flash to slide the ball calmly past the goalkeeper. At least we could relax a bit after that and enjoy watching Jason Pearce galloping down the wing every few minutes. Yeovil resolutely stuck to their task until the final whistle, winning a few late corners and building up that possession stat, but there were no further goals to entertain us.

The BBC is no great fan of Leeds United but I couldn't argue with the headline they used for the match report on this game. It read: "Ross McCormack's second-half goals lit up an otherwise drab Leeds performance against Yeovil at Elland Road." That just about sums it up. Once again it was difficult to assess just how good or bad this performance was from Leeds; maybe Prozone will provide the answer in the days to come. In his post-match comments McDermott noted, "If we can be there or thereabouts at Christmas it will be interesting. We have some good young players who are learning all the time and we are close to where we want to be." Where we are at the moment is 8th in the table with 20 points. Burnley still led the way with 33, closely pursued by Leicester and QPR. Then came Blackpool, Reading, Forest and Watford. Forest, in the 6th and final play-off spot, had only three more points than Leeds, having lost their last two games. McDermott was happy enough to declare that this was, "probably the best start I've had to a season", but it all seemed too much like the last few seasons to me. Leeds constantly tease us with a few good results to get us near those elusive play-off positions, only to then blow it and fall away again. As always I would travel to Charlton hoping for the best but fearing the worst. For now though, we'd beaten a team we were expected to beat. Yeovil are now rock bottom of the table, slipping behind Barnsley who got a decent point at Ipswich on Friday night, and Sheffield Wednesday who finally, at the 13th time of asking, got themselves a league victory by thrashing Reading 5 – 1 and maybe saving Dave Jones from the chop.

Brian McDermott's parting shot to reporters after the game was to congratulate Marius Zaliukas on a solid start although he added he was, "Not too keen on him nutmegging someone on the edge of our box so we did have a word about that", and then as an afterthought he added, "in Lithuanian". At least he's still got his sense of humour!

After the Lord Mayor's Show

The temperature on the dashboard of the big Peugeot read four degrees as I arrived in the multi-storey car park at Stafford station. It was cold, which came as a shock as this winter had thus far been so mild. I was about to climb aboard the 08:55 London Midland train to Euston for which I'd forked out £38 including a 'free' one day Travelcard for the capital. I was meeting up with the Leeds United family in the Lord Moon of the Mall again en route to the game at The Valley this afternoon.

I was nervous about the timing for this trip as London was likely to be very busy; the various events surrounding Remembrance Day were taking place today and tomorrow while this afternoon would also see the three and a half mile procession of the Lord Mayor's Show, making its journey from the City to Westminster and back. London would be installing Fiona Woolf, only its second ever female Lord Mayor in almost 800 years and the monster procession would include over 7,000 participants including 21 bands, 150 horses, 23 carriages carts and coaches, and hundreds of other vehicles. This was all due to be trundling its way around the streets of London between 11:00am and 2:30pm, exactly the time I was aiming to be in the Lord Moon! There was clearly something going on 'darn sarf' as there was standing room only left on the train not long after I grabbed a seat, but while the underground was also heaving, I still exited Charing Cross tube station pretty much on schedule at 11:15am. In fact the only problem I had was making the dash around the edge of Trafalgar Square to the pub on the Mall in the pouring rain with no waterproofs! It looked as though it had been raining for some time down this way as the roads were awash with huge puddles and the bus drivers were clearly enjoying ploughing through them and soaking unwary pedestrians. Slightly damp therefore, I skipped up the three or four steps into the pub to begin another very pleasant pre-match session.

I was one of the first to arrive today and I could only spot one friendly face initially, Dave, who I met for the first time here before the Millwall game a few weeks ago. But gradually they all began to arrive, and by midday the place was rocking as usual. I met another Chris for the first time; he introduced himself by suggesting he would probably get the accolade of furthest traveller today. Chris had flown in from the Falklands only this morning, landing at Brize Norton just after 8am and then dashing to his home in Epsom before heading here; that made my trip on a crowded train from Stafford and five stops on the tube seem pretty straightforward! We got chatting with Mike as well, another new face to me, a decent bloke who knew my area of Staffordshire and Shropshire well despite now being based in the South.

Later I spoke with big Tim from the Surrey Whites; he'd been at the 'Leeds on the Road' event last night in Charlton. Whilst he said the first half of the evening with McDermott, Redfearn and Gibbs was really interesting, he was disappointed with the input from the panel of Leeds ambassadors – Messrs Lorimer, Gray, and Matteo – who he reckoned were all very negative and backward looking. I made a mental note that I must attend one of the future events to see for myself. At least Tim currently looked the part...sporting the early growth of a Movember moustache!

I spent most of the time in the pub with Adam and Conor, discussing everything from possible team selections and former players to the latest names in the ever growing list of celebrities being sent on trial for sex offences; one minute we were debating Ryan Hall and the next Stuart Hall; Max Gradel and then Max Clifford! The three of us decided to aim for the 1:39pm train out of Charing Cross to Charlton to allow time to grab some food at the ground.

It was only while we were stood on the train waiting to leave Charing Cross that the first rumours began to circulate that the game might be off. Conor picked up off Twitter that referee Keith Stroud had ordered a pitch inspection at 2:15pm and that already the kick-off had been put back to 3:30pm. My heart sank. In my long history of watching football there have been very few instances of getting to a ground only to find the game postponed. In fact I could only think of one; I had a vague memory of my chum Brian and me driving up and down the

M6 one very wet Saturday many years ago, desperately trying to find a game that was still on.

I've since spoken with Brian about that saga and he reminded me it was January, 1995 (His football records and diaries have to be seen to be believed!). We'd set off down the M6 heading for the Walsall v Darlington game but learned en route it was called off due to heavy rain and a waterlogged pitch. Brian then came up with a game at Witton Albion that the radio was telling us was still on, only for us to find that too was called off by the time we'd retraced our wheel tracks back up the M6. A bloke at Witton told us he was heading to Mossley where their game, "was definitely on", but weary and wet by this time, Brian and I called the hunt off and headed home.

Back to the present, and most of the punters on the train at Charing Cross were just as taken aback as we were. Yes, it had been raining this morning, but it could hardly be described as torrential. The Valley pitch did have previous though; it was only a couple of months since the Addicks' game with Donny Rovers was abandoned due to a water-logged pitch while every other game in the capital that day was concluded without drama. I couldn't make my mind up if I would prefer the game to start and risk abandonment or whether I'd prefer it to be called off now. The 3:30pm kick-off already meant I would need a dash of Olympic proportions to try to make my pre-booked ride on the 18:46 back to Stafford.

It was somewhat ironic that when we arrived in Charlton the weather there was actually very pleasant with the sun doing its best to force its way through the clouds. Nigel grabbed me just outside the station (I have no idea how he manages to find me on these trips...he would make a first class stalker) and he and I made our way to the ground while Adam and Conor called at the fish'n'chip shop up Charlton Church Lane. I was starving too, but my more pressing need was to find somewhere to have a pee and I'd assumed we'd be able to get into the ground by now. Sadly, we know what assume makes though don't we? (*ASS* out of *U* and *ME*). The gates at entrance 4, the away entrance, were still firmly shut, locked in fact. That was a problem. I asked a couple of stewards if there were any toilets outside the ground, a pretty stupid question I admit. But many had obviously raised the same query and I was readily directed, "behind the block of flats at the end of Valley Grove". I jogged back up Valley Grove, passing several van loads of coppers; no doubt waiting to see if they would be getting a full afternoon's overtime or just a couple of hours; it might make all the difference to their Christmas celebrations. I poked my head inside one of the vans and asked, "Where can I have a pee without being arrested?", and after the inevitable jokes and, "You'll just have to hold it mate", they too directed me to a car park behind the flats. There was an attendant at the gate in an orange Hi-Vis jacket and, before I could even ask, he waves an arm pointing over to the fence and there I can see a long line of Leeds lads, backs towards me, and clouds of steam rising from the shrubbery behind the fence they were relieving themselves through!

Having sorted that pressing need, I then queued at the little burger stall that I remembered from last season did a mean cheeseburger. It was gone 2:30pm by this time and the gates were still not open but a text from Mark told me, "Game on. Keith Stroud the ref. Get to the bog. MOT." He'd rung me while I was heading for the makeshift toilet facility to check I knew the game was in doubt but I had to cut him off and focus on the job in hand (literally) at the time.

It was in the queue for my first burger (it was so bloody good I couldn't resist a second!) that I saw the line-up. I was chatting with a couple of ladies in front of me and one of them had the official tweet on her mobile screen. We knew there was a doubt over Stephen Warnock, he'd limped out of the Yeovil game, but looking over her shoulder I could see there was another name missing as well, there was no Alex Mowatt. It would later be revealed that Mowatt had picked up an injury in training and so there were starts for Danny Pugh at left wing back, his first of the season, and Michael Brown in midfield, only his second start. A third change saw a full debut for Dexter Blackstock, replacing Matt Smith. It looked like the same 5 – 3 – 2 formation.

When Michael Brown's name was mentioned the bloke behind me in the burger queue began to sing the Michael Brown song: "Number one is Michael Brown, number two-ooh, is Michael

Brown..." You know the one. I commented that Brown played well enough in the game against Chesterfield, even scoring a decent goal, and in the run of games he had last January and February he was often in the running for Man of the Match. This chap wasn't having it though, as far as he was concerned Brown was too old and was a Warnock favourite who'd effectively been granted an extended contract only through Warnock's loyalty, not merit. Many fans will say the same but I still maintain they are commenting on Brown's reputation and history, not his performances for Leeds on the pitch. We would see how he gets on today. Danny Pugh also has many detractors, again in my view without real justification. The side would line up:

Kenny
Peltier Lees Wootton Pearce Pugh
Murphy Austin Brown
Blackstock McCormack

The subs were Cairns, Tonge, Green, Smith, Poleon, Zac Thompson, and Marius Zaliukas.

I wondered if we would ever see Alex Cairns get any game time; his only appearance thus far being the second half against Blackpool two years ago, the infamous Rachubka game. I wasn't sure if this side would be strong enough to turn over a Charlton team that was in decent form. They'd not conceded a goal in over 460 minutes of football, not since the third minute of their game with Forest on 1st October, and they were unbeaten in five.

Lots of people had been looking back in the record books to see how our start to this season compared to previous ones. The stats showed that Leeds had amassed 20 points from the first 14 games, and would you believe that in two of the last three seasons our return was identical. The odd year of the most recent four was the 2011/12 season, when we had 22 points bagged from those first 14 games. That suggested a remarkable consistency, even though those results have been achieved under three different managerial regimes! It was a consistency that failed to get us into the top six by the end of any of those seasons though; the closest we got was in 2010/11 under Simon Grayson, when we missed out by just three points to finish seventh. If this season was to be any different we all knew that we had to be winning games like this one today, there would be far more difficult games ahead you would think.

Nigel and I pushed and scrimmaged our way through the crush of fans congregated at the bar outside the South Stand - the design of this place is ridiculous, and dangerous – and then wandered down to our seats in row A1; it was the very front row of the stand. Whatever transpired in this game, I was going to get a great view of it! The pitch was in a dire state, the stretch of the byeline just a few yards in front of me was just mud, squelchy brown mud, as was the area around the goalpost nearest to us. I wondered if it would play a part in the outcome of the game.

The teams took up their positions around the centre circle for the traditional one minute's silence on this Remembrance weekend and as usual it was immaculately observed, although I still felt the tribute at Elland Road last week with the playing of The Last Post was a much better way to do it. Just after 3:30pm and finally we had a game to watch; it would prove to be a cracking encounter with more ups and downs than the average…, well, average Leeds game!

Once again Leeds had sold out their full ticket allocation and over 3,000 of us packed the South Stand; figures published this week in the YEP confirmed that Leeds were easily the best supported team away from home in the Championship this season[1]. It was still disappointing though to see empty seats in the home sections, with a total attendance of only 17,601 in the ground. It was the 3,000 Leeds fans that were celebrating just 17 minutes into the game.

Tom Lees found himself out on the Leeds right wing, just inside the Charlton half over to our left. He launched a long diagonal ball to the edge of the area where Blackstock rose to flick it on with the top of his head. Stealing in behind was

[1] http://www.yorkshireeveningpost.co.uk/sport/leeds-united/latest-whites-news/leeds-united-formula-needed-to-end-travel-sickness16218125Ross

McCormack and a jubilant Ross stabbed it home from six yards. Simple when you know how.

The pitch was clearly difficult but both sides soon came to terms with it and if anything the home side played the better football and carved out the better chances. Simon Church was unlucky to see one strike come back off a post and another point blank shot brilliantly stopped by Paddy Kenny, who was immediately saluted with his chant of, "Paddy Kenny's having a party!" The Leeds fans were already contemplating having a party tonight if we could just keep a clean sheet and assuming it didn't rain again. That went out of the window on the stroke of half time. An in-swinging free kick from out on the Addicks' right wing was headed away but only as far as Hull City loanee Cameron Stewart. He was all of 25 yards out but he watched the ball all the way on to his right foot and then volleyed it on the full past Kenny and into the top left corner. It was some goal. This would not be the last time we would see Stewart this season. All square at half time, but Charlton unlucky not to be a couple of goals to the good.

Scotty Wootton had gone down a couple of times during the first half and so it was no surprise he didn't reappear for the second. Marius Zaliukas took his place. Three minutes into the new half, and following another long diagonal ball, we were bemused to see Danny Pugh latching on to a header from Ross McCormack and then racing into the box at the far end of the ground. Then Callum Harriott makes a clumsy challenge on Pugh and sends the Leeds man bodysurfing on the saturated turf. We all shout, "Penalty!" at the tops of our voices although none of us could possibly judge the incident from almost 100 yards away. Mr Stroud though has a much better view and points to the spot! Ross McCormack picks the ball up and tucks it under his arm as he always does and this time I was pretty confident he'd score; his own confidence must now be sky high, unlike the last time we saw him put the ball on the spot. Sure enough, Ross blasts the ball into the roof of the net. I wondered what Gordon Strachan was thinking now, having just announced his Scotland squad sans our Ross! Once again 3,000 Leeds fans were bouncing up and down, counting chickens and assuming we'd now go on to win this game and build on that all important momentum. "How sh** must you be we're winning away", blasts out from the South Stand and Ross McCormack gets his own personal salute to the tune we borrowed for Dexter Blackstock just two weeks. It crossed my mind that maybe Ross was shaken into action by that episode. Who knows? Anyway, surely we could hold out this time and take the three points?

It was proving to be a very strange game; Leeds were now ahead 2 – 1, but it was still Charlton having the bulk of the possession. They would end the game with a massive 64% of it! This time we held the lead for just over twenty minutes, although that was largely due to yet another world class save from Paddy Kenny, who somehow stretched to tip a deflected shot over the bar, just yards away from me.

Then in the 70th minute, we saw the latest example of our inability to defend the simplest of situations. Simon Church appeared to be well marshalled by Lees and Peltier, out towards the corner flag on the Charlton left but suddenly Church got between the two defenders. He then stopped on a sixpence allowing Lees and Pelts to get goal side again before beating them a second time. By this time Michael Brown has arrived by way of reinforcement but Church still manages to get to the byeline and knocks the ball across goal past all three of them. Addicks' captain Johnnie Jackson is then quicker to the ball than Zaliukas and the ball is in the net. 2 – 2!

The home fans were now ecstatic of course; they were going through the same rollercoaster of emotions as we were and for a few minutes the rest of the ground came alive again. For my part, I would've accepted a draw if offered at this point as the momentum was clearly with the home side. But no one had mentioned this to Ross. Another of those long diagonal balls we're so fond of is pumped into the Charlton area and we can see the luminous boots of Dexter Blackstock as he hangs in the air to knock a header across to the back post. Ross is harrying his marker and just nudges him out of the way. Somehow, the ball drops over the defender's shoulder and lands perfectly on Ross's right boot just three or four yards out. From there it rockets into the roof of the net. 3 - 2 Leeds, but still 20 minutes, give or take a few, to go. Now the thought uppermost in our minds is that we desperately want to hang on to what we've got...three bloody points. It would now be a disaster to give them up again having got so close. The minutes pass slower than a really slow thing and still any neutrals in the ground would easily spot that the home side was playing better than we were, except in the shooting department where we were standing three from three; all three of our shots on goal had gone in. The board goes up showing four minutes of added time and we all glance at our watches to make sure we're in a position to remind Mr Stroud what to do in about four minutes' time. But Stroud has now blown his whistle for a free kick to Leeds, about 20 yards out and to the right of goal, and Ross McCormack is standing over the ball again. I nudge Nigel and tell him Ross is going to score again, "He's got two '4's on his back, this is his hat-trick of fours, it's meant to be Nigel, it's meant to be". "Dream on Sir David, dream on", comes the reply. And the rest, as they say, is history. Ross takes four of his little steps and then curls the ball straight through a gap in the defensive wall into the far corner of the net. Game, set, and match-ball to Ross.

At the end of the game, Ross grabbed hold of the ball and held it aloft before tucking it under his arm and applauding us. It was another one of those new Hi-Vis Mitre Fluo balls, so perhaps I can live with the colour scheme after all. Incredibly, Ross had never before scored a professional hat-trick, let alone four in a game. I wonder if Gordon is watching Gillette Soccer Saturday this afternoon with a furrowed brow.

The final BBC stats for the game revealed that Charlton had 64% of the possession, 17 shots to our nine, four shots on target the same as Leeds, and six corners to our one. In the record books though, it will read Charlton 2 Leeds United 4. Paddy Kenny must take credit for his two breath taking saves, while Pugh and Brown both had excellent games. Ross of course was the difference between the two sides with his faultless finishing, while everyone else played their part without excelling. It was a nice way to go into another international break.

It took an absolute age to get out of the ground as it always does at The Valley and then when we got to the station we had a long wait there before a train arrived. I was nervously watching the minutes tick by as the train crawled along towards London Bridge where Adam had recommended I get the underground. Adam and Conor were also headed for the Northern Line and when they alighted at Kings Cross they wished me luck; I had just less than ten minutes to do one more stop to Euston, climb the several escalators up to the main rail concourse and then sprint along to platform 17. Breathless and sweating, I arrived on platform 17 at 18:45. For some reason everyone was queuing on the platform and the train doors were not yet open so I actually would have had a few more minutes. Eventually we all clambered on board and of course as I was at the back of the queue there was no chance of getting a seat. So I stood with a load of Evertonians making their way back to Liverpool via Crewe; they'd been to their game at Palace – a nil-nil draw. They were a brilliant set of lads and a few lasses, all ages, all with really thick Scouse accents. They had a full size brown leather holiday suitcase packed with all their booze supplies and they offered cans and bottles to the other passengers. Sadly I had to refuse, as I had the car waiting at Stafford, but I could have had anything from cans of beer, lager, whisky, Jack Daniels, you name it, they had it. I even spotted a bottle of ketchup in the case, presumably for the "sarnies" which emerged like magic out of tin-foil parcels later in the journey! I chatted with a couple of the lads and eventually plucked up the courage to ask what they did with the suitcase while they were at the game. Obvious really, I don't know why I didn't think of it; it goes in a left luggage locker at Euston, to be collected on the way back! Now that is what I call planning an away day!

So, despite my fears, this game didn't fall into the category of "After the Lord Mayor's Show" at all. In fact, it proved to be a rip-roaring show in its own right. When all the weekend's games had been completed we were right up there in the mix. We were also the form team in the league, level with Burnley having taken 12 points from the last six games. Everything was to play for and as BM wanted, "We were there or thereabouts".

Seventh Heaven

It was a strange international break. There was good news and bad for me. The bad news was I managed to get to see Worcester City this week. I stood on the Aggborough terracing, frozen stiff, watching as they feebly capitulated 3 – 0 to a Leamington FC side that was supposedly also battling to get away from the wrong end of the table. City did manage to knock lowly Ramsbottom United out of the FA Trophy the following weekend though.

There was good news coming out of Leeds in respect of an anticipated bumper crowd for the Middlesbrough home game, and a whopping 6,800 ticket allocation that Blackburn had given us for the game at Ewood Park the following week; an allocation we looked likely to sell out! GFH were pushing hard to get Elland Road full for the Boro match with all sorts of attractions booked for the afternoon of the game. The Teessiders were sure to bring a big contingent as well to witness the first game in charge for their new manager Aitor Karanka, while Katy Kerry was also appearing…that's Kerry, not Perry….Katy Kerry is apparently a Perry look-a-like who performs a tribute act. Let's hope the "Roar"[1] comes from us and not them on Saturday.

> *You held me down, but I got up (hey!)*
> *Already brushing off the dust*
> *You hear my voice, you hear that sound*
> *Like thunder, gonna shake the ground*
> *You held me down, but I got up*
> *Get ready 'cause I had enough*
> *I see it all, I see it now*
> *I got the eye of the tiger, the fire*
> *Dancing through the fire*
> *'Cause I am a champion, and you're gonna hear me roar*
> *Louder, louder than a lion*
> *'Cause I am a champion, and you're gonna hear me roar!*

[1] http://www.metrolyrics.com/roar-katy-perry-ml-video-gtw.html

Then came a rumour that another takeover bid was in the offing. LUST began the rumours by tweeting that they were investigating the possibility of bringing forward some form of supporter ownership of the club. They were talking about maybe persuading the club to sell a 10% stake, which they valued at £2m. They also claimed that a "wealthy interested party" would match pound for pound any investment LUST could muster, up to another £2m. They wouldn't name the party concerned.[1] Then there was a different rumour; that another consortium was manoeuvring into position. This one was said to include The Chief no less. Lucas's name was mentioned and immediately Leeds fans in their hundreds were drooling all over Twitter at that possibility. Former Leeds director and regular hypothetical consortium member Adam Pearson was also said to be in the frame. But was there any truth in this one? According to GFH, no; dailymail.co.uk reported GFH claiming: "We are watching with a mixture of bemusement and interest the report suggesting any credible takeover bid has been made. No serious approach has been made by any members reportedly concerned".[2]

Well, that could mean anything really! It suggested to me that, as they'd already told us a while ago, they *were* talking with someone, but not the rumoured Radebe/Pearson combo. In fact on Monday 18th November, the Yorkshire Post published an article claiming that a £7m bid for a stake in the club had been made *and* turned down and that bid was said to be from a consortium of Yorkshire businessmen but that neither Pearson nor Radebe was involved.[3] It also suggested though that Radebe had been discussing his own separate involvement with the owners for several months. It was hard to know what to believe. I was sort of hoping nothing major changed for the foreseeable. I wanted to cling to the hope that we could push

---

[1] http://leedsnews.blogspot.co.uk/2013/11/lust-fan-share-update-matched-funds.html

[2] http://www.dailymail.co.uk/sport/football/article-2508351/Leeds-United-owners-turn-bid-club-consortium-involving-Lucas-Radebe.html

[3] http://www.yorkshirepost.co.uk/sport/football/leeds-utd/leeds-reject-7m-bid-and-left-puzzled-over-radebe-link-1-6250270

on and make a promotion challenge this season with what we already had, not risk yet another 'new start' and have to waste at least another season in this increasingly familiar Championship. I want to visit some different grounds!

A few days before the Boro game, Lucas Radebe came out into the open and made a lot of media people look very silly when he confirmed in a BBC report that he had indeed been part of a consortium bid for a stake in the club.[1] If everyone is telling the truth then there must be dozens of consortia circling around Elland Road like buzzards hovering over road-kill! In the programme for the Boro game, chairman Nooruddin would describe the £7m bid as no more than "a cheeky distraction".

In other news, we heard that Jamie Ashdown was going to have to have another operation on his, "troublesome toe", while Gordon Strachan did eventually give Ross the call to join up with the Scottish squad when Jordan Rhodes withdrew with an injury. Ross got the last twenty minutes of the friendly against the USA, ironically replacing Rob Snodgrass. The game ended goalless. Ross then withdrew from the squad before the Scotland game in Norway (Scots won 1 – 0) with a hamstring injury. For their part, our England heroes came up very short at Wembley against a much fancied Chile side that ran out comfortable winners, 2 – 0, and then lost again a few days later to a predictably efficient German team. Already the sceptics were vocal, declaring England to have, "no chance", in Brazil next year.

The Middlesbrough game weekend began as early as Friday afternoon for me, as Mrs W and I set off up the M6 headed for Altrincham. We were meeting up with my eldest lad, Mark, and his girlfriend Jess at their flat, before making our way to the Salford City Red's stadium, or the A J Bell Stadium, as it's now called. The attraction there was the visit of Worcester Warriors, who were playing Sale in the Aviva Premiership. The rugby union playing Warriors, like the football team from my city of birth were also bottom of their league and already seemingly doomed to relegation at the end of the season. It was maybe a last opportunity to see them play at the top level.

---

[1] *http://www.bbc.co.uk/sport/0/football/25020276*

Come 9:30pm on Friday night and I wished I hadn't bothered! It was a bitterly cold night and the four of us, Moi-Je, Mrs W, Mark and Jess, stood on a freezing terrace watching possibly the worst game of rugby I've ever witnessed. Worcester were totally outplayed by a very ordinary Sale side and lost by 26 – 10. They even shut the bar before the end of the game, thus restricting our beer intake. Mark and I could only hope for better fare at Elland Road the following afternoon.

We set off from Altrincham at 10:15am; it was another cold morning with frost on the windscreen but a fabulous clear blue sky overhead, as we headed first to Warrington to pick up my regular passenger, Bogdan. Then it was a straightforward trip across the Pennines to Leeds. All the talk in the car was about how this was another of those potential turning point games; a win would continue our march up the table with a top six spot probably our reward but a defeat would stop us in our tracks and bring out all the doubters again. I was really nervous about it. I'd become used to Leeds going on a good run and getting within touching distance of the top six only to then stumble and fade away; we'd done it numerous times over the last three seasons. I've described it before as very much like a game of snakes and ladders. I bumped into Jo (of the Clown fancy dress outfit at Watford last season) in the Pavilion, and mentioned this to her. Jo was having none of it. "I'm really confident today", she told me, "I'll Tweet you later tonight to remind you that you said that", I told her, still fearing the worst.

The usual gang gradually assembled around our table in the Pavilion – NottinghamWhite, PockWhite, +15, BarlowBoy, Pecky10, Martin and his three boys, Nigel, Mark, Bogdan and I all tried to chat about the game. I say 'tried' because there were quite a few distractions going on. On the big screen to one side of the Pavilion we could watch the Sheffield Wednesday v Huddersfield game; while on the screen at the other side was the Rugby League World Cup semi-final between New Zealand and England. But more distracting than either of those was the latest 'Fosters Live' stage show, a raucous rock band called 'Radio Mojo'. I had thought this particular experiment had been abandoned, as we'd not seen or heard anything more of it since the Burnley game back in September. Then, as now, the noise coming from the band on stage made it all but impossible to converse around the table and we all avowed to write to the club to try to get this particular innovation stopped for good. They were a decent enough band playing some great old classic rock numbers but it's just unnecessary; folk want to talk football and chat with mates not listen to rock music.

The team news came through as usual not long after 2pm. It was very much the line-up we all expected given the recent injuries to Byram and Warnock who, though now recovered, were not considered ready to start a full game. Hence there were only two changes to the starting eleven down at The Valley; Scott Wootton was still out with the injury picked up at Charlton so Zaliukas continued at the back, while Alex Mowatt was now fit again to replace Michael Brown. Hence the team was announced as:

Kenny
Lees Zaliukas Pearce
Peltier   **Pugh**
Mowatt Murphy
Austin
McCormack Blackstock

Subs: Cairns, Varney, Brown, Tonge, Smith, Byram, Poleon.

It was good news that the hamstring injury that forced McCormack to withdraw from the Scotland squad had cleared up and good to see Sam Byram at least back on the bench. Ross was sure to be a popular target for the wrath of the Boro fans today, having rejected their advances earlier in the season. Aitor Karanka's first Middlesbrough line-up had no real surprises, with many names in it now very familiar to me from recent Boro games like ex-Leeds men Jonathan Woodgate and Frazer Richardson, goalkeeper Jason Steele, and the usually troublesome Marvin Emnes. They also had one of my favourite Championship players, the unpredictable but usually excellent Albert Adomah who'd tormented us many times in his days with Bristol City. Aitor Karanka's CV included a previous visit to Elland Road in a Champions League, second group game, back in November 2000, when he was an unused substitute for Real Madrid. We lost that one 2 – 0.

Gradually the Pavilion emptied out as many of its patrons stepped into the cold to make their way over to the ground. Mark and I hung on until the rugby finished. Huddersfield had beaten the Wendies 2 – 1 earlier, and so our attention had turned to the rugby, in which England were defying all the odds by leading New Zealand 18 points to 14, with just a few minutes to go. New Zealand were piling on the pressure though and every England tackle was greeted by a huge roar from the not insignificant numbers still hanging on to watch. With just thirty seconds of the game left, England gave away a silly penalty, and from the resulting play conceded a try. The Pavilion punters groaned as one and then fell silent as the conversion went over to win the game for the lads in black. As the cameras panned around the pitch, showing the England players collapsing to the ground, bloodied faces now streaked with tears, Leeds fans quaffed the last dregs of their beer and headed out for their own battle. England's disappointment somehow felt familiar to us Leeds fans, but I was clinging to a more positive thought today; Jo said we'd win didn't she?

Inside the ground the atmosphere was excellent. As predicted, over 30,000 were inside Elland Road, including a large contingent from Teesside. Apparently the Katy Kerry performance went down well with the kids in the Family Zone before the game – maybe we can get future Fosters Live events scheduled over there, and not in our Pavilion! Today was also the nearest home game to 27th November, the second anniversary of the death of Gary Speed; a specially made banner was being paraded around the ground as the teams emerged from the tunnel. There had been plenty going on all around the ground to keep everyone entertained. We now just needed the team to do the business on the pitch.

Once again, this could not be described as a game of open attractive flowing football, but Leeds were again mostly workmanlike and efficient. It was a noisy start to the game as Leeds fans at both ends of the ground did their best to annul the efforts of the 2,000 or so Boro fans over in the West Stand who, predictably, were mainly intent on hurling abuse and phlegm in the general direction of Ross McCormack. Both sides had early chances, which only served to crank up the volume even further, and then as the clock on the big screen ticked over to 11 minutes, we began to chant the Gary Speed tribute once again. The screen showed a picture of Speedo with the simple legend, "1969 – 2011", and it was left up there for the full eleven minutes while we all joined in the, "Oh Gary, Gary, Gary-Gary-Gary-Gary-Gar-y-Speed" tribute. For a split second I thought we were going to get a repeat of that amazing coincidence (was it just coincidence?) at Forest two years ago, when Snodgrass scored exactly as we stopped chanting Speed's name. This time, first McCormack had a shot blocked and then Blackstock hammered a shot just over the angle of post and bar. It was not to be.

In the 35th minute though, we *were* in a seventh heaven of a kind, as Ross McCormack scored his seventh goal in three games. Danny Pugh had a great effort well saved by Steele, who pushed the ball away for a corner, on the Leeds left wing. Murphy played the corner short to Alex Mowatt who instantly delivered one of his now trade-mark left footed crosses to the back post. Tom Lees out-jumped his marker to loop the ball back across for Blackstock but it just went over Dexter's head. Instead, it bounced up in front of McCormack who stooped to nod it home just inside the post. Ross just couldn't resist jogging towards the Boro faithful, thumping his chest and grabbing the Leeds badge on his shirt, prompting another volley of phlegm from the Teessiders. After a while, the Kop came up with its response to this despicable treatment of our Scottish goal-scoring machine with a chant of, "He said no Boro, he said no. He said no Boro, he said no", to the tune of 'Kum ba yah'!

In the 42nd minute, I started to get that déjà vu feeling again. A Leeds clearance up-field towards the South Stand was headed wide towards the Boro right back position by the normally adept Daniel Ayala. On this occasion though Ayala got a bit of a shock, as his right back wasn't where his right back ought to be! Instead the ball fell into acres of clear space just outside the corner of the Boro box and Dexter Blackstock was off after it like a greyhound chasing a hare. Jason Steele spotted the danger and he too was doing a greyhound impression as he sped off his line to try to clear the ball. Blackstock was quickest though, and knocked the ball past Steele while the Boro keeper got his timing all wrong and crashed his shoulder into Dexter who predictably went down in a heap holding his head after a triple salko. The Kop was up on its collective toes shouting, "Penalty!" as from where we were, about a hundred yards away, we knew it must be close to the box. But suddenly we see Mr Gibbs feeling around in his back pocket and he's clearly not just scratching his ample arse. Eventually, he finds what he's looking for....his red card! He's sent Steele off. The déjà vu feeling brought to mind that Bournemouth game here at the start of October. Then as now, McCormack gave us the lead, that time from a penalty when the Cherries' keeper was sent off for bringing down Noel Hunt (remember him?). In that game of course, the ten men from the seaside then proceeded to batter us and got themselves a deserved equaliser, only for Dom Poleon to save our blushes late in the game with the winner. Surely nothing akin to that would happen again would it? Jo told me we'd win this game remember, though she didn't say how! In fact this game did pan out in an almost identical fashion.

At half time we were all in a state of hysteria watching Mike doing the penalty competition. Mike sits just behind me on the Kop and this must have been at least the third or fourth time he'd been picked out and he just isn't getting any better! He was faced this time by the tiny Leeds United U12s keeper and though he scored from two shots, he also gave us a fabulous impression of an England player in a world cup penalty shoot-out! Hilarious!

The Boro came out in the second half all guns blazing, and an alien landing in the car park and drawn towards the lights of Elland Road would have been hard pressed to know it was ten v eleven out there. Leeds were still making chances…and missing them, as we often do, but Boro too were giving it a right go. It took the Ramsdens' sponsored (the pawnbrokers not the fish'n'chips) Boro only six minutes of the second half to level the scores. The goal was a well-crafted effort that came from nothing. A ball to their right wing found the dangerous Albert Adomah who proceeded to motor down the line. His curling low cross in behind Leeds' back line was met on the full by Mustapha Carayol's right boot and the ball rocketed past Kenny to bury itself in the roof of the net. The air was blue on the Kop, as we all began to consider the possibility that we were about to pass up yet another chance to break into that top six section of the table. I was already rehearsing my Tweet to Jo while the Boro fans were reminding us, "We've only got ten men!"

Amazingly though, Leeds did not appear too phased by this latest setback and if anything we started to look a much better side for the next few minutes. Leeds began peppering the Boro goal with shots and crosses with Austin and Mowatt both going close; Mowatt's effort was a lovely left foot shot that was destined for the bottom right corner, until substitute keeper Jayson Leutwiler got his left hand to it, turning it around the post for a corner. The first corner was cleared away for a second and this time Alex Mowatt played it short to Lee Peltier over to our left. Peltier played a one-two with Alex and then shifted the ball onto his left foot. He sent in a perfect cross to the back post and there was none other than JP Dog, Jason Pearce, rising above his marker to power a header past Leutwiler into the top corner. Boy was that a popular goal! JP immediately ran back towards the dug-out to celebrate, with his team-mates trailing in his wake, while I hugged Mark and high fived everyone around. I could see PockWhite, aka Pete, and +15, aka John, celebrating a few seats away, John trying desperately to capture these fabulous moments on his tablet computer through a sea of waving arms and pumping fists. He did a good job too, as he would later prove by posting his video of JP's goal and the goal celebration on the LUFCtalk forum.

With ten minutes left, Matt Smith and Sam Byram joined the fray, with Blackstock and Pugh going off. Blackstock had not had a particularly good game, other than getting Steele sent off; his role being mainly as a target man today and he got very little change out of Woodgate and Ayala in the centre of the Boro defence. Pugh had a decent game but picked up a booking midway through the second half, no doubt the reason for him getting the hook. Michael Brown then replaced Luke Murphy with just a couple of minutes left as McDermott tried to run down the clock. There were a few nervy moments but we got there in the end.

Middlesbrough, like Bournemouth before them, had the bulk of the possession and pushed us all the way despite the imbalance in numbers, though having said that, Leeds did muster 19 attempts on goal today compared with just nine by the visitors. It was not yet champagne football but it was another win, a fifth in seven outings, and when we looked at the league table later that night, we'd see the name of Leeds United in sixth spot, with 26 points; now only nine behind the three top teams; Burnley, Leicester and QPR, all tied on 35. After the game, Brian McDermott told the BBC: "It's good to be in the top six but I would rather be even higher. There is much more to come from the team".

By the time I got home and logged onto Twitter, Jo had beaten me to it; she tweeted: "Told ya we'd win ;-) x".

After the disappointment of seeing the Warriors lose, and then that last minute heartbreak for the England rugby league lads that we watched in the Pavilion, I had just one more hope for the weekend. I logged onto my Worcester City account. I nearly fell off my chair as I read: "Stalybridge Celtic 1, Worcester City 2"; City were off the bottom! This was not a bad day at all; I poured myself a generous Glenkinchie and sat back down with the lap-top. The Wembley arch appeared on the screen, some news item about the Rugby League Semi's down there; Australia had trounced Fiji 64 – 0 in the second semi to set up an Oz v New Zealand final next Saturday, at Old Trafford. But it got me thinking about the Championship Play-Off final at Wembley next May, and I couldn't resist just tapping that into Google. I read the details showing on the screen and then wrote an entry in my 2013/14 diary for Saturday, 24th May, 2014. It read simply, *"Play-Off final?"*

"It was poor son"

Still the talk about new investment in the club was the main fodder filling Leeds United social media sites. But each time we got actual news it bore little resemblance to the rumours that preceded it. On 26th November it was announced that club MD David Haigh had dipped into his own deep pockets to find £1 million to invest in the club, apparently to bolster the transfer fund being prepared for the upcoming January window. The investment had been made through Haigh's recently established company 'Sport Capital'. Then rumours began to circulate that Haigh himself was involved with yet another consortium that was on the brink of buying the lion's share of the club from GFH; a takeover no less. On the morning of our trip to Blackburn the official website confirmed:

"GFH Capital, majority owners of Leeds United FC, have granted a period of exclusivity to the investors in readiness for the transfer window. The two parties have signed a share acquisition agreement for the purchase of shares in the club with GFH retaining a significant stake. The consortium includes a number of high profile businessmen, and does not include any previous owners or players of the club. It is anticipated that the investment will be in place for the January transfer window and will see existing Chairman Salah Nooruddin and Managing Director David Haigh remain at the club for the long term."

The statement concluded:

"The announcement is the culmination of many months of negotiations by a team led by David Haigh".

I was even more confused. So, it seemed that Haigh, and a group of like-minded fellow businessmen were buying the club, or most of it, from GFH, presumably paying GFH more than they paid for it in the first place but manoeuvring themselves into the position of owners so that they, and not GFH, would see the bumper profit if Leeds get back to the Premiership. I wouldn't think other investors in GFH would be very happy with that! It was also revealed by the YEP that the rejected £7m bid made last week was from a consortium including the Chief Executive of 'Welcome to Yorkshire', Gary Verity, and former Manchester United employee Mike Farnan. Lucas Radebe had been supporting that bid although this latest YEP article now said that David Haigh wanted him to join his new regime as an International Ambassador.[1]

Mark and I weren't aware of any of this as we made our way from his Altrincham flat heading for Blackburn. It was a good job really, as we had enough to think about when the Sat Nav somehow directed us onto the A675 and then demanded that we head towards and through the tiny village of Tockholes in the West Pennine Moors. It was a lovely journey mind, through fabulous scenery, if perhaps not quite as quick as our intended route up the M60, M61 and A666 would have been. As we passed the Royal Arms pub in the village, we witnessed a traditional pre-Christmas scene no doubt being replicated in villages all over the country as a few lads with a tractor heaved a huge Christmas tree into position.

Our intention was to park on the A666, halfway down the hill between the Golden Cup pub and Ewood Park stadium, exactly as we did last season, but when we arrived we were stymied by the fact that this year the local police had liberally sprinkled 'No Parking' cones all along the road. It was just one of those little annoyances that we footie fans face week in week out. It hadn't put some folk off though, as there were a few cars parked there, but closer inspection revealed that the owners would be getting their own early Christmas gifts from the constabulary in the form of the fixed penalty notices already stuck to their windscreens! We drove to the Golden Cup and found a perfect roadside spot down a little lane right opposite for free; they were charging a whole blue beer voucher to use their car park!

Inside, the pub was just as I remembered it, friendly and welcoming, with plenty of bar staff on and both Wainwright Bitter and Thwaites' Original amongst the beers on tap. There were already dozens of Leeds fans enjoying the pre-match atmosphere – a positive one today after the recent run of three

---
[1] http://www.yorkshireeveningpost.co.uk/sport/leeds-united/latest-whites-news/haigh-s-closing-in-on-leeds-united-takeover-1-6289134

consecutive wins. Mark and I sat down and chatted with three lads from the Ilkley Whites; James, Mick 1 and Mick 2. Mick 1 told us he'd been following Leeds home and away since 1974. Through a nearby window we could see some of the Sussex and Surrey Whites stood chatting outside; Andy, Cliff, Paula and Mike, Wayne, were all out there and Mick 1 mentioned he recognised a couple of them from the pre-season tour of Slovenia. Mick 1 also told us that Michael Mowbray, he who wrote the excellent 'Route 66', was one of their fellow Ilkley Whites. I was pleased to be able to report that I'd read and very much enjoyed that book during the summer. It documents Michael's journey around all 66 (well, it was 65 in the end as one club folded before he got there, but 'Route 65' doesn't have the same ring about it!) football grounds in Yorkshire, during the 2011/12 season. I then bumped into Andrew, author of the regular post-match blog, 'Travels of a Leeds fan', (http://leedsfan.blogspot.co.uk/) on one foray to the bogs and then also met Dave and Gary, who would you believe, are two more lads who share my passion not only for Leeds United but also for Worcester City! Gary reminded me that the City were playing Telford in the FA Trophy today; I'd forgotten the next round came up so quickly. I popped out to have a chat with the Surrey and Sussex folk at one point too, and asked where their driver, Simon, was. "He's having a kip in the car in the car park", Andy informed me! This is all part and parcel of a Leeds away day, a day when over 6,800 lads and lasses would be enjoying themselves somewhere or other around Blackburn, drinking and chatting with good friends, having a sing-song, before we all congregate in the Bryan Douglas Darwen End Stand for the next instalment of this never ending Leeds United Odyssey.

The team was expected to be unchanged by the majority of the Golden Cup patrons, so it was a bit of a surprise when we learned that Luke Varney was starting alongside Ross McCormack in attack. There were rumours initially that Dexter Blackstock had been recalled by Forest but eventually we learned that he was in fact carrying an injury. Other than that it was the same side that just about saw off Middlesbrough. Blackburn were known to be a difficult side to score against, particularly at Ewood Park, where they'd only conceded one goal in their last five league games, so the loss of Blackstock was a blow. This game ended 0 – 0 last season, and that was my forecast in the LUFCtalk Prediction League, although I didn't have any money on it with the bookies today. The concourse under the away stand was absolutely crammed full when Mark and I arrived and after another quick sortie to the bogs we made straight up to our spot on row 29, near the back of the lower tier. We were just to the right of the centre of the pitch and the view was excellent. We had the big screen away to our right hand side and there were Leeds fans as far as the eye could see. As Leeds kicked-off, I scanned around the other three sides of the ground and was again surprised that those sections were nowhere near full. The crowd would later be reported as 20,267, in this 31,367 capacity venue. As so often, we had more than a third of the support in the ground.

The sound of 'Marching On Together' was almost deafening as the game got underway and we did our bit to push our lads on as they attacked the goal at the far end. It was another game where it became clear very early on that there wouldn't be shed loads of goals and it would probably be decided either by a defensive error or a flash of brilliance up front. The game was also being spoiled by a very fussy referee who only seemed to have one arm; the one that regularly pointed towards us in the first half. I'd checked the details of the officials earlier in the week and found that the referee was a Mr Craig Pawson, a relative newcomer to big games but recently appointed to the Premier League's Select Group. Having been overseeing non-league games as recently as two or three years ago, I'd been concerned that this game would test his nerve as his every move would be scrutinized by almost 7,000 Leeds fans. I was right to be concerned. I'd also spotted during my researches that the two liners were named Perry and Tankard and cleverly (I thought!) tweeted that I hoped they wouldn't drive us to drink. It was in fact Mr Pawson who would do that. The main problem was with Luke Varney. Time and time again Varney would challenge for the ball in the air and every time Mr Pawson would blow for a foul. As Varney was our main aerial threat this was a bit of a problem. This week had seen the media full of the latest revelations and accusations about match-fixing, with the Daily Telegraph having 'trapped' one alleged 'fixer' into revealing how it all worked during a meeting at a Manchester hotel that was secretly filmed and then broadcast on national TV. Arrests had been made and both players and match officials were said to be involved in the fixing of lower league and non-league games. Watching Mr Pawson at work, it was hard to resist the temptation to believe that he might well have been bunged a few thousand quid to set a new world record for free kicks given against the away team! In truth, I'm sure that wasn't the case...he was probably just another one of those "sh** refs" we always get, and we told him so several times during the game. It shouldn't have mattered overly much anyway, as just after the half hour we should have taken the lead. A long high ball down field was for once met by Varney's head without intervention by Pawson's whistle and a neat little header inside found Ross McCormack, back to goal, on the edge of the area. Quick as a flash Ross deftly back-heeled the bouncing ball into the path of Danny Pugh who was now clean through on goal, eight yards out. Pugh let the ball bounce and really only had to steer it past the keeper. Instead, Jake Kean in the Rovers' goal stuck out his right leg and deflected Pugh's shot over the bar. He should have scored and he knew it; he would have kicked himself...but would probably have missed that as well.

In the 40th minute, Varney was penalised for the 4th time and Pawson showed him a yellow card. At this point the free kick count was seven to Rovers, none to Leeds. In the 41st minute Pawson actually gave a free kick *to* Varney and the Leeds fans spontaneously lifted the roof off Ewood Park with a mighty and very ironic cheer, while a few Rovers fans very wittily broke into a chorus of "Sh** refs, we always get sh** refs!". Then, just as the half was coming to a close, Leeds seemed to have mentally already gone in for their half time cuppa. We give away three corners in the final four minutes and from the last of them, needlessly given away by Danny Pugh who could have just let the ball drift out of play, we concede. As the ball floats across it somehow finds its way onto the right foot of

Tommy Spurr and although he fails to hit it sweetly it still bobbles through a crowd of players into the net. Same old Leeds, same old Leeds; we'd just switched off, just bloody switched off!

The second half saw Leeds try their best to get back on terms but our best just wasn't good enough and Mr Pawson continued to blow seemingly every time we got within striking distance of the Rovers goal. Brian McDermott took off Varney and Peltier after an hour and Smith and Sam Byram tried their luck. But it was then the turn of big Matt Smith to regularly fall foul of Pawson's whistle. Every time the ball was lofted into the Rovers' box it looked for all the world as if Matt was being hauled to the ground by his marker, but each time a free-kick was given against him, much to the increasingly vocal annoyance of the Leeds fans. Dom Poleon was given the last ten minutes in place of Luke Murphy but had no impact. Rovers were only prevented from doubling their lead by another magnificent save from Paddy Kenny, turning away a vicious shot from Josh King that otherwise had an appointment with the top corner of the net. In the final minutes Paddy romped towards us for a Leeds corner and that got the adrenalin pumping for a few seconds, but nothing came of it and the game was over. Brian McDermott joined the players to salute us and we were generous in our applause for them, even giving a rousing "Oh Brian McDermott" to the boss. Then, as the rest of the players trooped off the field, Ross Mac walked purposely towards us and stripped off his shirt. On his tee shirt was printed, "RIP Moody". Richard 'Moody' Ismail was a well-known and popular Leeds fan who'd been brutally attacked outside a Sheffield bar just over 12 months ago. Moody had passed away last Sunday, 24th November, having spent all that time in hospital as a result of the attack. A murder enquiry had thus now begun with the suspicion being that the attack was football related. It was a fine tribute by Ross.

This game just proved to me once again how important it is to a) take your chances when they appear and b) not make silly, sloppy defensive errors. We managed neither today and that cost us in a game that, to be perfectly honest, was little different to the Yeovil, Charlton, or Boro games, all of which we won; in each of those games there was nothing really to choose between the two teams and arguably the opposition had more of the ball, as did Rovers today. In those other games though, we were more 'efficient' and clinical, although it has to be said that we still made defensive errors in them all. There was no doubting the part the referee played today as well, and as we sped back down the motorways Mark asked me what I thought of him and if I knew who he was. I couldn't help myself, I just couldn't resist; I started to giggle uncontrollably; then I turned to him and said slowly, shaking my head, "He was poor son".

On Sunday morning, I flicked through the various reports on the game and saw that Brian McDermott once again claimed that he "didn't think we deserved to lose". Well, sorry Brian, much as I like what you're achieving with the side, that is a bit too trite. I know what he means – he's merely expounding what I keep saying about how close these games are and how it is hard to say one side or the other "deserved" to win or lose. But, at the end of the day, we had the opportunity to win, but fluffed it, while Rovers took their chance; so surely we did deserve to lose, didn't we?

On the Daily Mirror website, on Sunday morning, the Red Bull rumour was being given another dusting off. Under the headline: "F1 giants Red Bull are poised to take over Leeds United", they quoted an article that apparently appeared in the Sunday People saying: "Arab owners GFH Capital have been trying to sell a chunk of the club and are close to a deal with a local group willing to put in around £7million. But People Sport can reveal that mega-rich Red Bull are interested in buying United outright. GFH would ideally prefer to stay in control, hoping that promotion to the Premier League will eventually give them a return on their outlay. But Red Bull, who have dominated Formula One thanks to the exploits of world champion Sebastian Vettel, want full control – and have been told that £40m is the asking price."[1]

[1] _http://www.mirror.co.uk/sport/football/news/red-bull-poised-leeds-united-2871263_

I wanted to believe it....but I didn't know if this story had wings or not.

I just can't let the Blackburn game go without referring you to one more blog that I found while researching this chapter. It was written by a former Cardiff City season ticket holder who gave up following the Bluebirds when they were 'rebranded' red. These days he travels all over Europe "to experience the craziest rivalries and supporters" and on Saturday he chose to be at Ewood Park with the Leeds fans. The whole article is well worth a read, particularly if you're not familiar with the regular circus that is Leeds United away from home. If you think football is losing its way I would urge you to follow @BenDudley88 and have a look through the rest of his website. This is just one paragraph that will give you a flavour of the humour and passion that travels everywhere with our great club:

"One incident long after the game had finished demonstrated the commendable attitude that Leeds fans have to supporting their team, despite the fact that they are, more often than not, terrible at the actual football side of things. I was amongst 300 or so Leeds fans waiting at Mill Hill station, waiting for a connection back to Blackburn Central to head home. First of all a train arrived on the opposite side of the station, heading towards Preston. Several of the more drunk Leeds fans got on this service anyway, despite the fact it was heading in completely the wrong direction. Those who remained on the platform began doing the conga up and down the outside of the train, singing "do do do, you're getting on the wrong train!" This was followed by a reworking of their earlier chant, as they bellowed "Let's pretend our trains arrived", counting down from ten and leaping around the platform like they'd just won the European Cup."[1]

---

[1] From the article: "A day with 'Dirty Leeds' by @BenDudley88
http://supportersnotcustomers.com/2013/12/02/a-day-with-dirty-leeds/

Wigan and Watford

On the Monday after the Blackburn game, Owen Coyle was sacked as manager of our next opponents, Wigan Athletic. He was the third Championship managerial casualty in as many days, coming hard on the heels of Dave Jones being removed by Sheffield Wednesday and David Flitcroft by Barnsley. Both Wednesday and the Tykes were in the bottom three and so there was little surprise they felt the need for a change, but Wigan were sitting comfortably in mid-table, so Coyle's exit was more of an eye-opener. The worrying thing for Leeds was that both the Owls and the Tykes had won their Tuesday night games – their first outings since their respective sackings – with Wigan coming to Elland Road on the Wednesday night no doubt hoping for the same instant response!

A crowd of 25,888 turned up to see this game, a fantastic figure for a mid-week pre-Christmas match and the best Championship crowd for this round of fixtures. GFH had come up with the novel idea of offering a free second ticket to all season ticket holders for this one as they continued to produce new initiatives aimed at filling the ground and getting as much support as possible behind the team. This one had clearly worked and probably boosted the overall income from the game once those free ticket holders had bought a few beers, fed themselves, bought a programme and visited the club shop.

Despite having succumbed to defeat at Blackburn at the weekend, there was no panic being shown by McDermott who made just one change to his personnel. Luke Varney had not looked much of a replacement for the injured Dexter Blackstock at Blackburn and so it was no surprise to see Matt Smith replace him. Perusing the programme before the game, I was surprised to note that Smith had in fact featured in all but three of our games this season albeit more times as a sub than a starter. Still the only players to have been on the pitch for every minute of every game were Paddy Kenny and Jason Pearce and it was no coincidence that I also had those two down as our best players of the season so far. Ross McCormack wasn't far behind them either, having featured in at least part of every game and Ross had just been announced the Sky Bet Championship Player of the Month, having scored seven goals during November. Ross needed just two more now to reach 44 in his Leeds career; 44 also being his shirt number of course. The side lined up as follows:

Kenny

Lees Zaliukas Pearce

Peltier   **Pugh**

Mowatt Murphy

Austin

McCormack Smith

Subs: Cairns, Varney, Warnock, Brown, Tonge, Byram, Poleon.

Leeds were ahead as early as the 14th minute and it was that man McCormack again, scoring his tenth goal in the last nine games. A right wing corner from Alex Mowatt found Marius Zaliukas at the back post and his downward header bounced up perfectly for McCormack to hook towards goal from close range. It was blocked by a defender but had clearly already gone well over the line. It was the perfect start. For the rest of the half both sides pretty much gave as good as they got in another close fought contest and I was already wondering if we had taken the all-important chance that would settle the game. In the second half, Wigan attacked the Kop end and worryingly they began to dominate possession, although without creating many clear cut chances. The half was not yet ten minutes old when the visitors made their first changes bringing on James McClean and Grant Holt; the latter looking to be packing a few more pounds than he had in his Norwich City days. Maybe he'd already tried out some of the special priced pies on offer around the ground today in honour of our visitors' reputation as the pie capital of England. Holt soon began throwing his considerable weight around and I am sure I wasn't the only one beginning to wonder if we were about to witness him score yet another goal against us as he frequently did for the Canaries.

Wigan made their final change in the 66th minute, bringing on Callum McManaman to replace Nick Powell, to try to up the pace, while Leeds were actually doing their best to slow the game down as much as possible. At one point the ball went dead just in front of me, going straight to a ball boy sat behind the byeline; it was a chance for the lad to take his time, maybe fumble the ball and waste a few seconds. But instead he lobs the ball straight back to Kenny in the blink of an eye. Paddy was beside himself and mouthed something along the lines of, "What the f*** are you doing?" He placed the ball down on the corner of his six-yard box and then as he walked slowly back to get ready to take the goal-kick he stared pointedly at the lad with a look that would have felled a small tree. Thankfully, Paddy has probably now forgotten the incident, as in the 76th minute Leeds took a two goal lead and with it the three points. Ross McCormack lined up a free kick just outside the left corner of the Wigan area and when he curled it right-footed low towards the back post everybody missed it; it nestled nicely in the corner of the net. Jason Pearce had initially wheeled away celebrating the faintest of touches on the ball and the announcer had actually proclaimed it have been JP's goal. But later that evening it would be credited to Ross. No doubt Ross had handed over a wad of notes to persuade JP he'd imagined the touch he thought he got. There was the usual flurry of corners to endure in the final few minutes, but this time Leeds got through unscathed for a relatively comfortable 2 – 0 victory. Once again, no one at Elland Road this evening will be madly searching for the online highlights or making glowing references to champagne football in their diaries, but it was another three points and another difficult looking game negotiated without too much bother. It was a fifth consecutive home win and of course Ross McCormack did now have his 44 goals for Leeds; the number we see on his back every week.

On the evening following the Wigan game, Thursday, 5th December, 2013, news broke on TV that Nelson Mandela had passed away at his Johannesburg home at the age of 95. Coincidentally, the name of Mandela was already firmly in my mind this evening as I'd been reading my signed copy of

Lucas Radebe's book, in which The Chief makes several references to his fellow countryman and hero, *Madiba*. In fact, Lucas recounts the story of how, during Mandela's visit to Leeds in 2001, the great man had embraced The Chief at a luncheon in the City, proclaiming to the other guests, "Here is my hero," much to the embarrassment of the Leeds captain. The front cover of the book carries that quote by Mandela. After the news of Mandela's death, it was announced that at every English game the following weekend there would be a minute's applause by way of a tribute to the former South African leader. The Leeds game this weekend would take place on Saturday 7th December, against Watford, and I knew the Mandela tribute at Elland Road would be a particularly moving moment for me on that date. December 7th is of course also the anniversary of the death of Billy Bremner who died two days short of his 55th birthday back in 1997. The front cover and a large part of the content of the programme for the Watford game this weekend would be given over to tributes to Billy. But December 7th is also the anniversary of the death of my mum, who, like Mandela, also made it to 95, before she passed away, two years ago.

We had our friends Sheila and Brian stopping with us this weekend; they went off to the Stoke v Chelsea Premiership game on Saturday while I made my way to Elland Road. Our Chelsea supporting guests would then be heading off to London for the Champions League game with Steaua Bucharest next Wednesday and then Chelsea's home league game with Palace the following Saturday. Brian is pretty committed to following the Blues.

As usual, I picked up Bogdan from his flat in Warrington on my way through to Leeds and we made straight for the Pavilion. Peter Lorimer's guests were Eirik Bakke and Gunnar Halle, two of our former Norwegian players who were helping to host a big party of their fellow countrymen during and after the game today. Mention was made during their interviews that in this fixture last season Leeds were stung by the Hornets in a 6 -1 defeat. I couldn't see there being six goals today but dutifully placed my usual 4 – 0 bet having spotted that the odds were 50/1 again. Watford were going through a dodgy spell at the moment, having lost their last four home league games, although weirdly they'd drawn their last three away! It was a very strange sequence of results indeed and with so many Championship clubs deciding this was the time for change I'm sure Gianfranco Zola was looking over his shoulder. Watford have some useful players though, none more so than the dangerous Troy Deeney up front. They might also still be smarting from that surprise home defeat we inflicted on them last May, when we thwarted their hopes of an automatic promotion spot, forcing them into an ultimately unsuccessful attempt at promotion via the play-offs.

Once again there was just one enforced change in the Leeds side with the return of Sam Byram in place of the injured Tom Lees. It meant McDermott was continuing to persist with his 5 – 3 – 2 formation, albeit with yet another different pairing of wing-backs; this time Byram and Pugh. Matt Smith continued up front with McCormack, and now looked set for a long run in the side since the knee injury to Dexter Blackstock had forced him to return to Forest and thus cut short his loan spell.

While I stood applauding with the whole of Elland Road, remembering the lives of Nelson Mandela and Billy and even joining in with the chant of, "There's one Billy Bremner", that sprang up from the back of the Kop, I was actually thinking about my mum. I hoped that one of her sayings didn't come back to haunt me today; she would always say to me before any trip to see either Leeds or Worcester, "You know they never win when you go!" By the time the half time whistle went today, not only did I feel sure that once again my old mum would be proved right but also that I may well be witnessing another Watford six goal haul; as the players trooped of the pitch we were already 2 – 0 down.

Troy Deeney had opened the scoring as early as the 12th minute, when he latched onto a loose ball ten yards from goal and beat Kenny at his near post. Then, in the last minute of the half, Leeds conceded again, with the Hornets swarming from one end of the pitch to the other. Alex Mowatt clipped a Leeds free-kick into the Watford area from the right wing, only to see it headed away. Hector Bellerin collected it, turned, and then sprinted down towards us in the Kop. Bellerin only joined Watford a couple of weeks ago on loan from Arsenal, and he wasn't even listed in the Hornets' squad in the programme, but he looked a class act as he pushed the ball past Byram and then left him for dead as he rushed onward. When he got to the edge of our area he flicked the ball across to Christian Battocchio and the Italian Under-21 international jinked one way and then the other around two Leeds defenders before sweeping the ball past Paddy Kenny and into the net off the inside of the post. Watford had only had two sights of goal…but both had ended up with the ball in our net. My resolve had been broken. At 1 – 0, even though we were not playing very well, I still had the hope if not the expectation we could find just one chance from somewhere to escape with a point; but at 2 – 0 I felt all hope had been abandoned. But football is a funny old game as we are reminded so often!

Right from the start of the second half Leeds looked as if they had suddenly found their mojo. It was the proverbial game of two halves; as different a performance from the first half as chalk is to cheese. For the first time this season (with the possible exception of some spells during that Birmingham game) Leeds attacked with purpose and guile. We actually looked a very formidable attacking force. Suddenly crosses were coming in from both wings with Pugh and Byram storming towards us at every opportunity. Matt Smith looked like a colossus in the middle and it was his head rising highest to meet most of what was thrown in there. All over the pitch Watford players were finding white shirts in their faces as soon as they got the ball and challenges were flying in from all angles. The Kop and the South Stand immediately picked up on this transformation and suddenly the noise at both ends of the ground was deafening. Shots and headers rained in on the goal just a few yards in front of me. In short, this was exciting stuff! Now, if we could just get a quick goal.

Only four minutes into the new half we had one. Ross McCormack is buzzing everywhere and at one point turns to the Kop and implores us to keep the noise going. Then he tries to whip in another right wing cross but this time he scuffs it low and it bobbles and ricochets through to Danny Pugh who takes it on his chest to the one side of the area, just over to my right. He seems to have knocked it too far and it looks like it will run over the byeline for a goal-kick, but at the last minute he lunges forward and just sweeps the ball towards goal with his left foot. The goalkeeper is as surprised as we are to see the ball fly over his head and into the roof of the net from the tightest of angles. Now we have a game on! Danny hardly celebrates as the players all dash back to the other end for the restart. Within seconds the ball is back in the area in front of us and Leeds are piling forward again. MOT belts out from the Kop again and then, "We are Leeds", and the South Stand can be heard echoing our efforts; the whole stadium appears to be up on its toes urging Leeds forward. The atmosphere is brilliant and clearly too much for someone in our vicinity as a beery fart makes its presence felt. We all vent our anger at the anonymous perpetrator of the foul odour but it's somehow really funny as well in a hysterical sort of a way; it's hard to be angry while also being hyper about what's going on down there on the pitch. It doesn't seem more than a couple of minutes since Ross put that previous ball in for Danny Pugh but now he's out on that right wing again and this time he clips the most perfect cross towards the back post and Matt Smith is absolutely towering over his marker to thump a header into the net. As Smith lopes across goal to celebrate with McCormack, the ball bounces invitingly in front of him and he lashes it high into the corner of the Kop. Surely he should get booked for that I think to myself but the referee thankfully ignores it. From being down and out we are now level and suddenly that sixth home win on the trot seems more than a possibility. MOT belts out even louder than before and everyone is hopping up and down bellowing and screaming "Come onnNNNNN!" at the top of their voices. Watford re-start the game once more and immediately lose the ball; Leeds sweep down towards us like a tidal wave; a tsunami of white shirts with legs and arms pumping. "Attack, Attack, Attack-Attack-Attack", is the cry now and then a moment of celebration as we all jig up and down singing "Let's go fu***** mental, la-la-la-la!" Rudy has a header palmed away and then hammers the rebound at the now overworked Jonathan Bond in the

Watford goal. Leeds win two corners in quick succession and from the second the ball eventually falls at the feet of Alex Mowatt who absolutely thunders in a shot that nearly decapitates a defender and then crashes against the underside of the bar before bouncing away to safety. It's war out there; Leeds are bombarding the Watford goal with their heavy artillery, all the visitors can do is try to launch the ball up-field in that 'have it' manner of Peter Kay. Watford try to stem the tide by making a couple of substitutions, each taking far longer than it ought to, each designed to eat up valuable seconds as well as to halt Leeds' momentum; to some extent they succeed. Gradually Watford get a foothold in the game once more and for ten minutes Watford give as good as they get. But this lull may well have played into our hands. Out of nothing, Luke Murphy launches a long ball down the middle, over the top of the Watford defence and Ross McCormack magically appears underneath it, all on his own; where did he come from? He nonchalantly touches it on the first bounce past the oncoming keeper and into the net. This is what heaven must feel like!

"Ross McCormack - Ross McCormack - Ross McCormack", is the chant that salutes our goal machine now as he celebrates his 16th goal of the season in this, only the 22nd game; his 10th goal in the last six games!

Whether Leeds decided to sit back and try to see the game out at 3 – 2, or whether they were simply drained by the superhuman effort they'd put in during this second half, we will never know. Whatever the reason, we were nowhere near as dominant in the last 15 minutes as we were in the previous half-hour and I was nervous that we'd give away another goal. In the 85th minute a long range shot from George Thorne, another recent loanee not listed in the programme, was spilled by Paddy Kenny, and Troy Deeney nipped in to score from the rebound. In the last minute of the game we could easily have lost it if it had not been for a last ditch sliding tackle from Marius Zaliukas, who came from nowhere to nick the ball off the toes of Joel Ekstrand who only had Kenny to beat, six yards out. Even before Watford had scored their equaliser though, I'd already decided that a point would be a great outcome. At half time we were down and out but this second half performance was mostly magnificent and could surely prove to be a turning point in our season. If I was McDermott I would be sitting the players down in front of a big screen on Monday morning to watch that second half, to show them what they are capable of, and to try to put a finger on exactly how they did it. A draw was a fair result but if we can replicate this second half performance in the coming weeks and months, and maybe if David Haigh can see his way to pay for a couple of top notch January signings, then this might just be a historic few months in the history of Leeds United.

We all applauded and cheered the players as they took their bows at the end of the game and I strained my eyes to read the other results coming up on the big screen at the far end of the ground. It wasn't the Championship that interested me today though, it was the Premiership. I wanted to know what sort of a mood my mate Brian would be in when I got home. Not good was the answer; I could see, "Stoke City 3 Chelsea 2", flickering at me in the distance just below "Manchester United 0 Newcastle United 1"; the latter result bringing a huge roar from the Elland Road faithful.

At the end of this round of games, with most teams having played 19 games, the top of the table looked like this:

Burnley	P19 GD 17 PTS 39
QPR	P19 GD 12 PTS 39
Leicester	P19 GD 10 PTS 38
Derby	P19 GD 14 PTS 34
Nott'm Forest	P19 GD 07 PTS 31
Reading	P19 GD 06 PTS 31
Blackpool	P19 GD 02 PTS 31
Leeds	P19 GD 06 PTS 30

The players line up for the tribute to Nelson Mandela

"You should've gone Christmas Shopping"

Christmas was on the horizon. Last weekend saw the draw for the third round of the FA Cup, with a trip to Rochdale for Leeds to look forward to on 4th January, while Kian Egan of Westlife was crowned king of the jungle. This weekend would see the crowning of the latest X-Factor winner on ITV, while I'd be rooting for Peter Crouch's missus, Abbey Clancy, in the BBC's Strictly Come Dancing semi-finals, now that Ola Jordan and her celebrity partner Ashley Taylor Dawson (Hollyoaks apparently!) had been voted out. Yes folks, this is how we know that Christmas is just around the corner in modern Britain.

On planet Football, match fixing was still the big topic of conversation. Sam Sodje, a one-time Leeds player for a short spell in 2009, had been arrested after apparently admitting on film to have gotten himself sent off in return for a £70,000 "fix". To earn said red card, Sodje allegedly had to punch Oldham's Jose Baxter in the crown jewels not once but twice before getting the referee's undivided attention during a League One game between Portsmouth and Oldham, earlier this year. Blackburn's DJ Campbell was amongst six other people arrested following this latest revelation.[1]

The only news in Leeds this week concerned another absence being granted for El-Hadji Diouf, this time to attend the memorial service for Nelson Mandela in South Africa. Dioufy is absent from work more than your average peer from the House of Lords (another story in the news this week). Much as I've been a great fan of Dioufy in his time at Leeds, I really hoped he wasn't being paid for all this time he was spending away from the training ground. In his Donny pre-match press conference, Brian McDermott confirmed there was no immediate possibility of Diouf featuring in a game precisely because he had done so little on the training pitch lately, but he

---

[1] *http://www.dailymail.co.uk/news/article-2520102/Its-50-000-red-card-Three-arrested-footballers-filmed-admitting-fix-matches-betting-fraudsters.html*

still did his best to defend the Senegalese Player saying: "He has got some personal stuff going on as well which I have given my blessing on. ...Nelson Mandela gave him the African Player of the Year award so it is really important to him that he was there. Who am I to refuse him something like that?"

There was a flutter of excitement on Twitter when it was announced that Leeds had signed the highly thought of Southampton youngster Gboly Ariyibi, until the end of the season, and he was said to be already training with the first team squad. A video of him doing the rounds on social media suggested he was a decent winger and a good crosser of a ball; he reminded me a bit of a very young John Barnes. Watch this space. Dribs and drabs kept appearing suggesting that one member of David Haigh's new consortium about to take over the club was Andrew Flowers, Chairman and Managing Director of Enterprise Insurance, the Leeds shirt sponsor. Flowers was known to be a huge Leeds fan and on the strength of that alone we would soon see rumours that Max Gradel was again a target for the January transfer window. Mind you, following a reported visit by Haigh to Salzburg, rumours also began circulating again about the Red Bull connection and, because of his association with the energy drinks giant, even that Thierry Henry might come out of retirement to play for us...

It was a relief to get back to the football and I arrived in my usual parking spot on Lakeside Boulevard in Doncaster, a few hours ahead of our next game. The threatened Siberian winter had still not materialised and although it was very windy it was a beautiful clear morning. I went for a stroll around the ground and along the edge of the Lake, stopping to admire the excellent Andy Scott sculpture at the one corner of the stadium. I'm getting pretty familiar with this part of Yorkshire, this being my fourth visit to Donny in three seasons; we'd won the previous three, including the 3 – 1 victory in the League Cup here in August. Having done my circuit of the Keepmoat, I headed for the nearby Beefeater and spent a couple of hours enjoying the pre-match banter with all the usual suspects while sipping a couple of pints of Pepsi Cola; I was nursing a pre-Christmas party hangover from the previous night!

Once again Brian McDermott stuck with his now familiar 5 – 3 – 2 formation, and again there was just one change in personnel, with Sam Byram surprisingly relegated back to the bench now that Tom Lees was fit after his one match absence. That meant Lee Peltier returned to the right wing-back spot after deputising for Lees at centre back against Watford. This was the ninth successive game in which McDermott had used the three centre back formation since Wootton, Lees and Pearce were all picked for the Birmingham game. It seems to have been very successful too, as we've suffered just two reverses in that period, both by the odd goal; 3 - 2 at Huddersfield and 1 – 0 at Blackburn. Five players have been ever present starters in that run – **Kenny, Pearce, Murphy, Austin, and McCormack,** while **Alex Mowatt and Tom Lees** have missed just one game each and **Lee Peltier** just two. **Matt Smith** failed to start in three games – losing out twice to Blackstock and once to Varney, while **Danny Pugh** now seems to have wrestled the left wing-back shirt from Stephen Warnock. Sam Byram has filled in a few times when injuries required and Michael Brown deputised for Mowatt once at Charlton. **Marius Zaliukas** now seems the preferred partner for Lees and Pearce since his arrival in the side when Wootton was injured, even though Scotty is now fit again. Those are the only 16 players to appear on a starting team sheet since we lost at Derby more than two months ago. My guess is that if everyone is fit, McDermott's first choice starting eleven would be the names I've highlighted and indeed that was the side to face Donny today.

Doncaster have been unpredictable of late and languished in 20th spot in the table as this game kicked-off. They'd beaten two of the leading lights in the Championship – Leicester and QPR – in recent home games, but slumped to a 3 – 0 defeat at Bolton last Saturday. A quick look down their squad list on the back of today's programme told me that Billy Paynter was still here and he was named among the subs. We weren't brave enough to sing, "If Paynter scores we're on the pitch", this time, after what he did as a sub in August responding to the same refrain earlier in that game. That day he powered a header home within seconds of his arrival.

The wind was clearly going to be a major factor today; it was blowing a real gale. Leeds lost the toss and Doncaster unsurprisingly decided to make Leeds attack towards their own fans in the first half with the wind at their backs. Once again Leeds had sold out their full allocation of tickets for this game and over 4,300 of us were stood in the North Stand as the south wind pushed Leeds forwards and us backwards. We pretty much picked up where we left off against Watford as we bossed the first 45 minutes, although come half time we only had one goal to show for our obvious superiority, and that was a worry.

The game was only 19 minutes old when we opened the scoring; it was a classic Matt Smith goal. Rudy Austin was fouled over on the Leeds right wing, out to our left, and as usual it was Alex Mowatt who trotted over to take it. His left foot in-swinger was allowed to float on the wind deep into the Rovers' six-yard area where Smith was bravest, throwing himself low at the ball to head home. It was just reward for our early domination of the game and we should have built on it to have been out of sight by half time. That we didn't was mostly down to rank poor finishing, an affliction that continues to frustrate us despite Ross's recent potency. McCormack, Austin, Mowatt and even Danny Pugh all had opportunities which on another day, with a different pair of boots, may well have gone in.

As in the Watford game last Saturday though, the second half was a totally different affair. This time, having excelled in the first 45 minutes, we then all but capitulated in the second period. Admittedly the wind was assisting Rovers now, but only because Leeds seemed to think that lofting the ball up-field against it was a sound method of defence. It wasn't of course, and time and time again Donny won the ball back and began another onslaught towards us. Most of us thought Theo Robinson had equalised when he burst through the defensive line to ram the ball past Kenny, and the Rovers players were well into a manic celebration before the linesman to our left suddenly raised his flag for offside. The flag was so late it was almost in the next game but referee Phil Dowd upheld the linesman's call. After the game Rovers manager Paul Dickov would complain:

"I've had the benefit of replaying the incident about 20 times on the video and Theo is clearly a yard on side. But the late flag has baffled me as much as anything else. It looked as if the linesman thought he was on side but changed his mind when Theo scored. It's a massive decision because we were all over them at that stage and had we got a goal it could have changed the course of the game."

I've seen comments from Leeds fans over in the East Stand who are adamant that Robinson was offside...but they would be wouldn't they?

Alex Mowatt was now regularly being robbed of the ball in midfield and so McDermott responded by bringing Michael Brown into the fray just as he did for the Charlton game, when Mowatt was injured. As always, Brown revelled in the situation and immediately set about getting some telling tackles in. Shortly after he came on he suddenly found himself one on one with the last Donny defender....albeit well inside our half. He pushed the ball past his man only to be unceremoniously hauled down in a cynical last gasp challenge that earned the Donny exterminator a booking. We were all beside ourselves at being robbed of the chance to see Browny's little legs run the length of the pitch to score; the conversation around me for the next few minutes was about how far he would have got before he collapsed of exhaustion and why wasn't the Donny defender sent off as he was the last man between Brown and goal.

In the post-match stats on the BBC, Leeds would be reported as having just 32 per cent of the possession, and believe you me, it was way less than that for the second half. But as we've seen so often with Leeds, that doesn't seem to count for much; as Mrs W always says, "It's not the size of it; it's what you do with it!" Leeds probably only had two brief opportunities in this half, and yet we put them both away. The first was a magnificent move down the Leeds left wing. It began with Rudy Austin passing it forward to McCormack. He laid it off to Danny Pugh and then got the return pass right on the left

corner of the Donny box. He ghosted past one defender, outpaced a second, and then stroked the ball past the keeper at his near post. It was McCormack at his impudent best and a sign that his confidence is still sky high. This all happened in the 76th minute and it effectively killed off what remained of Rovers' ambition. Rudy Austin got the third just before full time when he met a McCormack cross on the half volley with his left foot and drove it firmly inside the near post. That was the signal for a mass exodus of the ground by the Rovers supporters who streamed away no doubt wondering what they had done to deserve such a result; a result that flattered Leeds but a result that pushed us into those all-important top six places. I couldn't help thinking how this was a great reward for all the traveling Leeds fans, fans who'd probably been, like me, to Reading, Newcastle, Millwall, Derby, Huddersfield and Blackburn, to see us return empty handed every time, with just the McCormack win at Charlton to celebrate in all that time. We made the most of it! We told the couple of dozen Rovers fans who remained that they, "Should've gone Christmas Shopping", and then suggested that they, "Should've brought on Paynter", before breaking out into a rousing chant of, "Leeds are going up, na-na-na-na-na-na, Leeds are going up, going up, Leeds are going up!", a chant that always makes me a bit nervous, so often have I seen it proved wrong in the past.
Brian McDermott was typically honest in his summary of the game when he spoke with Thom Kirwin afterwards on LUTV. "Yeah, that was tough. First half I thought we were good, we were comfortable enough; thought we might have gone in 2 – 0 up. They had the wind second half and we couldn't get out".
By Sunday night Sam Bailey had won X-Factor and had released her first single, "Skyscraper", while Abigail Marie Crouch (née Clancy) reached the heady heights of the 'Strictly' final next week. Leeds had one more summit to conquer before we could enjoy our turkey dinner; a home game with Barnsley next Saturday. Danny Wilson had been recruited by the Tykes, 15 years after he left them. Barnsley have messed up a few of our Christmas and New Year holidays in recent years.

Gold, Frankincense and Myrrh

Gianfranco Zola became the sixth Championship manager to leave his club this season as he walked away from Watford following last Saturday's home defeat by struggling, and also manager-less, Sheffield Wednesday. It was the Hornets fifth home defeat on the trot and left them mired in mid table. Meanwhile, Barnsley, our next opponents, had filled their managerial hole by appointing Danny Wilson on Tuesday this week. Once again, for the fifth time already this season, Leeds would face a team having a 'debut' manager in charge; the good news was that only Derby's Wally had extracted all three points from such a game against us.

Barnsley have proved a bit of a bogey side for Leeds in recent years and indeed we'd only beaten them once in the last six attempts. Matches against the Tykes will always bring back memories for me of that night at Oakwell on Tuesday September 14th, 2010. It was right at the start of my own personal odyssey documenting Leeds' attempts to get back to the Premiership and it was the first away game of that season that Mark and I had been to...along with 6,730 other fanatical Leeds fans. We'd journeyed up to Barnsley that day full of excitement and anticipation and then experienced one of the biggest highs of our lives as Jonny Howson fired us into a third minute lead – a lead that put Mark in the money as he'd picked out Jonny for first goal. For 42 minutes that night we'd enjoyed one of the best atmospheres I have ever seen at any game anywhere...and then it all went horribly wrong. Barnsley equalised just before the break and then in the second half added four more before Davide Somma got a late consolation goal to make the final score a resounding 5 – 2 to the Tykes. To go from that initial high to the depths of despair during a single game was a devastating transformation and one that I will never ever forget; we have seen highs and lows before and since of course, but for me it was the most extreme swing of emotions I have felt, matched perhaps in recent years only by that famous day when we overcame all the odds to beat Bristol Rovers to win promotion to the Championship a few months earlier. We've played the Tykes around this time of year in each of the previous two seasons, and neither of those went well. On New Year's Eve two years ago we were humiliated 4 – 1 at Oakwell; Ricardo Vaz-Te scoring a hat-trick coming off the bench; it was the game that would eventually be seen as the beginning of the end for Simon Grayson, as Leeds fans booed the team off the pitch. Then last season we saw an almost identical scenario play out in another game at Oakwell, this time on January 12th. Once again Leeds fans booed the team off the pitch after one of the worst displays I have ever seen from a Leeds team, or any other team come to that; it was the game Ross Barkley, (now acknowledged as future England material and doing great things in an Everton shirt), made his loan debut for us. We lost 2 – 0 and as the old saying goes, "We were lucky to get nil!" It was the beginning of the end of Neil Warnock's reign at Elland Road. So, there is plenty of recent history in this fixture. As I drove alone to Elland Road for our latest encounter with the Tykes, it crossed my mind that defeat this time could also, in the fullness of time, be seen as a turning point in the reign of Brian McDermott. I quickly dispelled such thoughts from my mind and pretended I hadn't seen that solitary magpie on the verge outside McDonalds as I turned into the car park…

As I walked down Lowfields Road, I spotted David Haigh stood outside the hospitality entrance to the East Stand, opposite Don's statue. He was dressed in a very blue business suit (much like the type that the Don used to wear funnily enough!), Leeds club tie, and slightly incongruous brown shoes; he was tapping a message into his mobile phone. I wondered if it was perhaps an e-mail to the Football League to ask if they'd yet agreed his takeover, or maybe it was to Max Gradel's agent, or even Red Bull owner Dietrich Mateschitz. How appropriate is it that a bloke called 'Diet rich' became the owner of a company famed for making a best-selling energy drink?

Haigh may have just been gauging how successful his latest initiatives had been in bringing the crowds back to Elland

Road. There were promises of gifts being handed out inside the ground by the three wise men, Haigh, Nooruddin, and Patel, and cheap beer was promised in the stadium concourses. One lucky season ticket holder would get the cost of his ticket refunded, while there were rumours of free mince pies in certain bars too. You have to hand it to this GFH lot; they are not short of ideas! They seem to work too; over 31,000 would be packed into the old stadium again today and I have never seen such queues for the bogs! Probably all that cheap beer I guess, most of which was now swilling about on the bog floor. There were no surprises in the team selection today, with the same side that started at Donny turning out again. That meant Sam Byram continued to warm the bench with his dodgy hips alongside El-Hadji Diouf who made a surprise return after all that had been said about him this week not being ready to play. As we belted out MOT for the first time with the teams lined up in front of the West Stand, I looked carefully around the ground. The 'Cheese Wedge' was full, over in the south east corner, as was the majority of the West Stand and the lower tier of the East Stand. Two sections of the East Stand upper tier, up there in the gods, were full too. Yes, this GFH crew know a thing or two about marketing and their various gifts and offers had once again done the trick. Sadly, the Leeds team couldn't provide the real Christmas gift we all wanted; three points.

Leeds began the game well enough, attacking the Kop in the first half with plenty of vigour. In the opening few minutes Matt Smith had two glorious chances fall to him but he proved to be far less adept at sticking the ball in the net with his feet than he usually is with his head. The first chance he made for himself, as he neatly cushioned a long high through ball from Jason Pearce on his chest, brought it down on his right foot, but then hammered it too close to the keeper, who instinctively got an arm in the way. A few minutes later he was through again but this time his feeble shot was more reminiscent of Granny Smith than Matt Smith as an in-form Jack Butland in the Tykes goal saved easily. As the half wore on, my 5 – 0 bet (I know, I know, it's even more outlandish than 4 - 0) looked more and more unlikely as the chances became fewer and further between and Barnsley looked the more dangerous side. At half time there was a mad rush to the loos again as that cheap beer began to weigh heavily in bladders all around the ground and by the time I got to the bogs behind the Kop they were queuing twenty yards from the door. Inside it was not a pretty sight as the urinal troughs overflowed and balding hairy blokes paddled along fighting for a spot on the front row.

In the Leeds dressing room, Brian McDermott was hatching a plan to undo the Tykes' stubborn resistance and as we took our places back in the stands, surreptitiously eyeing the front of our trousers for evidence of 'splash back', we could see Sam Byram and Michael Tonge warming up on the touchline; we soon worked out that Peltier and Mowatt were missing. Tonge had not seen first team action since the Derby game and so this was his first taste of the 5 – 3 – 2 formation; it was not surprising that he struggled to start with although he did grow into the game as the minutes ticked by. Leeds continued to have the better efforts on goal but without ever looking likely to beat Butland, who easily dealt with a stinging Danny Pugh effort and a twenty yard effort from Tonge. Once again a very poor referee was not helping either side as he randomly decided whether a challenge was fair or foul; Keith Stroud is usually better than this but today he was more than worthy of the predictable "sh** refs" chant that eventually belted out from the Kop as we all got totally bemused by his decisions. McDermott tried one last roll of the dice as he switched to 4 – 3 – 3, bringing on Dom Poleon for Luke Murphy, but the young striker saw far too little of the ball in the few minutes he was on, something becoming a regular theme. In the 84th minute, Stroud finally got one decision right as he red-carded Marcus Tudgay for a terrible attempted tackle on Marius Zaliukas. There was no advantage for Leeds though as we were effectively also down to ten men with Marius limping his way through the last few minutes. It ended as it began, 0 – 0.

As I went for another battle of the bogs straight after the game, the most frequent comment I heard was, "We'd have lost that sort of game in the past", said in a mildly optimistic sort of a manner. I tended to agree. It was once again not a fantastic game, or a great performance from Leeds, but at least we were solid at the back and, on another day, we'd surely have taken one or two of those early chances. The only slight worry was the sight of Zaliukas limping away at the end of the game, as he was once again my man of the match. In my mind he is the reason we are now looking much more organised in defence. To lose him as we enter the Christmas and New Year run of three games in a week would be a potentially mortal blow.

The toilets were by now a total disgrace. Most of the troughs were overflowing with a steaming golden stream of urine that was rapidly turning the area into a paddling pool. We were jammed in three deep all along both walls and an old chap called Frank was going ape, having just been shoved in the back and having thus splashed all down his trousers. "Don't worry Frank", one of his mates consoled him, "it'll be dry by the time you get home mate". Everyone other than Frank fell about laughing. Clearly our three wise men had delivered their gifts; all around me I could see liquid gold, Frank incensed, and mirth!

On the radio going home, I learned that Peter Crouch had scored for Stoke in their 2 – 1 win over Aston Villa this afternoon and he was apparently now travelling down to London to see his missus perform in the Grand Final of Strictly. (Do you agree it's ironic that a bloke named Crouch is so tall?) Later in the evening, I watched a recording of the show and was happy to see Abbey complete a Crouch double, performing a fabulously sexy rock and roll show-dance routine to win the famous 'Strictly' glitter ball. I then checked the non-league football results and was amazed and overjoyed to see that Worcester City had pulled off an unlikely 1 – 0 win at home to high flying Harrogate Town. All in all not a bad day again; I wandered into the study to get myself a celebratory malt. A few days of festive cheer at home could now be enjoyed with the family, before Mark and I set off for the seaside on Boxing Day. It was all shaping up nicely.

Zaliukas and Kenny wish each other a good game

The Three Wise Men did the trick again in attracting a bumper crowd in for the Barnsley game.

Blackpool

My Christmas this year was once again held at chez Watkins, and very pleasant it was too. But you know, I sort of felt this year it was merely a temporary distraction between two important Championship games and not the most celebrated church festival of the year. I'm not a religious person and hence Christmas for me has always been just a fun time of year when I drink and eat more than usual, spend more time with friends and family than usual, and when Slade, Roy Wood's Wizard and The Pogues and Kirsty MacColl monopolise the radio. Of course the fact that I spent a couple of days over Christmas writing up the Barnsley game kept Leeds firmly in my mind and then Christmas night, once the Turkey dinner and Christmas pudding had been polished off, I was already thinking about the trip up to Blackpool; in particular how many hours I had left to get my blood alcohol levels back within legal limits before I got behind the wheel.

The Blackpool game was another live on TV match, our fifth so far this season; this one kicking off at a most peculiar time of 5:15pm on Boxing Day. By mid-day, Mark and I were on the road, enjoying the most un-Christmas like weather I could remember for many years. Wind and rain had been battering the south of England causing all manner of flooding and disruption, with many homes left without power on Christmas Day, but the Midlands and the North escaped reasonably unharmed. The temperature was still in double digits as we parked the car in our usual Blackpool roadside spot, just a five minute walk round the corner from Bloomfield Road. Our first task was to find Martin and Daniel; it was Dan's 18th birthday a few days ago and we'd promised him a pint. Right on cue my phone beeped signalling a text from Martin; "We're in The Castle mate", he'd texted. Useful information as long as you knew where 'The Castle' was…which we didn't. These days it's no problem though, and Mark soon found it on Google, just at the end of Central Drive, behind Blackpool Tower. We headed to the promenade and walked along the sea front bracing ourselves against the wind that was whipping up the waves in the distance. It was spitting with rain too as a friendly doorman in an orange Hi-Vis jacket pulled open the door to the pub and we stepped into a very familiar world full of Leeds fans. It seemed like everyone was in a complete frenzy and we soon discovered why. Up on the big screen we could see that Man U were currently leading 3 – 2 at Hull, in a televised Premiership game, and Hull were pressing for an equaliser; everyone in the pub was urging them on in their quest. Martin told us that Hull had been 2 – 0 up at one point and hence the intensity with which the Leeds fans were willing them on. Suddenly, a Hull player is through on goal in the inside left channel and as he pulls the trigger the whole pub rises as one ready to celebrate, only for the keeper to smother the shot. Man U held on to their 3 – 2 lead and The Castle clientele switched their attention to the disco that was rattling out dance tunes at the back of the pub.

Mark and I had a couple of pints with Martin before we headed off to the Auctioneer, a Wetherspoon pub on Lytham Road. Last season the Auctioneer had been rammed for several hours before kick-off but this year when we arrived at about half three there was plenty of room and we got a table to ourselves. There was a great atmosphere in there though with mainly Leeds but also a few Blackpool fans all coexisting without problem. A couple of coppers came in at one point, spotters from the West Yorkshire force, and they quickly got into the spirit of Christmas by allowing various patrons to have photos taken wearing their helmets! Then a bloke dressed head to toe in tangerine leant over our table chanting, "We hate Man U", at the top of his voice and telling us how, "The 'Pool' hate Man U as much as Leeds yer know". I thought about trying to explain to him that no-one, absolutely no-one, hates Man U as much as Leeds fans, but decided that would be unnecessarily controversial and instead just shook his hand and suggested he get the Blackpool fans to sing about Man U at the game and we'd join in.

The Travels of a Leeds Fan blog man, Andrew, said hello; he was with his regular blog companions The Happy Chocker and the Quiet One (you must read the blog as mentioned before) and at one point I was savaged by Simon from the Surrey Whites who were strangely short of numbers today. Eventually, Nigel arrived and we sat and chewed over the prospects for the game; most of us thinking a draw would be a decent result. Then we headed off to the ground.

The Blackpool match was a loyalty game; tickets went on sale initially to fans who'd already attended seven or more away games this season, and then every few days the requirement was dropped by a game until the tickets sold out. Surprisingly it got down as far as four games and there had still been tickets available in the week before Christmas, though I assumed they'd all gone now. It was interesting to see the list of games attended on the ticket section of the Leeds website; I was very surprised that only 121 people had been to every away game this season for example – I would have expected that figure to have been higher, though it did exclude the 350 or so away season ticket holders. It's hard to know what the club can do to ensure that limited ticket numbers are allocated fairly – the loyalty system is OK but it can be abused by folk claiming their ticket and then passing it to a mate who doesn't have the required number of matches under their belt to get a ticket in their own right. On rare occasions you might be required to show a membership card with the ticket but almost never do they bother to check that the number hand-written on the back of the ticket matches the number on the membership card. If they did, I am sure they would find a significant number who were not actually entitled to have a ticket! I had no such problems of course, as I'd only missed one away game in over three seasons, while Mark had managed five so far this term. Mark, Nigel and I stepped outside the Auctioneer to begin our walk to the ground and were immediately hailed by a bloke asking us if we needed any tickets, while a few steps further on we bumped into a couple of lads we know who were looking for tickets, proving my point!

Inside the ground, we all squeezed into the little Portakabin bogs – totally unsuitable for the numbers Leeds bring here – and then Mark and I left Nigel in the huge queue for coffee while we went to place a couple of bets. I went for a 2 – 0 Leeds win with McCormack to score first; a 40/1 offering from the Ladbrokes' shed. Mark refused to declare what he was going for.

Since we'd bought our tickets at different times because of the loyalty mechanism, they were not together, so we had a look at both tickets before choosing Mark's R 87 option which, since it was right on the edge of a walkway, gave us more space to squeeze two people in. As always, the Leeds support was magnificent. We had something over 1,700 for this one and that filled the whole of the one side of the ground. They still haven't redeveloped this side of the ground which remains a temporary stand that has all the characteristics of a bouncy castle when everyone gets excited, and we were all excited even before the game kicked-off! The substitutes were still having a kick-about as the teams came out and Luke Varney was given a rousing chant of, "If Varney scores we're in the sea", which he seemed to take in the spirit it was meant, holding his arms aloft to conduct our efforts before generously applauding us. There had been a few injury doubts before the game – Zaliukas in particular was a doubt following that despicable last minute challenge by Barnsley's Marcus Tudgay that earned the little Tyke a red card. Thankfully though, Marius was declared fit and played. Luke Murphy was suspended following his fifth yellow of the season last Saturday and unsurprisingly Alex Mowatt was rested, the youngster having looked very tired in recent games. Hence our midfield today included Brown and Tonge. The rest of the side was as in recent games with Peltier and the revitalised Danny Pugh continuing to hold down the wing-back positions. The full side was thus:

Kenny
Peltier Lees Zaliukas Pearce Pugh
Austin Brown Tonge
McCormack Smith

Subs: Cairns, Byram, Wootton, Varney, Poleon, Warnock, Ariyibi.

Probably the most interesting name in there was that of Gboly Ariyibi, the young winger signed only a couple of weeks ago. How we would love to see him marauding down the wing.

As the game kicked-off, with Leeds in their now rarely used light blue shirts, there were plenty of tangerine seats visible all around the ground. It never ceases to amaze me how even the smallest of Championship grounds fail to completely fill for a game against Leeds. 15,552 would be the official attendance – some 1,200 less than the stated capacity. Right from the start it was only the Leeds fans that could be heard and we must have been a fabulous sight with everyone absolutely bouncing...well, in this stand we had no choice really! Up along the back of our stand was a long row of Leeds flags, giving added colour to the scene. The lads in blue were giving us plenty to shout about too, as we carved out a few chances and looked really comfortable with the ball, frequently getting both Peltier and Pugh motoring down the wings to the byeline. The Ince family came in for plenty of stick from the Leeds songsters – father Paul, the manager in the dug-out and son Tom out on the pitch. Each time Ince junior got the ball he was regaled with, "Your Dad's a c*** and so are you", while later on a rather less politically correct version of, "Your Dad's a c***, your Mum's a slag", had even one or two of the Leeds fans shaking their heads in embarrassment. Fortunately, Tom Ince wasn't seeing much of the ball in the early stages as it was the visitors who were in control of the game. In the 25th minute we made that control count. Michael Tonge broke down the Leeds left wing and then held the ball up while Danny Pugh arrived. Pugh overlapped outside Tonge and then almost on the byeline he whipped the ball across to the back post. As the ball floated across the face of the goal a bloke behind me nearly deafens me with a cry of, "This is in, this is f****** in", even before it arrives on Lee Peltier's head, but he called it spot on. Pelts rose and got just enough on the ball to send it looping over the outstretched hand of the keeper, and it dropped neatly in the opposite corner. Cue celebrations the like of which I have rarely seen this early in a game. The rickety stand felt like it was built on rubber as we all jigged up and down going "f****** mental" while the other three sides of the ground fell even more silent than they were a few seconds earlier. There was little to choose between the sides for the balance of the half but it was noticeable that the Leeds defence seemed well in control of the usually fleet of foot Blackpool forward line. As always, the main problem for Leeds was we failed to hit the target very often...in fact we only managed the once, Peltier's header, while Blackpool didn't have a single shot on target in the first half. Not surprising therefore that the Leeds choir broke into song about it with a chorus of, "Shot on target, we're in the sea!" about midway through the half.

As the teams came out for the second half, I spotted Dan and Martin making their way along the front of the stand – Daniel carrying a bottle of Coke and Martin, clearly three sheets to the wind, somehow managing to carry a steaming meat pie in one hand and a hot dog in the other! Dan saw me waving and he began to manoeuvre Martin up the steps towards us, I was sure that either Martin, the pie, or the hot dog, or more likely all three, would go crashing to the floor at any minute but somehow he made it and squeezed himself past me into a vacant seat. He then proceeded to demolish the pie, offering one final bite to me before popping that into his mouth as well when I gracefully declined. Meanwhile, on the pitch, the fare was nowhere near as tasty for Leeds fans as the home side began to pile on the pressure, although Marius Zaliukas was looking imperious at the centre of the Leeds defence and I couldn't really see us conceding. I'd just said as much to Mark when Blackpool won a free kick out on their left wing. Eventually the ball is lofted into the Leeds box where it's headed away but only as far as Tom Ince, it had to be him didn't it? We were right behind the flight of the ball as he hammered it back towards goal and we could see Paddy Kenny in full flight ready to palm it away. Then, horror of horrors the ball takes a big deflection off the head of Marius Zaliukas and ripples the back of the net.

Suddenly, Bloomfield Road came alive as the Tangerines' fans found their voices and we tried to encourage our lads to dig deep for what was sure to be a difficult last 25 minutes. The atmosphere was fantastic and the game was end to end for a few minutes as both sides went all out for the win. There were some tasty tackles flying in too, mostly from Blackpool, but another very suspect referee, Scott Mathieson this time, seemed to have left his cards at home. Then suddenly a ball is lofted over the top of the home defence and Ross McCormack outwits Kirk Broadfoot but before Ross can get a shot away Broadfoot has hauled him to the floor. The challenge was just on the edge of the box so we were not surprised to only get a free kick but we were gobsmacked when Mathieson only shows a yellow card. Blackpool had already had eight red cards this season, and this really should have been a ninth. Ross himself took the free kick and predictably it came to nothing. The game could have gone either way after that but by the final whistle only three shots on target would be recorded in total – one of them being Lee Peltier's headed goal and two from Blackpool including their equaliser. Once again our lack of creativity had been highlighted as a problem, as well as our often appalling shooting skills. Rudy Austin had one great chance that he completely fluffed, as he has done with at least two or three shots every game. It really isn't good enough. In the last minute of the game some justice was done when Broadfoot lunged into a dreadful tackle on Zaliukas to earn a straight red card. It was a carbon copy of the Tudgay tackle on Marius last Saturday, and again I prayed that Marius wasn't too badly hurt. As happened on Saturday, it was too late for Leeds to take any advantage of the extra man, and so the game ended all square, 1 – 1.

A final memory of this game was the sight of the local police filming the Leeds fans as they always seem to do here. Many of our lads began to film the police filming them, holding up their mobile phones and chanting, "If you film us we'll film you back". The police were unmoved by the finest wit Yorkshire had to offer.

Leeds had played well for the majority of this game, and but for that wicked deflection off Marius's bonce we'd have taken three points off one of the better footballing sides in the division. We were now fifth in the table with 35 points and unbeaten in five games in December so far. Among the other results this Boxing Day was a 4 – 0 thumping for Millwall at Watford, a thumping that cost Steve Lomas his job after just six months leading the Lions. That was casualty number seven of this increasingly competitive Championship season and the fifth to go in December alone! Before we get too excited though, we should remember that Neil Warnock was ousted for a record not dissimilar to that of McDermott in the first half of the season – 35 points from 24 games.

The Castle in Blackpool, with the Tower in the background

Rocket from Derbyshire destroys Leeds

Our final game of 2013 was at the City Ground, Nottingham, scene of a Boxing Day humiliation last season when we were taken apart 4 – 2 by a rampant Forest side. I hoped for a better outcome this time, even though both teams were in very similar positions now as they were then – just on the fringes of the Play-Off places. Forest had leap-frogged Leeds into fifth with their excellent 2 – 0 win over QPR on Boxing Day, giving them 36 points and pushing us down to sixth.

This was another logistical puzzle for me as Mrs W and I were partying in Worcestershire the night before the game. Hence it was an unusual trip up the M42 and M1 on Sunday morning that got us as far as the Donington Park service area for a quick pit stop. I could not believe my eyes as I strolled across the car park; stood outside the main entrance was none other than 'Welsh' Andy, having a crafty fag. Talk about a small world! Andy had travelled up from Surrey with Wayne and his young son Dean; I bumped into Wayne in the Costa Coffee queue a few minutes later. He reminded me there was a diversion into Nottingham as work continued on the A453, work that will be ongoing right through to 2015 according to the signage we passed later on. It wasn't a problem going in, but we'd find it a nightmare after the game, working our way back to the M1.

I parked up just along the road from the Notts County Social Club on Meadow Lane, where I'd arranged to meet Chris and his lad Brandon and Chris's Uncle Gez. We wandered in not long after mid-day and already there was a smattering of Leeds fans in there. Mrs W wasn't coming to the game and she went off to the shops after first sampling a chip butty in the club – she told me her mum would be well impressed when she passes on the information that I treated her to a Sunday lunch of chips and a buttered bap! I know how to woo a girl.

I set off on the 15 minute walk to the ground at about 2:15pm – it was a bright crisp day with a mostly blue sky. The temperature now was about five or six degrees, slightly warmer than the freezing conditions we encountered when we left the village of Earls Croome in Worcestershire this morning. Just before we joined the M5, I became aware that the steering on the big Peugeot had gone very, very light and just as I was about to exclaim how icy the road was we came upon one car rammed into the hedge and another sideways across the road while a police car with its 'blues and twos' going was desperately trying to snake its way along the road to warn oncoming vehicles. This was ten o'clock in the morning as well, so goodness knows how bad it had been first thing. We managed to tip-toe around the fracas and once on the motorway it was fine.

The concourse under the Bridgford Stand was just as cramped as I remembered it from previous visits. The design of these places really does belong in a bygone age. The whole area is no more than ten metres wide and in that space there are people queuing for food and drink, folk trying to get in and out of the toilets, others just stood chatting in the middle and still more trying to get to their respective stairwells to go into the stand. Add to that the usual throng of lads trying to have a sing-song and you can imagine it's absolute chaos! Having struggled to the nearest stairwell, a helpful steward then pointed out that I would have to fight my way back through to the other end of the concourse to stairwell 16, which I have to admit was printed on my ticket, had I bothered to look! Eventually I got to my seat in row I, in the corner of the ground, with the nearest goal over to my left and not far from the Forest fans on my right, separated by a few rows of empty seats and a goodly number of stewards. It was not a bad spot and I was only about ten yards from the nearest corner flag.

A chap behind heard me discussing possible team selections with Nigel who'd found his seat just a few yards in front of mine. The guy told us there was just one change from Blackpool with Luke Murphy coming straight back in for Michael Tonge who went back to the bench. Alex Mowatt was thus being rested for a second game, with Michael Brown retaining his place. Among the Leeds substitutes again was Gboly Ariyibi.

Forest also made just one change from the side that beat QPR, and that meant they were persisting with big Greg Halford, a central defender normally, in attack; he'd scored against QPR. It looked as though Leeds won the toss and elected to turn the sides around, so Leeds would attack our end in the first half. It seemed a strange decision, although the upper tier of the Bridgford Stand above our heads is a Forest section. There was plenty of early banter between the two sets of supporters – Leeds had brought 1,968 in a near capacity crowd of 26,854 and initially at least we were the most vocal. The early exchanges included, "He's Jimmy Savile, he's one of our own", "There's only one Don Revie", and a rousing chant of "Scabs, Scabs, Scabs!", in which the Yorkshire lads revelled in reminding the Forest fans that it was their kith and kin whose lack of support in the '74 miners' dispute probably helped ultimately break the strike. The Forest fans retaliated with a round of, "Clough was better than Revie", and a great rendition of the words to the Forest anthem, 'Mull of Kintyre'; "City Ground, Oh mist rolling in from the Trent, my desire, is always to be here, oh City Ground", not lyrics that exactly roll off the tongue easily but gustily sung by the Forest fans nonetheless. It was a great atmosphere all around the ground.

It was another forgettable first half from Leeds. As so often this season the opposition were just, well, just better on the ball than we were. The portly Andy Reid and the former Arsenal midfielder Henri Lansbury were the stars of the show, running Leeds ragged for 45 minutes. The giant Greg Halford was putting himself about too; in the first minute of the game he raced in chasing an under-hit back-pass from Zaliukas and crashed into the legs of Paddy Kenny as the keeper put his body on the line. Kenny was down for almost three minutes and would subsequently require Marius to take his goal kicks. It seemed inevitable that Leeds would concede and in the 25th minute we did. Michael Brown brought down Reid on the Forest left and despite his protests received a yellow card for his trouble. Reid waited over the ball and as soon as he was given the OK by referee Linington, he swung the ball over to the back post. There was something predictable about the way Greg Halford rose to head the ball sweetly over Paddy Kenny, despite both Jason Pearce and Zaliukas jumping in front of the big defender. To be fair, we no longer concede this type of header anywhere near as frequently as we once did, but it was still a reminder that, good as our defence usually is these days, we are by no means perfect even in that department. The noise from the Forest fans around the ground was impressive; we were of course effectively surrounded by them with that tier above us full of home fans. We did our very best to compete and gave MOT an airing or two but the Forest fans were not without humour too, as they replied with, "One nil to the famous team!" At this stage I feared the worst and thought we might be on the end of another City Ground hiding.

Somehow though, despite the overwhelming possession enjoyed by Forest, they failed to increase their lead before half time and we could at least hope for one of those famous McDermott rallying cries to get us going. I slumped down in my seat and looked around to see if I could spot any familiar faces and my eyes soon alighted on RamseyWhite, sat just a few seats away. We both rolled our eyes at each other as if to say, "Here we go again".

The second half began with Forest still pressing forward, but gradually Leeds worked their way into the game. Matt Smith had a towering header miss by inches and then Forest's Gonzalo Jara Reyes was booked for a desperate challenge. The Leeds fans began to sense there was still a chance of at least a point here and we cranked up our volume another notch. McDermott then stoked the fire a little more by sending on Ariyibi and taking off Michael Brown. That was a positive move that really got us going. We all strained to have a good look at our new '27' as he began his work on the right, at the far end of the pitch. Within seconds of coming on he tricked a Forest defender into fouling him and earned his first roar of approval. Forest responded with a substitution of their own, bringing on Matt Derbyshire for Djamal Abdoun and then McDermott raised the stakes further, sending on Sam Byram in place of Lee Peltier. Byram and Ariyibi looked made for each other and immediately we appeared a far more positive outfit. Suddenly we can see number '27' and a pair of tangerine boots in acres of space and we all begin to tip forward as Ariyibi unleashes the first shot of his Leeds career. It's to be hoped he improves though; this one slices off one of those orange boots for a throw in. Forest show their strength in depth with a second substitution of their own, sending on Chelsea loanee and rising star Nathaniel Chalobah. Both sets of supporters are now giving it everything and there's a bit of a ruckus down to my right; a few Forest fans are ejected and a steward is sat on the floor rubbing his head. As Arsene Wenger would say, "I didn't see the incident". The action is non-stop on the pitch and out of nowhere Andy Reid lets go with a left foot shot that thunders against Paddy Kenny's left hand post. Leeds quickly get the ball up field again and suddenly a gap appears in the Forest back line; Marius Zaliukas is up with the attack and again we begin to tip forward as he threads the ball through for the unmistakeable figure of Sam Byram. From where we are, 100 yards away, Byram appears to hit a shot at goal, or maybe it was a low cross, it's hard to tell. Jamaal Lascelles is in the centre of the goal and he hooks the ball away with his left foot as he falls to the ground, with his keeper stranded at the front post. Amazingly, the ball strikes the keeper full on the chest as he tries to get out of the way and it bounces back into the danger area in front of goal. Ross McCormack can hardly believe his luck as it arrives at his feet and quick as a flash he rifles it just inside the post. I believe the phrase these days is, "OMG!" As unlikely as it seemed at half time, we were now level; we were going to get away from the City Ground, mist rolling in from the Trent and all, with a point! It is a magic moment, up there with the best I can recall; a top ten feeling for this season. I glance up at the clock away to my left; 83 minutes have gone. We have the momentum and time to win it, but more importantly we need to keep what we have. I start to shout, "Come on Leeds, work", at the top of my voice and I'm vaguely aware that in the few seconds of our celebrations Forest have made their final substitution, bringing on Simon Cox for Jamie Mackie. Forest have kicked-off again but few of us are watching the game, most are goading the Forest fans just a few yards to our right. I am though, I can see Matt Derbyshire receiving the ball about 25 yards out on the Forest right and I'm halfway through shouting, no pleading, "Tackle him, MARIUS TACKLE..."

Before Marius can get his foot in, Matt Derbyshire has shifted the ball onto his right foot and has absolutely rifled it into the top corner. If the net hadn't stopped it, it would probably have knocked me out as it was heading straight at me. Had Paddy Kenny got a hand to it he would surely have needed a wrist brace for a week; he didn't get close. The City Ground exploded, while some of the Leeds fans near me merely sank down in their seats. Many others stared in disbelief at the celebrating Forest players or looked up to the heavens as if to say, "Why us?" It was a real Leeds United moment, one of those moments we Leeds fans should be immune to, so often have we suffered them. A few seconds of glory and then the moment is snatched away by the gods and waved in our faces like a winning celestial betting slip. The frustration affected everyone; out on the pitch Rudy Austin and Paddy Kenny were having a go at each other with flailing arms and harsh words, neither of which would help the cause. I looked at the big screen again to confirm that we were still only in the 84th minute and something in me began to cling to the hope that we could find another goal; I even told myself that this time of year often sees daft games where the ball just keeps flying into the net at both ends, teasing the fans of both sides. I tried to tell myself that it was only fair that we got one back as we'd worked so hard in this second half. "Fair", hark at me, when did "fair" ever play a part in a Leeds United game?

We did our best to encourage our lads forward and McDermott sent on Dom Poleon, no doubt hoping that an inspired substitution would be the final twist, but to be honest the Leeds players were shell-shocked by that Derbyshire rocket and we frittered away the last few minutes of normal time and then five minutes of added time by failing to get the ball into the Forest half and by giving it away too easily. The players clearly felt exactly as we did – totally deflated.

As only football fans can, by the time we began to climb away from our seats, we were reconciled to the fact we'd lost. We'd cursed our luck, grudgingly accepted Derbyshire's shot was, "One hell of a strike", and acknowledged Forest were a decent side, a better side than us. Already we were calculating that a win against Blackburn on New Year's Day, would give us four points from two away games and one at home, not a bad tally in anyone's book. It's what football fans do to ease the immediate pain. We had to win that Blackburn game otherwise this would be yet another totally abysmal Christmas from a football perspective, no different to the last two in fact.

Mrs W had texted to say that the spare key she'd picked up from home yesterday before our trip to Worcestershire, was not in fact the spare key to my car that she thought it was, she was now standing by it in the freezing cold and could I please, "Wee n walk fast". I dashed into the bogs as instructed and then began to jog back towards Meadow Lane. A few of the Leeds fans spotted me and wanted to know why I was rushing, so I had to stop and tell the 'key' story a few times and then when I stopped on the bridge over the Trent to take a photo of the ground, 'Welsh' Andy threatened to tell Mrs W that I'd, "wasted a few more valuable seconds on a snapshot", knowing she was gradually freezing to death! Mates eh!

By the time I'd defrosted Mrs W and we were crawling along in the road works towards the M1, I'd already got over the defeat. My chosen option for dealing with this one was that there was nothing we could do about that Derbyshire goal; it was just one of those things. In any case, was it that important in the scheme of things? On the radio came the news that Michael Schumacher was fighting for his life in a Grenoble hospital having suffered severe head injuries in a skiing accident. That put things into context for me very quickly. As a huge Ferrari Formula One fan for as long as I've been a Leeds fan, 'Shumi' was a hero for me during his five consecutive championships at Ferrari. Coincidentally, my son Adam bought me the book 'Shunt, The story of James Hunt' for Christmas. The first chapter, 'Death – the unexpected", told the story of Hunt's final days and how he died of a sudden heart attack at home having just spent the weekend with his two young sons. Hunt was 45 years old when he died. Michael Schumacher had been skiing in the French Alps with his teenage son, Mick, when the accident happened; it would be Michael's 45th birthday on January 3rd…

Another disappointing visit to the City Ground

New Year, same old Leeds

Day one of a new year and the first day of the latest transfer window saw Leeds welcome Blackburn Rovers to Elland Road; first game of the second half of the season. If we could repeat that first half season in the next four months we would almost certainly be in the play-offs. Rovers had squeaked past us 1 – 0 at Ewood Park, just weeks ago. The importance of the transfer window to Leeds could not be overstated as we faced our fourth game in 11 days with what we expected to be pretty much the same starting eleven. We'd learned that Paddy Kenny felt unable to continue on Sunday, but was persuaded to carry on despite the leg injury suffered in the clash with Halford because the only other keeper we had available was Alex Cairns, who had only 45 minutes first team experience. McDermott was openly stating he'd given four names to David Haigh, the four players he'd like in the January transfer window. El-Hadji Diouf was not available again either, this time he'd gone back to Senegal because his mother-in-law was ill...It was becoming a joke, and not a mother-in-law joke.

As I sat in the Pavilion with Liz and Bogdan, discussing the upcoming game, I became more and more convinced that we must win it. The last two Christmas's had both been diabolical in terms of results and we know what happened to our managers during the weeks and months that followed in both seasons. Surely the same would not happen again? But a defeat today and it would be a win-less holiday period that would leave us on 35 points from 24 games; exactly the same tally we had last year. So many things had changed on and off the pitch at Leeds in the last 12 months that it was hard to comprehend that the actual results would be no different. Funnily enough, the atmosphere in the Pavilion seemed very familiar to last season when we faced Bolton Wanderers on January 1st and I can vividly remember thinking how vital a win was then as I tucked into a free mince pie. The free mince pies were out again this year, and they tasted as if they were from exactly the same batch! A similar 1 – 0 victory would do me. Last year it was courtesy of a Becchio penalty; we didn't play well but it just about kept the wolves at bay following that 4 – 2 thrashing at Forest and a humiliating and embarrassing 2 – 0 defeat at Hull City. A win today would in fact make this Christmas seem not too bad at all.

It had been raining pretty much all day in Leeds and although the game was never in doubt with our superb drainage system, the referee did go through the motions of a formal pitch inspection. Anthony Taylor pronounced the game good to go just before 2pm. The team news filtered through courtesy of Daniel's Twitter feed. Once again McDermott made just a couple of changes; Byram started in place of Peltier and Mowatt was back after a two game rest, replacing Michael Brown. I had hoped to see Ariyibi on from the start but at least he was named among the substitutes again. Paddy was declared fit but was clearly still limping and once again he wouldn't take any goal kicks. Blackburn had the £8 million man, Jordan Rhodes, up front; he was second in the Championship scoring charts with 15 goals to Ross McCormack's 17. In the Blackburn midfield, was 22 year-old Tom Cairney, currently on loan from Hull City and a former Leeds United Academy player. Cairney had been at Leeds from the age of seven until 16, when he was released as Leeds considered him, "too small". Alongside Rhodes was Rudy Gestede, on loan from Cardiff City. Blackburn were just four points behind Leeds in what was becoming an increasingly congested mid-table and had endured a similarly fruitless Christmas, drawing at home to Sheffield Wednesday on Boxing Day and then losing 3 – 2 at home to Birmingham City.

Over 30,000 turned out to watch this one, including almost 2,000 Rovers fans and once again the various incentives offered by GFH appeared to be doing the trick. The stadium looks so much better when it's almost full and the atmosphere is always good when there's a big crowd. Only a few sections of the upper tier of the East Stand were empty. I just hoped that Leeds could put on a decent performance to ensure that the 10,000 or so "floating" fans came back next time.

For the first ten minutes or so, Leeds did their best to entertain us as they surged forward with pace and purpose, but a shot from Rudy Austin that was blocked was our best effort. For Blackburn, the 'too small' Cairney looked big enough to me, as he began to run the Blackburn midfield and he also delivered their corners, one of which resulted in a header just over the bar. I was already concerned for my slightly tongue in cheek bet of 5 – 2 to Leeds at 100/1.

In the 13th minute, Jordan Rhodes got the opening goal; good news for my fantasy league points as I have him as my captain, but bad news for Leeds. It came with an assist from that midget Cairney. He slid a perfect ball through the Leeds defence and Rhodes strode confidently onto it before tucking it past Kenny. Someone in my vicinity suggested that a two-legged Kenny may well have got down a bit more smartly but someone else confirmed my thought that it was a pretty good finish from a top class striker. There was lots of head shaking going on both on and off the pitch as the Leeds players forlornly trudged back to line up for the re-start.

Leeds were not looking good again and despite the odd occasion when we got within striking distance, it was mostly Blackburn playing all the football. As always, they seemed able to control the football with their first touch, always had a man in space to pass to, attacked with pace and generally managed to fashion some sort of attempt on goal each time they went forward. By contrast, Leeds' first touch was usually scrappy and often resulted in giving the ball straight back, the man with the ball always looked isolated and under pressure, and frequently we'd lose the ball well before fashioning any sort of a shot on goal. In short, Blackburn had better footballers than we did, a trait that many other teams would exhibit over the coming months.

It was no surprise therefore when on 36 minutes Blackburn doubled their lead. A few seconds earlier, 'Tiny' Cairney had floated a corner into our near post where Matt Smith looked to be in prime position to head it away. Incredibly, we watched in horror as he appeared to duck out of the way and it was only a mad scramble behind him that got the ball out of play for another corner. Smith looked bemused as many of us shouted to him to, "sort it out", and, "get the f****** thing away for f*** sake". As Cairney prepared to take another corner just away to our right, in front of the Kop, Smith took up exactly the same position at the near post. I then watched as if in slow motion as Cairney sent over an identical cross and once again Smith appeared to get out of the way rather than try to head the ball. This time Rudy Gestede was hurtling in to smash a header in from a couple of yards. I was left open mouthed, just gawping at what had just unfolded in front of my eyes. It didn't make sense. It was all too much for Craig; he immediately set off for his half time cigarette, muttering that he'd, "seen enough of this bol*****". I sometimes wish I smoked.

Half time came and went and the only surprise was that Craig came back before the re-start. He muttered something about placing another £5 bet at half time, and that reminded me that my bet was technically still "in play". On the big screen at the far end of the ground a notice went up telling us we could now get 20/1 on Leeds winning 3 – 2, while Mike suggested we would get a cracking second half's entertainment if my 5 – 2 bet was going to come up! I thought it was about as likely as me popping in the Pavilion after the game for another of those stale mince pies!

Brian McDermott's brain was clearly working overtime trying to come up with an answer to Blackburn's superiority and his first change was to send on Gboly Ariyibi for Luke Murphy, at half time. It soon became clear we had also ditched 5 – 3 – 2 in favour of 4 – 4 – 2, as Sam Byram was now operating more as a traditional right winger, with Ariyibi on the left and Rudy and Alex in the middle. I felt we might get overrun in midfield doing that but what do I know? Nothing as it happens because for a while at least Leeds got on top. Matt Smith fired a shot across goal that he maybe should have done better with and then the ball came quickly to Ariyibi but his rushed lob was too high. In the 53rd minute though, the Leeds pressure paid off. Ross McCormack did well on the right wing and he pushed a clever ball inside the Rovers full back for Sam Byram. It looked as if Sam would just fail to get to the ball but somehow, as the keeper approached him to block the way to goal, he toe-ended it across and Smith was left in front of an open net to get his eighth goal of the season. Suddenly the mood around Elland Road lifted and the noise was incredible – it was another taster of just what this place could be like if we can ever get on a real roll. Everyone was going mental, although one person was going mental for a different reason to everyone else. Craig leans across to me and shouts, "That fu***** bet I put on at half time; I put five quid on Blackburn to win 5 – 0" Everyone within hearing distance fell about laughing at that one; "That'll teach ya, yer daft bugger, that'll teach ya for betting against us", I wailed through the tears of laughter that were now coursing down the side of my face. "It's only five quid", he said, trying to play down the folly of what he had just done! "My bet's still running mate", I teased him.

Chances came and went for both sides, but time was running out, especially for my 5 – 2 bet. In the 70th minute we came closest to an equaliser when yet another Matt Smith effort rebounded to Alex Mowatt, eight yards from goal, with just the keeper to beat. Mowatt has scored a few goals for the reserve sides but has yet to break his duck for the first team and that didn't change as his fierce strike cannoned off the cross bar. I am sure we will see a Mowatt goal before the season is out though. Dom Poleon was sent on again in the 77th minute, replacing Tom Lees, but as on Saturday, he failed to really get going in the short time he had. Dom must be getting heartily fed up of just getting ten minutes every week. Rhodes almost put the game to bed when he headed onto the bar late in the game and by this time Blackburn were just closing the game out very professionally. Players went down every time there was a challenge and every throw-in took an age. Another dire refereeing performance from Anthony Taylor didn't help either. On one occasion Ross McCormack appeared to be held back as he chased for a one-two in the area but Taylor waved play on and then he stood and watched as McCormack and Scott Dann squared up to each other and several other players waded in with handbags. Taylor was of course the referee who made the headlines earlier in the season when he missed the fact that Chelsea's Samuel Eto'o had kicked the ball away from Cardiff keeper David Marshall illegally and then allowed the goal from Hazard that resulted. Taylor was condemned for that but then ends up at Elland Road; proving beyond doubt that we do always get "sh** refs". The last time we saw Taylor at Elland Road was that game against Boro in 2011 when he sent off Max Gradel and Jonny Howson and Boro's Tony McMahon, so we should have known what we were getting. I've often also wondered why a referee from Wythenshawe, Manchester, is allowed to referee Leeds' games, knowing the depth of feeling against all things Manchester in Leeds and vice versa.

At the end of the day though it was not Taylor's fault we lost, he didn't help, but Blackburn were the better side on the day. On the BBC website on 2nd January, I spotted that Blackburn had moved quickly to sign up both Tom 'Tiny' Cairney and Rudy Gestede, on three and a half year contracts. While at Leeds…well, nothing yet.

And so it did indeed transpire that on New Year's Day 2014 our points haul from the first 24 games would be 35, exactly the same as last year. Someone also told me that over the last three years only three teams in the whole of English professional football have accumulated less league points than Leeds during the Christmas period, although I confess I've been unable to confirm that one. We were now in eighth spot (ninth last year at the same time) but were still only a single point outside the Play-Off places. There is plenty of time left of course but it's hard to avoid the conclusion that we have to get some quality in soon; as the saying goes, "If you always do what you always did, you will always get what you always got". This set of players is a hard working bunch but there are too many sides currently better than us, we need to improve our quality; even then it's going to be tough to get one of those coveted top six places. Brian McDermott had publicly stated he'd given the names of four targets to the owners and he even told us that one of them was well down the road to signing already. It was believed that one was Cameron Stewart, a winger who'd recently been on loan to Charlton from Hull City. He was the bloke who scored that fabulous 25 yarder against us down at The Valley, in November.

'FA' Cup success this year…

Paul Lambert, the less than charismatic manager of Aston Villa, grabbed the headlines on the eve of the 3rd round when he said that Premier League clubs could do without the distraction of the FA Cup. Implicit in his comments was that he considered Premier League survival far more important than winning a cup game because of the money that's available in our top Division these days. His comments were pretty much backed up by the fact that many Premiership clubs fielded 'weakened' sides this weekend. He did so himself and was rewarded with a 2 – 1 home defeat by League One side, Sheffield United. West Ham fielded a young side for their televised game at Forest too, and they got whacked 5 – 0 by a full strength Forest side that still looked a great bet for promotion, if they could continue to play like that; it made our 2 – 1 defeat there the other day look a much better result than it seemed on the day. Maybe Billy Davies would get the job done this season.

There was never any question in my mind that Brian McDermott would start with anything other than his best available side for the trip to Rochdale, which effectively meant some combination of the 16 or so players we'd been using in the last couple of months. I travelled to Spotland Stadium with Mark feeling that ought to be a more than strong enough team to see off even the pluckiest League Two side…

Mark and I had both been to Spotland before; Leeds played a pre-season friendly there in 2011 when we won with a 30th minute Max Gradel goal and a great cameo performance from Alex Mendy, a trialist in the side that day; I wonder what happened to him? So we pretty much knew the local geography and arriving just after mid-day got ourselves a prime parking spot on Willbutts Lane, just a few yards from the ground. We wandered down to the Ratcliffe Bars, one of the two drinking establishments that adjoin the ground and that were recommended on footballgroundguide.com. A sign outside informed us, "All fans welcome", and indeed we were warmly welcomed by a couple of very friendly bouncers on the door. We noticed some young lads in Rochdale tracksuits getting out of a Ford Fiesta in the car park and Mark joked they were probably Rochdale players; the two heavies informed us that it was actually no joke, and that all the Rochdale first team apparently have a club car and they are all Fiestas; "The team always park here on match days", they told us. Sure enough, as we looked around the car park there were quite a lot of Ford Fiestas already there. I mused that the travelling Leeds players will probably have left Audis and BMWs at Elland Road today, not Fiestas, while the Villa Premiership lads probably drove home in their Ferraris and Bentleys after their game; such is the gulf between each level of English football. It's only 34 miles from Leeds to Rochdale but in football terms there are light years between them.

There was hardly anyone in the Ratcliffe when we first walked in, though it filled up rapidly over the next hour or so, and by about 1:45pm it was absolutely rammed. Until more Leeds fans arrived, we passed the time talking with a very friendly group of Rochdale fans, who'd all journeyed up from Harlow in Essex, this morning. The one chap explained he used to live just along the road from where we now sat, but despite having moved south years ago he still travels all over the country following his beloved 'Dale'. Bizarrely, another of their number unzipped his jacket to show me his red Swansea away top! He explained he was born in Swansea but had lived in the Harlow area since he was four years old; he further complicated things by explaining that his second team was Leeds! *"There is pleasure sure in being a footie fan that none but footie fans know"* to corrupt a favourite saying of mine.[1] The Swansea lad told me he felt the game today would go either of two ways; either Dale would nick a one or maybe a two goal win or Leeds would hammer them five-nil. I replied that I couldn't see Leeds scoring that many but that I really didn't see this as a cup upset as we would almost certainly play our best eleven. He gave me a knowing wink at that and as a final comment merely warned: "They play some decent stuff do the Dale tha knows".

[1] *"There is pleasure sure in being mad that none but madmen know"* John Dryden, The Spanish Friar, (1681); Act ii, scene i

There was one other factor that could transpire against Leeds today; their manager Keith Hill. It was Hill who was the Barnsley manager on that terrible day at Oakwell when they hammered us 4 – 1 on a freezing cold New Year's Eve, two years ago. The Rochdale fans have apparently christened Hill 'Baldy Mourinho', their own special one. The omens were certainly not all in our favour.

Gradually, as the Ratcliffe began to fill, I saw more and more familiar faces. The three lads from the Ilkley Whites, Mick 1, Mick 2, and James, who we met at Blackburn, joined us at our table and then Liz, Bogdan and Nigel appeared. On my way to the food counter at the far end of the big open room I spotted Marc and Shaun the Norwich Whites stalwarts, RamseyWhite and his usual crew, PockWhite and Martin, and then Andy, Lily and her mum. It seemed everyone was here despite the recent fall off in our form. None of us had a clue at this time that our support was about to be tested to the limit.

As Mark and I worked our way through a plate of home-made potato and meat pie and chips, Bogdan was first to pick up the team news on Twitter. It was more or less the same side we were now very familiar with; just a couple of changes from the defeat at Elland Road last Wednesday. Alex Mowatt was missing presumed injured and his midfield spot was filled by Sam Byram, allowing Lee Peltier to slot back into the wing-back role Sam occupied on Wednesday. Scotty Wootton was recalled for his first game since Charlton, relegating Tom Lees to the bench again. The full side therefore lined up as:

Kenny
Peltier Wootton Zaliukas Pearce Pugh
Byram Austin Murphy
McCormack Smith
Subs: Cairns, Lees, Brown, Tonge, Poleon, Ariyibi, Hunt.

It was the first time we'd seen Noel Hunt in a match-day squad since Derby, back in early October.

Since our tickets were all in completely different areas of the Willbutts Lane Stand, Mark, Nigel and I made our way to an area that appeared to be less populated than most and we just squeezed ourselves in. It just happened to be near the half way line, and only three or four rows back from the pitch. More familiar faces were near at hand; none other than Gary Edwards, perhaps our most famous fan, was stood just a couple of rows behind us. There were 3,413 of us in all, another sell out allocation, and we filled the Willbutts Lane Stand that runs all down the one touchline. The mood was expectant and early in the game, with Leeds kicking towards the Sandy Lane Stand to our right, we belted out the first rendition of MOT with typical gusto. Sadly, if you could have graphed our enthusiasm and optimism levels for the next 45 minutes, they would have been seen to decline in a straight line from the opening minute down to zero by half time.

Everyone had been warned that Rochdale are a decent footballing side, but none of us was prepared for the way they tore into us from the start of this game. Rochdale sat just four points behind their division leaders, Scunthorpe, and were the third highest scorers in League Two, so they were clearly a good side...but they were only a good League Two side; we are Championship. Our old green and scaly friend, the alien visitor, would have guessed it was actually the Blue and Black striped shirts that belonged to the Championship side. Within eight minutes of the start, Rochdale had the ball in our net, after a slick move saw Joe Bunney burrow his way through our defence to stab the ball home. This proved to be just a warning though as it was flagged offside.

Sam Byram did look dangerous for Leeds on the rare occasions he was able to venture forward in his new right wing come right midfield role, but twice he was chopped down mercilessly by Dale defenders who were quite prepared to take a booking to stop his progress. Two yellows were duly handed out. Matt Smith had a decent header cleared off the line too, as he met a Danny Pugh free kick. But this was the extent of our ambition in those first 45 minutes. The rest of the time Rochdale moved the ball about quickly and accurately and looked far and away the more likely to score. The shouts from the Willbutts Lane Stand grew steadily more and more aggressive as the Leeds players were made to look distinctly inferior to the home side and there was no escape for the likes of Peltier, Wootton and Byram, who were all plying their trade just a few yards away from us on the Leeds right. I did have to laugh at one comment aimed at Lee Peltier, which he must have heard, when a bloke yelled out, "F****** hell Peltier you're more f****** dingbat than wing-back!" Mark's vitriol was mainly directed at Matt Smith, who looked lumbering and clumsy and spent more time standing offside than doing anything positive; time and again either he or McCormack would be flagged. Mark eventually declared in respect of Smith: "He should never be allowed to wear a Leeds shirt again", so meagre he considered the big man's contribution. As half time approached, Leeds seemed to be reliant on just hoofing the ball away towards Smith, and each time he would either fail to get to the ball or fail to retain possession if he did win it initially. A new chant goes up, "Shot on target, we're on the pitch", after a long period when both teams failed to trouble the goalkeepers, but there was a certain inevitability that Rochdale were going to score as we moved into added time in the first half. Peter Vincenti, playing out on the Dale right wing, had looked sharp since the start and deep into added time he swung over the most perfect cross to find Scott Hogan, who'd got himself a yard away from the sleeping Zaliukas. Hogan's leap and header were perfect, and the ball flew across Paddy Kenny to bury itself in the corner of the net. The Leeds fans were silenced, while three sides of Spotland erupted in a cacophony of noise and bouncing bodies. The Leeds players looked totally distraught and suddenly drained of all enthusiasm for this game. Unsurprisingly, as the half time whistle sounded, 3,413 mouths drowned it out with boos and obscenities.

I slumped down into my seat, while Mark went off to the bogs, and only got up when Steph introduced himself to me. Steph was just back from a holiday in Bangkok during which he'd been working his way through my books and tweeting me most days with comments. He'd tweeted the other day that he'd try to find me here. His view on this game was that the last thing we needed was a draw so he'd rather we lost 1 – 0 than have to face a replay. I would have taken a draw myself. Ever the optimist, I would have loved another Premiership side in the next round, however unlikely it seemed at this point in time. Mark returned with eyes streaming and coughing his guts up, complaining that the bogs had once again been turned into an unofficial smoking shelter.

Leeds began the second half a little better and we managed a few forays towards the goal to our left. But as the half wore on, Leeds play became more and more predictable and Rochdale gradually took control again. The harder Leeds tried, the more error strewn was their play and the more verbal the abuse from their fans. "Brian, Brian, make a sub", was the plea from the fans, as we realised the players on the pitch were just getting nowhere. Another little flurry of activity by Leeds saw a drive from Danny Pugh well saved and then a curling shot from Ross Mac looked destined for the top right corner but just shaved the post. Whether in response to our calls, or if McDermott had it in mind anyway, we'll never know, but in the 75th minute he made the first change. He withdrew Scott Wootton and sent on Noel Hunt. I looked around at the anguished faces behind me and it was clear the sight of Noel Hunt coming on was not met with universal approval. "What the f*** is Hunt gonna bring us?" cried one chap shaking his head. Elsewhere I could see Simon from the Surrey Whites stood in the gangway with his head in his hands, and the look on Gary Edwards' face was one of utter disbelief. The change appeared to make no difference whatsoever, and it was the home side that was now peppering the goal to our right. The irrepressible Vincenti rasps a shot just wide of Kenny's right hand post and then Dale win two corners in quick succession. The Leeds fans are starting to fear a second goal and a chant of "What the f*** is going on?" breaks out from a section somewhere up behind us. Shots are now raining in almost non-stop on the Leeds goal; Vincenti with a header, and then Lund with a shot that just misses the target. Then Paddy Kenny makes a wonderful save, turning a Vincenti drive around the post. Then the inevitable does happen and Rochdale double their lead. And what a goal it was too. Graham Cousins had only been on the field for 12 minutes and maybe that's why no one picked up his run. He was all on his own on the right wing and had plenty of time to assess his options and then float a measured ball across to Ian Henderson, also in acres of space on the edge of the box. He hit the ball on the volley with his right instep and directed it perfectly over the outstretched gloves of Paddy Kenny, into the top right corner of the net. All hell broke out at that point as the Leeds fans let rip into the team with everything they could think of. "We worked all week for this", was the first of many telling chants to rise from our ranks. It was clear that many fans felt there was a lack of effort and interest from the Leeds players. "The fans turn up, the players don't", succinctly put that feeling into words and then the chant I've heard before on those awful visits to Barnsley in recent years: "We're sick of it we're sh**", blasted out. A bloke just behind me nearly deafened me with a shout of, "You're just not fu***** interested Peltier". It only served to make the players even more erratic as they were clearly now spooked by the volume of abuse that was coming from just yards away in this tiniest of grounds. The Dale players are now knocking the ball about the field with supreme confidence and the Leeds fans begin to shout, "Olé", with each successful Rochdale pass. Dom Poleon has materialised onto the pitch at some point in the last few minutes and it takes me a while to work out that it's Lee Peltier who's missing; I'd wondered why it had gone quiet behind me! Another world class save from Paddy Kenny just keeps out another strike from Henderson and I start to tot up in my head how many great saves he has made today. This is another all-time low in the history of Leeds United. I can hear blokes saying it was like Histon and Hereford all over again, and to me it felt just like those Barnsley horrors and that appalling display up at Hull last season. It was a truly miserable experience.

There was only one more act that remained in this macabre show and that was sure to come at the final whistle when the fans would undoubtedly boo and jeer the players off the pitch. On cue, the whistle goes, and once the huge roar from the home fans has died away the Rochdale air is filled with more abuse and booing. Mark is just staring out at the pitch, not saying a word; I too am speechless, while Nigel rabbits on next to me something about, "I keep telling you we are not good enough Sir David, this was bound to happen sooner or later...." I just wished he would shut the f*** up. I didn't want to hear any of that, not now; I was in mourning for God's sake. I suddenly spot the players all turning to return to the safety of the dressing room and that incenses me even more than Nigel's constant moaning which is still going on; I can tell because I can see his mouth moving but I have somehow blocked it out and can't hear it. I start to manically shout out towards the players, "Hey, what about us, don't just f****** disappear!" I felt they had to come over to us and face the music, I knew it would be difficult for them but I was convinced it was the right thing to do. So did Brian McDermott. Eventually he appears out of the middle of the players and strides purposely towards us, hands held above his head. Now and again he turns to the players to make sure they are following. Eventually, all the players are lined up alongside him, all applauding us, while half the Leeds fans continue to shake their fists at them and hurl all sorts of abuse in their direction. I honestly don't know what to do but find I'm actually applauding them. In my mind, I am acknowledging that at least they've had the decency and guts to approach us and thank us for being here. There is no universally accepted gesture they could make that says, "Sorry, we f***** up", but the look on their faces told me they knew full well and this was the only thing they could now do; applaud us for our support, recognising that we'd once again done our bit even if they'd failed to do theirs. After several seconds, McDermott turned and led his players away to the tunnel, and as they turned there was a loud chant of, "What the fu***** hell was that?" I hoped it was meant as a reflection on the game and not on the players coming over to thank us.

The emotion was now affecting me and it was some time before Mark or I spoke. I spotted Pete, aka PockWhite, coming out of the bogs and just clasped his hand; I hoped he'd washed it. Neither of us spoke. In fact, it was eerily quiet everywhere as we left. As we drove away from the ground we passed under a bridge over the road that had the legend: 'Rochdale, birthplace of cooperation' painted on it in huge white letters. This referred to Rochdale's history as the birthplace of the cooperative movement and the site of the first cooperative shop opened by the Rochdale Pioneers in 1844. I saw the irony in that as I pondered how the cooperation between the club and the fans of Leeds United had just suffered a catastrophic breakdown. But I knew it wouldn't last long; come next Saturday we'd all be at Hillsborough, ready to get behind them again and we'd once again all be 'Marching on Together'. And if the events of today serve as a wake-up call to the club and the players then it will have served some purpose. Rochdale might yet again be seen in days to come of the 'Birthplace of Cooperation'.

That was certainly the way McDermott was rationalising it. In his post-match interview he said it was, "probably the worst moment I've had as a manager or player. I lost a play-off final and I didn't feel as hurt as I do today. We now have to show what we are made of, show some character and bounce back."

On LUTV, McDermott was asked, "Brian, why were you outplayed by a League Two side today?" There was a long silence, and then the interviewer jumped in again. "Are you angry?" Eventually McDermott spoke:

"I'm not angry, I'm focussed. I'm thinking about the question, they had more about them than we did today...

"Right at the end when we went over to our supporters to thank them for coming and we got what I knew was gonna come...that's gonna be a driver for me in the coming weeks. We need to invest in this team. This team needs help, it seems to have run out of steam...we need to invest and do it for those people who came to watch us today...I've just told the players, you've got to remember that moment on the pitch at the end there 'cos that was one of the worst in my football career".

So, that was the extent of our cup run this season and there is now just the Championship to focus on, which may prove to be a good thing. In comparison with the last two seasons though it was hard for me not to conclude that far from being at the same level, as I'd thought we were the other day, we were actually now worse; at least last year we had a bit of a cup run and even knocked out Spurs. But that was it for this year; sweet f a cup success this time.

Spotland Stadium, lowest point of the season...so far

Leeds fans smiling...before the kick-off obviously

All at sixes and sevens...again!

It was now public knowledge that Andrew Flowers, MD of Enterprise Insurance, was indeed a member of the Haigh consortium that was in the process of purchasing 75% of the share capital of Leeds United from GFH. Haigh made a statement on Tuesday on the official website, confirming that Flowers was part of the deal. It also confirmed that Sport Capital Limited was the vehicle being used for the transaction and that Sport Capital had already put as much as six million pounds into the club for general running costs. Haigh confirmed that funds were in place to support any transfer window activity, although the required approval of the share transaction by the Football League had not yet been given.[1] As usual with Leeds United, this whole deal did seem to be taking far longer than it ought to. We then learned that the transfer of Cameron Stewart had run into problems. Apparently someone had realised at the eleventh hour that Stewart had already played for two teams this season, Charlton and Hull City, and therefore he was not allowed, under FIFA rules, to play for a third, except by way of an emergency loan. It could only happen with Leeds United!

Also on the official website (OS) was a plea from the club to create a "Sea of Gold" at the Wednesday game by asking every fan to wear one of the gold away tops. They announced big price reductions on the shirts to try to get fans to buy one in time for the game. They wanted a sort of 'Golden Wonder'...I just hoped it would mean our passing would be a bit more "crisp" than it was at Spotland! I also felt that expecting everyone to wear a gold top was milking it a bit...

Finally this week, GFH announced they'd signed a partnership agreement with the San Francisco 49ers, the NFL outfit, and Twitter was immediately awash with pictures of scantily clad 49ers cheerleaders! As the 49ers are one of the biggest global marketing outfits in world sport this did seem a bit of a coup

http://www.leedsunited.com/news/article/1gsp4gds73kn51a63idizy8tv2/title/investment-update for Leeds and anything that helped increase club revenues had to be a good thing. I had of course been to see the 49ers when we were in San Francisco in the summer of 2012 and the family were already 49ers fans as a result of that one visit. I've also never been averse to cheerleaders at the football.

On Tuesday night, Leeds were due to take a strong side to Chester City for a friendly and I had every intention of going to watch it, not only to see our players but also to see how Ross Killock and the Turner twins were performing these days. Killock, Nathan and Lewis Turner are all currently on loan there and getting rave reviews. Then news came through that it was cancelled due to the ongoing wet weather which had rendered the Chester pitch unplayable. Leeds were clearly intent on getting match time in though as they then quickly set up a game at Skrill Conference North side, Harrogate Town, for Wednesday night. Harrogate was of course the side that Worcester City beat the other day. Of course we are unsure exactly what Brian McDermott was trying to achieve in this game but he took and played a side that included Cairns, Dawson, Wootton, Drury, Stephen Warnock, Ariyibi, Noel Hunt and Dom Poleon. Harrogate used a total of 21 players themselves...not all at the same time obviously...and beat Leeds 3 – 1 with three second half goals. The solitary Leeds goal came from Dom Poleon as a late consolation. So, who knows what that achieved? It was certainly no confidence boost, as it was watched by 1,300 spectators, most of whom would be Leeds fans eager to see that the Rochdale debacle had been well and truly put behind us. It may well have merely confirmed once again that we desperately need some new faces. Right on cue, the following morning we had one. The OS announced that Cameron Stewart had now signed on an emergency loan until the summer and had already agreed a three year contract that he would sign at that point. Before the day was out, pictures of Stewart wearing his squad number '28' shirt were all over the Leeds website. It was a signing that met with almost universal acclaim – a winger with pace, who can score goals, as witness the one he thumped past us at The Valley this season, and with time on his side at just 22 years-old. There was no other transfer news on the website yet, although Twitter was convinced that ex-Reading winger Jimmy Kebe, currently at Palace, and current Reading striker, Ashley Barnes, were both on the point of coming to Elland Road. I was not absolutely convinced that it was the right move to load us up with McDermott's old cronies from Reading, especially Barnes, who it would take me many games and goals for Leeds before I could ever forgive him for raking the faces of Lees and Byram in a game at Reading a couple of years ago. Every time I've seen Barnes, I've considered him a conniving, cheating sort of a player, all elbows and studs...but maybe a bit of aggression is what we are missing up front, perhaps Matt Smith could learn a bit from him. Anyway, he hadn't signed yet.

In fact, within the next few days, Barnes would sign for Burnley, while Jimmy Kebe was indeed announced as a Leeds player and he was allocated squad number '38'. Both Kebe and Stewart were said to be in contention for a start at Hillsborough, despite only having spent a few hours with their new team-mates and in the case of Kebe, having played little first team football this season. I was doubtful either would start as surely they just would not be up to speed and it would mean a new formation to learn presumably? I was sure McDermott wouldn't risk it...

It was another glorious, bright, clear morning as I drove up to Sheffield. The USA was continuing to suffer with horrendous snow conditions and temperatures way below zero, while over here temperatures had stayed in positive territory all winter and the only problem had been the amount of rain we'd had in some parts. This morning though, the sun was shining and the sky was blue, and I was soon parking the old Pug outside the White Horse pub on Halifax Road, to the north of Hillsborough. I'm a creature of habit and parked here last year when Mark and I sampled the delights of both the White Horse and the Railway, which is a bit further down the hill towards the ground. I had no plans to drink at all today though as I was on my own and it was just too early. So I set off down the road knowing it was all downhill from here...little knowing at the time how literally and metaphorically that phrase would prove appropriate!

The Hillsborough game last season was the night of that infamous incident when Aaron Cawley got onto the pitch and pushed the Wendies' keeper Chris Kirkland in the face. I'd been reminded of this on Twitter in recent days as the miscreant popped up claiming he had a ticket for the match, despite a life-time ban from Leeds games. There had been other trouble on that October Friday night too, and it had all transpired to ensure that Leeds were only given 3,100 tickets this time, way short of the 5,300 we got last season. We were to be housed in the upper tier of the old West Stand, while the whole of the lower tier would be kept empty to give Kirkland plenty of breathing room. I did a circuit outside the ground and took a few photos and then stood outside the away turnstiles, reading the programme in the sun. It was still early, but there were plenty of Leeds fans already making their way inside the ground and many familiar faces said hello on their way in. Mick and James were the first, the Ilkley lads I now keep bumping into. Then Martin and Ty and the boys rolled up, eager to get inside. They informed me that the bars inside were serving beer up until kick-off. @MOTForever was next, and he told me that both Stewart and Kebe had been named in the starting eleven. I was shocked by that and couldn't see the sense of it at all. I was even more surprised when I checked the team on my own phone and saw there was no Matt Smith in the side. So, let me recap. We'd recruited two pacey wingers, one of whom had virtually no game time so far this season, put them both straight into the side after just one training session together and then put our target man and best header of a ball on the bench. Up front we would have the tiny figure of Ross McCormack against one of the biggest defences in the division. Just didn't make any sense to me, especially since this game was so important to show that Rochdale was only an aberration. The full side today would line up as:

Kenny
Peltier Lees Zaliukas Pearce Pugh
Kebe Austin Mowatt Stewart
McCormack

Subs:
Cairns, Warnock, Byram, Brown, Poleon, Smith, Varney.

Inside the ground I did try to get myself a beer, but gave it up as a lost cause after spending ten minutes scrimmaging in the concourse with 3,000 other Leeds fans, all of whom seemed way thirstier and more dedicated to the challenge than me! It was hopelessly crowded and at times resembled a riot in a prison block as we were crushed up against the wire fence that separated the counter from its customers. The 'prize', if you could be bothered to put up with the aggro, was bottled Carling, insufficient incentive for me to risk life and limb I'm afraid. Instead, I made my way through the crush to stairwell 'z' and thence on up to my seat on row 24. I was about five or six rows from the very top, and apart from a couple of supporting pillars either side of the nearest goal, the view was pretty good.

Hillsborough is a fine old stadium, a traditional ground with four mammoth stands on each side. It boasts a capacity these days of 39,732 and thus is just a bit bigger than our own Elland Road and indeed is actually the biggest English ground currently outside the Premiership, with ER second behind it. In fact, the capacity was a bit higher until shortly after our visit last season when they took out a row of seating in the lower tier to keep the fans further away from the pitch and the temptation to attack the nearest goalkeeper. It was from that area that a minor pitch invasion, including Cawley, took place after Tonge lashed in our equaliser last season. They've played football here since 1899, and it became known as Hillsborough in 1914, having been 'Owlerton' prior to that; hence the Wednesday nickname of "Owls". Two mascot 'Owls' were trudging around the pitch while the players went through their pre-match warm up routines. Don Revie would have considered that bad luck...he wasn't fond of birds. Talking of omens, how about this one: Tomorrow, January 12th, is the 22nd anniversary of a game that took place between Wednesday and Leeds in our last First Division title winning season, a game Leeds won 6 – 1. Those old enough to remember it will recall that it was also a live televised game – a rare event in those days, and Lee Chapman grabbed a hat-trick. I did toy with the idea of placing a 6 – 1 bet, just for the hell of it. In fact the number six kept cropping up everywhere I looked this week; when I checked out the 49ers website the other day, I spotted that their current catch-phrase is: "The quest for six", referring to the fact that they are in line to maybe this year finally grab their 6th Superbowl title. We had gone five games without a win too, so if we lost today that would be another half dozen statistic and look closer at those previous five games and you'd see we'd conceded six goals in them. I would kick myself if Leeds did now score six today, unlikely as that seems.

There were some other birds on the pitch before kick-off today; a local group of half a dozen cheerleaders performed a dance routine, each dressed in the Wednesday strip. With our 49ers connection I look forward to seeing some scantily clad ladies on the Elland Road pitch in the not too distant future.

From my vantage point, high above the pitch, I had a great view of the Leeds formation. As we lined up, it looked to me like a very definite 5 – 4 – 1, with McCormack stood on his own furthest up the pitch, Mowatt and Austin behind him and the two new lads wide on the wings. I shook my head to myself as Wednesday kicked-off and launched their first attack towards us. I was still shaking it four minutes later as a ball was threaded through the centre of our static defence and Jacques Maghoma beat Tom Lees to the ball. Fortunately he overstretches and tumbles over before troubling Kenny. McDermott and many learned media commentators would later say that we were in fact playing a 4 – 3 – 3 formation with Stewart and Kebe operating as traditional wingers either side of Ross…Whatever, Maghoma's early effort was a clear warning that it didn't really matter what the hell formation we played if we still defended like numpties. Wednesday, like Rochdale last week, are a big, powerful side, and they were not afraid to mix it physically with us. Lee Peltier and Maghoma both tangled in the first minute, Peltier leaving his opponent prone on the pitch holding his head. Then the huge figure of Reda Johnson launched himself at Jimmy Kebe, flattening the Leeds wide man in front of referee Lee Probert. Probert took no action, despite it looking to me as if Johnson had shoulder charged our man very high. Then Ross McCormack got the better of Miguel Llera but was hauled down from behind. This time Probert did book the Wednesday man. It all began to feel like the Rochdale game – as soon as we even looked like getting through we'd be chopped down, while our own defence never looked quite as 'determined'. It was clear from very early on that our formation had no chance of undoing the home side. Kebe looked exactly what he is – short of match practice. He didn't deserve the vitriol he was getting from some fans just up behind me though – claiming him to be a, "Lazy bas****", amongst other things, but I confess he did spend an inordinate amount of time falling to the ground under the slightest of challenges. Stewart looked little better on the other side, as he scurried after one long ball after another while McCormack darted here there and everywhere but in truth didn't achieve anything. Several Wednesday players were looking very good though. Johnson was always prepared to support his front men and kept popping up all over the pitch, while in the middle, Kieran Lee was running the whole show. Up front they had the dangerous looking Sunderland loanee, Connor Wickham. Several times their slick passing was too good for us and it was only by good fortune we lasted as long as we did. In the 20th minute we were behind.

Connor Wickham, who seemed to be in charge of everything Wednesday did, launched a free kick into the Leeds box from out on the Wednesday left wing. Tom Lees heads the ball away comfortably enough but then the Leeds defence does its headless chicken routine. The ball fell at the feet of Kieran Lee, to the right of the box, and as every member of our backline charged out he deftly chipped the ball over to the back post where two Wednesday players were waiting for just such a delivery. To me, looking on from about a mile in the air, I could only conclude that the two Owls had flown offside, and indeed I could see Lee Peltier on the opposite side of the box with his hand in the air appealing to the liner. When I watched the TV replay later that night though, it was clear that Peltier himself had played them both on as he had ambled slowly out, seconds after the rest of the backline. Reda Johnson had all the time in the world to control the bouncing ball and then steer it past Kenny, just as Danny Pugh finally spotted the danger and tried to get his foot to the ball. It may even have been Pugh's boot that got the final touch. It was another of those goals that just looked embarrassing; one player with his hand up, all the rest looking over their shoulders wondering what had just gone wrong. I could see ten heads in gold shirts drop as one; a sea of gold despair not Golden Wonder. On the TV replay later, summariser Andy Hinchcliffe would conclude that Johnson's marker was Zaliukas and MZ had just gone AWOL.

As always, the Leeds fans shook themselves down and soon reasserted their dominance in the singing stakes with rousing renditions of 'MOT' and 'We are Leeds', while on the pitch Leeds' one dimensional style continued to dictate that balls would fly up to McCormack, Stewart, or Kebe, only to immediately be given away, as they were all just too lightweight to hang on to the ball. If we tried to play the ball through midfield, then it would be Mowatt who invariably got caught in possession or Austin who would aim the ball at a seemingly invisible Leeds player. We were just as poor as against Rochdale but thankfully Wednesday were not quite as good as the League Two side. It was obvious McDermott would have to change this formation in the second half and it seemed only logical to get Matt Smith on to try to give Stewart and Kebe something to aim at…not that either was seeing much of the ball. The danger with all that though, was that we would presumably have to sacrifice one of our three central defenders to get Smith on, and at the moment, if anything, we seemed in need of two or three more, not one fewer, to cope with the constant attacks from the flying Owls. In the fourth minute of stoppage time, at the end of the first half, it all seemed pretty irrelevant as we conceded again.

Marius Zaliukas had looked a world beater when he first arrived, back in early November, and the five wins in seven games we then enjoyed I thought owed a lot to his presence in the side. In the run of games since then, in which we'd failed to win in the last five, I equally felt he had a part to play in most goals we'd conceded! Today would only confirm my belief that, for whatever reason, Marius Zaliukas had lost his form. It could be argued that Zaliukas should have done better for the first goal today, there was a case for saying that Johnson was his man, but equally there were several others at fault. But he was there again at the centre of the storm for their second. It was Marius who played a suicidal ball to Rudy Austin who was immediately dispossessed by Reda Johnson, albeit well into the Wednesday half. But then the Owls sprang forward down the inside left channel and eventually had both the marauding Johnson and Kieran Lee behind the Leeds defence, with Zaliukas and Lees both drawn towards the ball as it's slipped through to Lee. It's then the simplest of tasks for Lee to roll the ball across the face of goal for Atdhe Nuhiu to slide in at the back post. Again, it was all too easy, and the sight of Leeds' defenders hopping about and chasing towards the ball like a bunch of under 11s was too much for many Leeds fans; hundreds immediately stomped off to the concourse, either to the bogs or because they'd forgotten that there would be no Carling on sale at half time!

Predictably, many of those that remained booed the team off again, but I detected a tone of resignation this time. At Rochdale it had been plain anger but this time it was almost as if the Leeds fans knew nothing much had changed so they actually expected the same outcome. What they wouldn't have expected was what followed in the second half.

Every now and again over the last few seasons, Leeds have been totally annihilated, often admittedly when other events transpire against us; sending-offs or injuries usually, or a dire referee. Last season it was a 6 – 1 home reverse to Watford, when Jason Pearce saw red. The season before it was that 7 – 3 reverse at home to Forest and the Blackpool 'Rachubka' 5 – 0 fiasco; and before that both Barnsley and Preston put us to the sword. With the Leeds defence clearly at sixes and sevens again today, it crossed my mind that we might just be about to see another such humiliation. But then I remembered that Matt Smith was on the bench and surely we'd change the formation to accommodate him in the second half and that ought to bring some rewards…

Sure enough, at half time, McDermott made the change everyone expected. Matt Smith lined up for the second half and from my lofty position it was clear to see that we now only had a back line of four – Peltier, Zaliukas, Pearce and Pugh. Tom Lees had been sacrificed to allow us to go to 4 – 4 - 2. Did I suggest earlier that Smith could do with some lessons on aggression from Ashley Barnes? I withdraw that suggestion.

Within a few seconds of the restart, Jimmy Kebe gives away a free kick just outside the corner quadrant over to our left and Chris Kirkland goes across to launch it up-field. Marius Zaliukas rises to head it back deep into Wednesday territory where that man Reda Johnson (there really did seem to be more than one of him on the pitch!) rises to head it back again. Matt Smith comes charging across to make a challenge but arrives a good half an hour late and clatters into Johnson from the side. Johnson is a huge bloke, a Goliath of a man, and every bit as tall as Smith, but on impact he goes down like a rag doll hit by a speeding truck, and rolls about on the floor holding his head. In my book, it was very similar to the challenge by Johnson on Kebe earlier in the game that went unpunished. This time though Premiership referee Lee Probert begins fishing in his top pocket whilst manoeuvring himself so he's facing the TV cameras (watch it again if you doubt me!); out comes a red card. Once again, when it rains on Leeds it really does pee down in torrents and it was immediately obvious that we would now need a minor miracle to get anything from this game. Three minutes later Wednesday scored their third goal and it was clear the miracle shop was as firmly shut as the half time bars.

There was an element of bad luck about this one for Leeds too, as Jason Pearce appeared to be blocked by a Wendies forward just as the ball broke to Connor Wickham on the left corner of the box. That gave Wickham the time to steady himself before rifling a shot that crept past Paddy Kenny, down at the foot of his right hand post. We were only five minutes into the second half, but already significant numbers of Leeds fans were leaving. Karen, Nick and Craig all brushed past me, faces like thunder, heading for the exit; they all acknowledged me and I gave Karen a comforting peck on the cheek as she went by. They'd seen enough; "I can't watch this bo***** any more Dave", Craig sighed, and down the steps they went.

I spent the last forty minutes of the game joining in the chanting, which got ever more inventive and humorous. We sang about our dream of a team of Michael Browns and got to number '100' with that. On the pitch, Wednesday scored a fourth in the 66th minute, just a few seconds after Sam Byram was sent on in place of Peltier. The fourth goal was hilarious as well; little Chris Maguire seeing his weak free kick ricochet off Rudy Austin, wrong-footing Paddy Kenny and sneaking into the net just inside the left post. When your luck is out...
I was now chatting with some lads from the Hope Inn coach who were passing a silver hip flask round; I could smell the lovely aroma of whisky. We sang, "We're gonna win five – four" and, "How sh** must you be, you've only scored four", before the old classic, "Let's pretend we scored a goal" when we all count down from ten to one before going mental as if we'd just scored. Externally we were all still having fun, but inside we were all hurting and if everyone else was anything like me we were all just beginning to accept that there was no way in the world we would be getting promoted this season; we may or may not be coming back to Hillsborough next season, but that didn't depend on us, it more depended on whether this Wednesday side was actually good enough to stay out of the relegation places for the rest of the season. It looked as if their temporary manager, Stuart Gray, would get the job full time after this result, but I wasn't sure the Wendies were actually that good, it was just that we were dire, and boy was the luck going their way? I did wonder if they'd used up a full season's worth today and I was certain we were due some.
In the 79th minute we were five down, as our man Zaliukas was at it again. This time he lamely went into a challenge for a bouncing ball just inside the Wendies half with substitute Caolan Lavery; Lavery predictably came away with the ball and headed straight for our box with MZ in pursuit, skipping along like a six year-old chasing a bouncing ball in the back garden. At the edge of the box Lavery checked, side stepping first Alex Mowatt and then Danny Pugh before scuffing the ball towards goal. Unsighted, Kenny could only watch in horror as the ball slowly struck the left post and crawled over the line. We sang, "What the f*** is going on", for all of a few

seconds, but our heart was not in it anymore and instead we told the Sheffield fans, "We're gonna win six-five", and then gave a splendid MOT for good measure. The top broke off the hip flask and whisky spilled on to the concrete floor; all the lads fell about laughing, and then another Wednesday strike smashes against our right hand post. We are all laughing hysterically now, the whole situation was farcical! We debated whether McDermott and the players would be brave enough to come over to us at the end of the game and I confessed that I thought it unlikely. We move into added time and Wednesday score again. We were truly at sixes and sevens now, looking like a junior team playing Barcelona. Reda Johnson is still plying his trade as if his life depended on it and he wins the ball on the left wing and lumbers forward. He rolls a simple ball to the edge of the Leeds box but Zaliukas is there first to beat Lavery to the ball. Then, incredibly, MZ contrives to get himself all tangled up and Lavery wins it back, turns towards goal and curls the ball into the far corner. Six – nil! On the TV replay later, I watched in a daze as commentator Bill Leslie asks the world, "...and once again what can you say about that Leeds United defending?" answering the question himself with, "other than atrocious! Zaliukas, what *is he* doing here?"

The game ended and a few of the Leeds players ventured over the half way line towards us, but they came nowhere near as close as they did at Rochdale. Sam Byram was there and Ross and amazingly they both got some decent applause but then Rudy joined them and the mood turned decidedly ugly as he was roundly booed and fists shook in his direction. No other players came close but then Brian McDermott appears and he does march right down towards us, hands over his head applauding. Weirdly, he's only got one glove on; "Maybe he's only half applauding us", I joke, thinking it was a really funny line; no one laughs. A few lads somewhere amongst us did start to chant, "What the f****** hell was that", but then it was drowned out with applause and then I was astonished as most fans joined in a chant of, "Oh, Brian McDermott"! Incredible support! Eventually McDermott turned away and disappeared down the tunnel with the last few players who'd watched all this unfold from the safety of the half-way line.

For now, McDermott seemed to still have the backing of the majority of fans; I could only assume it was mainly the sending off that in the minds of the fans was disguising our abysmal performance. The rank poor defending was probably forgotten for the time being. I slumped down in my seat and watched thoughtfully as the stand gradually emptied, still amazed at just how resilient the majority of Leeds fans can be – years of practice I suppose. At one point a whole line of lads came bouncing down the steps from the back of the stand doing the conga and singing, "Oh, Oh, Oh, Let's all do the Conga!" all the way to the exit!

It was still only 3pm when I arrived back at the car and set off towards the M1, so I was able to listen to all the footie action on 5 Live on the way home. The commentary match was Cardiff v West Ham. I was fascinated listening to the way West Ham were dominating the play. After all, they'd come into this game, a vital bottom of the Premiership six-pointer, on the back of a 6 – 0 thumping at Man City in mid-week, and having been dumped out of the FA Cup by Forest last weekend. Sound familiar? Ever on the look-out for an omen, I wondered if Leeds could somehow respond in exactly the same way next Saturday when they host Leicester City, the Championship leaders, at Elland Road. West Ham beat Cardiff 2 – 0.

When I got home, I fired up the lap top and began to sift through the various reactions to our latest humiliation, as well as checking what damage had been done to our league position. We would end the day in 11th spot, four points behind Brighton in sixth, but now a whopping 19 points adrift of Leicester at the top. On Sky later that night, I saw McDermott interviewed and he was clearly angry. "That is humiliating today and is erm, you know, erm, what can I say after last week when we said everything after the Rochdale game. That was worse. So, we have to get this right and erm, that's what we will do starting tomorrow morning". Good luck Brian, good luck with that. In his interview on LUTV he would talk about the need to get back to basics, something I've mentioned often before. It would be easy to write this result off as just bad luck, certainly everything did go against us, including the sending off, which realistically would only have been a yellow on another day. But, I also felt this result had been waiting in the wings. We've not played well for months and in fact we had picked up most of our points in games that could equally as easily have gone against us. Almost all of our games this season have been close encounters, where more often than not we've been outplayed. We'd been punching above our weight. The real problem today though was our diabolical defending, we just have to get the basics of defending right; tackling, marking, tracking. We also need to get the basic ball skills right – controlling the ball, finding space, picking out a pass, and ensuring when we do get sight of goal we can hit the bloody target. These are all basic skills that, for whatever reason, we've not been good at…and not only this season either. Those faults have been apparent for years! As to the right formation, for me that now has to be 4 – 4 – 2. We now have wingers available but more than that we need to get one extra body in midfield which is where we're losing possession. Today for example we only had Austin (who looks knackered) and Mowatt (who just now seems out of his depth and too easily dispossessed). It will be fascinating to see what team BM puts out next weekend but I was certain he already knew it and would be putting it through its paces all week. We have to be ready by 12:15pm next Saturday; the Leicester game was yet another one to be screened live and McDermott could not afford another humiliation in front of millions on TV.

Out-Foxed

In the aftermath of the Hillsborough horror show, most talk the following week was centred on Brian McDermott. Was he good enough to get us out of this mess? The jury was out. On the face of it, he remained focussed and committed and believed he could sort it. Yet he'd given that impression after Rochdale too. A similar humiliation against the Foxes on Saturday and I felt he might just be gone, one way or another. Surely he would not be able to overcome the sheer embarrassment of a third capitulation, and even if he could, would GFH, or whoever was currently running the club, be able to? I doubted it. There wasn't much going in our favour at the moment though; on Tuesday the Football League refused to overturn Matt Smith's red card from Sheffield, so he would definitely miss the next three games – all home games, against Leicester, Ipswich and Huddersfield. As yet there were no more reinforcements by way of new faces either. A few names were being bandied about but then there came an allegation that GFH had stepped in to block the proposed signing of Ashley Barnes before he was snapped up by Burnley. Apart from my own personal satisfaction that it was the Lancashire club and not Leeds that would benefit from his flailing elbows, I was as concerned as the next man to establish why GFH had blocked it, if indeed that was the case. The transfer of ownership to Sport Capital, Haigh, Flowers et al, had still not been confirmed; as with all ownership changes at Leeds, this one was just going on, and on, and on. No one appeared to know what the delay was, but what was clear was that, for the time being at least, Bahrain still had control of the petty cash. The YEP published an article suggesting that the club had agreed a fee of £500,000 for Barnes only for certain individuals in GFH, the ultimate parent company, to then refuse to sanction the spending of the money.[1] As usual Leeds United was being made to look a laughing stock, an embarrassment to its loyal and long suffering fans.

[1] *http://www.yorkshireeveningpost.co.uk/sport/leeds-united/latest-whites-news/leeds-united-deal-for-brighton-s-barnes-blocked-by-gfh-1-6376046*

Haigh was sufficiently aware of the fans disquiet that he posted a statement on the OS by way of reassurance. He told us: "everyone was working towards a successful conclusion sooner rather than later". LUST popped up again too, Chairman Cooper reporting that he'd spoken with Haigh on Wednesday morning concerning the fans "impatience" and Haigh told him that all that remained to do was, "crossing a few 'Ts' and dotting a few 'Is." ...LUST's punctuation...not mine I hasten to add! At least McDermott himself seemed convinced that David Haigh's consortium was the right move forward for the club. In his press conference after the Hillsborough game he told us: "The people who want to come in are spot on for this club. The only thing they want is for the good of Leeds United, so it is very important that we get it done and as quickly as possible".

In another of those incredible Leeds United coincidences, two Scotsmen were being celebrated in the news at Elland Road this week. On Monday 13th January, the Leeds United website broke the news that Bobby Collins, the inspirational captain recruited by Don Revie at the start of his reign in 1962, had died at the age of 82. The fans would get their chance to pay tribute to Collins before the game on Saturday. The Leeds player who'd be leading the team out for that game would be another diminutive Scotsman, Ross McCormack. News filtered through on Twitter on Thursday afternoon that Rudy Austin had asked to be relieved of the arm band and Brian McDermott had taken that in good faith and passed it to Ross. It was hardly a surprise to anyone who'd witnessed Rudy's performances lately and we could only hope that without the pressure of leading the side in these troubled times, his play on the pitch would improve; always assuming he continues to be selected of course. Whether Ross could fulfil the role any better remained to be seen, but having a Scot of a vertically challenged nature leading us had never been a problem in the past. All of our greatest captains had shared these characteristics as well as the wee man's red hair; Bobby Collins, Billy Bremner, and Gordon Strachan had arguably been our three best skippers. They were, like Ross, also feisty fellows. The secret of their success may well lie in the animal kingdom, where it is a well-known fact that the smaller the creature, the greater is their pound for pound strength. The dung beetle for example is a little beastie famed for breaking down elephant dung into perfect balls, often many times their own body weight, which they then push all the way home. It is said that a male beetle in search of a mate will create the biggest balls of all to show off their strength. I can think of no player in the current Leeds squad with bigger balls than Ross! Anyone who's prepared to dump his Christmas rubbish in a busy roadside layby complete with his own address prominent on the packaging must have some huge cohonas!

I travelled up to Leeds early on Saturday morning trying my best to be positive and trying to look forward to the game, hoping it would be a new beginning and not the third part of a dire trilogy. In the Telegraph.co.uk this morning an article had revealed that this was Brian McDermott's mentality. He has apparently posted up a banner at the training ground that proclaims: "The secret of change is to focus all of your energy not on fighting the old but on building the new"; it's one of Socrates' apparently! [1] It is McDermott's way of trying to focus on the future and not to constantly regret the passing of our historic past which he believes has haunted the club for years. He wants us to respect the past – hence the Revie style tracksuit tops, the pre-match wave and the like – without being held hostage to it. It was equally applicable to the need to break out of our current rut and McDermott had promised a back to basics approach to reforming his side, accepting that he'd made mistakes but was now going forward with something different. That something different would presumably be a different looking team, and when I picked up Bogdan in Warrington on the way through to Leeds it was the main topic of our conversation. What formation would McDermott play? Would Zaliukas retain his place in the side after his disastrous display last week? Who would partner McCormack up front? Neither of us had much of a clue to be honest.

[1] http://www.telegraph.co.uk/sport/football/teams/leeds-united/10581000/Leeds-United-still-haunted-by-errors-and-former-glory.html

It was only 10am as we showed our season ticket cards at the door of the Pavilion and so we had another hour or so of discussions before finally getting to see the team on Bogdan's Twitter feed just after 11:15am. Out went Zaliukas, Pugh, Peltier and Mowatt, while in came Byram, Warnock, Michael Brown and Luke Varney. The full side, in 4 – 4 – 2 formation was:

Kenny
Byram Lees   Pearce Warnock
Kebe   Austin Brown Stewart
Varney   McCormack

Subs: Cairns, Peltier, Wootton, Diouf, Murphy, Poleon, Mowatt.

When you stopped to think about it, there was a lot of logic to this side. We had to go 4 – 4 – 2 to get that extra manpower in midfield; we had no Matt Smith up front; and Zaliukas had a nightmare last time out. Most agreed that Danny Pugh was unlucky to lose his place but we surmised that BM wanted a more natural defensive full back rather than the more adventurous Pugh; the inclusion of both Brown and Austin also had the look of, "let's be tight and strong in the middle"; while Varney was probably in there because of his undoubted ability in the air if either Kebe or Stewart could get to that byeline. I personally was still concerned about playing both Stewart *and* Kebe and I'd have had Murphy in there instead of one or other of the new men. In general though, the Pavilion punters seemed happy that this was McDermott making the best of limited options. I still felt Leicester would just nick the game as I really couldn't see how we could improve that much in a week despite all the talk of back to basics and pride in the shirt and even the fact that McDermott apparently picked his side on Tuesday as soon as he knew the appeal of Smith's red card had been turned down. We've had three days to work with this side but Leicester were top of the league, and they destroyed Derby last week, 4 – 1. Everyone was unanimous that the important thing today was a solid, decent performance; no more humiliations, and in that vein I'd plumped for a 1 – 0 win by Leicester in the LUFCtalk prediction league. I did have a little wager on a 1 – 0 Leeds win in the Pavilion too at 8/1 just to show my colours!

Before the game there was a definite air of new beginnings and the ending of eras. Ross McCormack led out his team carrying his own little lad, who was one of the several mascots today; then he had to dash back to line up for the tribute to Bobby Collins, having carried his own "wee man" back to the touchline. On that touchline stood many of Collins' former team-mates, who all applauded with everyone else in the stadium as Bobby looked down at us from the big screen over the simple legend: Bobby Collins. 1931-2014. The line of former players stood in front of the West Stand, reminded us all of that great Revie side once again; it will take more than a few words from Socrates to get us to only look forwards and not back. Jack Charlton and John Giles were there as were Lorimer, Reaney, Norman Hunter, Mick Jones and Eddie Gray, all household names in any home that had a football supporter in it in the late 60s and early 70s. They are all now in their own 60s or 70s of course but it's a sign of the team spirit that group had that so many come back when one of their own needs their support. It was a fine tribute.

The most fitting tribute today though, would be a Bobby Collins type performance, and for the opening half an hour that is exactly what we got. On the TV show recording that I watched the following day, a very serious and determined looking McDermott told the viewers before the start, "We're ready", but it was clear that Leicester were ready too. In the second minute of the game, Leicester's no nonsense full back Paul Konchesky pulled back Jimmy Kebe as he was about to break free of the Leicester back line. At any other time in the game it would surely have been a booking but even Mike Dean thought this a bit early to be taking the limelight. Konchesky got away with no more than a wagging finger from Dean. In the fourth minute David Nugent kicked out at Jason Pearce as the two came apart after a challenge. An incensed Stephen Warnock spots it and immediately appeals to the linesman who does eventually flag for a foul, but Dean pleaded the Arsène Wenger and again no card was issued.

Leeds were rampant at this stage and Leicester were doing everything in their power to stem the tide. The Kop and the South Stand were enjoying the opening minutes too, vying with each other to give the best support to the lads in white. In the fifth minute, a wayward clearance is sliced out to the Leeds left wing and Varney is onto it in a flash. He picks out Ross McCormack in the middle and the skipper's glancing header has Schmeichel beaten all ends up only to smack into the back post and rebound to safety. It wasn't all one way traffic though and in the seventh minute Leicester's Jamie Vardy stole in behind Jason Pearce to crack a shot that hit a Leeds' post. But this proved to be the only serious attempt the Foxes could manage in the first half. The game was being played at a phenomenal pace and Leeds immediately went down the other end and we saw Schmeichel flailing at a cross ball. It came out to McCormack who instinctively clipped it back over the Danish keeper, only to see it headed off the Leicester goal line. Leicester continued to defend 'robustly' while Leeds continued the onslaught, and in the 17th minute, McCormack had the chance of the game. Konchesky, who was having a nightmare game, played a loose ball across the edge of his own box, completely failing to see Ross McCormack running in between him and his intended target. Ross was in, one-on-one with Schmeichel, in front of the Kop; his debut game as skipper, twelve yards out. He could have taken it around the Dane and slotted it in the net but instead he tried to clip it to Schmeichel's left. By nothing more than a coincidence, Schmeichel's left hand just happened to be in the precise spot that McCormack's shot was aimed at and the ball is palmed away. There were other good Leeds' chances in that frenetic first half, including a Tom Lees header that grazed the bar with Schmeichel again beaten, but Mac's was the best. When I watched the Sky TV recording, I was not surprised to see that Leeds had ten shots at the Leicester goal in that first half, four of which stretched Schmeichel, while the Foxes could only muster three shots, none of which needed any acrobatics from Paddy Kenny. As the Leeds players trooped off the pitch at half time, it was to the sound of applause rather than boos after an excellent first forty five minutes, but it was hard to escape the thought that Leicester would be better in the second half and that maybe, just maybe, we'd missed our opportunity to win this one. Above all though, the team had given us the performance we needed to restore our belief in this group of players and in Brian McDermott's management.

The second half was a far more even affair, although it began in a similar manner to the first with Leicester adopting a "thou shalt not pass" mentality in their defending. In the first minute of the new half, Liam Moore had both arms wrapped around Luke Varney, bringing the Leeds striker to the ground, but the very short sighted Mike Dean waved play on. On the Sky show, summariser Andy Hinchcliffe is beside himself telling viewers: "I can't believe the assistant right in front of that incident did not give Leeds United a foul!" Within a minute, Knockaert has tripped Warnock and Dean had no choice but to show the cunning Fox a card. From the free kick, Wes Morgan viciously clouts Varney across the head to give yet another free kick and earn another yellow card. Leicester were clearly determined to keep Leeds out at all costs. We could learn a lot from the way they defended in this game.

Chances were fewer and further between in the second half, and it looked nailed on to be a nil-nil draw. And then McDermott decided to make some changes. Leicester had already made their three substitutions, including the introduction of their latest signing, the irrepressible 40 year-old Kevin Phillips. They also had Liam Moore limping around the pitch having had a brief encounter with the Leeds woodwork. For 85 minutes Leeds had looked comfortable in this game, in fact we'd dominated at times. Why would anyone want to change the side for the last five? I am sure both Luke Varney and Jimmy Kebe were tired, probably all the Leeds players were tired, but was it really necessary to take them off for the last five minutes? Why interrupt a successful formula? Or was it one of those occasions to allow a player to take an individual bow after a good game? Whether it played any part in the events of the final two minutes, no one will ever know. But for the record Varney and Kebe were replaced with Peltier and a very overweight looking El-Hadji Diouf. For a couple of minutes Diouf strutted his stuff on the right wing and even whipped in a decent cross at one point, while the ageing Phillips was also involved in everything Leicester were doing at the other end. Phillips had one shot himself, albeit straight at Kenny; set up a shot for fellow sub Andy King that went narrowly wide, and then played a central part in the defining moment of the game. Liam Moore stabbed the ball low across the Leeds box from the Leicester right wing, over to our left as we stood on the Kop. Kevin Phillips shaped to hit it but then stepped over the ball, allowing it to run on; David Nugent nipped in front of Tom Lees. While Nugent was alert to the situation as the ball broke from the challenge, Tom Lees was down on his backside again and Nugent was able to toe-poke it past a very slow reacting Kenny and Pearce to win the game. In some ways it was a cruel blow; we had given everything this afternoon against a very good side, and, had we been more accurate in front of goal, should already have been two or three goals to the good. We had seemingly got over the Christmas wobble when we were just crap, and had reverted to the type of performance we saw pre-Christmas; tight games in which we would get points if we put away our chances or in which we would give points away if we made stupid errors at the back. This was an example of the latter. When Mike Dean brought the game to an end, we watched as the Sky TV officials gathered up Ross McCormack and Kasper Schmeichel in the centre of the pitch for the end of game interview. The interview went on while we all applauded the rest of the players off the pitch with a genuine show of approval. That it was Schmeichel who was handed the SkyBet man of the Match award surprised none of us.

The stats confirmed that Leeds had 14 shots, with Schmeichel saving four of the best efforts, including that one-on-one with Ross, while Leicester had just one shot on target all day...the one Nugent poked into our net two minutes from the end. Yet it was the Foxes who had hunted down the three points and Leeds who would leave the field after suffering a fifth straight defeat. After the match McDermott was clearly disappointed; "they've nicked that game today, we should have been three up at half time." He also confessed that, "That's the first time today that I've been able to put a team out since I've been Leeds United manager to achieve what I'm looking to achieve here...how we've lost it I do not know". He explained that today's formation, and the way the team played, was much more like what he was trying to create at Leeds, the type of team he knew was needed to get out of the Championship, and that he'd used at Reading to such good effect. He, like the rest of us, was still devastated that we'd failed to get the three points though.

As usual, Bogdan was waiting by the car in the Hoxton Mount car park after the game; we both jumped in and, eager to get away and on the road home, I spotted a gap in the cars waiting in the queue leading to the exit onto Wesley Street. I fired up the car and stuck the old Peugeot into the gap. As the minutes then ticked by with no further movement, I spotted Simon and his car load of Surrey Whites slide past on our left; I could see Wayne through the rear off-side window and Simon in the driver's seat both gesticulating at us, pointing and laughing hysterically. Knowing the lads as I do, I assumed they were having a laugh by telling me there was no way I was getting out before them because their line was moving quicker than ours, which it was. I gesticulated something very rude back to them and laughed... It was only when another car went past to our left that I suddenly twigged what the Surrey lads were actually trying to tell me...I'd only gone and pulled out behind a car that was still parked up with no one in it! I was going nowhere in that line! I felt like a right prawn and quickly manoeuvred past the parked car and joined the queue down Wesley Street, behind Simon's black motor. That will take some time to live down...I just know the lads will have fun retelling that again, and again, and again!

On Christmas Day, Leeds sat fifth in the Championship table with 34 points, eight points behind Leicester in 3rd. By the end of today, 18th January, five games later, Leeds were in 12th with just one additional point on 35. Leicester were now top, 22 points ahead of us. Once again, the Christmas and New Year period had proved our undoing. The top half of the table now looked like this:

Leicester	P26 GD 20 PTS 57
QPR	P26 GD 15 PTS 52
Burnley	P26 GD 19 PTS 51
Derby	P26 GD 16 PTS 47
Nott'm Forest	P26 GD 13 PTS 44
<u>Reading</u>	<u>P26 GD 09 PTS 41</u>
Brighton	P26 GD 07 PTS 39
Blackburn	P26 GD 00 PTS 37
Middlesbrough	P26 GD 08 PTS 36
Ipswich	P26 GD 06 PTS 36
Wigan	P25 GD 02 PTS 36
Leeds	P26 GD 00 PTS 35

Quite what the rest of the season held for us, I was no longer sure. What I did know was that two wins in the next two games were vital to stop the current slide. First up was Ipswich in ten days' time, as we had a day off on Saturday while most of our peers were involved in the fourth round of the FA Cup. Then it was our old friends, the Tesco Bags from Huddersfield.

It was not a good weekend for the 49ers either; their bid for a 6th Superbowl title came to an end when the Seattle Seahawks beat them 23-17 in Sunday's NFC Championship game. The Seahawks would go on to win Superbowl XLVIII, thrashing the Denver Broncos 43 - 8 in New York on Feb 2nd.

"Come si dice in italiano... 'what the f*** is going on'?"

The rumours surrounding the takeover got a whole lot wilder this week. There was nothing official coming out of the club on the subject – indeed the most exciting announcement on the official website was that we could get free postage and packing on orders placed online with the club superstore this coming weekend! But with just a few days left in the transfer window, the fans were getting ever more restless; believing that something must have gone seriously wrong with the consortium's 'agreed' deal. We'd been told that the timing of the takeover by Haigh would not adversely impact the bringing in of players during the window, yet everyone now believed that GFH in Bahrain had indeed blocked the purchase of Ashley Barnes, presumably because they felt there was doubt the Haigh takeover would be completed at all. Neil Warnock once famously told us: "You wouldn't add a conservatory in the middle of selling your home would you?" Then, out of the blue, or at least out of the Daily Mail, came rumours that a certain Massimo Cellino, the infamous and erratic owner of Italian Serie A side, Cagliari, was about to gazump Haigh and his followers with a bid of his own for Leeds.[1] The Mail's slant was that Cellino was replacing the Haigh consortium and buying the 75% on offer himself, although that was swiftly followed by an alternative interpretation that said Cellino was only replacing a member of the consortium who'd dropped out. If either scenario were true, it promised yet more violent ups and downs in the Leeds United roller-coaster, as Sig. Cellino is known to be a colourful character. The Italian, who nowadays lives in Miami USA, is said to be extremely superstitious and in particular, like most Italians, has a dread of the number '17' and certain colours. I understand that Michael Brown is dead set against the Cellino bid while Paul Green and Aidy White have concerns too!

[1] *http://www.dailymail.co.uk/sport/football/article-2543655/Cagliari-owner-Cellino-steals-march-race-takeover-Championship-Leeds.html*

As Friday progressed, the fury over the lack of information being given about the current status of the Leeds takeover, or TOMA II or even Tomageddon as it had variously been dubbed, was positively boiling over on Twitter, while articles continued to appear all over the Leeds fan websites speculating on how Massimo Cellino might be involved. We learned all about the Sardinian 'King of Corn' from an article by Phil Hay in the YEP[1], it presumably being easier to get the inside leg measurement of an Italian living in Miami than it was to find out what was going on in a boardroom in Beeston. Then, incredibly, the ire of Leeds fans was ratcheted up a notch further, as Sky Sports broadcast the news that West Ham had tabled a bid of £3.5 million for Ross McCormack. All the vitriol that had been aired only a few months ago when Boro made their unsuccessful attempt to grab McCormack was rolled out again with similar threats to boycott the club if GFH dared to let the talismanic front man leave. The Tweets were not all angry mind; there was plenty of humour too. The funniest I saw was by @jamesjamesbrown: "Do you think #WHUFC are trying to take advantage of the #LUFC free P & P offer @haighdavid is running this weekend?" Eventually, later on Friday night, Salah Nooruddin came to the rescue with a rare tweet, telling us: "I'd like to reassure all #lufc fans that we're working hard for the club and can confirm we've rejected an offer from West Ham for Ross". The McCormack rumours would continue for days to come and there would even be a suggestion that the Hammers may tempt us with a swap deal. I could imagine the conversation between Big Sam and McDermott: Allardyce to McDermott: "How about Cole for McCormack?" McDermott to Allardyce: How many bags?"

I was beginning to tire of reading vile and abusive tweets aimed at Haigh and the club over the takeover and McCormack – it was just another opportunity for "keyboard bravery"; the chance for small minded folk to say on a public platform things they would never dare to say without the

---

[1] http://www.yorkshireeveningpost.co.uk/sport/leeds-united/latest-whites-news/massimo-cellino-is-the-king-of-corn-after-leeds-united-6393750

relative anonymity of the internet; things that would potentially get them served with slander notices if spoken in public.

I tried to ignore all this for a few days, and focussed instead on my third love, Worcester City. (If you're wondering, I thought I'd better slot the family into that list...I'll leave it to you to determine the order!). City had a league game at Altrincham on Tuesday night, so I hooked up with Mark and spent a fabulous evening watching them thoroughly outplay the home side and come away with a deserved 2 – 1 win. In a crowd of only 547, there were just ten of us supporting City, including a couple of lads I'd come across through Twitter; Lee and Mick. Lee had told me on Twitter that the City had been playing some "beautiful football" recently, since the addition of three new faces in the team. He was dead right too. This was a third consecutive win, and it took City out of the relegation places in the Skrill Conference North, and was achieved with some scintillating play on a boggy pitch in the pouring rain. Our second goal was one of the best I have ever seen; Daniel Nti cut inside from the inside left channel on the edge of the box and curled a delightful right foot shot that swerved and dipped into the top right corner, leaving the home crowd stunned. At the end of the game all the Worcester players and staff came across the pitch to applaud the ten of us who'd made the trip. It must have been one of the few occasions where there were more players than fans! The following Saturday, while most of our peers were playing in the FA Cup 4th round, Leeds of course had a day off, so I drove up to Ellesmere Port to see the City play Vauxhall Motors. That was a culture shock! Rivacre Park is tiny; originally it was the works pitch for the Vauxhall car plant on the opposite side of Rivacre Road, but today the club is a stand-alone outfit that plays in the Conference North. Both ends of the ground are completely open to the elements and there are just two minuscule stands, one on each touchline. Saturday was horrendous weather-wise; I drove through a hail storm of biblical proportions complete with forked lightning and the wind blowing a gale. Consequently, it was impossible to play any decent football and it became the proverbial game of two halves; the side defending against the wind unable to get the ball out of their own half! City lost by a single, scrappy, second half goal, scored by a bloke who should have been sent off in the first half. He'd blatantly stamped on a City player's head as he followed through, having pushed him over in the first place. The referee "bottled it" and only produced a yellow.

It had been a long ten days; so much had happened off the pitch that it was a relief to get back on the road to LS11 for some football on the Tuesday night for the Ipswich game. I picked Bogdan up as usual and within a few minutes of setting off from Warrington I had Mark on the phone telling me he'd meet me in the Pavilion, as he'd got a rare early finish from work. He didn't have a ticket of course so Bogdan swung into action calling ahead to Liz to ask if she could drop by the ticket office. Within minutes Liz had texted to say she had bought said ticket and amazingly had procured the seat next to me on the Kop! It was the seat Mark used to have when he had a season ticket. That did suggest that it wasn't going to be a bumper crowd tonight.

In the Pavilion, the shambles that is currently all things Leeds United continued, with Lorimer interviewing Mick Jones. For some reason Mick didn't seem to be quite up to speed with recent events at Elland Road and in response to Lorimer's question as to who Mick would chose to partner McCormack up front tonight, our legendary striker went into a long justification for playing Matt Smith! Lorimer was clearly embarrassed to have to break the news to Jonah that Smith was still suspended! The rest of us in the Pavilion were also struggling with the same question, though we all knew it wouldn't be MS. The problem was that a rumour was circulating that Luke Varney was talking with Blackburn (or was it Blackpool, no one was quite sure, but it definitely had 'black' in it) about a move away from Leeds. If that was not the case, then everyone was agreed the team should be unchanged from the one that so gallantly fought against Leicester ten days ago. If Varney *was* talking to someone then surely he wouldn't be risked in the side tonight? Sure enough, when the team was announced it was the same side that played the Foxes with the exception that there was indeed no Varney.

That proved to most of our satisfactions that Varney was on his way out and the Blackburn interest would be confirmed by McDermott after the game. McDermott also explained that it was Varney who had asked not to play tonight, "in case he got injured". In his post-match interview with McDermott, Eddie Gray was astonished to hear that, and he as good as said it wouldn't have happened in his day! The second striker role went instead to El-Hadji Diouf, making only his second start of the season. There was, shall we say, a muted response to that amongst the Pavilion's punters. It once again highlighted just how short of quality players we were; Noel Hunt was the obvious choice for me (even though I'm far from being his biggest fan) but he is still coming back after a hamstring injury. He did though score yesterday in a 5 – 2 win for a Leeds reserve side against a Hull City XI, in a behind closed door workout at Thorp Arch. Matt Smith scored a hat-trick in that game ironically enough. Other than that we had Dom Poleon or the option to play someone like Jimmy Kebe up top; very limited options really, and it showed just how important it was to get the takeover finalised to enable McDermott to call for reinforcements...

It was not the greatest atmosphere in Elland Road tonight, as Mark and I took our places on the Kop. There were a number of spare seats in our vicinity and the crowd would eventually be reported as 20,461, still not bad for a wet Tuesday night but not enough to generate the sort of noise we all crave. Indeed, the singing of MOT as the game got underway was very low key.

In fact, low key would be the watchwords for tonight, as once again we were treated to the sight of two very average Championship sides going about their business in an average manner with very few clear-cut chances being created and few moments to raise the temperature on a chilly night in West Yorkshire. The first half was mostly forgettable, with the exception of a double save from Paddy Kenny that reminded us how much we owe him for keeping us in matches this season, a season in which both he and Jason Pearce remain the two players to have been on the pitch for every minute of every game. Rudy Austin had his obligatory shot at goal, and this one was half decent, forcing the Town keeper into a good save at the foot of a post.

I read a statistic on a new site this week called 'ViewFromTheKop.co.uk.' The site breaks down the stats of all Leeds' games by individual player and there are some real gems on there. The one that caught my eye was Rudy's shot count for the season...64! The Beast has started all bar two games this season but he's managed to convert just two of those attempts into goals. Quite why the Kop insist on shouting, "Shooooooot", every time he gets the ball, God only knows! For the record he would manage two shots tonight with no further reward.

In the bogs at half time the mood was not good. "Who do ya think is gonna buy us Ted?" I heard one lad say to his mate. "What this fu***** circus?" his mate replied. "Fu***** Billy Smart wouldn't touch this f****** team of f****** clowns". And that pretty much summed it up really.

The second half provided similar fare to the first. There were a few spells of decent football from Leeds and odd glimpses of what Cameron Stewart was all about, as he showed his undoubted pace out on the left wing, attacking the South Stand. He tried a couple of his long range shots that we know he has in his locker but both were well blocked before they reached the intended target. On the other wing, Jimmy Kebe was still having trouble coming to terms with life at Leeds with another below par performance that got the Kop increasingly agitated. He would be dispossessed of the ball five times in this game according to @VFTKop. Nigel told me at least 300 times that this would be a nil-nil draw and I have to admit it did look likely that, barring some calamitous mistake, no one would score. Just for the fun of it though, I told him I was certain somebody would break the deadlock shortly.

It is one of those old football clichés that when you are down, nothing, absolutely nothing, will go in your favour. This is undoubtedly true and Leeds' lack of luck in recent weeks has proved it beyond doubt. Paddy Kenny has been a hero all season long for Leeds and there was hardly a blemish on his record, but he will not be too happy with his efforts to stop

David McGoldrick's 57th minute shot in this game. For me though, Jimmy Kebe must take a sizeable chunk of the blame too. Kebe intercepted the ball on the edge of his own area and played a simple one-two with Michael Brown as he moved towards half way. But it was a lazy, aimless run, and he then tried to flick the ball around Ryan Tunnicliffe with little conviction. Predictably the ball just bounced off Tunnicliffe's ankle and the Ipswich man was away, with Kebe just ambling after him. (Presumably this was one of the 5 dispossessions.) My alien friend would have been easily persuaded that Kebe was in fact not a footballer at all; just a visitor who happened upon this game and joined in, not really knowing what he was supposed to be doing. Tunnicliffe pushed the ball wide to McGoldrick and he checked inside both Byram and the bemused Kebe to let fly from all of thirty yards. McGoldrick didn't even connect well with the ball and it bounced five yards from goal, in line with the left hand post as he would see it. From my viewpoint, just a few yards behind Paddy's right hand post, the ball beat Paddy and seemed to ruffle the side netting. But then I watched in amazement as the ball suddenly appeared over the goal line *inside* the net. Surely it was an illusion? Some magic trick such as that bloke Dynamo would conjure up, like squeezing someone's mobile phone through the neck of a Coke bottle. Eventually the Ipswich players began to celebrate and several Leeds players had their heads in their hands; I realised then it was no trick. We all gawped up at the big screen in the South Stand and then we too had our heads in our hands as we saw a slow motion replay of the ball sneaking past Kenny inside the near post. Bugger! There were a few shouts of, "Kenny, you useless tw**", and such like, but for the majority of us this was just Sod's Law in action. Either that or Paddy was part of one of those match fixing syndicates we keep reading about. The contagion of bad luck that has mortally injured Leeds United lately still showed no signs of abating and Paddy was no more immune to it than anyone else in and around the club.

Gradually the Kop shook itself down as it always does and despite the obvious depression we tried to lift the visibly shaken troops out on the battlefield. Even we lost it for a moment when Kebe gave the ball away feebly yet again and a brief chant of, "What the f*** is going on", rose from our ranks. The old chap who sits on the front row down below us, the one with the flat cap and a Macron jacket, was up on his feet demanding, "Throw me a f****** shirt McDermott, I could do better than this shower of sh***", while someone else suggested the boss throw us eleven shirts and give a few more of us a shot at it. Nigel acknowledged that I'd been right about the fact it wouldn't be nil-nil, but was disbelieving when I now told him I was convinced we'd win the game and that we'd now reached the ultimate nadir of our fortunes and things could now only get better. Even he began to believe it though when only five minutes later we were awarded a penalty.

Cameron Stewart was away down the left wing on another of his lightning quick sprints but he looked to have overrun the ball as he reached the byeline to the left of goal. Luke Chambers was steaming after him and suddenly seemed to lose his footing, sliding down with both his legs wrapped around the feet of Stewart. Both players went down in a heap and instantly referee David Webb (not usually a name known for charity to Leeds as anyone who remembers the Chelsea player of the same name would surely agree) pointed to the spot. For once I was convinced that McCormack would score this one but more for dramatic effect than anything else I turned to face the rest of the Kop instead of watching the spot-kick. I might well do that again; it was a fabulous experience seeing 5,000 initially nervous faces suddenly change into a sea of bouncing smiley ones!

No doubt sensing this might be a turning point in our fortunes, McDermott immediately sent on Dom Poleon and Alex Mowatt, for the older legs of Brown and Diouf, and the injection of youth did keep Leeds on the offensive for the final half an hour, although without achieving the breakthrough we all thought was coming. It ended 1 – 1, and at least that also brought to end our run of five consecutive defeats.

I bade farewell to Mark and joined Bogdan in the car, waiting for the queue to begin moving; having made absolutely sure the car in front of us was occupied and intending to set off! Bogdan quickly found some of McDermott's post match comments on his mobile. Most telling was: "The football's been peripheral these last ten days". Later I would watch his full LUTV interview with Eddie Gray and it became clear just how much the off field antics were weighing on his and the playing staff's shoulders.

"This is tough here at the moment", he began; "I'm not just talking about on the pitch, but off the pitch too. I've had one of the toughest weeks I've ever had in football at this football club; it needs to be sorted…we need the ownership sorted out, full stop. It's filtering down to the players, down to the crowd, and it's very, very straight forward. I personally have gone through a hell of a lot these last few days; there's a lot of stuff that's going on that shouldn't happen".

More information on exactly what that "stuff" was, came when Andrew Flowers finally broke radio silence and issued a statement to the Yorkshire press. Phil Hay's article, under the headline: "Leeds United takeover in disarray", was updated the morning after the game.[1] Flowers told the world that the basis of Sport Capital's failure to complete their takeover was that a revised and lower bid they'd put forward, due to adverse findings from their due diligence process, had not been accepted by GFH. Flowers had then gone on to criticise GFH for their consideration of a bid by Cellino. The Italian connection was thus confirmed. Flowers told the YEP: "We are convinced this [Italian bid] will not be in the interests of the club, the manager, the players or the fans. We must ask the question whether the prospective preferred bidder understands anything about the culture of Leeds United, its fans, its heritage or British football."

Once again Leeds United was in melt down. Even Cellino seemed to be back-peddling as he was supposed to be at the Ipswich game but was later said to have flown out to Italy instead. As I scanned Twitter, there was even talk that if no one was prepared to buy Leeds from GFH the club could end up in administration again. I idly wondered what the Italian was for, "What the f*** is going on?"

[1] http://www.yorkshireeveningpost.co.uk/sport/leeds-united/latest-whites-news/leeds-united-takeover-in-disarray-updated-1-6402484

Ipswich Town at Elland Road

Life of Brian

After weeks of very little in the way of official news on the state of the takeover, on Thursday 30th January, two days before the Huddersfield game, we were inundated with statements. None of them boded particularly well for the club though.

First, David Haigh finally came out and admitted his hat was being removed from the ring. On his personal website he told us that one or more of his backers had failed to stump up the promised cash and he, "ultimately didn't feel able to deliver the financial backing we had hoped was agreed to take the club forward". He was also scathing of the treatment he was receiving from certain quarters and in words reminiscent of a certain Ken Bates he complained: "At the same time neither my life nor my job have been made any easier by the personal intrusions and abuse directed towards me on social media or by some of the smear campaigns against me personally". Only the dreaded word "morons" was missing!

GFH quickly followed with their own statement, talking about "continued discussions" being ongoing, albeit not telling us who those discussions were with. They too were clearly of the opinion that the press and social media weren't helping the process as they pleaded: "We would ask all fans to ignore the media speculation surrounding investment and be assured that we remain as committed as ever to the club and ensuring any new investment is in the best interests of Leeds United for now and the future". So, it looked like Cellino may well be in the driving seat with his potential bid, although there were rumours that the Farnan, Verity, Pearson, and recently announced Red Strike Marketing man Frank Devoy, consortium was still mulling over another approach.

An article in the Yorkshire Post explained just why Brian McDermott had been so incensed by the goings on at Elland Road when it described how representatives of Cellino had turned up at Thorp Arch to watch a training session. Apparently, Gianluca Festa, the former Middlesbrough and Pompey defender and close ally of Cellino, also requested that he be able to sit on the Leeds bench for the Ipswich game, presumably to provide advice and not as a sub! This was ultimately refused. Meanwhile, more and more potted biographies of Cellino began to appear, noting how he has been through 36 different managers during his 20 year reign at Cagliari and how he was currently awaiting trial in Italy on charges of embezzlement. He had already been convicted of two counts of fraud many years ago. Quite how GFH thought he was going to pass the Football League's Fit and Proper Person test was beyond me. With Flowers a key part of the now defunct losing bid, I also wondered how long the Enterprise shirt sponsorship would last! I could see us going out in 'skins' on Saturday!

On the same day we were reading all about this, in Leeds Minster the funeral was taking place of Bobby Collins. If there is a heaven, they will be building quite a side up there, with Collins now linking up once again with his midfield protégée Billy Bremner under the astute leadership of Don Revie. Quite what the three of them would think about how the club they built to greatness was being slowly dismembered and discredited by one set of suits after another, we could only guess. If it is possible to turn in a grave, those three will surely be spinning.

And so we arrived at Friday, 31st January, 2014, transfer deadline day, and the day before our Yorkshire derby game with Huddersfield. The day began as most deadline days have for Leeds fans in recent years, with absolutely no expectation of us featuring on Sky Sports today; not a chance of a mention from Jim White. Throughout the day the rumours continued about Cellino being on the point of taking over the club and this was strengthened when LUST published a statement on behalf of Mike Farnan's consortium, which we now learned had been dubbed 'Together Leeds'. It was short and to the point and told us that the offer they made back in November was actually worth a lot more than the laughable £7m reported in the press. It concluded: "In recent days, before and since the collapse of the Sport Capital bid, we have re-engaged with GFH, and offered significant investment into the club. We are hopeful of those discussions being allowed to progress to a successful conclusion. We thank everyone for the huge support shown to us, particularly this week." On the face of it one could conclude their bid still had some legs, yet the "being allowed" bit suggested to me that it all depended on GFH not already being committed to Cellino's offer...

On Sky, there had been a couple of mentions of Ross McCormack, first suggesting there may still be a late bid coming, most likely from Cardiff, but then Ross himself made a statement that Sky broadcast in which he said he was very happy to continue to play at Leeds under Brian McDermott. Many of us sat back in our arm chairs at that point and poured ourselves a celebratory beer. Well, I certainly did! Ross was stopping put and the takeover would no doubt rumble on for a few weeks yet; we could now concentrate on beating the Dog Botherers tomorrow.

And then all hell broke loose...There had been a few rumours knocking about that Brian McDermott's position was in jeopardy, and some speculation in the Yorkshire press that if Cellino did indeed become the majority owner of Leeds then he might well want his own man in the big leather chair at Elland Road. But it was no more than tittle tattle for the most part by the usual ITK (In The Know) suspects who like to stir things up on Twitter. But then, at 7:45pm precisely, Phil Hay of the Yorkshire Evening Post tweeted: "CONFIRMED: Brian McDermott sacked by #lufc"

Wow! Just Wow! My lad was watching the Sky Sports deadline day programme in the other room when I spotted the Phil Hay tweet but when I mentioned it to Adam he scoffed and said: "I wouldn't believe that, there's been nothing on Sky". Almost as soon as he uttered the words, Jim White was proclaiming: "We understand Brian McDermott has been sacked by Leeds United." They had Tony Cottee in the studio and immediately put the cameras on him and asked what he thought. It was almost cruel to throw that at him out of the blue and he gave a stock answer about it not being too unexpected because of the poor results Leeds had suffered lately! Clearly neither he nor any of the other presenters had been briefed about the goings on at Leeds with Cellino, Haigh, and Farnan, as absolutely no mention was made of that angle.

However, you have to hand it to Sky, once alerted to a story they are all over it like a rash and within ten minutes they had Ross McCormack on the phone talking live on the programme!

Ross might have got away with his initial comments saying things like how "gutted" he was at the sacking and how he wished McDermott all the best and that he was very close to him, but then the interviewer began to probe. They knew of course that Ross had said he was happy to be at Leeds, "as long as McDermott was there", that being the gist of his earlier statement. It was inevitable though that the Sky man would now explore if Ross's position had changed now that Brian would seemingly *not* be there. Ross gave sufficient openings for any club to now give his agent a ring and I did wonder what his future at Leeds would be now that he'd put his head above the parapet. Surely his comments will have annoyed GFH; or Cellino, if he'd already got his hands on the rudder. At one point Ross also mentioned, "the new owners", although it was unclear if he was referring to the fact there were new owners already in, or whether he was just referring to the obvious fact that there would be new owners at some point. Sky was convinced they were onto a scoop now, and from the phone call with Ross they cut immediately to their roving reporter in Cardiff who grabbed a random fan and asked: "If you could say anything to Ross McCormack tonight, what would it be?" Predictably the bloke pleaded into the microphone in a thick Welsh accent, "We need you Ross, come down and help us avoid relegation".

Twitter understandably went crazy. There was plenty more abuse for David Haigh, who was considered to have messed everything up, but also for GFH and Cellino. Fans were divided as to whether they should boycott the game tomorrow or turn up in their hordes and protest. It hadn't finished yet though, and soon there were rumours coming through that Andrew Flowers had promised to withdraw the Enterprise shirt sponsorship as soon as that became contractually possible. There was even a report on Sky Sports News that Flamingo Land had told them that they were considering withdrawing their sponsorship of the academy as a protest against the sacking of McDermott. Did GFH have any idea what they'd started? Did Cellino have any idea what he was coming in to? I doubted it somehow!

In the event, despite Sky claiming that six or eight clubs had expressed an interest in snatching Ross away at the eleventh hour, no deal was done. It merely remained to be seen if his outspoken, if honest, comments would mean whoever was picking the team for the Huddersfield game would pick him or not! Ross's final tweet of the night was a rallying call to the players and fans to be united for the game tomorrow.

Surprisingly, the game with the Dog Botherers (Terriers) was a normal 3pm kick-off, so I set off from home just after 10am and arrived at my usual car park spot almost bang on mid-day. I joked with the attendant on the gate, suggesting it was all his fault that the club was in a mess and he denied it and blamed Tom Lees. He (the attendant that is, not Tom Lees) informed me there were Leeds fans already protesting outside the ground and there was a threat of a pitch invasion. I rolled my eyes at that; the last thing we needed was to exercise the minds of the Football League's disciplinary committee. Several of the Surrey and Sussex Whites were spilling out of Simon's people carrier as I left the car park, so I said a quick hello to them before heading off to the Peacock. Liz had said she was joining a few folk in there today by way of a more peaceful protest against GFH by not adding to their coffers in the Pavilion. I'd said I wasn't prepared to change my normal routines but had agreed to pop into the Peacock for a quick pint. As it happened, I didn't see Liz in there as she was running late, but I did have a chat with James, the Ilkley White and his mate Josh, before jogging on down to the Pavilion. Birkybulllufc was stood at the entrance collecting for the Red Cross, so I said hello to him and dropped a few coins in his bucket on the grounds that we may need them later on if the protests turned into a riot!

Clearly, few folk had decided to boycott the Pavilion; it was already mobbed and even busier than usual. The word was that over 30,000 would be at the game today and it looked like most of them were supping beer in here, taking full advantage of the temporary Theakston and Leeds Brewery counters. It was difficult to have a chat with anyone though as once again there was a band playing; that particular initiative clearly not yet having been abandoned despite our complaints. The "Primates" were a decent enough rock-band but...and this may just be me showing my age...they were far too loud; it had my ears positively ringing. That was more than my mobile phone was doing though, as I'd forgotten to charge it this morning, so I was reliant on others passing their phones to me to let me read the constant stream of tweets from Phil Hay at the YEP. In no particular order, Hay told us Festa had picked the team today; McDermott had picked the team today; McDermott was to be reinstated and was going to watch the game from the directors' box; Cellino had been at Elland Road last night; irate fans had barricaded his taxi in the ground; McDermott was taking legal advice and had been advised not to attend the game; several Italian players had been signed last night just before the deadline; Paul Hunt (CEO) had been sacked last night; Paul Hunt had been reinstated; David Haigh had resigned: David Haigh had un-resigned; and a very nice billionaire, a Leeds supporter all his life currently living in Yorkshire, had swooped in this morning with a suitcase full of cash and had bought the club. OK, I made that last one up; this is Leeds United for goodness sake.

My main concern for the game was another rumour that did the rounds last night. It suggested that Gianluca Festa would be responsible for the team selection and that he'd decided to make "several" changes from the side that drew with the Tractor Boys last Tuesday...blimey, was it only last Tuesday? I couldn't see how we could make lots of changes and still produce a side capable of beating the Terriers. Fortunately, when the team was announced it had a very "McDermott" look about it and we would later hear it was the side he'd penned on Friday. It was:

Kenny
Byram Lees Pearce Warnock
Austin Mowatt Murphy
Stewart   **Kebe**
McCormack

Subs: Cairns, Peltier, Wootton, Brown, Poleon, Hunt, Tonge.

So, there was actually just the one change from Ipswich; Luke Murphy coming back in for his first game since the Rochdale debacle; Michael Brown made way for him. Having seen the team, I really felt we were in with a chance; in fact I had a sneaking feeling Leeds could get a big win here – always expect the unexpected with Leeds. My regular 4 – 0 bet was placed with more than the usual degree of hope.
The atmosphere inside the ground was electric; a crowd of 31,103 was second only this season to the opening day against Brighton; why the extra folk were here was anyone's guess; anti Cellino? Pro McDermott? Anti GFH? End of an era? Start of an era? Who knows? I strained my eyes up towards the directors' box, high up to my left in the East Stand, but couldn't see anyone I recognised; there was certainly no sign of Brian McDermott's distinctive bald pate or any flash Italian suits. The air was full of Brian McDermott's name though as the Kop and the South Stand vied to outdo each other with several early renditions of, "Oooooooh, Brian McDermott", and, "We want our Brian back". In the home dug-out, over on the touchline to my right, the unmistakeable figures of Nigel Gibbs and Neil Redfearn were clearly in charge of the Leeds troops, with no sign of Uncle Festa.
Sadly, the first half played out like many of our games thus far this season, if you exclude the few when we have been very, very bad, and the even fewer when we have been very good. It was all very ordinary stuff, played in a swirling wind between two ordinary sides. It was not for lack of effort, certainly not in the Leeds ranks anyway, where Ross Mac was doing his best to lead by example with his seemingly boundless energy. But little he tried came off apart from one sublime back heel near the touchline in front of the couple of thousand Huddersfield fans in the West Stand. It put Jimmy Kebe into the clear but nothing came of his cross. It all looked like hard work and there was little to distract the fans from their regular salutes to Brian McDermott. There was one warning for us when Oliver Norwood hit a shot from distance that was as near as damn it a replica of the Ipswich goal; this time though it

struck the post instead of sneaking just inside it. A few mouths tasted heart for a split second though. Then in the 25th minute we found ourselves conceding the opening goal of a game for the seventh consecutive game. It all looked far too easy. A slide rule accurate pass was played diagonally into the Leeds box from the right; Danny Ward had time to control the ball and then lash it across Kenny into the far corner with Sam Byram no more than an interested observer, albeit only inches away. It was a desperate moment. I'd detected a degree of optimism before the game – most people, including me, were either expecting, or maybe just hoping, for a response from the team today. "Let's do it for Brian", was I am sure in many minds, while others just felt we were due a change of fortune. The Huddersfield goal would have been enough to finish off the toughest of teams in our situation and would have silenced most sets of fans...but not us. Whatever else we are, we are not quitters! We may get knocked down more than most, but we always get back up...bloodied but unbowed.

We needed a bit of luck this time though; we winced as Nahki Wells poked the ball wide of the post with just Kenny to beat and then watched nervously as Sam Byram made a last ditch interception. But deep into added time at the end of the first half, McCormack was Johnny on the Spot again, as a long ball was allowed to bounce in the Huddersfield box and although Jimmy Kebe failed to make contact, Ross did, and he hooked the ball over the line from close range. It was perfect timing to keep just the faintest of hopes alive.

The phrase, "a game of two halves", is a much used and often maligned cliché in the game of football; we've had a few good halves this season including Birmingham (first half), Watford (second half) and Leicester (first half). Today's game was another excellent example of the phenomenon. We should also mention that other well-worn footie cliché, "It's a funny old game", at this point too.

This was Jimmy Kebe's fourth game for Leeds, and for the previous three and a half, including the first half today; he'd been, without putting too fine a point on it, crap. I'd seen a video interview with McDermott recently though, in which BriMac told the interviewer that he was sure Kebe would come good but he was a confidence player who needed to feel wanted and loved. He may just now begin to feel the love of the Leeds fans. With just five minutes of the new half played, and with Leeds suddenly looking rampant, Alex Mowatt rediscovered his mojo to thread a defence splitting ball through to Ross Mac. Ross, ever alert, replicates his first half back-heel to Kebe, steaming through the centre. This time Kebe takes it in his stride, touches the ball over the outstretched leg of a defender and then arrives just in time to lift it over the sprawling figure of Alex Smithies in the goal just a few yards in front of me. It was a class goal, it was the sort of goal Arsenal were scoring all the time this season and it completely changed the complexion of this game. I did feel sorry for Kebe, in that even now it was not his name the Kop were bellowing, it was that of the man who brought him here, Brian McDermott. But even so, Jimmy suddenly looked a yard quicker and two feet taller.

Confidence came flooding back to the Leeds players who were now marauding down both flanks in a manner we haven't seen since the days of Gradel and Snoddy. It was an open game though and the Terriers were living up to their nickname too with a couple of half chances going begging. Leeds really needed the security of another goal to keep the momentum and belief with us and, in the 62nd minute, we got it. It was another goal that would not have looked out of place at The Emirates. Rudy slid the ball forward to Sam Byram on the right; Sam could have tried his luck but the angle was tight and the keeper well placed. Instead, he spotted the run of Ross McCormack at the back post and just rolled the ball across Smithies, and Ross slid it home. For the second time today he raced to a corner of the ground tugging at the badge on his shirt, kissing it and showing it to the fans.

There was only one side in this game now and every Leeds player knew it and had a swagger about them. Jimmy Kebe was a revelation, gliding around the pitch with an ease we had not seen until now; Cameron Stewart looked dangerous every time he got the ball and came close to getting his first goal; while Murphy and Mowatt began to dominate the midfield area. It was actually quite emotional watching it, it was almost as if a long lost son had suddenly come home; we knew he was still alive, just hadn't seen or heard from him in such a long while!

On 72 minutes it was 4 – 1 and I began ruing my decision to stick with that 4 – 0 prediction – why on earth do I always believe we will not concede? The livewire Stewart works some magic on the left of the area just below the Kop and pulls the ball back firmly across the six yard line to the back post. All the luck is now on our side, it's as if the luck monitor has finally realised that he's been handing it out only one way, against Leeds, for too long, and was now evening things up. The ball arrives at the feet of Ross on the right corner of the six-yard box and he side foots the ball back across goal where it thumps against the post and rockets into the net on the other side. A Ross McCormack hat-trick, just hours after that phone interview in which he appeared to have given up on the club after hearing of the sacking of his boss and mentor. You couldn't script it! No one would believe it! There were few things left that could possibly make this any more emotional for me…but there was one.

In the 82nd minute, Rudy Austin hooks a long high ball over the back of the visitors' defence. Alex Smithies makes an instant decision to come for it, even though it was clearly dropping well outside the box. Huddersfield defender Anthony Gerrard makes the same call and once again lady luck has a say in it too. Sandwiched in between the two Terriers is Ross Mac, just making a nuisance of himself really, but just being enough of a nuisance to make Smithies think he has to go for the ball. It looks as though Smithies is going to punch it at one point but he then seems to realise that would only get him sent off so he sort of tries to shoulder it away. All three players collide and fall in a heap, while the ball falls at the feet of young Alex Mowatt, 22 yards from goal in front of the Kop. Quick as a flash, Mowatt lifts the ball back towards goal on the half-volley and it just creeps in under the bar, It was an accomplished finish that belied his youth and was very similar to Ross's effort against Leicester which was headed off the line. I've felt for some time now that a goal would make all the difference to Alex, give him the confidence to push on to greater things. As we all cheered and bounced around like lunatics, I confess I started to well up.

The Theatre of the Unexpected had delivered again. The club was still in chaos; we had no idea who'd be leading training on Monday morning and we had no idea whether the Football League would allow the "agreed" deal between GFH and Cellino to be ratified. But hey, we'd just played 45 minutes of champagne football and we'd beaten our Yorkshire rivals 5 – 1 in a derby game. The Wendies must have felt like this three weeks ago.

On the official website, a brief GFH statement that was posted during the game read: "The club would like to make it clear that Brian McDermott remains our first team manager. He has not been dismissed from his post as has been suggested and we look forward to him continuing in his role with us in taking Leeds United forwards." The story went as follows: Cellino had initially told the press he had had no alternative but to sack McDermott who had argued against everything the new owners wanted to do; presumably things like having a complete outsider sat on the bench for a game before the deal was even signed! Hence a lawyer acting on behalf of Cellino's company, Eleonora Sport Limited, rang McDermott on Friday night and told him he'd been dismissed. GFH then found out and twigged of course that the firing was not authorised or legal even; the company doing the firing was not yet even BM's employer; hence the statement from GFH correcting that error. The problem I had was in believing BM would return, knowing presumably that if the Eleonora purchase of Leeds was ratified by the FL then he may well be sacked again, legitimately this time! McDermott was said to be taking advice from the League Managers Association, the managers union. If you put this in a book nobody, but nobody would believe it, although I suppose it would make a pretty good comedy movie, 'Life of Brian', maybe? But it's all true, I can assure you; and it isn't finished yet.

For the record, Leeds finished the day in 11th spot in the Championship, a full eight points outside the play-offs, although with one game in hand over sixth placed Reading. On Saturday evening the Football League at least confirmed they were aware of the intended sale of the club to Eleonora Sport Limited, with a statement saying: "The Football League has begun "preliminary conversations" with Eleonora Sport Limited over the potential change of ownership". It was said they would adjudicate next week.

Sky TV was camped in Leeds on Monday to see how this story was going to pan out. We saw Brian McDermott driving his beige 4 X 4 into Thorp Arch to take training at 9am, so that was the first question answered; at least BriMac was going to give it a go. The rumour mill was now suggesting that David Haigh's Sport Capital outfit was in talks with Mike Farnan's Together Leeds consortium, presumably to see if they could together come up with a deal capable of matching Cellino's bid, or, in the event of the Football League saying "no" to the man from Del Monte, maybe getting GFH to accept their combined offering. It was a nervous few hours while we waited to see if the FL would render this new initiative irrelevant by just rubber stamping the Cellino deal. I'd decided in my own mind that the best scenario was that the FL refuse to sanction the Cellino takeover in which case there seemed some possibility that the Haigh/Farnan combo would succeed and they had already pledged to keep BriMac; surely that was the best of all worlds? My only doubt was whether the UK bid would have the same financial resources to throw at the club as the Italian had promised. For now, I was prepared to, "Always look on the bright side of life", as the 'Life of Brian' continued to play out on my TV screen.

Where have all the flowers gone?

I imagine that any Leeds United fan able to, was sat watching Sky Sports at 1:16pm on Monday afternoon; I know I was. Brian McDermott was sat alone at a small desk festooned with microphones, dressed in his Leeds United tracksuit and swigging regularly from a bottle of water. He'd arrived at Thorp Arch this morning despite suffering a flat tyre on the way and reported he'd taken training as usual as the team prepared for Saturday's lunchtime game at Yeovil, another live on Sky TV game. Bryn Law opened the questioning, asking Brian to explain exactly what the timeline had been over the weekend. His initial answer confirmed what we already knew; he'd received a call from Chris Farnell, a lawyer acting on behalf of the Italians, on Friday evening, telling him he was being "relieved of his duties". McDermott thought this was strange. On Saturday, the team picked by McDermott was changed by Gianluca Festa but then it was altered back again after GFH told McDermott he was reinstated. In the meantime, McDermott had taken advice from the League Managers' Association and Paul Gilroy QC, and had sought assurances from the owners, GFH, that he would have complete control over all football matters at the club as long as he was manager. He'd received these assurances in writing and hence was prepared to resume his position. He praised Nigel Gibbs as "a class act" for the manner in which he'd looked after the team on Saturday. He would not comment as to whether he felt he would remain the manager if Cellino won the battle for the club, saying only, "I can't answer that". In fact, the only thing we learned was that there was an Italian player at the club, Andrea Tabanelli, brought in late on Friday, but the club was unsure if he was cleared by the Football League to play or not! Typical of his manner though, McDermott stressed that if the player's contract was confirmed he would be given, "full respect", and every opportunity to prove his worth. McDermott came across with great dignity and I hoped all parties watching would realise what an asset he could be to the club in the coming years, if given the chance. McDermott said a couple of times that some high profile people in the game had advised him he should walk away but he told us all he wouldn't do that, saying: "This is Leeds United, and I am Leeds United's manager and I want to be Leeds United's manager".

Late on Monday I saw the first article that seemed to confirm there was hope that the new Haigh - Farnan alliance may still have a chance of beating Cellino in the race for the club. It was by well-known football journalist David Conn and he reported that the new alliance was due to meet with GFH officials in London on Tuesday morning. He also felt there was good reason to believe that Cellino *would* pass the Football League's owners' and directors' test, formerly the fit and proper persons' test.[1]

The meeting on Tuesday came and went with little official comment but then around 6pm another torpedo was launched at the good ship Leeds United. Andrew Flowers went public with confirmation that he had petitioned for the winding up of the football club! The Financial Times had first spotted the winding up order going through the system and reported that it was lodged on 29th January, the day after the Sport Capital bid, of which Flowers was a part, fell by the wayside. The fact it was left in place to proceed was taken by most observers to mean there was now no possibility of Flowers' latest involvement in the joint SC TL bid coming to anything. Not long after 10pm, Tuesday, GFH posted a hastily put together response on the Leeds United official website. It read:

"The winding up petition by Enterprise Insurance, a sponsor whose managing director, Andrew Flowers, claims to support the club, is misconceived and an abuse of legal process. It is being vigorously contested by the club's lawyers.

As there were no valid grounds to issue the petition **we can only assume that Mr Flowers is seeking to influence the deliberations of the club's owners and management in relation to the take-over negotiations.**

Under the ownership of GFH Capital Leeds United has always met its financial obligations, and it will continue to do so".

[1] http://www.theguardian.com/football/2014/feb/03/leeds-united-massimo-cellino-football-league

When I read that, I was taken aback at the strength of the middle paragraph and one of the lawyers must have then had second thoughts too; the section highlighted was removed sometime around 11:30pm.

If the events over the weekend had been a shambles, this latest twist was more akin to a pantomime and the jokes came thick and fast. @Brinpaul tweeted: "Removing the Enterprise Insurance logo from our shirts will be a long and arduous process; or two washes as it is also known. #lufc!!" It was a reference to the way the printing on our Macron shirts always falls off after a couple of rounds with the washing machine. *"Who exactly was winding who up here?"*, I wondered, as I shut the lap top down and crawled to bed, imagining Leeds fans all over the country, possibly all over the world, doing the same.

So, Andrew Flowers was gone, and coincidentally so had his near name sake, Andy Flower, the England cricket coach. He'd stepped down in the fall-out over England's dire performance in losing the recent Ashes series in Australia, 5 – 0. The Rev Paul Flowers, disgraced former chairman of the Co-op Bank was also in more bother too; bailed recently on various drug charges! Pete Seeger, the US folk artist, died last week; his most well-known song being of course, "Where have all the flowers gone"! A re-release might be appropriate!

If you believed the rumours, the need for GFH to come to an agreement with someone, anyone with any cash really, was getting ever more urgent. The word was the club was losing more than £650,000 a month and the imminent accounts for 2012/2013 were said to report a loss of around £11 million. The YEP then revealed in yet another Phil Hay article, that Cellino had already pumped £1.5m into the club by way of a loan.[1] Indeed, it seemed all the main players had loaned money to the club. Certainly there was evidence that Haigh, Cellino and Flowers by way of Enterprise Insurance, had all got a financial interest and it crossed my mind it would be necessary for the club to repay all those loans to any parties who failed to win this battle.

[1] http://www.yorkshireeveningpost.co.uk/sport/leeds-united/latest-whites-news/cellino-s-1-5-million-loan-to-leeds-united-1-6418724

This was probably the reason for Flowers' winding up order, to make sure he staked his claim early! It was another ironic twist that the date set for the WUO hearing was March 17th; that date ought to get Cellino's attention!

So, with Flowers seemingly out of the running, we all assumed that Cellino would be our new owner. But come the Wednesday before the Yeovil game (yes, we will get back to the football eventually!) we'd still had no word from the Football League as to whether Sig. Cellino would pass their Mickey Mouse test or not; though most punters reckoned he would.

There was also word that Mike Farnan had not actually thrown in his towel yet either. Flowers had done though, although he refused to go quietly. In a statement on the Wednesday evening he claimed GFH were effectively overseeing a "fire sale" of the club, and he told the YEP: *"Both myself and my company, Enterprise Insurance, have been enormous financial supporters of the club for the last few years and while we may understand the commercial expediency which leads the owners to accept the superficially attractive Cellino offer, we remain firmly convinced this deal will not give the club the stability or investor commitment it badly needs."*[1] Or in other words, he thought it was all wrong and it would end in tears but he wasn't prepared to pay as much as Cellino obviously was.

Rumours spread that the £1.5m loan from Cellino had been used in part to pay the salaries for January and in part to pay the final £140,000 owed to Crewe Alexandra for the signing of Luke Murphy; had that not been paid Crewe were considering imposing an embargo on the player preventing him playing for Leeds until the debt was cleared. Other local businesses in the Leeds area were not as fortunate, as the club had apparently told them their invoices, some going back as far as October last year, would not be paid until the ownership issue was sorted! There was even talk that a new Astro Turf pitch at Thorp Arch couldn't be completed as the installation team hadn't been paid.

[1] *http://www.yorkshireeveningpost.co.uk/sport/leeds-united/latest-whites-news/leeds-united-flowers-out-of-takeover-race-leaving-path-clear-for-cellino-1-6420899?utm_medium=twitter&utm_source=dlvr.it*

Right up to the eve of the Yeovil game there was still word coming out of the Mike Farnan camp that he was willing to show his proof of funds if GFH would just return his calls. My guess was GFH had no interest in his 'proof of funds' unless Farnan was willing to make a comparable offer, which he seemed reluctant or unable to do. Meanwhile we were told that in Italy, Cagliari had been sold by Cellino, thus removing one more potential obstacle, the ownership of more than one football club and Cellino suddenly had many more millions going spare. Cellino told the Financial Times he was sure he would pass the Football League's owners' and directors' test and was due to see them next week when he flew back to the UK. Finally, around mid-day on 7th February, Salah Nooruddin, and then Hisham Alrayes, MD of GFH Capital, both posted statements on the official website to the effect that GFH had now exchanged contracts with Eleonora Sport Limited, a UK company owned by the Cellino family, for the sale of 75% of the club. Hence the club now had new majority owners, subject only to that Football League approval which they all hoped would follow next week. Since Cellino himself only owned 9.5% of Eleonora it was hoped that the FL approval could now be circumvented anyway. The statements confirmed that David Haigh would take-over as CEO, with Paul Hunt now seemingly gone for good, while Nooruddin would remain as chairman.

Cellino was clearly wasting no time in trying to win over the fans as he'd already told the FT that as well as meeting the Football League next week he was also going to the bank to arrange the purchase of Elland Road! He made it all sound very straightforward; Day one: buy 75% of Leeds United for £25 million…Elland Road for another £17.5 million…pay off those local businesses…get that Astro Turf pitch finished. Day two: create an expanse to separate the waters and call it the sky! Or was that someone else?

Meanwhile, in a soggy corner of Somerset, Yeovil Town FC were asking for volunteers to help put back the plastic sheet that was covering their ground, protecting it from the latest round of storms that were battering the south of England. I'd checked with my sister, Gill, who lives in a village not far from the ground, and she told me the game would probably be on but the weather forecast for the day of the game was not good, with more heavy hail and rain forecast. There was not much I could do other than set off and hope for the best. It was another 12:15pm kick-off, for the benefit of yet another Sky TV live broadcast, so I was setting off from home at 6am to ensure I was at the ground, or a nearby hostelry, by about 10am.

My drive down to Somerset was uneventful, apart from a strong wind that threatened to lift the Peugeot off the M6 and deposit it in a waterlogged field nearby. In the end though it wasn't the wind that got me off the M6, it was the West Mercia Constabulary. They'd closed the motorway at junction 11, forcing me to take a diversion through darkest Wolverhampton, which added 45 minutes to the trip. So, after a four hour drive, I arrived at The Hollies Hotel in the pretty little village of Bower Hinton, where I was due to pick up Nigel; he'd travelled down by train from Dewsbury yesterday. Bower Hinton is just six miles from the village of Muchelney, in the Somerset Levels, a name now familiar to the rest of Britain as the village that had been cut off by floodwater since the end of December. Only this week, Prince Charles had visited the village and surrounding areas – going into Muchelney by boat and then touring around on a trailer hooked to the back of a tractor! The evidence of the flooding is still all around, with thousands of hectares of land still underwater. I'd first spotted it when I left the M5 at junction 25; the sun was out just at that moment and for miles to my left it looked just as though tin foil had been laid in the fields, so bright was the reflection coming off the vast stretches of water. I hoped those volunteers at Yeovil had kept that pitch covered!

Arriving at the ground at around 10:30am, we quickly found a roadside parking space just opposite the ground, in the entrance to an industrial unit and then walked to the Arrow pub, which was suggested on footballgroundguide.com as the most likely watering hole in the vicinity. It was clearly the pre-match venue of choice for Leeds fans as it was already bursting at the seams. All of the regular Leeds away-day travellers were in there and I spent a very pleasant hour or so chatting and supping a couple of pints of the excellent Ringwood Bitter and the much less excellent EPA; the latter brew tasting and looking like it was the urinary output of a swarm of incontinent gnats.

Huish Park is a tiny little football ground that really has no place in the English Championship. It has a capacity these days of 9,665 according to footballgroundguide.com, of which 5,212 can be seated. For this game Leeds had been given, and had sold, 2,100 tickets. Most were for the one uncovered area, the Copse Road End, behind one goal, while a smaller number of us were housed in the adjoining section of the Screwfix Stand that runs along one touchline. From that you will gather that I was in a covered section. With more rain forecast, and a gale force wind blowing towards the Copse Road End, Nigel was not looking forward to taking up his spot on the uncovered terracing! It was purely luck and not sound planning that meant I was in the stand – when I'd ordered my ticket I automatically chose the first option, which just happened to be the seated area with a roof.

Predictably there was tremendous support for Brian McDermott as he took up his usual position in front of the home dug-out; both sections of the Leeds fans joining together in a rousing rendition of the "Oooooh, Brian McDermott" song. McDermott had entrusted the same team to begin this game as started against Huddersfield, even though he now had Matt Smith available again after his three match ban. I did wonder if Smith should have started the game as I looked around the Yeovil side and noticed that half of their players seemed to be about eight feet tall! Or maybe that was the effect of the green and white hoops they wore! Even the rather attractive girl band 'Viva Pitch' looked enormous dressed as they were in the home shirt and not much else, whilst gyrating on the pitch before kick-off. One of the giant Yeovil players was the dangerous Ishmael Miller, on loan from Nottingham Forest. His Wikipedia reference says he is only six foot three. Yeah, and I'm only five foot five!

Right from the start of this game it was clear there would only be one winner...the wind. It reminded me so much of that

Worcester game up at Ellesmere Port the other week, another ground with open ends and tiny stands that allowed the wind to pass straight through uninterrupted. It was blowing straight into the faces of our fans behind the goal to my right, the end Leeds were trying to defend in the first half. The objective had to be to keep the score at nil-nil until the second half when we'd have the same advantage. It was comical. Every time Paddy Kenny tried to take a goal kick the ball would refuse to stay on its spot and at one point I thought one of the other players would have to lie down with a finger on the ball as they used to do in rugby before the advent of the kicking-tee. It was no surprise that Yeovil dominated the territorial battle with most of the game fought out in Paddy Kenny's half. Corners were a nightmare; the ball had to be driven at 45 degrees away from goal and still it would often end up sailing over the cross bar. This was a game to get through unscathed, for the team and the fans! After seven minutes it became even more farcical as the heavens suddenly opened and icy water was jet-propelled towards those hardy Leeds fans cowering behind Kenny's goal. The fans in the roofed section with me saw the funny side of this and sang, "We are dry, we are dry, we are dry", and then, pointing at the hapless lads and lasses over to our right, "You only sing when you're swimming!" Fair play to them, they came back pointing at us and suggesting our support was "f****** sh**", while several lads in the centre block stripped off their tops and began twirling them around their heads! Then they sang, "We can't see a thing, we can't see a thing, we're Leeds United, we can't see a thing!" This was Leeds fans at their humorous best.

It all got more serious though in the 32nd minute. Yeovil won yet another corner out on their left wing, and this time the delivery was perfect. That midget Miller got himself free of the attentions of Rudy Austin and rose to power a header into the corner of the net. This was now the eighth consecutive game in which we'd conceded the first goal and even with the atrocious conditions I felt it was a sign something is not right in our defence still. In fact, I have to say that I was disappointed with our play throughout the first half in this game. There is a tried and trusted way of playing against the wind and that is to keep the ball on the ground and play it short. Leeds didn't appear to change their modus operandi at all. I wasn't the only one starting to get annoyed either. Not long after the goal, another chant of "Ooooh Brian McDermott" went up, but when it did there were a number of blokes muttering things like, "F****** sort this out McDermott for f*** sake". The recent events at Elland Road had greatly increased McDermott's reputation as a man of dignity and honesty, and he was generally regarded as a "jolly good egg" and decent bloke. But there were many fans now, like me, who were just beginning to wonder if being a nice bloke was enough. On the pitch a few of his players were failing him too. Alex Mowatt was having a stinker, and those delightful through balls he played in his first couple of games early in the season now seemed nothing more than distant memories. His partner in midfield, Luke 'the million pound man' Murphy, was little better; while Jimmy Kebe was the Kebe we saw in his first five and a half games for us and not the superb Rolls Royce version we saw last week in the second half v Huddersfield.

Just before the break, Leeds had a big let off. There were just seconds left of the first half when Kevin Dawson was brought down in the area by Sam Byram. There was no complaint from any quarter, least of all Sam, who had just got his feet tangled up as he slid in for a tackle. He brought Dawson down cleanly with the ball long gone! Leeds had amazingly not conceded a penalty all season so far and I really thought big Ishmael Miller would dent that record. I didn't see him look up at the scene behind Kenny's goal, but if he did it must surely have put the willies up him! 1,600 or so Leeds fans were hooting and hollering and waving scarves and shirts around their heads as Miller tried to spot the ball. It took him an age before he was confident the wind wouldn't disturb it and then he ran straight at the ball and powered a full bloodied shot towards goal. In these conditions it was always going to be a dodgy strategy as the ball was bound to lift, and lift it did. The ball cannoned off the top of Paddy Kenny's crossbar and disappeared out of the ground! The Leeds fans went even more berserk as the ref blew for half time!

The obvious change for me was to bring Matt Smith on for Mowatt and to go 4 – 4 – 2 as opposed to the 4 – 3 – 3 or 5 – 3 – 1 (it's the same formation just depends whether we're attacking or defending!) we'd been playing first half. Most lads making the half time pilgrimage to the bogs thought we should be strong enough with the wind advantage to turn around the one goal deficit.

Sure enough, only ten Leeds players took straight to the pitch from the tunnel while big Matt Smith waited on the half way line for his cue from the referee. Within seconds of the restart the wind once again influenced the game.

Ross McCormack is slowly becoming an icon at Leeds United. He has even won me over now. I used to think he was overrated and wasteful in front of goal and until recently I was not a fully paid up member of the 'Ross must stay at any cost' club. But in recent weeks he's grown into a true leader at the club and I now think he is a good choice as captain. By his own admission, since the birth of his son he's matured tremendously and this is showing in his play; he is an intelligent player too. Yeovil keeper Marek Stech collected the ball and shaped to clear it up-field; it was his first clearance against the wind. Ross knew exactly what was going to happen and he stood expectantly right on the edge of Stech's area. The ball leaves the keeper's boot in the usual manner and for a moment looks to be sailing towards half-way. But then the wind gets hold of it and it boomerangs back towards Stech. It fell to earth right at Ross's feet. He was facing the wrong direction initially but he has the turning circle of a uni-cycle and in an instant he had the ball on his right foot on the left corner of the box. He looked up and then delivered a perfect curling shot into the far top corner of Stech's net. It was a wonderful strike and Ross enjoyed milking the applause of the 2,100 Leeds fans at close quarters with much badge tugging and kissing again.

Leeds did play much better in this second half while Yeovil had no answer to the conditions and Leeds carved out several very good chances, albeit we missed them all. Jimmy Kebe was the most culpable, put in the clear by McCormack but then completely losing his composure as he blasted the ball high over the bar from fifteen yards, in much the same manner as Windy Miller had done earlier. Kebe was also still having a mare all over the pitch – at one point seemingly totally unsure what he was supposed to be doing as he constantly passed the ball in short one-two's with Sam Byram; Byram clearly getting more and more frustrated with his more senior teammate. Kebe did have a hand in creating the goal that would prove to be our winner though, going down easily under a challenge to win a free kick, about forty yards from goal and just three or four yards in from the touchline in front of me. Stephen Warnock shaped to take the kick and I will forever believe his intention was to find Matt Smith at the back post. Warnock gently clipped a long high ball towards the far side of the penalty area and inevitably the wind did the rest. Matt Smith initially did his best to reach it as did Marek Stech but it eluded them both to fly over their heads into the far corner of the net. Warnock stood with an arm in the air nodding as if to say, "I knew exactly what I was doing lads", but everyone else knew better and as the rest of the players joined him to celebrate there was a fair amount of laughter going on both on and off the pitch.

With chances regularly going begging and Kebe continuing to give the ball away, the game was still in the balance right up to the final whistle. Yeovil won a couple of late corners that kept us all on our toes but this time there was to be no late catastrophe to endure. At the end of the game, Sky had man of the match Ross and Stephen Warnock in the centre circle for the post-match interviews while the rest of the players took their bow from us. Brian McDermott, complete with two gloves this time, shook hands with his players and then walked towards the Leeds fans behind the goal and the usual mutual applause was ritually carried out. I remained unconvinced that this love affair will go on indefinitely but today there could be no real criticism as it was all about getting through the game, nicking the three points, and moving on. McDermott was now openly assuming that Cellino would be his next boss and in an interview after the match reported on the BBC website he said: "From what I can gather [prospective owner Massimo Cellino] is coming to the game against Brighton. Hopefully we will sit down and have a conversation and maybe a meal together and see where we go from there." Cellino also seemed willing to give BM a chance to prove his worth as he was reported in the Sun on Sunday newspaper saying: "I want to get to know the manager and help him. I hope he can help me as well. We are going to work together." In the same piece he reiterated what he told us last week about buying Elland Road. "When I am approved by the Football League I will go to the bank the next day and buy Elland Road." Stressing to the Sun how he was now intending to focus all his energies on Leeds he said: "If I was running a Fiat 500 in Italy, now I have the chance to run a Ferrari," adding, "I want to forget about Cagliari now. My heart is with Leeds." I am starting to warm to this bloke! Oh, and if you think his superstitions are nothing more than a load of old bunkum how about this: I spotted the Yeovil mascot parading around the pitch before kick-off; the Jolly Green Giant, or Big Jolly as he's known locally. Guess what number was on his shirt? You've got it! 17! It's definitely been unlucky for Big Jolly as the Glovers have only won two at home all season, and he got punched in the nose by a Forest fan here last October!

Leeds fans brave the elements in the Copse Road End

Brighton Rock

It looked very much like we'd seen the last of Paul Green and Luke Varney as both went off on loan to Ipswich and Blackburn respectively. That was the extent of the news on the Leeds website as I set off for Brighton; TOMA II seemed stuck in a kind of suspended animation.

For the first time since November, Leeds had not sold out their full allocation of tickets for this one, though there would still be almost 2,000 of us in the Amex for a Tuesday night game despite a forecast of yet more stormy weather. It is credit to Leeds fans that we're still able to take vast numbers away despite the lack of entertainment we've seen in recent months. Cut any Leeds fan in half and you'll see 'Leeds United' in the same way that 'Brighton rock' runs right through the famous south coast candy. I'd been thinking about this the other day when someone asked me why I still travel all over the country watching Leeds when the football is invariably rubbish and the team rarely wins. My answer was that a big part of an away trip is actually about meeting up with fellow fans before the game; sharing a few pints and dreaming of better days.

And so it was for the Brighton trip. Yes, part of me hoped we could keep our recent mini-revival going and we could come back north with three points, but mostly I was looking forward to meeting up with old friends and I was resigned to the likelihood we'd probably get beat. As far as I was concerned, if Leeds got into the play-offs this season it would be one of the most remarkable stories in the history of the Championship; matched only by the tremendous run Reading had two seasons ago to win promotion. Yes, I know Brian McDermott was the Reading manager that season!

Mrs W and Kentley the Stokie were in the car with me as I set off on the 226 mile jaunt to Brighton and despite the appalling weather and Kentley's inadequate internal plumbing that required a pit-stop every 45 minutes; we arrived in bright sunshine at 2:30pm. Kentley was staying in the same hotel as Mrs W and I were in tonight; the Umi, only yards from the exclusive Grand Hotel. It was £52 for a double room for the night at the Umi, including breakfast. The Grand was charging £179 for the same package...well almost; maybe the towels were a tad softer than the sandpaper at the Umi! The three of us had a quick walk along the sea front and then strolled on the famous Palace Pier, marvelling at the view looking back towards Brighton. The wind was blowing a gale but above us the sky was a glorious blue and the air was crystal clear. The sea below us, in contrast, was a dirty grey as huge frothy waves churned up the sand and stones like a giant concrete mixer.

Just as we were heading back to the hotel to check in, we spotted Nigel ambling towards us clutching a stick of Brighton rock; he'd come straight to Brighton from his hotel near Yeovil, arriving here yesterday. He reminded me that 'Brighton Rock' was also the name of a Graham Greene thriller, set here in the 1930s, and two subsequent films based on the book, released in 1947 and 2010. The term 'Brighton Rock' is used in the films as an analogy for the way Greene believed human nature was defined at birth and unchangeable. He thought it was written right through them, a bit like a Leeds fan has no choice but to follow the Whites from the cradle to the grave! The climax of the 1947 film took place on the Palace Pier exactly where Nigel and I stood.

I'd arranged to meet with my mate Andy 'the Shrimper' and Pecky, in the Fiddler's Elbow on Boyce's Street, at 4pm. It was the pub Pecky took me to last season; the one with, "The best pint of Guinness this side of the Irish Sea", and once again it didn't disappoint. The Shrimper was using this game to knock-off another of 'the 92', this being number 84; not particularly impressive I didn't think since I was with him for number 83 at Reading, as long ago as last September! It was a source of good-natured banter in the pub though as he confessed he began this quest as long ago as 1971! Over the course of the next couple of hours we were joined by Nigel and then RamseyWhite and we got through plenty of the black stuff as we put the world to rights.

At 6:35pm, Pecky suggested we ought to begin the walk to the station, where we'd be getting the train to Falmer which is right next to the Amex Stadium. While Mrs W made her way back to the hotel (she doesn't have Leeds United written right through her) Kentley and I popped into the Bright Helm on West Street, in case anyone else we knew was still there. Sadly, it had already emptied out and clearly everyone was working to a similar timetable as us.

Stepping off the train at Falmer, we got our first view this trip of the Amex; it was dark of course but the stadium looked majestic; yellow lights burning brightly against the navy sky. The Shrimper, Liz and I had seats together on the right hand side of the Leeds end, looking along the near touchline; we could see RamseyWhite up in row 'Z' behind us and Nigel a few rows in front. As I surveyed the scene inside the Amex I could see many of the usual suspects; the Surrey and Sussex folk were there in numbers as always; Simon and Wayne were stood up behind us and I'd bumped into Tim, Mike and Paula in the concourse. Martin and Daniel were also there of course. All we needed now was a performance to round off a perfect day…but I didn't expect one… and I wasn't disappointed.

Massimo Cellino was supposed to be here for this game, but we would learn from McDermott's post match interview that, "No, he wasn't here, he's in London; he's ill". It was probably a good job he wasn't here as I'm sure he would have felt even worse had he witnessed his new team's dire display… it made me feel queasy…then again that might have been the five pints of Guinness!

McDermott named an almost unchanged side from that which started down at the Huish. The only change was Danny Pugh in for Cameron Stewart; the latter having temporarily returned to Hull to create a break in his loan contract. That meant he could then resume his 93-day loan spell in ten days' time and that would almost get him to the end of the season. Potentially he'd only miss one more game, the last one, at home to Derby in May. It was a clever move that showed someone at the club has his or her wits about them despite the general impression of chaos and pantomime being portrayed in the media.

This was a forgettable game in every respect and unlike Graham Greene's novel, could not be described as a 'thriller'. I saw it called, "A dour game between two average sides", and that pretty much summed it up. Leeds fashioned nine shots in the whole game, half the number the Seagulls managed, though unusually Leeds did get four of theirs on target, compared to only two from Brighton. The difference though was that one of theirs went in. In the 64th minute, Leonardo Ulloa was given the freedom of the Leeds area and had all the time in the world to control the ball before tucking it neatly past Kenny. After the game, a downbeat McDermott would bemoan the fact that Leeds had not been alert enough to the Brighton throw-in that led to Kasenga Lualua's left wing cross that Ulloa converted. He said there were, "details we didn't get right", but other than that he felt there was, "nothing in the game, it should've been a draw". I cringed when I heard him say that; it should have been a draw only if we didn't make a mistake! I also felt we had as good as played this game again with ten men; Jimmy Kebe took all sorts of abuse from the fans for another dire performance.

So Leeds came away from the Amex on the end of a 1 – 0 defeat, just as Doncaster, Birmingham and Reading had done in the Seagulls' previous three home games. It looked like they had a formula that worked, even though they didn't look much more than a very average side to me. McDermott brought on Matt Smith, and later Noel Hunt, to try to conjure up an equaliser but it never looked likely and our brief little run of victories shuddered to a halt.

Despite the defeat I enjoyed my trip to the seaside and was already looking forward to Bournemouth at the end of March. For that one, Mrs W and I are down for four days. By then our season may be as good as over of course and I wondered if McDermott would even still be in charge.

As we drove back to the Potteries, storm clouds began to gather; not at Elland Road for a change, but directly over our heads. The promised gales and torrential rain began just as we arrived home; by 6pm we were in the eye of the storm. A tree in the back garden was blown down and then we lost our electricity when another fell onto local power lines. We'd remain sans power for the next 27 hours along with tens of thousands of homes around the country as we were hit by the latest of a number of violent storms that had been battering the country for weeks.

Final goodbyes

Massimo Cellino duly paid his planned visit to the Football League offices on Wednesday 12th February but instead of coming away with their blessing, he and lawyer Chris Farnell were merely given a long list of documents the FL still required to see. Hence there was no report of a visit to the bank the following day and no evidence that Sig. Cellino had been able to fulfil his promise to purchase Elland Road. Meanwhile, Cellino's 23 year-old daughter Eleonora was now the pin-up girl of thousands of Leeds lads as a photo of her rather fetching rear went viral on Twitter. It was sort of 'Pippa Middleton does Elland Road', if you can imagine that.

On Valentine's Day, we said goodbye to the great Tom Finney. Sir Tom, the Preston Plumber, was 91 years old when he passed away this week; one of the oldest surviving England international players. It was an opportunity to bring out some of the wonderful quotes made about him over the years. When Bill Shankly was once asked if George Best was as good a player as Tom Finney, the former Liverpool manager had replied: "Oh Aye, he's as good as Tommy...but then Tommy is nearly 60 now!" Fans of all clubs would say a final goodbye to Sir Tom in tributes at games in the coming days and then at his funeral in Preston Minster next week.

I spent the week leading up to the Middlesbrough game at a cottage in North Yorkshire, with Mrs W and a few friends. It was arranged originally to fill the gap between the Charlton home game and the Boro match to reduce the driving but the Charlton game was postponed to accommodate the Addicks' continued presence in the FA Cup. We spent the week walking and drinking and generally chilling out before driving on up to Darlington to stop with our friends Brian and Sheila, to take advantage of their ceaseless hospitality and to do even more drinking. On the eve of the Boro game we visited nearby Shildon National Rail Museum for a once in a lifetime event.

It was advertised as "The Final Goodbye", probably the last time ever that the surviving six glorious Series A4

Locomotives will be gathered together in one place. Only 35 of these steam legends were built and these are the last of the line. The star was Mallard, but five other similar legends would line up alongside her. Dwight D Eisenhower and Dominion of Canada had been repatriated from the USA and Canada respectively especially for the event and they were to feature with Mallard, Bittern, Sir Nigel Gresley and Union of South Africa. It was an incredible display of a bygone age when steam was king. Mallard still holds the world speed record for steam locomotives, having been recorded at 126mph, racing down Stoke Bank on 3rd July 1938. Tom Finney was then just 16 years old and still to begin his illustrious playing career.

It was an altogether more modern locomotive that carried me to Middlesbrough on Saturday morning. Brian decided he was going to find a pub in Darlington in which to watch the Chelsea v Everton game that was being shown on BT Sport; the Boro v Leeds game kicking off half an hour earlier than that one, at 12:15pm, it being yet one more game that Sky TV were showing live. In fact, three of our current run of four away games were all being screened live; the Brighton game being the odd one out. I really do hope Leeds get a fair share of the TV revenue from all these away games that are surely only being chosen because of our vast army of casual supporters who will tune in to watch. The Championship viewing figures were published recently, showing that Leeds are far and away the most popular team on TV. The average TV audience for a Leeds' Championship match is just over 400,000, whereas the next best is QPR with just 244,000. Hence the reason Sky chooses our games so often. The highest rated game so far this season was Leeds' home game with Sheffield Wednesday; attracting an audience of over 594,000 and Leeds featured in four of the top five highest individual TV audiences.

Brian dropped me off at Darlo station, at the top of Victoria Road, in time for me to catch the 08:59. It was a gorgeous day; crisp but with a clear blue sky that meant the sun was streaming in through the windows, warming me and the handful of Boro fans at the other end of the carriage. I could hear them discussing how Boro could set an unwanted club record today if they failed to score. Boro had not scored in their last five games; drawing three of them nil-nil and losing the other two without scoring. However, there is always an optimist in every group of footie fans and the one in this gathering pointed out that Boro had only conceded one goal at the Riverside in their last seven home games, due in no small part to the arrival on loan of goalkeeper Shay Given from Aston Villa. He'd kept eight clean sheets in his last eleven games. I was already thinking I should pop in the bookies on arrival in Middlesbrough and stick ten quid on a nil-nil draw! I subsequently forgot to do it.

The ride only took 25 minutes and so I was wandering around the streets of Middlesbrough by 9:30 in the morning; I was looking for the most likely watering hole. I checked out the Lord Byron on Bridge Street, where I've been in previous years but some coppers stood outside informed me it wasn't open yet and, "the Leeds fans have been sent over to the Isaac Wilson on Wilson Street; it's the only place that opens early enough for you lot!" I made my way to Wilson Street and soon found the Wetherspoon pub…it had four Police vans parked outside and a dozen coppers in riot gear! Wetherspoon pubs typically open at 8am for breakfast and then start serving alcohol from 9am. I made a mental note of that for future reference.

The Isaac Wilson is another link with rail history, it being named after a former director of the Stockton-Darlington railway who went on to control the Tees Engine Works that produced locomotives and other railway equipment for the area. Middlesbrough grew as a town only after the creation of the railways.

Once inside, the familiar sights and sounds of the Leeds travelling army greeted me; it seemed like ages since we'd gathered in Brighton just 11 days ago. At the bar I spotted Nigel; once again we'd not arranged where or when to meet yet here we both were, almost three hours before kick-off, in a town neither of us really knew our way around! We both ordered a Wetherspoon's Traditional Breakfast and a pint of Abbot Ale; a steal of a deal at just £5.48!

After a few more pints of the excellent 5% ABV Greene King brew, we set off for the ground, saying hello to a few of the many Leeds fans now gathered outside the Lord Byron on the way past. By now the wind had got up, and I don't just mean the effect of all that Abbot ale, although that was having its usual effect! It was decidedly nippy as we got closer to the Riverside although the sky was still a beautiful blue; a perfect backdrop to the ground and the towering 'Temenos' steel mesh sculpture that overlooks it.

Middlesbrough have now followed the lead of many clubs and similar to what Leeds did last season, have moved the away support further around the corner from where we used to be in the South Stand end. Hence my seat was about level with the edge of the penalty area at the south end of the ground. The far side of the South Stand now housed a very vocal section of the home support – complete with drummer as is becoming almost de rigueur in the Championship these days. Right from the start of the game, 3,211 Leeds voices made it clear that, "We're Leeds United, we don't need a drum", and when we got really pi**** off with it later in the game we told the drummer he could, "Stick yer drum up you're a***!"

Massimo Cellino was at the game with another of his sons, Edoardo, – though I'm pretty sure they didn't come on my train as the carriages and the seats were all finished in a deep shade of purple; the colour he has a fervent dislike and superstition of. I wondered what seat number he had up in the directors' box too; would they dare put him in seat 17? At Cagliari he renumbered every seat 17 as 16b!

By the end of the game he might just have been wondering what the hell he was buying; as yet again Leeds failed to get their act together and played out a turgid nil-nil draw that got the Boro their all-time record run of blanks. At least Cellino would not see this game reported as a 'purple patch' for Leeds. The display was all the more disappointing as Brian McDermott had promised us an attacking performance today and made five changes to the side that lost at Brighton. In goal we now had Jack Butland, signed on loan until the end of the season from Stoke City. He was straight in for Paddy Kenny who was struggling with an ankle injury. Admittedly two of the other changes were enforced, as Sam Byram had picked up a hamstring injury while Tom Lees was missing for "family reasons". In came Lee Peltier and Scotty Wootton. Up front Noel Hunt was paired with McCormack while Cameron Stewart reverted to the left wing, now that he'd "returned" after the little manufactured break in his loan spell. But even as late as Friday morning, McDermott was still telling us: "We have got to try and create as many chances as we can and hit the target as many times as we can. We'll be looking to get lots of crosses into the box as well". After the game, the BBC statistics would tell us that Boro had bossed the possession by 55% to 45%; had 11 shots to our 7 of which they had 3 on target to absolutely none from us. They had also won 6 corners to our 2. McDermott was regularly falling into the trap of promising performances that his team was simply unable to deliver. Cellino would surely see that as failure wouldn't he? I know I did.

In truth, both sides were poor, and in a dismal first half there were only 4 attempts at goal of which just one, a Butterfield shot from outside the box that Butland turned over the bar, was on target. It had all the hallmarks of a mid-table game between two very average sides; as a spectacle it was hardly worth the £28 we'd all forked out for our tickets let alone the cost of the travel. At half time, @MOTForever, stood just in front of me, wondered aloud how he was going to come up with anything to write in his blog about the game, so little was there to describe. The second half was marginally better but no player really stood out as having a good game. Even the few big names in the Boro line-up – Chalobah, Curtis Main and Kai Kamara – didn't look anything special. In the battle of the keepers, it was our own Jack Butland who was far and away the busier out of him and Given and in fact Sky TV awarded their Man of the Match chocolate football trophy to Butland for several excellent saves without which we might have got a real hiding. Very early in the game Butland had won over the Leeds fans and we immediately broke into a chant of "England, England's number one". Shay Given was saying his own final goodbye to the Boro faithful today, having been recalled by Villa, and we could see him handing the trophy over to Butland in the centre circle after the game before he waved farewell to the Riverside. This was the second time this season we'd seen Butland of course; he was on loan at Barnsley earlier in the season and kept a clean sheet against us in that nil-nil draw in December. I really should have put that bet on.

Leeds would end the day in 11th spot in the Championship, with 43 points, seven points adrift of the final play-off spot, albeit with a game in hand over the current occupants of that coveted position, Reading. McDermott was still saying that if we could get to the last ten games and be only four or five points adrift then all would still be to play for. But I couldn't see how this squad of ours could suddenly start picking up enough points playing like we did today. We just lack the flair to do it, and with TOMA II dragging on it was unlikely we'd see any new faces soon even though the signing of Butland had made a few of us sit up and take notice! If we could just find some outfield players of similar star quality, then maybe, just maybe, all was not lost. One thing I was certain about was that a performance like this down at QPR next Saturday would quite possibly earn us a spanking; and that would definitely be a final goodbye to promotion.

As I left my seat at the Riverside, I glanced up at the big screen in the corner of the ground to see the result of the Chelsea v Everton game. The screen proclaimed that game had also ended nil-nil. At least that meant that Brian wouldn't be crowing over a Chelsea win when I got back. He'd just settled down to watch the England v Ireland Six Nations game when I knocked on the front door. His first question as he peered round the open door was, "What was your score like?"

"Nil-nil, same as yours", I told him. He then furrowed his brow and in one of his many little mannerisms put his hand sheepishly over his mouth before he informed me: "We won 1 – 0 with a dodgy 93rd minute free-kick". And then it dawned on me. I'd completely forgotten that the Chelsea game ran half an hour behind ours and only then did I realise that the "result" I'd seen on the big screen at the Riverside was in fact just a latest score! Oh well, at least someone in the house was happy tonight!

Leeds fail to kick R's

Leeds fans all sat up sharply on Wednesday, as the news came through that Connor Wickham had been signed on loan for the remainder of the season from Sunderland. We'd last seen him in January of course, scoring one of Wednesday's six goals on that bleak afternoon in Sheffield. To most Leeds fans, Wickham was exactly the sort of signing they'd been crying out for, and, coming so quickly after the loan signing of the highly rated and fellow England under-21 player Jack Butland; it seemed to suggest that Cellino was footing the bill for the wages of these guys himself. This was as good as confirmed when we then learned that Cellino had dipped into his own pocket to pay the February salaries, just as he'd done a month ago for the January pay-out. News then came that Cellino had also paid back the £1.5m loan to Enterprise Insurance and thus the impending winding up order was withdrawn. The folly of that bit of financial mismanagement by GFH was revealed when it was publicised that it cost them around £100,000 in legal fees alone. Totting up all the figures, it was estimated that Cellino had now loaned around £6m to GFH and we were told that if the FL refused to allow his takeover that loan would command a ten per cent interest rate. The consequences of a "No" vote by the Football League were unthinkable for Leeds but still they continued to ponder.

I was thankful that at last we had a worthy strike partner for Ross McCormack. Wickham had looked a decent prospect at Wednesday, scoring eight goals in eleven outings. He was allocated the poisoned chalice of the Leeds number '9' shirt and it was rumoured he may even be available to buy at the end of the season for as little as £3m; he'd cost Sunderland £8m from Ipswich in 2011. Perhaps we'd finally found the true successor to Jermaine Beckford, the last successful wearer of the '9' shirt. In the four years post JB we'd seen four different players wear it, and between them they'd scored just eight goals! Billy Paynter got three; Jerome Thomas got one; Steve Morison got three; and then the unlucky Dexter

Blackstock got one earlier this season before injury cut short his loan. Not a great record for the most prestigious shirt number on the pitch. What could go wrong for Wickham?

On Thursday, I watched Tom Finney's funeral, broadcast live on a BBC website. It was a lovely funeral, if that is ever possible; many famous names from the world of football were there including Bobby Charlton, Trevor Brooking, David Moyes, Peter Ridsdale and Tommy Docherty. 'The Doc' read a eulogy to the great Preston winger, closing with the words: "You will never see the likes of him again as he was simply the best". Docherty played at Deepdale for nine years from 1949 to 1958 and was a team mate of Tom Finney who played there from 1946 to 1960. The brusque Scot is now 85 years old, but coincidentally on my desk was a photo of a much younger Docherty. As I watched Simon Grayson and members of the current PNE squad carry Tom's coffin from the church, I was flicking through the QPR programme from a 2-1 home defeat to Newcastle United in the old second division. It was my first and only visit to Loftus Road, back in September 1980. The cover picture was a very youthful looking Docherty, the QPR manager shaking hands with Wayne Fereday, then a youth player who'd just been handed his first professional contract. I was working in London at the time and really went to see two former Leeds players; Tony Currie was playing for the R's and Terry Hibbitt was in the Newcastle line-up. I would discover on Saturday that the ground had changed little in the intervening thirty three and a half years!

I was letting the train take the strain for this one, albeit was a bit of a strain rising to a 5am alarm call. I was on the 6:36am Stafford to London Euston Virgin service, a ride I'd secured online a few weeks ago for just £12! The return ticket, on the 15:46 London Midland 'crawler', only cost me £6, although it did take half an hour longer to do the trip. The reason I was setting out so early, was that this was yet another bloody Saturday lunchtime Sky TV game. They really were now taking the pee – five of our most recent eight Championship games have been scheduled in the 12:15pm slot and with just QPR to go we'd only won one of them! My records showed the QPR game was already our 10th live game of the season and Sky had announced this week that the Wigan and Forest games were also to be shown live. To date we'd won only two of the previous ones – Birmingham at home and Yeovil away. Having seen the figures recently, I understand that the TV audience is far greater for a Leeds game than any other current Championship side but even so, making us travel to places like Yeovil, Middlesbrough and London, to be there for 12:15pm, is ridiculous; thank God for Wetherspoon's early opening times!

I was taking a photograph of Marble Arch as early as 8:20am, en route to 'The Tyburn', another 'Spoon's pub, this one on the junction of Bryanston Street and the Edgware Road in W2. I love reading up on the history of their pubs, they all seem to be named specifically after local folk heroes and this one is no different. It takes its' name from Britain's most famous place of execution. The 'Tyburn Tree' stood on the spot now indicated by a stone slab on the traffic island opposite the Odeon cinema just along the road. The so-called 'Triple Tree' could 'accommodate' 24 persons; its most famous victims included Perkin Warbeck and Jack Sheppard. I'd love to tell you all about them but having just read their Wikipedia entries their stories cannot be done adequate justice here. I will tempt you to do your own research by merely saying that Shepherd's execution in 1724 was watched by over 200,000 people and his life and death were immortalised in John Gay's "The Beggars Opera".

In The Tyburn by 8:30am, I treated myself to another of those Wetherspoon traditional breakfasts that had gone down so well at Boro. I suppose I shouldn't have been shocked (but I still was) that it cost me £4.29 down here, a full quid more than the same menu choice up in Middlesbrough; a thirty per cent increase! I got my second shock when I stood at the bar on the dot of Nine o'clock asking for a pint of Abbot Ale, only to be told they didn't serve beer until Ten o'clock! I wondered absentmindedly if that was the reason everything cost more down here; they had less time to make their profit! I somehow made a £1.45 cappuccino last a full hour as I was certain I wouldn't be able to arrange a second mortgage on a Saturday morning…

Simon and the Surrey gang arrived pretty much bang on 10am, and 'Welsh' Andy, who still isn't Welsh, informed me they'd been drinking just down the road as they knew about the 10am prohibition in the Wetherspoon. Adam and Conor bowled in about the same time and slowly but surely the pub filled with Leeds fans of all shapes and sizes.

When the team news came through, courtesy of Conor's mobile phone, it was much as we expected. Young Conor's near name sake (the number of 'n's in the name Conor or Connor seems randomly allocated!) Connor Wickham, replaced Noel Hunt up front and Tom Lees returned at the expense of Scott Wootton.

Butland
Peltier Pearce Lees Warnock
Kebe Austin Murphy Stewart
McCormack Wickham

Subs: Cairns, Byram, Wootton, Smith, Hunt, Brown, Mowatt.

The team was beginning to take on the appearance of a half decent outfit, but for me there was still one piece of the jigsaw missing. We were not strong enough in midfield, or at least, not creative enough. This side was looking much harder to score against though, and hopefully Wickham will add firepower up front, but where was that telling through ball going to come from? Oh! And why was Jimmy Kebe still on the team sheet?

Just after half past eleven, the majority of fans in The Tyburn finished their drinks and set off to Marble Arch tube station. We'd once again done our jobs pretty well, as we'd drunk them dry of Abbot and IPA and I'd ended up drinking London Pride. I hoped it was the last time I'd be uttering that phrase today.

Our tube ride was a short one of just six stops west along the Central Line to White City. QPR have the unusual record of having played their home matches at more grounds than any other league side – more than 20 in their history – but have been playing at Loftus Road for most of the last 97 years. They had a couple of spells at the much bigger, but long since demolished, White City Stadium, built originally for the 1908 Olympics, to try to garner greater crowds. But they eventually settled back into the compact and bijou Loftus Road that boasts (?) a capacity of not much more than 18,000. This a team that was in the Premiership last season don't forget.

It seemed to me to be mostly Leeds fans walking from the tube station to the ground that gradually came into focus at the end of South Africa Road. On the left hand side we passed the wonderfully named "Batman Close" and a dentist's taking the same name; The Batman Dental Practice. One wag commented that with the prices down here they would no doubt be "Robin their patients" too. We had to walk past the main reception area, a huge vivid blue-painted monstrosity, and around three sides of the ground to get to our entrance in the School End where 1,794 of us would squeeze into the upper tier of the vertigo inducing stand. It's not high, but the slope is very steep yet still it's not possible to see the byeline if you're more than a couple of rows from the front. Before I got to my seat I had to pay a visit to the toilet block under the School Stand and once more I was amazed how such facilities get a license in this day and age of health and safety gone mad. I've pushed and shoved my way through many poor examples of concourses that are totally unsuitable for purpose...and this was a top five example. There must have been beer on sale somewhere down there as I could see many lads holding plastic pint pots; trying their best not to squeeze too tightly for fear of sending a jet of their expensive lager into the air yet tight enough to ensure they were not dislodged by a marauding elbow. It was carnage! There appeared to be only one male and one female block for the whole stand and there was room in ours for maybe twenty at a time. I've been in country ale houses with bigger facilities! During the game we would make our dissatisfaction with their ground heard by singing to the R's fans: "We've been to Yeovil, it's better than this" and for once we weren't making it up.

QPR were on a dire run of form. They'd lost their last three games and according to manager 'Arry Redknapp, were missing six of their best eleven players. Charlie Austin was out with a long term injury while Joey Barton was suspended. This was a great time to be kicking R's.

The ground looked pretty full, with few obviously empty seats, but the attendance would later be reported as just 16,448. None the less, the atmosphere was electric and there was a mood of optimism amongst the Leeds contingent. The weather was perfect too, although the bright sun was obviously causing a problem for the TV studio that was just over to our right. Within minutes of the start, a bloke could be seen taping up a makeshift sun blind that appeared to be made from black bin liners! I assumed it was Sky's Simon Thomas and Peter Beagrie I could see behind the glass.

Within ten minutes of the start we should have been ahead. Ross McCormack was chasing a lost cause in the inside right channel when Richard Dunne stuck out a leg and appeared to knock the ball away for a corner; indeed, the liner on that side pointed to the flag. But Ross, having been knocked over initially, rolled straight back onto his feet and was now appealing, cricket like, to referee Chris Foy for a penalty. To our bemusement Foy points to the spot! What a start this would be, one – nil up inside ten minutes. But first we had to score the spot-kick.

Against Bournemouth earlier in the season, McCormack missed a penalty. No shame in that; he's more than made up for it with his goals since and we eventually still won that game. But if you remember, I was a tad upset with Ross on that occasion for the manner of the spot-kick. He'd taken one against Millwall at Elland Road in March last year when he hit a very tame shot to the keeper's left; so in my view, to hit exactly the same penalty against Bournemouth was unforgiveable. I'd have bet my house on him not doing the same again today; but I'd now be homeless. His shot was a carbon copy of those previous efforts, just tamely struck with his right instep towards the keeper's left hand side. As in those other examples, this one was also easily gathered by Robert Green, he that we'd already told, "let his country down". It must have been a sweet moment for Green while McCormack was now ruing a third miss from eight attempts for Leeds.

The thing about Ross though, as I've mentioned many times before, is that his cohonas are huge, totally out of proportion to his diminutive stature. When Rudy was bundled over, 25 yards out and just four minutes later, there was no doubt who'd be taking the free-kick despite the presence of both Stephen Warnock and Connor Wickham. Warnock made as if to take it but stepped over the ball, while Ross clipped it right-footed over the wall. Green had it well covered actually, but the ball took a wicked deflection off a Ranger's head that sent it perfectly into the top right corner.

For the next 15 minutes, Leeds were on top and bossing the game. I was never quite sure if that was because we were playing really well or because the R's were so poor, because I have to say that all the usual Leeds faults were still there for all to see. Passes regularly went astray, our control of the ball was schoolboy-like, and our movement was lack-lustre at best. Everyone in a gold shirt was doing OK, but no one was really shining. When I say everyone, obviously I don't include Jimmy Kebe. He was having his usual 'mare. Neither I, nor most of the fans within my hearing, could understand why McDermott was persevering with him. He appeared almost frightened to get involved in the game and when he did his touch was appalling and his decision-making perplexing. We all know he has been a decent player in the past but he just isn't doing it for us and anyone else would surely be a better bet for the time being.

I'm not really sure what Harry did to change his team's fortunes but towards the end of the first half we faded and they began to look a much better organised outfit. It was no surprise when, just a minute before the break, they equalised. It was no surprise, but the manner of it was still annoying. Several Leeds players were caught ball-watching as the R's knocked passes to each other on the edge of our box at the far end of the ground. A short ball was then played in to Kevin Doyle, back to goal on the edge of the area. Jermaine Jenas ran through an open door to take the ball off Doyle and plant a shot in the bottom corner of Butland's net. It was far too easy; far easier than getting to the bog at this place anyway.

It took me the full fifteen minutes of the half time break to make my slow progress along that tiny concourse again; carefully squeezing past blokes gently holding pints of amber nectar and trying to hold back the heaving throng behind as I was in danger of trampling on a couple of small children. A line of coppers against the left hand wall was just adding to the congestion. I hadn't come across anything as bad as this since making my way through that corridor of uncertainty that lies behind the away end at Fratton Park.

The game had already restarted by the time I got back to my seat, and it was Rangers now bossing the game. There were few chances though, and the game was very disjointed with several lengthy stoppages for injuries. Most fans near me were now focusing their attention on Kebe, wondering just how long it would be before McDermott gave him the hook. Unbelievably it was Stewart who was taken off first, replaced by Alex Mowatt in the 70th minute. On 80 minutes the board went up again and there was more astonishment as Luke Murphy made his way off for Michael Brown. Presumably Cellino was now averting his eyes from the number '17' emblazoned on Brown's shirt...assuming he wasn't asleep by this time, or safely belted into a private car on its way into town, as the game had all but petered out. Still Kebe jogged around like he was looking for daisies, occasionally getting the ball and then losing it again through a poor first touch or a soft challenge. At one point a group of lads started urging Chris Foy to send him off and then Kebe stepped off the pitch to pick up and swig from a bottle lying just over the touchline. As he crossed the whitewash there was a bit of a cheer as several folk thought he was going off. Then there was an audible sigh as he threw the bottle down and walked back on. Finally, in the 90th minute, number '38' went up on the board alongside '25' signalling that even McDermott had seen enough and on came Sam Byram for the last few minutes. Most of us had now settled for the point and hoped there would be no last minute drama. It had been a good day out and a point away from home was always a decent return, even if we would be the first team in four not to beat this Rangers outfit. Then suddenly Clint Hill is behind our defence swinging his left boot at a loose ball. He lashed it across Jack Butland into the far corner of the net and the little ground erupted on three sides while 1,794 jaws dropped in the upper tier of the School End Stand. It was a false alarm; the linesman to our left had his flag held aloft and Hill was correctly flagged offside.

At the final whistle, most Leeds fans seemed to accept a point was a fair reward and we generously applauded our heroes as they and McDermott wandered over towards us to the usual chant of "Oooooh Brian McDermott". In the centre circle we could see Jason Pearce and Clint Hill being interviewed for TV and eventually it was Pearce who took the chocolate football; his reward for a man of the match performance. It was one of those games when any one of 21 players could have been given the accolade and there would have been no murmur of dissent. Had Kebe got it there would have been a riot and letters to Anne Robinson at 'Watchdog'.

As I wandered out of the ground I spotted several dozen Leeds lads dressed in bright yellow suits and black shirts with wide white ties. Each ensemble was topped off with a Messina, the distinctive Fedora often worn by the Mafia. It was a tribute to Massimo Cellino and was a sign that most of the Leeds fan-base is starting to warm to the idiosyncratic 'King of Corn'. He must be pleased with that but I daresay he has not been writing home about the football he's seen thus far in England. The sooner he's cleared for take-off the better and maybe he can inject some flair into the Championship. It was going to be too late to get Leeds into the play-offs this season though; the result at Loftus Road did little for either team. Leeds were now down in 12th spot with 44 points, 8 points away from Wigan who had steadily progressed up the table now that they had played their games in hand. Maybe I wasn't so far off with my pre-season prediction that Wigan would be going up after all. Leeds had 14 games to play, potentially 42 points up for grabs; but I just couldn't see how this team of ours could possibly win enough of them to claw back that 8 point difference. As in the last three seasons, we were all clinging onto the mathematical possibility of a play-off place, whereas in reality it was as good as over.

For the third time in 12 months, Ross tamely misses a penalty

Fortunately, his free-kick was a lot better

Chickens come home to roost

Leeds fans had their worry beads out again. With most now having decided that Massimo Cellino was actually not that bad a bloke after all, and with many of us looking forward to seeing more of his daughter's arse, we were perturbed to read this week of the latest obstacle that might still scupper his takeover of Leeds. A date had now been set of 18th March for a hearing in Italy over his latest indiscretion. He was facing charges by the Italian tax authorities that he'd engaged in tax evasion. He'd apparently taken his yacht, 'Nelie', (Presumably in honour of aforesaid daughter Eleonora) from the USA to Italy without paying the €400,000 import duty required. His Sardinian solicitor, Giovanni Cocco, no clown apparently, was confident no tax was due and the case would be thrown out. He argued that under EU rules Cellino was allowed to have the yacht in Italian waters for 18 months without tax being due, as it was registered to a USA company of which Cellino was allegedly an employee and the yacht was only visiting, not staying. It sounded like tax evasion to me though, especially as it was said the ownership of the yacht only transferred to the US company a few weeks before it set sail for Italy! Anyway, it was just one more thing the Football League had to consider and it seemed likely that at the very least they'd delay their decision until after the Italian court case, despite stating their next meeting was on 13th March.

Leeds had six players on International duty this week, ranging from young goalkeeper Eric Grimes, with the Republic of Ireland Under-19s, to Ross Mac with Scotland, who got an impressive 1 – 0 win in Poland. Jack Butland captained the England Under-21s in their European Championship qualifying victory over Wales; Rudy Austin was a key player in Jamaica's 5 – 0 win over St. Lucia; while Marius Zaliukas was with Lithuania in their 1 – 1 draw with Kazakhstan. Last but not least, Alex Mowatt was a 67th minute substitute for the England Under-19s, in their 3 – 0 win over Turkey. It was Alex's international debut. Thankfully all returned uninjured.

The mood in the Pavilion on Saturday was surprisingly optimistic. We were gathered at the Theatre of the Unexpected today for the game with Bolton, our first home game since that unbelievable 5 – 1 win over Huddersfield, five weeks ago. Since then, we'd played four away games and had only lost the one; that single goal defeat at the Amex. Bolton were down in 18th spot in the table and until a couple of weeks ago they'd been flirting with the possibility of relegation. They'd been hammered 7 – 1 just a few weeks ago at the hands of Reading; the Trotters' heaviest defeat in 31 years. Admittedly they came into today's game on the back of two comfortable wins, over Watford and Blackburn, but overall most had the odds in our favour. We were, after all, a much better organised outfit these days with Butland and Wickham in the side.

In the Pavilion, I sat myself down at a table with three lads from County Durham and I chatted with them about my recent visit to Darlo. Eventually WiganWhite, aka Alan, arrived and then gradually the usual crew appeared and we speculated mainly on the likelihood of Jimmy Kebe turning out today. I was adamant we wouldn't see him and that McDermott had finally seen sense by taking him off at the end of the QPR game. As usual it was Daniel who was on the ball and first to pick up the announcement of the team on Twitter. He informed us that Kebe was in the side!

A few minutes later the team was announced over the PA and when, "Number '38', Jimmy Kebe", was called out, there was an audible groan. There has seldom been a more unpopular player to pull on the White shirt. The only change to the side that played last week at Loftus Road was in the centre of defence, where there was no Jason Pearce for the first time this season. We were not aware of the reason at the time but would eventually hear he'd become a dad overnight with the birth of his first child, a son. Scott Wootton would come in to partner Tom Lees at the back.

There had been much speculation as to how many would be at this game. With Leeds play-off hopes all but gone, a home game with Bolton was not the most attractive fixture on the list but then again it was the first home game since Feb 1st and as a 'double header' with Reading here on Tuesday, there were many stopping over in Leeds to take in both games. Many of our Scandinavian fans were doing exactly that. In the event, a healthy 28,904 were inside the ground at kick-off, including 1,000 from Bolton. As the teams came into view from the tunnel, amidst the now de rigueur hoards of school kids waving flags, I gazed around the ground and was pleasantly surprised that all bar the East Stand upper tier was just about full. I looked long and hard towards the directors' box up in the East Stand to try to catch a glimpse of Massimo Cellino, or better still Eleonora, but the only figure I could see was David Haigh, Beeston Dave, as he's now known, sat at the back of the top section in the directors' box. The chap in front of me assured me that Cellino was here somewhere and since he looked about eighteen feet tall I took his word for it.

Quite what the Sardinian made of this game would become clear in the Sun newspaper the following day, and it would not make pleasant reading for Brian McDermott. The first half comprised another tedious 44 minutes with two poor sides struggling to assert themselves; there was little in the way of quality on show. After the game McDermott would once again categorise the first half as another one where, "for 44 minutes there was nothing in the game". I have to agree too, absolutely nothing happened...until the 45th minute. Then, just as at Loftus Road a week earlier, the Leeds defence went AWOL.

Many had already set off for a half time beer or fag, convinced nothing was going to change in the last few seconds; you would think as Leeds fans they'd have learned by now. Even the ground staff must have thought it safe to begin their half time routines as inexplicably a sprinkler head popped up in the Leeds penalty area just in front of the Kop and gave a quick spray before disappearing from view again. Then Neil Danns, he of the braided hair and regular tormentor of Leeds, brings the ball over the half-way line and makes progress towards us, with the Leeds defence back-pedalling like formation unicyclists. Danns then stabbed the ball forward and it clipped the heel of Scotty Wootton and diverted perfectly into the path of the onrushing Joe Mason who steered it past the startled Jack Butland into the corner of the net. In an instant, all of that pre-match positivity disappeared quicker than that sprinkler head and all I could hear was a cacophony of, "for f*** sake Leeds". Seconds later, referee Keith Hill blew the half time whistle and there was plenty of booing emanating from behind me. It was a comment not just on going a goal down in such a lame manner, but also on another tedious, uninspiring first half of football. Once again there was a strong case for taking this up with trading standards, so poor was the entertainment we were being served up with. You will know though that I am nothing if not a believer in coincidence and irony in our beloved game, and I clung to the hope that we were about to see a repeat of the Huddersfield game. We'd gone a goal down in that one before we scored deep into added time at the end of the first half and then went on to score four more in a brilliant second half, attacking the Kop to win 5 – 1. The symmetry of two '5 – 1' games at either end of our run of four away games was not lost on me either...

And so it proved to be; the game did end 5 – 1! Sadly, it was the Trotters who scored four more in the second half and Leeds that got just the one. It was not that Bolton suddenly turned into world beaters, indeed the match stats would report that actually Leeds had more of the game. We would record more shots; a total of 12 corners to their 2; and a 57 per cent share of the possession. But each time Bolton got the ball anywhere near our goal our defence just melted away or ran around like headless chickens. McDermott had recognised one thing we had all spotted – Lee Peltier was having a nightmare game. He was subbed at half time for Sam Byram. Whether we were all wrong and Pelts would have made any difference, we will never know. In the 52nd minute, Jay Spearing clipped a free kick towards the back post and Lukas Jutkiewicz thumped a header past Butland who had seemingly morphed into Paddy Kenny, rooted to his line. Four minutes later and Spearing was stood over a similar free kick, this time 15 yards further from goal. He delivered the ball to exactly the same spot though and this time the Leeds defence (Ha! is that what it is?) allowed the ball to fall at the feet of the giant Zat Knight who bundled it over the line with Butland again in no man's land. I could only surmise that Leeds were confused by the Bolton kit which was exactly the same hue of Day-Glo orange as the

Leeds' stewards' jackets; why is that allowed by the way? It must have been a nightmare for the liners. All this time, Jimmy Kebe had been doing his daisy collection routine and each time he miscontrolled the ball or stepped out of the way of an oncoming steward the Leeds crowd would shout obscenities and shake their fists at the hapless winger. In the 64th minute, McDermott finally spotted the elephant on the pitch, and pulled both his 'wingers' off. Stewart left first, replaced by Matt Smith, and then Kebe, to a huge cheer and applause from the Kop, replaced by young Alex Mowatt. The experiment with two wingers had lasted nine games; starting with a 6 – 0 defeat at Hillsborough and now ending with us 3 – 0 down at home to a very average Bolton side. We'd won just two of those nine games. Now McDermott reverted to a standard 4 – 4 – 2 formation, with the two giants in the middle at the front, Wickham and Smith, while McCormack plied his trade on the right side of midfield.

Leeds did now look a bit livelier, but the final ball was often wasted and at the other end, each time Bolton attacked, we looked fragile. It seemed obvious to me that the problem was not really to do with the wingers, poor as they were; it was still our overly generous defence. The same porous defence we have struggled with for three and a half seasons!

In the 72nd minute, it was 4 – 0, when a quick break down the Bolton left wing resulted in a first time cross and another unchallenged header in our six-yard box; this time neatly finished by Mark Davies. Once again it was almost comical to see Lees and Warnock looking around as if to say, "Where the f*** did he come from?", while wondering again why Butland hadn't claimed the cross. The Kop chanted, "What the f*** is going on?" With a minute to go the Trotters completed their knap hand with a stunning strike from Andre Moritz that rifled into the roof of the net off the underside of the cross bar. The Kop sang nothing; we were too stunned.

By this time, many Leeds fans had left the ground. It's a rare thing indeed to see our fans leaving Elland Road before the final whistle and this was the first time I'd seen it this season. It was the first time we'd lost a home game this season by more than one goal as well. In fact, you had to go back to the days of Neil Warnock to find the last home thumping; a 5 – 1 Capital One Cup defeat to Chelsea, and before that a 6 -1 reverse to Watford. Those could both be explained; Jason Pearce had been sent off against Watford (there is something to ponder, Pearce missed a big chunk of that match too!) and Chelsea; well Chelsea were just too good for us. There was no apparent reason for this hammering though, with the possible exception of Jason Pearce being absent again. We all know he's been a rock at the back this season and frequent man of the match awards have found their way on to his mantle-piece, but no player should be that vital to us.

Those Leeds fans that did stay were rewarded for their stoic support with a consolation goal in the dying seconds. It may be a template for more to come if McDermott has now ditched the winger system. Ross McCormack found space right on the touchline, in front of the East Stand, and his low cross found Matt Smith diving in to head home from close range, with the Bolton defence showing that had we been able to exert any pressure at all on them they are not much better than us! The Leeds fans, ever the humourists, sang, "You're not singing any more", in the direction of the temporarily silenced Bolton supporters over in the West Stand. They were on their feet and singing jubilantly just seconds later though when the final whistle blew. Final score: Leeds 1, Bolton 5.

I slumped down in my seat and watched silently as the players dutifully applauded us. I noted that when McDermott held his hands aloft towards us this time there was no, "Oooooh Brian McDermott", coming from the Kop. I did wonder if BM might throw in the towel tonight, or if Cellino might kick him out again. The following morning Cellino's words appeared in the Sun newspaper:

"We didn't even try to play and they made the fans ashamed.

"The players pi**** me off because they didn't fight for the club.

"For what they did today I would like to kick their arses one by one. They are guilty.

"They were without pride and should be ashamed of themselves. They are chickens".

Elland Road chaos

The beauty of this time of the season is that if you do drop a bollock there is soon chance to get back to winning ways as the games come so thick and fast. The downside is if there is something fundamentally wrong there is not much time to put it right. Brian McDermott was at pains to tell us that all was not yet lost and, "if we can get on a run we can do something this season", although at the same time admitting that was, "just talk". "All I can do", he told us in his pre-match press conference ahead of the Reading game, "is to get a result on Tuesday". Commenting on the booing by the fans on Saturday and the huge cheer that greeted Kebe's substitution, McDermott was philosophical. "The fans are fantastic; when we play at home we have got to give them something. I understand their frustrations; they pay good money to come and watch us play and they pay their money to watch us get results and perform."

If he needed any reminder as to how much a results business football is these days, he got it with the news that the longest serving Championship manager, Chris Powell at Charlton, had finally been sacked this morning, with Charlton having sunk to the bottom of the pack. I was surprised it had taken this long. The new man in the longest serving seat was now Nigel Pearson at Leicester; he looked secure for the foreseeable future though as his side were romping away at the top of the table, a full 13 points ahead of third placed Derby.

There was still no news from the Football League; worse than that though was the apparent cooling of enthusiasm for it all by Massimo Cellino. As well as his rant in the Sun over the weekend, he'd now told reporters he was refusing to commit any more of his hard earned (?) cash to the club until the Football League made their decision. He'd already put some ten million pounds into what he himself was now referring to as, "a black hole", and he said that was it, "finito", until he got ownership of the club. These were his parting words apparently as he stepped back on a plane to return home to Miami. The FL was still due to meet on Thursday but even then we were all sure we would still have to wait until that Italian tax hearing on 18th March before they would announce their verdict. With two home games in the space of a few days, my guess was that the cash flow would be positive anyway for a couple of weeks and that his gesture was more an attempt to put pressure on the FL than it was to put Leeds in difficulty. David Haigh, now either sacked by or resigned from GFH Capital, (it was impossible to tell which) told the media there was no shortage of cash at the club and administration was not even a remote possibility. Another rumour doing the rounds this week was that Cellino's sale of Cagliari had now fallen through. Apparently the Arabic buyers had pulled out and the word now was that Cellino had decided to keep it and would run both Cagliari and Leeds, assuming his ownership was ratified, in much the same way as the Pozzo family runs Udinese, Watford and Granada in Spain. At least that was the gist of an article I read in Italian with a bit of help from Google Translate! So, all the background uncertainty was still there as Mark and I set off from his flat in Altrincham, just after 4pm on Tuesday evening.

I got a phone call from Pecky10 just as I was about to leave home, telling me the M62 was closed and likely to remain so for some hours to come. Apparently a big accident had resulted in a car overturning on the eastbound carriageway. She suggested later that we take the A628 Woodhead Pass route through the Peak District National Park. "It's a lovely road too", she texted.

I discussed this with Mark on arrival in Alty, but news was already coming through on the radio that the A628 was now severely congested too, due to the world and his brother plumping for that alternative route. We looked at the map and decided to head north out of Manchester on the M60/M66 and to then pick up the A58. It worked well enough until we got to Ripponden, when the combination of all the westbound traffic now being diverted off the M62 to allow the air ambulance to land, and road works through Ripponden, created total gridlock. A kindly bloke and his wife, crawling past us in the opposite direction, suggested we retrace our steps and turn off down Elland Road (I assumed this was a different Elland Road to the one we were attempting to reach tonight some miles to the east!) onto the B6113 and work our way along the back roads to Brighouse before re-joining the M62 beyond the incident at junction 26. Again, it went OK until we reached the outskirts of Elland, home of the Brewery of the same name whose fine ales I have been known to sample. Sadly, the little B roads were just not up to the job and we ground to a halt. Initially, we'd laughed with a certain smug self-satisfaction as we could see all the trucks stuck on the M62 in the distance, over to our right. But as time went on and the radio broadcast that the motorway had reopened, we began to realise we would probably have been just as quick had we sat in the queue on the M62. I had a text from Kentley the Stokie later in the evening telling me that he had done precisely that and: "We made it with plenty of time! M62 reopened and it was virtually as quick as normal!" Excellent, pleased for you mate…not!

It began to look as though we'd miss the start but then I got a few tweets telling me kick-off had been put back to 8:15pm as many fans and even the match officials were stuck in the chaos all over Yorkshire. We continued to crawl along and at one point spotted a car with a Leeds United badge air-freshener swinging in the front window, squeezing past us going in completely the opposite direction. We gestured to the occupants asking if they were going to the game and if they knew a quicker route. Strangely, they burst out laughing, shaking their heads and rolling about in the car. They were either going home, having given up and considered we were mad still trying, or maybe their laughter meant they'd given up watching the team at all this season and they were just surprised anyone was still mad enough to want to watch such rubbish! It could have been either!

In the event, we eventually pulled onto the car park at Elland Road, LS11, at around 7:15pm, an hour before the rescheduled kick-off, but four and a quarter hours after I left home in the Potteries; and almost three and a quarter hours after we left Altrincham. It was officially my worst ever journey to Leeds. Mark and I grabbed a half pound cheeseburger each from the van at the bottom of Lowfields Road and then made straight for the bar behind the Kop. The burgers were excellent but pricey at £4-50, but did the job. They don't have much choice of beer in the non-members bar behind the Kop – Fosters or John Smiths is your lot - but we enjoyed a couple of ice-cold Fosters and then ruminated over McDermott's team selection.

He'd promised us changes during that pre-match presser, telling us: "We trained on Sunday and Monday; we've picked a team and there will be changes. Everyone is hurting and we have to put it right on Tuesday". Pleased to hear that Brian.

It wasn't the team *I* would have picked for sure. I wanted us to go with the 4 – 4 – 2 formation we ended with on Saturday, with both Wickham and Smith up top and McCormack in midfield. But BM had gone back to his old 5 – 3 – 2 formation, including his main three centre backs – Pearce, Lees and a recall for Zaliukas. Pugh was in at left wing-back, with Byram now on the right. Hence we lined up:

Butland
Byram Lees Zaliukas Pearce Pugh
Austin Murphy Mowatt
McCormack Wickham

Subs: Cairns, Wootton, Brown, Stewart, Poleon, Hunt, Smith.

That represented five changes from the starting line-up on Saturday, which is a lot, but whether it was the team of "men" he'd promised us was far from obvious. At least Jimmy Kebe was nowhere to be seen; ironically other than on the front cover of tonight's programme! Come on editors, get your act together! We would later be told that Kebe was ill, presumably with some kind of anxiety attack. He makes me feel ill every time I see him play.

Looking around the ground, it was clearly much less populated than for the Bolton game. The Reading fans just about filled the top section of the away area, while there were big gaps in the South Stand and the Cheese Wedge was completely empty. The official attendance was reported afterwards as 19,915 and I assumed that everyone had managed to get to the ground by kick-off time, 8:15pm.

Why most of us had bothered though was difficult to understand, as once again two mediocre sides battled to gain the upper hand. As he's done so often this season, after the game Brian McDermott would make his standard comment that, "there was nothing in the game in the first half", and I know he means there was nothing between the two teams. But the irony is that there was *literally* nothing going on in the game either. Well, almost nothing. In the 25th minute, there was the usual sight of the Leeds United defence in total disarray as Reading stole the lead.

In the previous few days, the world had been perplexed by the total disappearance of a Malaysia Airlines Boeing 777 aircraft, flight number MH370, somewhere over the South China Sea. It was a bit like one of those huge TV magic stunts where an illusionist can make large objects disappear. This time though we knew the plane took off with 239 people on board and had disappeared off radar screens in mid-air. But I swear to you, had it landed behind our defence tonight, no bugger would have noticed it.

A Leeds throw-in on our right wing, in front of the West Stand on the half-way line, finds its way back to Marius Zaliukas. Zaliukas, seemingly fully aware of his surroundings, casually sweeps the ball first time back into the no-man's land between Butland's penalty area and Jason Pearce. What both Zaliukas and Pearce fail to spot though is that Garath McCleary is racing towards the ball at a rate of knots. The ball dissects Butland and Pearce perfectly, and each clearly thinks the other has it in mind to hoof it away. Suddenly, Pearce catches McCleary out of the corner of his eye, but it's too late and the Reading man is past him and toe ending the ball past Butland. Our new on loan keeper takes an almighty swing at the ball with his right boot but completely misses it and lands in the standard Leeds defensive Kama Sutra position…flat on his arse. Ironic for a bloke called Butland really. McCleary walked the ball to the penalty spot before tapping it into the empty net. This was a snake's-belly moment for Leeds fans; it just could not get any lower than this…could it?

Well, funnily enough it could. The half time whistle blew and was followed by the now almost standard mild booing from the Kop as we settled down to our half time routines. No one could possibly have foreseen what was about to transpire out on the pitch in the second half.

Within nine minutes of the new half, Leeds were 4 – 0 down. That's FOUR – NIL for the sake of clarity. Less than a minute after the break, Royston Drenthe stood over a free kick, a couple of yards outside the Leeds box in front of the South Stand. This is the same Royston Drenthe who once played for Real Madrid but who eventually suffered from anxiety attacks after being booed by the Bernabeu fans...maybe Jimmy Kebe could benefit with a chat with Mr Drenthe. Anyway, Drenthe seems a pretty confident fellow nowadays and he curled a delicious left-footer around Leeds' wall and into the far corner of the net off the upright. It was just one of those goals; couldn't do much about it; two minutes later it was 3 – 0.

Leeds fans are still booing after the second goal when a routine cross is sent over from out on the Reading left wing; it takes one touch off a Royal's head before bouncing in the Leeds six-yard area. Once again it's like the Bermuda Triangle in there, but Nick Blackman is in there stooping to head home, with Butland doing a bit of a street dance spin on his goal-line. Immediately the Kop is asking the not unreasonable question: "What the f*** is going on?" again, while a disbelieving McDermott is roaming around his technical area no doubt wondering how that 777 disappeared and whether he could do the same..

But it isn't finished yet; another six minutes pass and we are 4 – 0 down! IT IS STILL ONLY THE 54TH MINUTE FOR CHRIST'S SAKE! Reading move the ball swiftly down their left wing again...well they would wouldn't they? They knew bloody well that Zaliukas was down there! A long ball bounces about two yards behind Zaliukas with Robson-Kanu at a good two yards disadvantage as they both race for the ball. In the space of those few yards the Reading man is suddenly a couple of yards to the good, clear on goal in the inside left channel and Zaliukas is...well, skipping along is the only way I can describe it. We saw this peculiar skipping action at Hillsborough when he lost out in a similar race up there all those weeks ago. The rest was just a formality as Robson-

Kanu steadied himself before crashing an unstoppable shot past Butland, just as Jason Pearce arrived on the scene. If it wasn't so serious it would be comical, but this was serious. We'd now conceded nine goals in only 100 minutes of football on our own patch! Leeds fans all around the ground picked up the next chant that began at the back of the Kop: "You're not fit to wear the shirt", everyone screamed. At one point Ross McCormack looked up at the Kop and for one millisecond I thought he was going to show his anger, but he obviously thought better of it. Then the whole ground picked up on the next chant, the one that's become so familiar on the last two visits to Oakwell, when Barnsley have ridiculed us: "We're sick of it, we're sh*t", rang out from all sides of Elland Road louder than I've ever heard it before. It was still ringing out as big Matt Smith began to warm up beyond the touchline in the north-west corner. At least he was without blame either today or on Saturday when he'd come on and grabbed that consolation goal.

Smith had only been on the field three minutes when his presence was felt, and it was all so simple. Ross, tight in the north east corner, laid the ball back to Austin on the right wing. Rudy sent the ball over first time to Jason Pearce who nodded it down and between two Reading defenders to find Smith waiting at the back post to prod the ball past ex-Leeds loanee Alex McCarthy. The huge cheer that went up from the Leeds fans was nothing more than ironic at this stage but as soon as Reading restarted the game Leeds were on the attack again. Suddenly, Rudy Austin had run onto a knock down by Connor Wickham, just over half-way, and Rudy was now powering his way towards goal. About thirty yards out he shifted the ball onto his right foot and let fly. The ball simply rocketed through the Elland Road atmosphere, bending away from McCarthy all the way into the top right hand corner. It was some goal and the cheer this time was explosive and full of admiration. It was enough to get everyone onside again – fans and players together – and for the next 30 minutes Leeds bombarded the Reading goal, while our fans raised the roof off Elland Road chanting, "Attack, Attack, Attack-Attack-Attack". The best chance fell to McCormack, as a left wing cross beat everyone to arrive with him at knee height at the near post, but so surprised was he the ball had made it to him that he just allowed it to hit him and bounce wide.

The game ended 2 – 4 and it was a strange few minutes as we tried to come to terms with the events of the past hour and a half. The determination and spirit that Leeds had shown, once Smith got his goal, was the dominant thought and so it was generous applause that the Leeds players got as they held their hands aloft to salute us. I could only wonder how things might have turned out had Smith and Wickham begun the game up front as I'd wanted them to; we will never know what difference that might have made. For now, Leeds needed to bottle the formula of the last half hour and forget the rest. They would need to replicate that period on Saturday when we go to Burnley, the second best side in the Championship.

Leeds had sunk to 15th in the table tonight, and no one was any longer thinking about the play-offs. Relegation was now the word on many lips.

Keep Fighting

Mark was with me again for the trip to Turf Moor, so once again I met him in Altrincham and we drove the 35 miles north up the M60 and M66, this time carrying straight on up the A56 and then taking the Manchester Road into Burnley.

We were early again, arriving in the car park otherwise known as the outfield of Burnley Cricket Club, just after mid-day. We parked at long-on to a right-handed batsman at the Football Ground End, for anyone who knows this famous old cricket club. Every year I come here, the outfield looks a little worse for wear, and this year it was all moss, as far as the eye could see. I was surprised that the square hadn't had its first cut of the year yet either; there was plenty of work to be done in the coming weeks before the first ball of the new season is bowled.

The reason for the early start was to get in front of a TV by 12:30pm when the Italy v England Six Nations match was due to start; England needed to win by 60 points to set Ireland the challenge of a big win in France to wrest this year's title from England. Mark ordered us two sausage and bean filled Yorkshire puds at the little kitchen area, before we found seats in the upstairs bar and settled down with our first pints. I couldn't believe how crowded it was! It was rammed, far busier than I could ever remember it. Luckily we spotted Nick and Karen sat at one of the little round tables and they offered us their seats while they went on a fag break. James and the two Micks, the Ilkley lads, sat at the next table.

The first disappointment was that Mark had cocked-up the food order; it arrived as plates of sausage, beans and chips, with no sign of the giant Yorkshires we were looking forward to. My second disappointment was that Mark had not got any cash with him! And the third disappointment was that come half twelve the TV was still showing Sky Sports and not the rugby on BBC. I was despatched to the bar for refills and to see if I could get the channel changed. Armed with another pint of Thwaites Bitter and a pint of Carling for the scrounger, and having sweet-talked the barmaid into putting the rugby on, we settled down to watch the match.

I have to say it was not easy to concentrate on the game as the only screen was fixed high up on the opposite wall, and the room was now crammed full with Leeds fans all nearing their own personal bests for beer supping. At one point, a group of particularly loud lads bouncing up and down in the middle of the room, decided it would be fun to launch their beers into the air. Suffice to say we all got a good soaking. I'm all for having a good time; we are on this earth only once and it doesn't last long, but when that involves spoiling the occasion for others it's gone too far. At the extreme, behaviour like that could ultimately cause the cricket club to close their doors to us, even though I'm sure they would loathe to miss out on the profit they earn from our visits. There are lots of old pictures and trophies on the walls around the club and it really would be a shame if they were damaged. Mark took one lad to task over the beer throwing incident and of course as soon as he stood up and his six foot six inch frame loomed over the lad, he was totally contrite and apologetic. But the damage was already done, most notably to my new black jacket that was now only marginally less beer sodden than the towels on the bar. Within minutes of the first episode, it happened again, so Mark and I decided to drink up and try the bar downstairs. I'm sorry lads, but if you do ever read this, just remember that we're all Leeds fans, but your behaviour does us no favours and spoils the party for the rest of us...and anyway, more to the point, why waste decent ale?

Downstairs it was a lot more sensible, although the only TV was a small set with a picture that resembled a snow storm on a dark night. Surrey White Simon quipped that a braille version was available on request. We watched the end of the game and England ran out 52 – 11 winners; not quite enough to set any points target for the Irish but they would still need to beat the French in France, later in the day.

This was a huge weekend of sport; as well as the conclusion to the Six Nations, in Australia the first race of the all new Formula One season was taking place, with Lewis Hamilton having secured pole position for the race in the early hours of the morning in his Mercedes 'Silver Arrow'. On each side of his Mercedes cockpit was inscribed, "#KeepFightingMichael", a reminder to us all that Michael Schumacher was still fighting for his life in a Grenoble hospital, almost three months after his awful skiing accident.

Mark and I made the short walk to Turf Moor with a long column of fellow Leeds fans and then made our way into yet another totally outdated football facility. Here, as at Loftus Road a couple of weeks ago, it was chaos in the concourse beneath the David Fishwick Stand, home to 3,587 Leeds fans for the next couple of hours. In fact, we had the biggest away attendance of the whole weekend; more than any Premiership side, including the likes of Liverpool at Man U, Chelsea at Villa, and Arsenal at Spurs!

Once inside, Mark grabbed a couple more beers at the little counter and we then found ourselves a space where we could drink without being jostled by the heaving crowd of fans that was engaged in the three main activities that take place in these dark concrete bunkers under football stands; queuing for beer; queuing for the bogs; and trying to watch one of the tiny TV's perched high above our heads. If Burnley are promoted at the end of this season, I presume many of the teams they will host here will bring three thousand or more fans, and those fans will, like us, have to suffer these inhuman conditions. With all the money that's being paid to Premiership players these days it's to be hoped Burnley will also find some cash to splash on improving this area. They were a Premiership club as recently as 2010 of course.

As we drank, we spotted many of the away game regulars squeezing past us; I had a quick chat with Jon, aka @flipper66, Carmel and Jo, Wayne and 'Welsh' Andy, who we'd seen with the rest of the SAS (Surrey and Sussex) Whites in the Cricket Club earlier. Martin and Daniel, Jack, and many, many more were also here as Burnley is always a popular trip. All the while, at the far end of the concourse we could hear the Leeds choir singing and chanting and could see plumes of lager and ale spilling into the air, just as it had done in the cricket club earlier.

Brian McDermott had finally seen sense and his starting eleven today was the side that began to restore our faith in the final half an hour at Elland Road on Tuesday. That meant it would be 4 – 4 – 2 today from the start, with Matt Smith replacing Zaliukas. For Burnley, Danny Ings was missing due to an injury picked up last week in their game with Blackburn. Ings and his strike partner Sam 'I was sh*t when I played at Leeds' Vokes, had scored 44 goals between them this season, so on the face of it Ings injury was a Godsend. His replacement was Ashley Barnes though, he of the flailing elbows and another frequent thorn in our side during his time at Reading. Incidentally, while Leeds were doing their chicken act against Bolton last weekend, a chicken also featured in Burnley's game at Ewood Park. Yet again a disgruntled Rovers' fan had smuggled a live chicken into the ground and onto the pitch, in protest against the Indian poultry firm Venky's controversial ownership of Blackburn. Burnley won that game 2 – 1, their first victory over their East Lancashire rivals in 34 years. Burnley were on a fine run of form, unbeaten in eleven, and still unbeaten in the league at home all season; the only Football League side still claiming that honour.

A crowd of 18,109 roared the game into action, with the Leeds fans in surprisingly good voice considering our recent form and the amount of beer most of them had shifted today, and it was Leeds who began the game on the front foot. In the opening minutes, Ross McCormack split the Burnley defence with a superb little pass to Matt Smith whose left foot shot was saved low by Tom Heaton. Minutes later and we ought to have been a goal up – how many times have I written that lately? Ross McCormack was put clear through on goal by a sloppy Burnley back pass, but, as we've seen so often, despite all his goals, he misses plenty too. This time he cheekily chipped Heaton but the ball struck the left upright and bounced across goal. Ross got to the rebound and shot again but that was blocked and cleared. This was all very encouraging; the more we could attack, the less time our suspect back division would have to cock things up. Just before the half hour mark the Fishwick Stand erupted as Leeds took the lead.

Yet again it was that man McCormack, showing that the odd miss or six was not going to dent his confidence or his ability to put the next chance away. Connor Wickham was playing on the left wing (very strange for a six foot five striker I thought) and was also being employed to hurl his long throws into the box at every opportunity. In the 27th minute he threw the ball long and flat into the area at the far end of the ground. It took the slightest of nicks off the head of Matt Smith before arriving perfectly at head height for McCormack who steered a powerful header inside the front post. Cue delirium! A beer fuelled calypso celebration exploded in the Fishwick Stand.

We held the lead for just 11 minutes, and the nature of the Burnley equaliser pretty much summed up Leeds United this season…well, any of the last four seasons really.

Danny Pugh was left stranded high up the pitch in the left wing position when a Leeds move broke down. It was left to our new six foot five winger to cover at the back as the ball was lofted over his head by Dean Marney to the overlapping Kieran Trippier. Unsurprisingly, Trippier got round Wickham easily and lashed the ball low across goal where Jason Pearce stuck out a leg and diverted it past Butland. It was another shocking goal to concede; another fiasco.

Leeds held out until half time and I just about did too. While the Leeds players trooped back to the dressing room, I dashed down to the Burnley smoking shelter, also known as the away end bogs. This is something else that just has to be sorted out; I've mentioned it before I know but sooner or later I am sure someone will bring an action against one of these clubs that refuse to police no smoking in their toilet areas. Most of us made a joke of it this time, but I did spot one irate gent demanding of a steward stood idly outside the bog entrance that he does something about it. It was choking down there, and the fact that there was just not enough trough room to cater for demand meant that everyone was queuing in there for far longer than normal, too. It was a nightmare and hardly surprising that some of our lads were using the hand basins as well. Premier League? You're having a laugh!

In that dressing room underneath the Fishwick Stand, most of the Leeds players could feel satisfied, proud even, of a decent first half display. The only player I felt was not really at the races was Alex Mowatt, who, in my opinion, has struggled for a long while now with the pace of Championship football. He started really well in his first few games and showed an eye for a defence splitting pass as well as being a decent crosser of a ball with his left boot. But he lacks pace, he's only got one foot and he's often brushed aside all too easily; he was today again and may even have been carrying a knock from one particularly heavy challenge. Quite who should replace Alex I don't really know, as we are not blessed with a multitude of midfield dynamos.

In the second half, Burnley quickly began to show us that despite their ground being totally unsuited to the Premiership their team may well propel them there this season. Gradually they began to dominate possession and they looked sharp and eager all over the pitch. Just after the hour mark, Brian McDermott also decided that Mowatt was struggling and for the first time in six weeks or so we got to see what Dom Poleon had to offer. One minute later we were a goal down.

It was no fault of Poleon I guess and in fact the problem this time appeared to be another of our young guns, Sam Byram. Sam is another youngster who, despite our great hopes, has recently been underperforming. He had a great season last year and of course walked away with virtually every award at the club's end of season dinner. This season he began slowly with that hip injury and lately he's often been found wanting in his defensive duties. So it was again today that he, like Pugh in the first half, suddenly found himself in an attacking position down the Leeds right wing, while the ball was quickly being shifted to the opposite end by Burnley's Ben Mee. Quick as a flash the ball arrived at the feet of Scott Arfield in our box and although his initial left-footed effort was well blocked, he was first to react to the rebound to lash it home with his right.

Three sides of Turf Moor went crazy; it was easy to understand why of course as suddenly the home side was in sight of another three points and they were a step closer to Premiership football again. I could only imagine how manic Elland Road will be when we eventually get as close to the Promised Land ourselves. Burnley looked as if they might be going back after just four seasons in the wilderness; we'll be taking at least eleven seasons if not more!

Leeds battled without further success for the last 25 minutes and at the final whistle our players got a fabulous reception from the fans with a long rendition of, "We all love Leeds" and then a few rousing choruses of, "Marching on Together". There was even an, "Ooooh, Brian McDermott", as the manager walked off the pitch ahead of his players, back to the dressing room under our feet. That is not to say everyone was happy. As I made my way out of the ground I heard at least one chap being very vocal about how, "McDermott is f****** rubbish", and, "why are they singing his name for f*** sake?" For most of us though, it was just a small positive that we'd not been battered today. There were still big problems of course, most notably with a defence that seems totally unfit for purpose, and we still have to see whether Sig. Cellino will be our new saviour. At the game today, a couple of lads unfurled a huge banner with the message:

RIDSDALE – YOU STARTED THIS NIGHTMARE
BATES – YOU WERE THE NIGHTMARE
MR CELLINO – PLEASE WAKE US FROM THIS NIGHTMARE
WE NEED YOU!!!

LEEDS UNITED – ENGLAND'S TRUE SLEEPING GIANTS

It pretty much said what most of us now believed and I read between the lines that there was also a nervousness that maybe the aggravation of this Football League approval and our lamentable recent form might cause Massimo Cellino to think again and maybe pull out of the deal. Surely that was not possible was it? This is Leeds United, everything's possible.

Not too much damage was done again by this defeat to our league position as many of the teams below us also lost today. We'd end the day in 14th spot, still stuck on 44 points, 13 points behind six placed Forest who were also on a dire run of form. But perhaps more importantly, we were now only 15 points above the relegation places. Next up was a home game against our old foe Millwall, a team also in great danger just outside the drop zone. "Millwall is now a f****** huge game", muttered Mark in the car going home, just before he fell asleep. I listened to the radio commentary as the Irish won their Six Nations game in Paris to nick the title from England. The following day I watched as Nico Rosberg, who holds both German and Finnish passports, won the Australian Grand Prix in one of those German Mercedes cars with "#KeepFightingMichael" written on the cockpit sides. As the German national anthem played, I thought again about Schumacher and the many times I'd seen him up on the podium while listening to that tune.

'Keep Fighting' was also the title of Paul Harrison's biography of our own Billy Bremner of course and it's a motto that is close to the hearts of all Leeds fans as we begin to contemplate yet another season in the Championship. It would be as well that the players remember it too; they did at Turf Moor, but recently we'd maybe been too ready to give up the fight too often. As Mark and I had walked back to the car after the game today, we came across Andy Hughes. He's known to be a big Leeds fan and of course played over 100 times for us between 2007 and 2010. He was having his picture taken with Leeds fans outside the ground. Now, Andy Hughes, he was a fighter!

Nelie and the Lions

Tuesday 18th March was due to be a landmark day for Leeds United. It was the day our fate was likely to be decided in a Sardinian court room. Massimo Cellino was still in the USA having decided not to be present as Judge Sandra Lepore sat in judgement over the case of Nelie the yacht and the €400,000 of import duty. As with all things Leeds United, when the verdict was given early on Tuesday morning, it was still far from clear what it meant for Leeds. Judge Lepore concluded that Sig. Cellino was guilty of tax evasion and that the penalty would be a €600,000 fine and the confiscation of Nelie the rigged yacht. When Cellino's lawyer Cocco the Clown asked Lepore if they could have leave to appeal the decision, Lepore surely replied: "Not on your Nelie…" It was at this point that we learned that further tax cases were being prepared against Cellino for similar offences; one for the import of a Range Rover and one for yet another yacht, this one going by the highly ironic name of "Lucky".

On the face of it, the game was up for Cellino, but immediately after this court proclamation, his lawyer, Sig. Giovanni Cocco, pops up to announce that his client did indeed intend to appeal the ruling. Where did that leave us? Any appeal in Italy was likely to take at least nine or ten months to be heard. Meanwhile, the FL issued a new statement: "The Football League has noted the outcome of the court hearing earlier (on Tuesday) regarding Massimo Cellino. We are engaged in an ongoing dialogue with his legal representatives in this country and cannot comment further at this time." Well, at least it wasn't "No"! But surely it was just a matter of time now before they did say "No". It was all about as clear as the whereabouts of that Malaysia Airlines 777 which was still missing or why a Teesside man had been left by the side of the A66 having had his penis cut off![1] Unsurprisingly the man was, "too distressed to speak about what happened".

---

[1] http://www.independent.co.uk/news/uk/crime/middlesbrough-man-found-with-penis-cut-off-too-distressed-to-speak-9199163.html

Meanwhile, at Elland Road this week, they staged an attempt to get into the Guinness Book of Records; over 7,000 local schoolchildren packed the East Stand for a maths lesson. I thought it was doomed to failure from the start...nothing ever seems to add up at Elland Road these days.

As if to prove the point, GFH sent a letter to the Football League in which they demanded an answer on Cellino's ownership. As well as telling the FL to pull their fingers out, the letter was also an attack on the other consortia still trying to get in on the Leeds United act. It could only have been clearer if it had contained a picture of a burning bridge! Phil Hay of the YEP posted a copy of the full letter from law firm Gibson Dunn.[1] The relevant paragraph read: "Neither we nor our client are aware of any other instances in which you have applied such rigour, which we note is against the unprecedented backdrop of the objections you have received from two failed bidders for the Club (Flowers and Farnan/Together Leeds), who have attempted to stop the takeover by ESL and the appointment of Mr Cellino as a Club Director." I very much hoped they had a plan B that did not require the involvement of Messrs Flowers, Farnan or Verity!

And if GFH and their lawyers weren't already doing their best to scupper their own relationship with the FL, the Yorkshire Post appeared to be making sure Cellino was blown out of the water. They published an article this week suggesting Cellino had strong links with a certain Pino Pagliara, a former Italian football agent banned by the Italian FA in 2005 for match fixing![2] That will help the cause. Thanks lads!

Once again the lead up to a game was being dominated by off-field talk and rumour; all stuff that Brian McDermott was increasingly suggesting was at least partly responsible for the poor performances on the pitch. I was less than convinced about that. The guest of honour at the Millwall game on Saturday, March 22nd, was Vinnie Jones and in his programme notes, McDermott told us he would get Vinnie in the dressing room before the game. I somehow doubted Vinnie would

---

[1] *https://twitter.com/PhilHayYEP/status/446906918096101376*

[2] *http://www.yorkshirepost.co.uk/sport/football/leeds-utd/new-leeds-owner-linked-to-match-fixing-agent-pino-pagliara-1-6509984*

allow such things to affect the way he approached a game. Ever on the lookout for a good omen, I checked the results from our Second Division winning year, 1989/90, Vinnie's finest hour. Almost to the day all those years ago, Leeds beat Pompey 2 – 0 at Elland Road with goals from Lee Chapman and, you've guessed it, Vinnie Jones. I watched all the home games in the final couple of months that season and still to my mind it was the most exciting season I can ever remember.

The Millwall game itself was nothing much to write home about. McDermott named an unchanged side from the one that started at Burnley, meaning Rudy Austin had shaken off an ankle injury picked up in that game. A decent crowd of 23,211 turned up and hopes were high that a similar performance to the last one would see us comfortably home against a Millwall side that was languishing in the relegation places, despite the arrival of Ian Holloway in January. Generally, the Lions' results had not improved since Holloway came in – they'd won just two of their 12 league games under the former Blackpool and Palace boss. But, one of those wins came just two weeks ago at much fancied Derby, so they couldn't be written off just yet. A win for Leeds though was now seriously overdue; we'd gone six without a win since that wind-assisted game at Yeovil and we'd only won two games out of 15 since Christmas. That was not much different to Millwall's record. In the Pavilion we watched as Derby thrashed Forest 5 – 0 and I wondered if that was 'job done' for Billy Davies.

Millwall started the game with a real urgency and looked by far the better team in the opening quarter of an hour; only a miraculous Butland finger-tip save from a misplaced Jason Pearce header kept the scores level. Leeds looked nervous and hesitant and I was seriously wondering if Vinnie had gone in the right dressing room before the game. Then, out of nothing Leeds had the lead. It came from another long throw, out on the left wing by Connor Wickham. Matt Smith stretched every sinew to get his head on the ball and it looped backwards over David Forde in the Lions' goal to drop over the line. Millwall could rightly feel hard done by.

Millwall regrouped again and continued to take the game to Leeds, attacking the Kop with the driving rain now at their backs and in my face. I love my seat near the front of the Kop, but if it rains and the wind comes from the South, I will get wet! In the 41st minute I didn't care though. A long ball down the Millwall left wing was met by a full bloodied sliding challenge from Tom Lees that sent the ball ricocheting back up the Leeds right wing; Ross McCormack was chasing after it all on his own. Ross took the ball on into the box and then slid it neatly between the legs of Forde from the tightest of angles for his 26th goal of this, his most prolific season to date.

At half time, Vinnie Jones was interviewed right in front of the Kop, only ten yards or so away from me and he delighted the fans by agreeing to sing a rendition of Marching on Together; the whole stadium immediately joining in. Oh, how we miss having a few characters like Vinnie in the side these days; perhaps that's the real problem behind our recent hidings. There's no one prepared to dig in and spill blood for the cause.

The second half began as the first had ended, with Millwall still looking the more accomplished of two poorly equipped sides. As so often this season, Leeds seemed amateurish in much that they did with the ball; failing to control it, misplacing passes, getting caught in possession, all the basic stuff we ought to take for granted that professional players can do. Exactly on the hour mark, Ian Holloway made a triple substitution in a sh*t or bust attempt to rescue something from the game. On came six foot eight inch Austrian striker Stefan Maierhofer, and everyone near me was having flash-backs to a Tuesday night in January 2011 when the similar shaped Nikola Zigic scored four goals for Birmingham to end Simon Grayson's reign. DJ Campbell (still on bail on a charge of match fixing) and Simeon Jackson also joined the fray for the Lions. Within 13 minutes of the substitutions, Millwall had scored. Maierhofer, back to goal on the edge of the Leeds box, chested the ball down and D J Campbell thumped a volley into the corner of the Leeds net. This was the type of moment in a game when we needed the guts and passion of a Vinnie Jones figure.

Brian McDermott then made his changes; bringing on Michael Tonge for Alex Mowatt in a move I was appreciative of and then giving the best player on the pitch – Connor Wickham –

the hook and bringing on Noel Hunt. What was that all about? Sometimes I fail to understand what is going on in the mind of our outwardly very intelligent looking manager.

As it happens, we survived. Millwall continued to throw high balls up towards Maierhofer and we all shuddered with fear as a number of late corners curled in towards our six-yard box. But with Millwall totally committed we could also have snatched a third.

The fear of our fans in those final moments was clear for all to see. Ian Holloway would tell the BBC in that fabulous accent of his: (Try reading it in his West Country accent)

"Leeds were on their knees. I've never sensed this place like that. They need to back their manager, get their life sorted out. They're a wonderful club but that ain't right. Stop causing havoc, support your manager who's a great bloke, and sort your life out. I've never been to Leeds and they (have) felt that wobbly. And that hurts, because they were there, and they slipped out the bag."

Maybe Holloway has the credentials to manage Leeds. He certainly seems to understand us, the fans. In contrast, Brian McDermott was nervy and irritated. He told us: "We're fighting for our lives as a club with the ownership situation. We want to get it sorted out as quickly as possible." I couldn't help thinking he would be better off spending his time concentrating on matters he could affect; getting the players playing the game in the right way. But what do I know?

At the end of the day it was a vital win and a vital three points that should, barring some miraculous results at the foot of the table in the coming weeks, see us retain our place in the Championship, always assuming we don't fall into administration if the Football League say no to Sig. Cellino and GFH run out of money. Little did I know that the papers would be full of such speculation again in the next few days while I was sunning myself in Bournemouth. We ended the weekend in 13th spot with 47 points; Leicester and Burnley still looked odds on to take the two automatic promotion places while Millwall, Yeovil and Barnsley continued to look the most likely three to go down.

Vinnie Jones at half time during the Millwall home game

Muppets

I'd been looking forward to the trip to Bournemouth for a couple of months. Mrs W and I had booked three nights in a hotel near the sea front for Sunday, Monday and Tuesday; it was my birthday on the 24th and of course the game at Dean Court was on the 25th. What could be more perfect?

We set off on the 194 mile drive on Sunday morning, stopping for lunch at a lovely little farm shop and café in the village of Cholderton on the A338, about ten miles north of Salisbury. Setting off again having enjoyed Sunday lunch of home-made scotch egg and cheese sandwiches (we know how to live it up) we arrived in Bournemouth early afternoon. The weather was gorgeous; brilliant blue sky in the main, with only the odd heavy dark cloud. It was chilly mind, the brisk wind making it feel much cooler than the ten degrees showing on the dashboard. Before we went to the hotel we decided to find Dean Court, which is actually nearer Boscombe than Bournemouth. In fact, the Club is still officially registered with the Football League as 'Bournemouth and Boscombe Athletic Football Club' although since 1972 it's traded under the shorter name of A.F.C. Bournemouth. It began life in 1899 as plain old Boscombe FC. These days the ground is officially called the Goldsands Stadium and it's a typical small modern facility. It was mostly rebuilt in 2001, with the addition of the temporary Ted MacDougall Stand at the south end being added as recently as 2013. It has a reported capacity of exactly 12,000. Leeds had sold out its allocation of just 1,388 tickets and we'd be housed in the south end of the East Stand along one touchline.

This was my first visit to Dean Court and my first visit to Bournemouth, so from that you will know that I was not at *the* game here on 5th May, 1990, the final day of the 1989/90 season when Lee Chapman scored with the header that secured our promotion to the old First Division with Vinnie Jones, Strachan et al. At around 4:45pm that day I was dancing around our front room celebrating as hard as the lads and lasses who were sweltering in the hottest May temperatures ever recorded, down in Bournemouth. Folklore has it that over 5,000 Leeds fans made the trip, of which just 1,700 had tickets for the game. It was a big game for the Cherries too, as they were relegated as a result of the defeat. Leeds fans are widely said to have been responsible for over one million pounds worth of damage in the town as the celebrations lasted all through the bank holiday weekend.

On Monday 24th March this year, my birthday, Mrs W and I drove to Poole Harbour and got the little ferry across to Brownsea Island. It was a lovely morning again although it was a test of our endurance to remain on the open top deck of the ferry as it made the twenty minute crossing in a biting gale. The attractions of Brownsea Island are many and varied; we did the two hour walk around the entire island and enjoyed every minute. The views back to the mainland were superb and it was one of the most peaceful places I've ever come across. The only thing missing was a sight of the red squirrels that are said to inhabit the island. Brownsea is most well known as the home of the very first Boy Scout camp, back in 1907, an event hosted by Robert Baden-Powell himself.

With time to kill until the next ferry back to Poole Quay, we decided to treat ourselves to afternoon tea in the little 'Villano Café' and as I enjoyed my Latte and a scone, I checked my Twitter feed for any news from Planet Leeds. I was surprised to see I had a Direct Message from @ingham37, otherwise known as TheHopefulLeedsFan or even Keith to his mates! It said simply; "This is a sorry state of affairs. The club's a mess!" I quickly sent him a message back asking what had happened and within a few minutes I had his answer. "at 11 o'clock ish the FL said no to Cellino and he's 14 days to appeal but he won't and were in the #%^# !"

As best I could I then tried to piece together the events of the morning by logging into the BBC Sport website on my smartphone. Sure enough that confirmed that Cellino's application to the FL for approval had been unanimously rejected. Contrary to what Keith initially thought though, the article I read gave the impression that Massimo Cellino *would* appeal the decision, something he had to do within 14 days for it to be considered. I really couldn't think on what grounds he could appeal though, as however narrowly you defined "dishonest", surely having your yacht confiscated and having to pay a fine for tax evasion puts you pretty much right in that category! There was other stuff being reported on the BBC too and it was not all bad news. Billy Davies *had* been sacked by Nottingham Forest after that 5 – 0 drubbing by East Midlands rivals Derby County at the weekend and astonishingly it appeared that Neil Warnock was favourite to take over that hot-seat. As I read on it seemed that Warnock must have already been appointed because he'd made his first loan move – bringing Lee Peltier in from Leeds! Blimey, he wasn't wasting any time! Still the news kept coming, and now there was more bad news as I read that Sunderland had recalled Connor Wickham! Bloody hell, I was marooned on an island and all hell was breaking loose! I might be in Baden-Powell territory but I was far from prepared for all this.

I suddenly became aware that Mrs W was staring at me and knocking on the table to get my attention: "I'm still here", she said, waving a hand in front of my face. "What's been happening?" I'd also spotted on the BBC news page that today was the London premiere of the new Muppet movie, "Muppets Most Wanted" and so I summarised the morning's events for her reporting that: "Cellino, Billy Davies, Peltier and Wickham have all gone… but the Muppets and Neil Warnock are back!"

We climbed back aboard the next ferryboat and continued our little cruise around Poole Harbour; the ferry does a big circle after stopping at the island, before arriving back at Poole Quay. The commentary pointed out all the posh houses at Sandbanks where these days most of the property is owned by footballers. It's said to have the fourth highest land values in the world. Maybe I should have popped over to see if anyone there fancied owning a run-down, debt-laden Championship club with no prospects.

The day of the game we went to Corfe Castle which is both the relic of a real castle and a village of the same name. Just as on the Monday, the weather on Tuesday morning was fabulous, but later in the day those ominous grey clouds would appear again... in both a literal and metaphorical way.

My old mate Nigel, who sits next to me on the Kop, was down for this one as well, and he was stopping at a hotel near the pier. He wandered over to ours just before Five o'clock and we drove the couple of miles to Boscombe, parking behind the Wetherspoon pub, 'The Sir Percy Florence Shelly', where footballgroundguide.com recommended away fans could gather. Apparently, this Percy was the son of the famous romantic poet of the same name and he lived in Boscombe Cottage, the oldest property in the area. Quite tame really after I bigged up Wetherspoon's for their heritage stories.

I worked my way through several pints of the excellent Cornish ale, 'Doom Bar", while Mrs W and I also indulged in the £5.99 meal and ale deal. Kentley the Stokie joined us as well and we whiled away the time pondering who might fill the gap left by the sudden recall of Connor Wickham by Sunderland. No one expected any other changes. As always, the pub was jam packed with Leeds fans eager to improve the local economy.

When news filtered through about the team, no one was particularly surprised that McDermott had turned again to Noel Hunt; he'd filled the Wickham role for a couple of games before the Sunderland man arrived, albeit in unspectacular fashion. The rest were the same as for Millwall and Burnley which again surprised none of us. There were a couple of interesting additions to the bench though, as young Lewis Walters took his place there for the very first time joining Aidy White who we'd not seen since the Newcastle United cup exit last September. White had obviously done himself no harm by scoring for the reserves earlier in the week and was clearly now recovered from the injury that saw his loan period to Sheffield United cut short after only eight appearances for the Blades at the end of last year.

Mrs W left us to go back to the hotel, while Kentley, Nigel and I made the short walk to Kings Park in which Dean Court is situated. The three of us picked out a spot with a few empty seats and decided to stand there together; all our actual seats were in different areas of the stand. Our position was right in line with the edge of the penalty area at the South Stand end. Apart from the fact the ground is so tiny (it looked pretty full tonight even though there were only 10,109 in here) the facilities are pretty good. The toilets were vast and clean and there was none of the usual scrimmaging we have seen at recent away games. At both ends of each stand, the Perspex wind-breaks were decorated with giant photographs from recent Bournemouth games and they looked fantastic. There was a decent atmosphere in there too, as the announcer welcomed the teams onto the pitch for the usual line-up and hand-shakes. Leeds were unusually wearing their home strip of all white, while the Cherries wore their familiar red and black stripes. At left back for the home side was former Whites hero Ian Harte and his face was also staring out at us from the cover of the Bournemouth match day magazine, which goes by the inventive title, 'MATCHDAY'.

Leeds' fans were in great voice and as the game kicked off, all the noise was coming from our 1,388 mouths. Within seconds of the start though, Danny Pugh had slipped and the Cherries tore through our defence. Thankfully, the dangerous Lewis Grabban must use the same studs as Danny and he hit the turf too, before he could hit the target. But it was a temporary reprieve only and just seconds later that dead ball expert Ian Harte was taking a corner just a few yards to our left. Watching the replay of the goal reminded me of my boys playing in their junior sides a few years ago. At a corner you always have a player lurking just outside the box to pick up any scraps and the defending team always needs to allocate someone to mark that player. If you watch this goal back you will see that Simon Francis is the Bournemouth player waiting just outside our box but we've decided not to bother to mark him! Harte spots him though and delivers the corner accurately onto his right boot. Francis hits the ball on the volley and it may well have gone in without further intervention, but to make sure, Yann Kermorgant sticks out a foot and deflects it into the net. Many of the Leeds based fans had travelled 254 miles to get to this game, spending a minimum of £100 during the whole trip, probably a hell of a lot more judging by the queues at the bar in the 'Percy Shelly'. But with less than two minutes gone we were already staring another defeat in the face. The last thing a team so far from base wants to do is give the home side an early boost. I was dumbstruck and the next half an hour was just a blur as I struggled to understand what the hell was wrong with our team. In the 18th minute we were two down as a driving run down the Cherries right wing ended with a simple ball across the edge of the area and Lewis Grabban being far more alert than Tom Lees to sweep the ball home. The Leeds players looked as mesmerized as I was; there was no anger, no shouting at each other, no "come on lads let's fu***** sort this out", no nothing. They just trudged back to their positions and it all started again. Ten minutes later and we were three down. Grabban finds himself in acres of space on the right corner of our box, shifts the ball to his left foot, and drives the ball low past Butland. Minutes later it could, maybe should, have been four, as Yann Kermorgant smacked a shot against a post.

There was a brief chorus of, "You're not fit to wear the shirt", aimed at the hapless Leeds players and then in response to the delirium of the home fans we sang, "You're nothing special we lose every week", but apart from that Leeds' fans were mostly arguing amongst themselves at this point. The lads in front of us agreed with me that we just do not do the basic skills of football very well and hence put the blame firmly on McDermott's shoulders and the coaching staff. Nigel was adamant that the players didn't care and just weren't trying. Kentley was more interested by now in a bonny looking girl in the next section he fancied!

The half time whistle brought a few minutes of respite and a chance to gather our thoughts. What could McDermott do to change things around? One of those lads in front of us wanted Lewis Walters brought on but I was certain he wouldn't be blooded in this scenario. I felt he was only on the bench as an introduction to the routines of a first team match day and that he was never intended to get a run unless we were already two or three goals to the good and he could play himself in with confident players around him. To throw him into this cauldron could damage him for life!

Both teams returned unchanged for the second half and the home side carried on in exactly the same bullish frame of mind taking the game to Leeds. It took them only six minutes to stretch their lead even further. Ian Harte over-hit his free kick but Matt Richie was first to react and he quickly gathered the ball and sent it back into our six-yard box; that hallowed piece of turf where Leeds defenders fear to tread. And so it was again today that two Bournemouth players were in there challenging for the ball and Yann Kermorgant rose to plant his header in our net again. A good number of Leeds fans immediately disappeared, presumably to get a few more beers down their necks to numb the pain. But strangely, the vast majority who stayed in the ground then seemed to come together in a defiant show of strength. A chant of, "We all love Leeds", began and quickly spread to every single Leeds fan and we chanted those four words over and over and over again. Periodically a different chant would go up, 'MOT', or 'YRA', but then after a couple of rounds of that the, "We all love Leeds", chant would start again. Whether it was coincidence or not I will never know, but slowly the Leeds players seemed to take heart from the support they were now getting and a few tentative attacks began. McDermott then reacted to it by sending on Aidy White and Cameron Stewart and withdrawing Murphy and the anonymous Noel Hunt. BM was back to his 4 - 4 - 2 formation with two wingers again, presumably forgetting how badly that ended last time we saw it against Bolton. But it seemed different now; Aidy White was steaming down the left wing every few minutes and a few crosses found their way into the box. Still that chant went on and on; I was joining in myself, only stopping when someone let off a yellow smoke canister a few yards away and we were engulfed in thick, choking smoke. The Leeds fans had now spilled out of the first few rows of seats and were right up against the barriers at the side of the pitch. A couple tried to climb the fence but were pushed back down by a line of stewards and police that was now in evidence in case of a pitch invasion. Every time a Leeds player came anywhere near us they were urged on with an even louder chorus of, "We all love Leeds", and a sea of waving arms demanding they give every last once of effort in the cause. It was like we needed just one goal to win a semi-final. One of the stewards was now joining in with the chant and everyone pointed at him and shouted, "He's Leeds". I could see the tiny figure of Jo down there at the front teasing him. Suddenly Butland launches a clearance to beyond halfway and Matt Smith seems to jump ten feet off the ground to nod the ball to Ross McCormack. Ross takes off with the ball seemingly tied to his boot laces; he ghosts past one defender, shifts the ball to his right foot and shoots. The net ripples and the roof comes off our stand as we roar like we've now got that all important semi-final goal and not just a consolation goal in a four-one rout in front of 10,000 fans. Ross McCormack grabs the ball and kicks it back towards the centre circle before running over towards the Leeds fans, right arm held aloft pointing at us. He then gestures to us that the goal was for us and we are all still bouncing up and down singing, "We all love Leeds"! It was a quite incredible show of support for a team that had done little to deserve it. Ross then raises both arms together and with palms facing the ground he bows and pays homage to his supporters again.

At the end of the game the Leeds fans kept on singing; the rest of the ground was virtually empty but most of the Leeds fans had stayed behind. Brian McDermott walked from the dug-outs on the opposite side of the pitch and he raised his hands as he applauded us. The rest of the players followed suit, seeming genuinely humbled that we were so forgiving of what for the first hour was a pretty dire display. Ross McCormack peeled off his shirt and brought it with him as he walked right up to the barriers in front of us before lobbing the shirt to someone in the crowd down there. Still the Leeds fans sang but now it was 'MOT' belting out and raising the roof. Once again I could only dream of being around when we finally do win our place in the Premiership back as we must surely do one day. It will be amazing if it's anything like this!

And that was my first experience of Dean Court. Despite the incredible show of public support on the terraces, many fans were openly discussing Brian McDermott's future as they walked back to their buses or cars. The general view was that he'd had his chances, probably more than he was entitled to, and he wasn't up to the job. "He's a nice enough bloke, but nice doesn't cut it", was pretty much the consensus. I myself thought his position was untenable now and felt sure we'd hear of his demise in the hours and days ahead. The only thing that might save him was that the Muppets at Elland Road had even more pressing things to sort out trying to come up with a plan B now that the Football League had seemingly scuppered Cellino's takeover.

Kentley, Nigel and I walked slowly to meet up with Mrs W, parked in Jefferson Avenue a few streets away, and we delivered Kentley and Nigel to their respective hotels. The good lady and I popped into our hotel bar for a final drink. On the TV screen in the bar, I saw that Manchester City had beaten Man U 3 – 0 at Old Trafford, which improved my mood a little. I then checked my phone to see how Worcester City had got on with their home game with Stockport County. They'd drawn 0 – 0, City's favourite score this season. They had lost just five of their last 14 games and were sat nice and secure in 15th spot in the table. News was also coming through that Malaysia Flight MH370 had almost certainly crashed in the Southern Indian Ocean and it was believed that pieces of debris spotted floating in the water were from the aircraft. I told myself that there were more important things than football to worry about in the world and a few glasses of Peroni later I almost believed it.

The calm before the storm as the players line up pre-match

A smoke canister erupts in the Leeds section to my left

Talking Italian

The first thing I did when I got home was to check the football websites and there was plenty of news coming out of Elland Road, as there always is these days. The BBC football website carried the rather worrying headline: "Leeds United owners look to fill wages shortfall".[1] GFH were apparently in discussions with Cellino and other third parties to try to raise almost £2 million to pay the March salaries due on Friday. GFH reckoned they had an agreement with Eleonora Sport Limited that it was the Italians and not them who were liable for all club costs for a period of six months, even if the takeover failed! The worry beads then got a real pasting as the ever reliable (?) dailymail.co.uk ran an article with the catchy headline: "Leeds in financial meltdown: No one to pay McDermott's and player wages as owners' row erupts... and a 10-point deduction looms".[2] According to The Mail there was now a distinct possibility that Leeds would suffer the pain of administration and a points deduction with neither GFH nor Cellino accepting responsibility for the Clubs finances. Meanwhile, Brian McDermott appeared to be trying to put the team's recent failures on the pitch, down at least in part, to the events going on off the field. He was reported as saying after the Bournemouth game: "What is going on off the field does affect the players. All of the talk is about who is coming in and are we going to get paid." Many of our fans felt it would be a travesty if the players *were* paid for the display down on the South Coast.

No one really seemed to know the exact truth of anything going on inside Elland Road, but lots of people were prepared to speculate. Even Ken Bates decided to put his two penny worth in when he aired his views on Radio Yorkshire. Astonishingly, he claimed that he'd been approached by the Andrew Flowers/ David Haigh consortium at the time of their

---

[1] http://www.bbc.co.uk/sport/0/football/26752394

[2] http://www.dailymail.co.uk/sport/football/article-2590314/Leeds-financial-meltdown-No-one-pay-McDermotts-player-wages-owners-row-erupts-10-point-deduction-looms.html

attempts to buy the club a few months ago and had agreed to put £1.5 million into their pot if it meant it would get the takeover over the line. He also criticised GFH, claiming his wife had, "to lend them a million pounds this time last year to pay the wages and why are they scrabbling around today trying to pay the wages tomorrow at the same time as they have borrowed money from David Haigh?" Any Leeds fans watching the video of the Bates interview would be grateful at least that Uncle Ken stated categorically that *he* would not be stepping forward to buy the club this time.

On Thursday this week, the Football League confirmed in an official statement that they had received a notice of appeal from Massimo Cellino. The appeal would be heard by an independent QC with the assistance of expert legal advice to unravel the details of the Italian tax case. We were in for another two week wait before we got the result.

Meanwhile, another club in a spot of bother was Nottingham Forest. We now learned that our mate 'Colin' had turned down the offer of a job there as he was concerned about interference from the owner, Fawaz al-Hasawi. Initially the Lee Peltier loan also fell through and he was then strongly linked with a move to Bolton instead, but by Thursday, Fawaz al-Hasawi announced that Pelts was indeed a Forest player. Stuart Pearce was next to turn down the apparently poisoned chalice of the Forest hot-seat although he would later agree a deal to take charge at the start of next season, presumably hoping they would get promoted in the meantime.

On Friday this week, even Gordon Taylor was wheeled out to comment on the Leeds United situation. It was all due to the threat that his members, our players, might not be paid on time. The Mirror carried a story[1] quoting Taylor as saying:

"Arrangements are in place with regards to payment and there is going to be some proportion of wages paid today and more next week. The players are OK with it. Leeds are a big club with a large fan-base and we have no reason to believe that things won't be sorted in the near future". That all sounded a

---
[1] *http://www.mirror.co.uk/sport/football/news/leeds-players-agree-wages-deferred-3294877*

bit blasé to me in the circumstances and of course there was no clue as to exactly who was loaning the club the additional money, as I assumed that the club itself still didn't have the readies.

Twitter continued to carry tweet after tweet worrying that we were about to enter administration again and everyone was checking the Football League rules on how many points we might lose this time and would it be this season or next with so few games left. Even that fantastic parody of Enrique Iglesias' 'Hero' by Chris Moyles about that 2007-2008 season was doing the rounds again:

> *We were docked fifteen points from the start*
> *It was tough but we never lost heart*
> *Through it all, with Dennis Wise*
> *We knew we'd prob-ab-ly survive...*

I could picture Moyles madly trying to write some new verses; something he could get out a bit sharpish before the end of the current tax year...The irony being that Moyles himself had been found by a tax tribunal to have avoided significant amounts of tax by using an illegal scheme which involved him posing as a second hand car dealer.[1] I wondered if he used the same tax accountant as Massimo and whether Cocco the Clown did his legal stuff too?

Friday night, before the upcoming Doncaster game, Jim White spoke with Mike Farnan, by telephone live on Sky. Farnan, seemingly the leading figure of the 'Together Leeds' consortium, evaded several Jim White attempts to get him to reveal just how much money TL would devote to the club but he did tell White: "We are a very good group, we're a very experienced group; we have the interests of the club at heart".

Just at the moment it would be easy to forget that Leeds do occasionally play football too and that we are not just a rich source of legal fees for the corrupt, unscrupulous and misguided. Such a game this weekend was against unfancied

---

[1] *http://www.theguardian.com/media/2014/feb/21/chris-moyles-used-car-dealer-tax-avoidance*

near neighbours Doncaster Rovers, another side struggling at the wrong end of the Championship and so in need of a few points.

The usual crowd gathered in the Pavilion and we nervously awaited the team announcement. While we waited we were entertained by Peter Lorimer and Paul Reaney who were waxing lyrical about something or other...we couldn't tell exactly what as the sound system had gone awry and it sounded as if they were gargling in a goldfish bowl. Maybe the sound engineers hadn't been paid. We'd heard that 'Showsec', the company that supplies many of the stewards on match days at Elland Road, had not been paid and they were threatening not to turn up today. If that meant there was no one to keep telling us to sit down on the Kop, then at least that was a result.

When the team was announced just after 2pm, there was just the one change from Bournemouth; Noel Hunt was dropped to the bench and was replaced by Cameron Stewart. We would line up:

Butland
Byram Lees Pearce Pugh
Stewart Austin Mowatt Murphy
McCormack Smith

Subs: Cairns, Hunt, White, Warnock, Tonge, Wootton, Poleon.

Quite why McDermott chose Stewart and not White was a mystery; at Bournemouth they'd both come on as late substitutes but it was White who'd looked by far the livelier of the two. The manager's mind works in a mysterious manner.

A decent crowd of 23,476 had turned up, either because of, or in spite of the off field troubles (they do say there is no such thing as bad publicity) and the Leeds fans were in good voice. In my mind I felt things could not get any worse and every game was approached as a sort of potential new beginning; a possible turning point; I think most Leeds fans felt the same. The lads and lasses in the South Stand certainly seemed on good form as they often led the singing, with the Kop for once lagging behind. But the efforts of the fans did not seem to be encouraging the players. Yet again it was the opposition who flew out of the traps and took the game by the scruff of the neck, while we looked like the nervous relegation threatened side we were fast becoming. Did McDermott actually have a point when he said all of the off-field stuff was affecting the players? Well, if he did, then matters were probably not helped when many fans in the South Stand suddenly turned round chanting, "Turn your backs on GFH", and then, as if to confirm McDermott's point, within a couple of minutes we went a goal down!

A Doncaster corner was headed away cleanly enough by Sam Byram, out to the Doncaster left wing. The Leeds defence, seemingly transfixed by the quality of Sam's header, ambled out, eyes glued to the Doncaster player out on their left who had now collected the ball. Meanwhile, Donny's David Cotterill was left in isolation on the other side of the pitch, just inching his way back to stay onside. We knew what was going to happen well before any Leeds player twigged it and sure enough the ball is lofted diagonally forward to Cotterill. I swear he had a look of mild surprise on his face as he controlled the ball, took a few steps forward, and then absolutely lashed a rising shot from the corner of the box. It was past Butland before you could say, "England's number one". Several Leeds defenders ducked out of its trajectory to avoid decapitation. It was another shocker of a goal to concede.

The Kop immediately broke out into its own protest against the owners, not quite as subtle as the South Stand; "F*** off to the GFH", rang out loud and clear from behind me while I swear I could see David Haigh shrinking into his seat up in the East Stand.

As half time approached, Donny continued to press Leeds back and I felt we really needed to get into that dressing room at 0 – 1 and then regroup. Equally, I was nervous that we'd concede again in the few minutes remaining; something we've done time and time again this season. There looked to be no particular danger as a simple ball was lobbed forward towards Billy Sharp, lurking in the arc of our penalty area; he was closely marked by Sam Byram. We all expected Sam to hoof the ball up field and clear the danger but suddenly Sam is adopting the Leeds defence default position, on his arse on the turf, while Sharp is living up to his name and is poking the ball past Butland, just as Tom Lees arrives on the scene...a few seconds too late as usual. Leeds had time for just one foray forward before the whistle brought the half to an end and it was met with a chorus of booing from the disgruntled Leeds fans. In this season of dire first half performances, this was right up there with the worst. Once again we'd probably already given ourselves too much to do, although the lads in front of me reminded me that we'd been in exactly this situation, 2 – 0 down at home to Donny, two years ago, in Neil Warnock's first game. We came back to win that one 3 – 2. As if to trick us all into thinking that was a possibility this time, we could see that SkyBet were offering odds of 28/1 on that result happening again today, up there on the big screen at the far end of the ground.

At least it looked like McDermott was going to go down fighting; at the start of the second half he sent on Aidy White and Michael Tonge, withdrawing Rudy Austin and Luke Murphy. It did smack a little bit of sheer desperation by the manager though; it was as though he'd started to peruse the rest of his squad thinking, "Who the hell else do we have around here that can play a bit?"

I saw a compilation of statistics recently that showed that Leeds' second half performances have been way better than our first half displays all season. If our games had ended at half time, our 37 games prior to this one would have yielded just 39 points and we'd be in the relegation places. Conversely, if the second halves had been separate games in their own right, Leeds would have earned 52 points from them and in that table we stood 8th! The next 45 minutes would prove the point once more.

From the first kick of the new half, Leeds were on the front foot. The introduction of Michael Tonge in the middle meant at last we had someone in there looking to pick out a pass, while out on the left wing Aidy White's pace was also unsettling the Donny back line. Leeds piled forward and were unlucky not to get a penalty when a Sam Byram cross was clearly handled and then in the 62nd minute we took the lead in our second half game.

Once again it was so simple that it was hard to understand why it doesn't work more often. Danny Pugh lofted a free kick towards the back post from out on the Leeds' left. Matt Smith rose well above his marker to head across the face of goal and Ross McCormack was well placed to head the ball past the Donny Keeper, Sam Johnstone. It was Ross's 28th goal of the season, 27 in the league. Had he put those two penalties away that he missed against Bournemouth and QPR he'd have his 30 for a season for the first time in his career.

The last half an hour saw Leeds lay siege on Johnstone's goal and at one point the keeper earned a yellow card as he hauled Ross down just outside the box. Had the incident happened a few yards further from the byeline he may well have got a red one. But for all of our possession and pressure we could not find that elusive second goal and at the end of the game there was more booing than cheering emanating from the stands. Over in the South Stand there had been another short turning of backs to the game just before the end and the Kop had issued a few half hearted, "To the GFH f*** off" chants but to be honest there was not much enthusiasm even for the protests. The Leeds fans were running low on emotion of any kind having had our hopes battered so often in recent seasons; we were exhausted.

We would end the evening in 15th spot in the table, on 47 points, 12 ahead of Barnsley in the third relegation position with eight games to go. With games against four of the bottom six still to come we ought to get enough points to stay up...

Monday 31st March was another day that left me thinking that no one was going to believe what I was writing in this resume of our 2013/2014 season. You think you have seen and heard it all and then...

It was the day of the Cellino appeal today and so many of us were constantly refreshing our Twitter feeds hoping to see a positive outcome. We got nothing all day on that front until the Football League posted a brief statement in the evening informing us:

"Massimo Cellino's appeal under the Football League's Owners' and Directors' Test has now concluded with the independent QC reserving his judgement".

Reserving his bloody judgement? What the f*** is that supposed to mean? No one seemed to know.

But in the meantime, one enterprising Leeds fan had amazed everyone by managing to ring Massimo Cellino at his home in Miami and then posting the sound track of their conversation on the internet for us all to hear! The call took place on Sunday night, the night before the appeal hearing, and was made by the owner of the Twitter handle @WhiteLeedsRadio, an independent Leeds United internet radio station. I listened to the 22 minute conversation twice, as quite simply I didn't believe what I was hearing the first time. Cellino was wary at first, asking, "Who are you", and, "What do you want from me", in his thick Italian accent but when the caller simply told him, "I am a Leeds United fan, a concerned Leeds United fan" that seemed good enough for Cellino to open up. And open up he did. With very little prompting, Cellino spoke for most of the 22 minutes, lambasting GFH, David Haigh, Brian McDermott and even Ken Bates, while lauding the Leeds United fans. He also told his young interrogator that, "the player from Reading [Noel Hunt] was on £25,000 a week!" He spoke good English but he sounded either very tired or slightly drunk and various journalists later confirmed that in their view there was no doubt the call was genuine. At one point he said that no doubt people thought he was a fool for getting involved with Leeds with all the trouble that the club was in but he explained that having experienced the Leeds fans first hand at Middlesbrough he was hooked and he wanted to help them after the horrendous ten years they had endured. Every other word was the 'F' word, a typical trait of Italian businessmen I've come across myself in my own career. In a truly insightful comment about the fans he said, "Fans are not for sale, they have feelings and you don't buy feelings. You can buy a bitch for one night, but you don't buy the love my friend".

On another day…

The general consensus ahead of the Charlton game was that Cellino may come to regret some of his comments during his ill-advised phone call and his advisors and legal staff were no doubt tearing their hair out at another example of the man's naivety; they would eventually contact the caller and get the SoundCloud recording taken down. But most Leeds fans were now even more supportive of Cellino. At last here was someone who spoke like the fans, felt like the fans, and appeared to want to get involved for reasons other than to make money out of the club. I was very much in the Cellino camp, though I still felt the FL decision would be upheld and we would need that plan B that didn't yet exist.

Mark was with me again for the Charlton game at Elland Road so it was another trip to Altrincham to pick him up before the onward leg of the journey to Leeds. Once again we got Mark the seat next to mine on the Kop, suggesting again there would not be a huge crowd. That feeling was increased when we walked into the Pavilion. This was a rearranged fixture of course due to Charlton's run in the FA Cup and apparently the Pavilion had been booked for another function. Hence when we got there only about a third of it was open. Lorimer would joke it was a cost saving measure to help pay the players' wages. Despite the limited room it was not very busy at all.

As before every game these days, the Pavilion punters eagerly awaited the announcement of the team, each of us wondering what the next changes would be as BriMac searched for a winning formula; we were all convinced there had to be some. McDermott didn't disappoint us this time either, dropping a total of four from the starting eleven on Saturday that so badly let us down in the first half of that fiasco. In came Wootton, White, Tonge and Stephen Warnock and out went Pugh, Murphy, Austin and Stewart. It looked like they would line up:

Butland
Wootton Lees Pearce Warnock
Byram Mowatt Tonge White
McCormack Smith

Subs: Cairns, Pugh, Murphy, Stewart, Poleon, Hunt, Brown.

For once I had no gripe with that at all and felt that Tonge and White in particular deserved a start after both giving promising little cameos in their substitute appearances on Saturday.
I wasn't going to bother with a bet today until someone on the table mentioned that 4 – 0 to Leeds was on the SkyBet sheet at 50/1...I know, I know, there is a reason for that...but I still couldn't resist! We'd scored four down at The Valley I reminded everyone...well, Ross did.
When we reached our seats there was plenty of room all around us and as I scanned the stadium there were big gaps everywhere. There were lots of unusual faces around too suggesting that many regulars were missing. The crowd would later be announced as 17,343, the lowest of the season including the Chesterfield League Cup game.
This was a big game for Ross McCormack – his 150th appearance for Leeds - and he almost set up Matt Smith in the very first minute, sending over a cross that the big striker just failed to connect with. It was not a great game it has to be said though and we had to wait for 25 minutes to see the first shot on target, a week effort by Smith from another Ross Mac cross. The first half faded out with no score and little in the way of goalmouth action.
It was another of those games after which McDermott was bound to say, "There was nothing in the first half", regardless of the final result. I felt we'd done OK and didn't look in any danger of conceding for a change but we certainly hadn't created very much going forward. But was that really reason enough for McDermott to take off Matt Smith and replace him with Noel Hunt? McDoughnut would later tell us he made the change to, "inject some energy into the team". I could relate to that but still felt Smith was the wrong player to take off. MS has scored 11 goals this season from just 18 starts and 17 late substitutions; surely it was madness to not have that threat on the pitch? Many other fans in my hearing had the same opinion and already I could hear the figure of £25,000 a week being snarled in the direction of Mr Hunt by the old chap on

the front row in the flat cap. He's usually a good barometer of general opinion.

Credit where credit's due though, in the opening minutes of the second half we did look more lively, and on another day we may well have taken the lead. Ross McCormack received the ball back to goal, mid-way in the Charlton half, turned, and from 25 yards let fly with his right foot. The ball swerved and dipped ferociously as it rocketed towards us in the Kop and it took the merest of touches from the keeper's upstretched fingertips. The ball smacked against the cross bar, bounced down just short of the goal line and away to safety. On another day… it would have hit the bar an inch lower and would have been in, but not today; it was probably just not going to be our day. This was confirmed beyond any doubt a few minutes later.

We were 100 yards from the action at the other end of the pitch but we could still clearly see that Jason Pearce was not quite tight enough to Reza Ghoochannejhad (honest). Ghooch, as he's known to his mates for obvious reasons, had chased a ball over the top of our defence and Pearce had tracked back with him, but as the Addicks' striker jinked right and left Pearce was a few feet too far away. It was a marvellous curling strike with his left foot though; it started way outside the far post and just crept inside it on arrival at the goal-line, having bent agonisingly around the right hand of Butland. FFS is I believe the relevant abbreviation these days.

It was a blow; but credit to fans and players alike they all kept going. Within a couple of minutes Noel Hunt was showing that energy BM wanted as he sped down Leeds' right wing before hammering a low ball across the face of goal. Ross Mac was steaming in to meet it. On another day…he would have met it on the half-volley and it would have ricocheted into the roof of the net. On another day, yes…but not today. Today, it rocketed just over the bar into the Kop.

With 20 minutes still to go McDermott made his final change, another 'sh** or bust' move to my mind; sending on Dom Poleon and taking off Scott Wootton. As the game moved into added time Leeds were piling on the pressure and the Kop was doing its level best to suck the ball into the net in front of us; if only we could rescue a point from this game then it might just be that turning point we've been looking for.

And then it happened. Ross McCormack went haring down the right wing and scuffed a low ball across goal with his right foot. Michael Morrison somehow gets his foot to the ball in front of Noel Hunt and hammers it at Jason Pearce's head, just to the right of the Charlton net. It cannons off Pearce and bounces back towards the penalty spot where Aidy White is sprinting towards goal with Diego Poyet (son of Gus who was watching from the stands) close behind him. Poyet pushes White firmly in the back and our number '14' goes sprawling. After the briefest of moments the referee was pointing to the spot and Elland Road was in raptures at last. A point! We were going to salvage a point! Never has a solitary point looked so juicy.

It took an age for the referee to book Poyet and to then make sure everyone was outside the area, and all the while Ross McCormack stood patiently with the ball tucked under his arm. I was pretty confident Ross was going to score this one; I assumed that since he'd missed three of his last six spot-kicks, he must have been practising after training every day, certainly since he missed the last one down at Loftus Road just a month ago. The management wouldn't let him take it otherwise would they? We had Stephen Warnock on the pitch, he who has a one hundred per cent record for us, so Ross must have been practising and scoring 99 out of a 100 at Thorp Arch if he was taking it. But no, this is Leeds bloody United we are talking about here, we don't do the obvious. Ross stepped up confidently enough and struck the ball firmly with his right foot, sending it skidding across the turf towards a spot just inside the keeper's right hand post. A spot where coincidentally, Ben Hamer's outstretched right hand was hovering. Ball duly struck hand and went away for a corner.

Unbelievable! Un-bloody-believable! Come on lads, own up, who's smashed a f****** mirror?

And that was that; a sixth defeat in seven games; we were officially the worst team in the Championship on current form. We'd remain 12 points ahead of that final relegation spot with most teams now having seven to play; 21 points to play for.

Cellino

Predictably, after the Charlton game there were more calls for McDermott to resign or be sacked. Equally predictably, McDermott was adamant he would not resign and that he just needed an end to the uncertainty around the club to start to improve our fortunes. Defiantly he told reporters, "We have to get ready for Wigan now and we have to get a result. I'm not giving up on this and the players won't either. Everyone has to be in it together". Well, we were all certainly in it, in it right up to our necks. All we needed now was the Devil to race by in his speedboat and the good ship Leeds United would surely capsize and sink in the swamp.

At least it did look as though the various parties were now stepping up the search for Plan B, just in case the appeal decision went against Sig. Cellino. The evening after the Charlton game, both Massimo Cellino and Mike Farnan separately spoke on Sky TV, explaining they were now talking to each other, exploring ways they might work together, whichever way the appeal decision went. Massimo talked of, "living a nightmare" while he waited for the appeal outcome and Farnan spoke of constructive discussions taking place with the Italian. There was some talk that under the purchase agreement Cellino had signed with GFH Cellino now had the rights to offer his shares for sale to a third party but that GFH required the sale to be at the same value as Cellino paid. It didn't make any sense to me, but then I was only a Finance Director for thirty years…Depending on who you believed, that purchase price, for 75% of the club remember, was either £25m or £35m. If it was indeed the latter then I will be seeking a dark place in which to sit for a few weeks with a damp towel over my head. Quite how and in what manner Farnan and Cellino could work together was beyond me; if Cellino won the appeal why would he need or want Farnan? And if he lost, then surely Farnan would not be prepared to pay what Cellino had paid for the shares?

But anyway, that was just a little bit of good news, that Cellino and Farnan were best buddies and seemed hopeful that whatever Cellino's appeal fate, they would find a way forward. Farnan stated again and again that he and his backers would not entertain administration, which he said was in no one's interest. But as with all things Leeds United there is always a Ying to our Yang and when McDermott gave his pre-Wigan game press conference he confided that he'd been subject to late night phone calls from irate Leeds United fans intent on abusing him. Terrific! The other bad news this week was contained in the latest set of accounts for the club that showed a loss of almost £10 million and suggested that at the date of the accounts, 30th June 2013, the club had built up debts of around £25 million!

All eyes this week though were on the appeal. First of all we were told that QC Tim Kerr would be announcing his verdict at 6pm on Friday night, so alarms were set all over Yorkshire for 5:55pm. Then we were told that wasn't right and there would now be a further delay, probably until Monday. Alarms were reset. As if to fill in the time, the YEP then published yet more revelations about the manner in which GFH had been running the club, and in particular the manner in which they'd tried to run Brian McDermott.[1] Seemingly it wasn't only a few fans that were abusing McDermott. Apparently, GFH had begun to get very nervous as our form collapsed after Christmas and they asked McDermott to present reports explaining the poor results. I actually saw nothing much wrong with this, as it's only what any right-minded owners would require of any business manager if the business results were failing. I guess this was just another part of the "stuff" McDermott referred to the other day, stuff that was affecting him and his players' performances. I actually felt the YEP was sensationalising it all a bit, though I did wonder what GFH would do with the "strategy to be undertaken, list of players and squad formation" that they wanted to receive 24 hours prior to each game. Then again, had this been carried out regularly maybe even someone in Bahrain would have posed the question, "What the f*** is Jimmy Kebe's name doing on there again?"

[1] http://www.yorkshireeveningpost.co.uk/sport/leeds-united/latest-whites-news/leeds-united-gfh-in-amazing-attack-on-whites-boss-1-6541471

As it was, the requirement was seldom fulfilled and it appears that David Haigh didn't pass some of the requests on, preferring to try to protect his under pressure manager as best he could. Maybe it was this that cost Haigh his contract with GFH.

Not many were very confident about the trip to the DW Stadium on Saturday to face in-form Wigan. I actually thought we might get away without a hiding though, as we managed to do at Burnley recently. Mark was with me again as we motored up the M6 early; it was another live on Sky, Saturday lunchtime kick-off jobby. This was another new ground for me; I'd been to the old Wigan ground, Springfield Park, in 1987, for our FA Cup quarter final that year against the Latics. Sadly, I can't remember much about it other than we won it 2 – 0. My programme collection also tells me I was there for a fourth division game with Bradford City, in September 1979, a game Wigan won 4 – 1, but again I can remember nothing about it or even why I was there! A clue may be that there were several familiar names in the Bradford team photo in the programme; Terry Cooper, Mick Bates and David McNiven, though research has told me that the Terry Cooper, who played in midfield that day for Bradford, was not the Revie Legend I perhaps thought he was! The DW is also home to the rugby league giants, Wigan Warriors.

Pre-match research told me that getting a drink near the DW Stadium would not be possible until 10:45am, when the Marquee, a bar at the ground similar to our own Pavilion, was due to open. A nearby pub, the Red Robin, was not supposed to be open until 11am either. As it happens, we arrived just before 10am and found a roadside parking spot right opposite the pub. It was spitting with rain at the time, so we sat in the car and fiddled with our mobiles; I checked the latest Twitter news while Mark placed his Grand National bets. I could see a group of lads pacing up and down outside the Red Robin's entrance and we surmised that maybe they knew something we didn't. Sure enough, within a few minutes the doors opened and the group of lads disappeared inside and we followed them in.

It's a decent pub, part of the Fayre and Square chain, and we passed an hour or so in there before adjourning to the Marquee. The Marquee was less appealing. It's built under one of the stands and in theory should be ideal as a place for away fans to drink. Unfortunately, like so many venues we visit, it just didn't seem prepared for the number of fans who turned up. By the time we arrived, they'd run out of draught lager, yet the queues at the bar were still horrendous and the bar staff seemed totally overwhelmed. Nigel had joined us by this time and we eventually managed to get a few bottles of Coors Light and a pint of Worthington's for Nigel and since we were in the land of the meat pie we all had one of those to soak up the beer. Most of the usual lads and lasses were by this time sampling the delights of the Marquee – Andy, Wayne, Mike and Simon were there, Nick and Karen, Wigan White and Max who I know from the LUFCtalk forum, and loads more. Paying a visit to the bogs before we left, I noticed 'Welsh' Andy looking the worse for wear and being looked after by Wayne. The bog floor was a death trap as it was now very wet either with water or...well, let's just hope it was water. Poor old Andy had apparently slipped in there and gone down like the proverbial sack of spuds.

The final short walk was to the away entrance and thence into the North Stand. For a ground that was only opened some fifteen years ago and one that has graced (?) the Premiership for the last eight seasons or so, I couldn't understand why it didn't seem to be coping with 3,400 Leeds fans very well. Yet again the concourse under our stand was absolutely rammed and it was a struggle to inch your way along to the right stairwell, let alone try to get into the toilet block. I am convinced that sooner or later there is going to be an emergency in one of these places and the ensuing panic is going to bring back all those issues raised by Hillsborough and Ibrox that we thought and hoped were long behind us.

Finally, Nigel, Mark and I made it up into the stand and then we found ourselves a space right near the front; once again we ignored the actual seat numbers we were all allocated as they were all in different rows. As the teams came out to the usual fanfares and flag waving we buttoned up our jackets to keep out the rain that was still gently wafting in towards us.

We'd picked up the team selection from a couple of lads sat in the Marquee, one of them handing us his mobile. Once again our Brian had tinkered a bit with the side from Tuesday night.

Butland

Wootton Lees Pearce

Byram   Warnock

Tonge Brown McCormack

Hunt   Smith

Subs: Cairns, Zaliukas, Murphy, Mowatt, Stewart, Poleon and Pugh.

I have set out the side as I thought it would play – so in my mind it was a 5 – 3 – 2 formation, though to be honest it could equally have been a 4 – 4 – 2 with Wootton and Warnock as full-backs and Byram right mid-field. I confess having watched the game I was none the wiser.

Wigan had been my pre-season favourites to go straight back up to the Premiership this year and although they'd struggled early on they had now started to justify my faith in them. They sat comfortably in the play-off positions and next weekend they faced Arsenal, at Wembley, in an FA Cup semi-final. They were of course the Cup holders, having beaten Man City last year in the final as well as knocking them out of this year's competition in the last round. They are clearly a decent side and under new manager Uwe Rosler have steadily climbed the Championship table. Previous manager Owen Coyle was sacked just before the Latics went to Elland Road in December, losing to the Whites 2 – 0 with two McCormack goals. Something similar would have been fantastic today.

But it was not to be. This was another pretty unmemorable game of football; following the typical template of Championship matches where neither side was really any better than the other. There would be a total of just four shots on target in the whole game and we managed just one of those, a tame Michael Tonge effort. The game was settled in the 33rd minute when our defence let itself down once again.

James McArthur won the ball out on the Wigan right wing and was allowed to run unchallenged almost to the edge of our area having played a neat one-two with ex-Leeds man Stephen Crainey. Eventually Tom Lees sticks a leg out and nicks the ball off his toe but only prods it a couple of yards outside the box where Martyn Waghorn hits it first time with his left foot. It was a weak sort of an effort that went all along the ground but somehow Butland saw it late and although he got his right hand to it his wrist wasn't strong enough to keep it out and he merely diverted it into the corner of the net. It was not the action of an England goalkeeper.

That was pretty much the only action of the first half, a half that hardly kept the 16,443 fans in the ground interested, so goodness knows what the TV viewers thought. The Leeds fans once again seemed resigned to another defeat as soon as that shot crept past Butland and they spent the rest of the half coming up with ever more inventive chants. We began with the obvious "You're nothing special we lose every week", and then as the Wigan drummer began to pound out a beat we told the Latics fans that "We're Leeds United, we don't need a drum", although it was handy to keep time for several other chants. In the 14th minute the score board signalled a minute's applause to remember Chris Loftus and Kevin Speight, the two Leeds fans so tragically murdered in Turkey, 14 years ago to the day. Wigan fans on all sides of the ground joined with the Leeds fans in the applause which was great to see. Early in the game all the Leeds fans turned their backs in a mini protest against GFH and later chanted "The Football League's corrupt, the Football League's corrupt, and now you're gonna believe us…the Football League's corrupt" in one final attempt to sway the verdict in the appeal hearing perhaps. A rumour was going around that the reason for the delay in the appeal decision was that the Football League didn't want it to affect today's game. More likely they didn't want a demonstration live on Sky TV! With all this in our minds it was easy to forget there was a game going on. It was still 1 – 0 at half time, the only 'flare' on display being a bright blue one launched onto the pitch from somewhere in the Leeds contingent, the acrid smoke once again choking off the singing.

The second half was much the same, the only difference really being an increasingly bizarre set of decisions coming from referee Neil Swarbrick that sparked another, "The Football League's corrupt", chant. Time and time again Leeds were penalised for minor tugs and pushes, yet when a Wigan player clearly hauled Stephen Warnock back with a high tackle that would have earned ten minutes in the sin-bin had this been a Warriors game, Swarbrick waved play on! McDermott took Hunt off in the 69th minute to give Dom Poleon another try out but once again he failed to make much of a mark on the game. Hunt was as ineffectual as ever and, if true, his twenty five grand a week wage looks more outlandish with each passing game.

The Leeds fans all stayed behind long after all the Wigan fans had left and we continued to sing MOT and, "We all love Leeds", until all the Leeds players had disappeared down the tunnel. There was no particular anger today; I think everyone had expected us to get well beaten. Hence a 1 – 0 score line was seen as a relative success.

As Mark and I made our way the short distance back to the car, Mark suddenly stops and peers more closely at his iPhone screen. "Cellino passes Owners' and Directors' Test appeal" he reads. "Are you sure?" I ask, peering over his shoulder. "Yeah, think so, it's all over Twitter". Then another tweet pops up saying that the Football League will make an announcement at 5pm and then within seconds yet another one suggesting it would be 3pm! I refused to get excited yet. But as we crawled along in the traffic trying to escape Wigan more and more tweets began to come through saying it was a done deal and Massimo Cellino was indeed the new owner of Leeds United. When Mark spotted a tweet from Mike Farnan saying just: "Congratulations Cellino #lufc #MOT !!!!", even I began to dream.

Eventually we heard confirmation on BBC radio as the commentator interrupted his description of how Crystal Palace were hammering some more nails into Cardiff City's relegation coffin; Palace would win the game 3 – 0 and almost certainly we would be making that awful trip to Cardiff again next season.

In an exclusive article given to the Sun, Cellino was saying all the right things; he told Leeds fans, "I will make your club great again", and he promised to return the club to the Premiership by 2016 and to buy back Elland Road and Thorp Arch as soon as next week! He was due in London on Monday when he promised to give a full press conference to outline his immediate plans. All Leeds fans should remember well exactly where they were at 3pm on 5th April 2014; in years to come it may well be a "Where were you?" moment.

A 'Where were you?' moment for Leicester City fans occurred around 5pm on the day of our game at Wigan as the Foxes secured promotion back to the Premier League when QPR and Derby both lost. The good news for Leeds was that released a further £200,000 payment in respect of Kasper Schmeichel's transfer from Leeds in June 2011. Massimo might be grateful for that in the coming months.

Me outside the DW stadium before the Wigan game

One 'F' in fiasco

After experiencing the euphoria of believing Cellino was home and dry on Saturday afternoon, reality kicked in again on Sunday when I realised there could still be a few twists and turns to navigate. In particular, I read an article by David Conn for the Guardian which confirmed my original understanding of how the Italian tax case came about. It confirmed that the suspicious part of the whole saga was how Cellino had only set up the USA Company, 'Freetime Miami', a short while before sailing Nelie the yacht to Sardinia. Hence it did look very much as though that was a manoeuvre specifically designed to evade the import duty. As explained in the Guardian article, QC Tim Kerr had only upheld the appeal as there was as yet no documented evidence that Cellino's actions were "dishonest". However, it was also clear that he wasn't ruling out the possibility that there could be such evidence in June, when the written reasons for the "conviction" over the unpaid tax were due to be published by the Italian judge. If those written reasons documented that Cellino was "dishonest" in setting up that US company, then the Football League would have evidence of dishonesty and would be within their rights and rules to disqualify Cellino. The article also explained how the purchase price was arrived at. The business was bought for £11m (presumably the estimated value of any assets the club has such as the value of the playing squad and any other physical assets together with any goodwill payment) plus another £23m to pay off the debts of the club. That at least made a bit more sense.[1]

We all waited patiently on Monday to hear what Massimo Cellino had to say; he was due to arrive in London and give a press conference and we were told he would definitely be at Vicarage Road on Tuesday night for the Watford game. The next act in this increasingly chaotic pantomime though, was an input from the players; well, if the Daily Star is to be believed anyway. The often controversial paper published an article

[1] http://www.theguardian.com/football/2014/apr/06/massimo-cellino-football-league-leeds?CMP=twt_gu

online under the headline: "EXCLUSIVE: Massimo Cellino facing revolt from Leeds stars...and he wants to axe McDermott".[1] I read the article in disbelief. I had to keep telling myself that this was just a red-top rag trying to stir up a hornets nest...but if it was true, I would be aghast. It basically told us that the players were so upset at the way Cellino had "bad-mouthed" them after recent displays and how he'd disclosed contract details of certain players that the squad regarded Cellino as a "hate figure". A "senior source" at the club was quoted as saying: "I can't see the players running through brick walls for the new man coming in. There is trouble ahead and it could get very messy indeed." Unbelievable! I hadn't noticed many brick walls being disturbed at Rochdale or Hillsborough or Elland Road in any games since Christmas; who the hell do these players think they are? I was really angry and was just desperate to believe there was no truth in the article. Whereas I initially felt that the players would go out on Tuesday night and sweat blood for the cause under the new regime, I was now not so sure. I did have to concede that Cellino had been very wrong to name players and salaries – it was yet another stupid and naïve act of a maverick owner – but in my book, to threaten revolt, thus taking their annoyance out on the fans, is just not acceptable. Once again I couldn't get rid of the thought that there are so many aspects of football these days that I just detest.

With no sensible trains returning to Stafford from Watford on a Tuesday night, I'd decided to drive to this one but I did have company as Kentley the Stokie was hitching a lift. We met at junction 15, leaving his motor in the Holiday Inn car park, and then drove the 160 or so miles to Watford. It was an uneventful trip and with Kentley talking non-stop for three hours the time soon passed! We parked in the Watford Girls Grammar, where Mark and I parked a couple of years ago, although we nearly reversed out again when we discovered they were now charging £7; "We're not leaving it the week mate", I protested!

[1] http://www.dailystar.co.uk/sport/football/373258/EXCLUSIVE-Massimo-Cellino-facing-REVOLT-from-Leeds-stars-and-he-wants-to-AXE-McDermott

We headed straight for the Oddfellows pub, in Fearnley Street, that is about midway between the Girls' Grammar and the ground; again, I've been here before on previous visits and remembered they usually have a BBQ going in the beer garden at the rear of the pub. Over the course of the next two and a quarter hours I met dozens of folk I know from my travels away with Leeds. Sat in the bar when we arrived were Keith and Gill the good folk from Southend; I've bumped into Keith a few times this season – most notably at Ipswich way back in August when I met him at the Beer Festival and then saw him again after the game with a tear in his eye celebrating a famous victory. The hope and optimism we all had that day seems light years away now. Adam, Conor and his girlfriend Imogen were next to arrive – it was Imogen's first ever football match! What a game to start with if the Cellino era does ultimately prove successful! I spotted Steve and Stu across the room and they came over for a chat; Andy and Lily were there, PockWhite's mate Martin joined us, and the other Martin and Daniel arrived; everyone was there! The only problem was that once again our thirst was greater than the pub's capacity to quench it so the Stella ran out quite quickly and the Doom Bar pumps looked to be only for show! Oh, I do have one more complaint about the BBQ as well. The cheeseburger I had was absolutely superb…but it was also the smallest burger I have ever seen if I exclude those one bite efforts you get as nibbles at posh Christmas drinks parties! We all had a fabulous time though and everyone was convinced that the players would all be going balls out for a victory to get Cellino off the mark. Conor spotted the team announcement on his Twitter feed just after 7pm.

Butland
Wootton Lees Pearce Warnock
Poleon Tonge Brown Mowatt
McCormack Hunt

Subs: Cairns, White, Pugh, Smith, Murphy, Zaliukas, Stewart.

I had this sneaking feeling that Dom Poleon would get a start – he's had so many late substitutions recently but we'd never really given him the chance to get the pace of a game. Now was his chance. There was rather too much Hunt in this team for me though and an excess of Mowatt too.

I made my way up to find my seat and was incredulous to find it was right next to RamseyWhite, aka Phil, so we mulled over the team together while I demolished a hot-dog bought from the counter down in the concourse – another concourse incidentally totally unfit for purpose. This one gets the record for 'narrowest concourse in the Championship' although strangely it didn't seem as crushed as many of the others I've suffered recently. Leeds brought 1,789 today out of a total attendance of 16,212.

Kentley appeared to take his place next to us just before kick-off and Martin and Daniel arrived in the row in front. The Leeds choir was in great voice and there was an early rendition of the Cellino tribute: "Cellino-oh-oh, Cellino-oh-oh, he comes from Italy, don't pay no VAT, Cellino-oh-oh Cellino-oh-oh", or that's what it sounded like anyway!!!!Even the first MOT was a rip roaring, ear bursting version that almost lifted the roof off the Vicarage Road Stand. Out on the pitch the Leeds players looked up for this one. We were in our all white strip too – some fans had voiced an opinion that the mustard coloured away strip just didn't cut it and was bringing us bad luck, so many were pleased by this; I guess they'd conveniently forgotten that we'd just lost four out of the last five games at Elland Road wearing white, conceding a ridiculous 13 goals! Anyway, Cellino was in the stand; he'd spoken with McDermott before the game and hadn't sacked him, so let's get ready to rumble!

We didn't rumble for very long. In fact it looked very much like Watford had rumbled us. Within seconds of the start, the Hornets were buzzing all over the pitch; the ball was pinging about like the pitch was a giant bagatelle board and the Leeds players were already looking a yard short of pace. Wootton in particular was being given a right run around by Ikechi Anya who was turning him inside out in the right back berth. With barely eight minutes gone, Watford keeper Manuel Almunia takes a goal kick. It lands on half way and a Leeds player hoofs it back into the Watford half. The next few seconds were a blur. Watford play three quick short passes and then, almost without looking, a Watford midfielder clips the ball down the left wing over the head of Scotty Wootton. Anya gets to it first and once again turns Wootton one way and then the other before standing the ball up at the back post. Two Watford players were being marked by three Leeds players but it was Almen Abdi who got up unchallenged to thump a header past Butland. It was our old friend the six-yard box header. Two of the three Leeds players are Warnock and Mowatt and Warnock makes it clear for all to see that he felt Mowatt should have been tracking Abdi. Mowatt listened to the bollocking for all of a nanosecond and then just turned his back and jogged away, leaving Warnock just staring at the youngster, slowly shaking his head. Our bubble was already burst. It had been unreasonable to expect our poor side to rally and suddenly become world-beaters just because a man called Cellino had arrived...even if he had now paid the rest of their wages for them. We are just not very good footballers!

The Watford fans were jubilant and their plucky mascot, Harry the Hornet, was banging his drum for all he is worth. Fair play to the Leeds fans they started to use the drum beat to back their own songs and slowly we were back on-side with the team, albeit we did tell the home fans "You're nothing special, we lose every week", just in case they were getting ahead of themselves and thinking they were now heading for the play-offs. In truth, Watford were at best average themselves ...but we were way, way below average.

On the half hour, Ross McCormack suddenly believed he was Wayne Rooney or David Beckham, as he spotted Almunia off his line and tried to beat the keeper from the half way line, but the ex-Arsenal man back-peddled and easily caught the ball just in front of his line. It would be our only shot on target in the first half. Within a couple of minutes, Watford were attacking us with pace down the flanks again and we succumbed once more. Anya collected the ball in the left wing corner, touching it to the overlapping Riera who then played it low across the box. The Leeds defence then assumed that was Anya's work done for the night, I assume they thought he was off to his hotel or something and they proceeded to ignore him while they focussed on the player with the ball on the other wing. When the ball inevitably comes swinging back in it is of course the now unmarked Anya who nods it past Buckland. It looks to me like Mowatt is the one who should have tracked back with Anya and Warnock obviously thinks so too; once again he appears to be giving young Mowatt a bit of a rollicking and once again Mowatt appears to be not arsed one little bit.

Over on the touchline, it was annoying me to see McDermott stood quietly with his hands in his pockets while the Hornets' boss, Beppe Sannino, was going bananas with his lads who were two-nil up! I have no idea whether it makes any difference if your coach jumps up and down and swears a lot but it would make me feel better and all the fans near me were now doing it! Having said that, it wasn't proving to be much of a birthday for our Brian – he was 53 today.

Half time came and went and the hapless Mowatt was withdrawn for Cameron Stewart who I am sure is a footballer but I am just not sure what kind. He made little difference anyway. In the 67th minute we were three down and I did at least spot McDermott half-heartedly kick a water bottle into the dug-out. He was just about to give Noel Hunt the hook and send on Matt Smith. I'd already discussed with Ramsey why on earth Smith wasn't on earlier when it was clear the Poleon – Hunt combo was having no impact; two little uns wasn't working so we might as well try one big un! Anyway, back to the 67th minute: How many 'F's are there are in fiasco?

The normally reliable Jason Pearce makes a sloppy header out to Tom Lees in the Leeds right back corner, under pressure from a Hornet. In fact, Tom plays the ball so hurriedly that it looked for all the world as if he thought he might get stung! The ball cannons off the attacker into the air and is picked up by a second Hornet who touches the ball forward to Troy Deeney. There is no danger; 23 other defences in the Championship would know what to do; only one would not...ours. Lees and Wootton have Deeney trapped between them but neither attacks the ball; instead all three players are just shimmying towards the Leeds net doing a sort of 'Jake the Peg'. When they reach the corner of the six-yard box, that

Bermudian Triangle of perpetual fear for Leeds defenders, Deeney puts his foot through the ball and it rockets past Butland into the roof of his net. Even McDermott would say after the game that it was a shocking goal to concede and, "it should have been cleared".

That was the signal for the angst of the Leeds fans to be aired once again with that "We're sick of it, we're sh**" chant and then to the home fans, "How sh** must you be you've only scored three". We briefly told our players they were, "not fit to wear the shirt", and, "You don't deserve your wages", too, as we did at Rochdale and Wednesday amongst a few other places in recent months. It was all very sad. At the end of the game we still managed to give a huge rendition of MOT and several rounds of "We all love Leeds" but it sounded almost as if we were singing it to ourselves, for ourselves, and maybe for Mr Cellino. McDermott did briefly come towards us applauding but then he quickly turned on his heels and sought the sanctuary of the tunnel. The players looked dazed as they stood in a line, hands above their heads, perhaps incredulous that they were not being lambasted. We had made our views heard during the game of course, not least when sarcastically shouting, "Olé", as we strung a few passes together, or cheering fanatically when we got an odd shot on target, however weak it was. When the majority of fans were doing that I was uncomfortable, something was telling me that was not actually helping the cause. If our players were low in confidence surely that would only make it worse? Or could it not get any worse? Perhaps not.

I'd chatted with Andy J at half time and he told me how he just felt Watford had far better footballers than we did; how Watford, like many other Championship teams, just did the basics much better than we did. After the game, McDermott seemed to agree when he said: "If you don't do the basics right, which we're not doing at this moment in time, you don't get the result." Looking towards the next game, now a vital potential "six-pointer" against lowly Blackpool, McDermott said, "We need characters to go out and play on that pitch on Saturday"; the reporter asked him without any trace of irony, "Do you have eleven of those Brian?"

All the way home I kept asking Kentley to check Twitter to see if Cellino had sacked McDermott; I was absolutely sure he would. But there was nothing of the sort. There were a few quotes from Cellino saying how he was going to be very hands on at the club, even, "looking after the grass", and, "driving the bus", but he appeared to be saying that McDermott had the rest of the season to prove himself. I was just no longer sure our Brian had it in him to lift this group of players; surely we needed someone in that changing room to get some fires lit? Maybe Cellino would do that too. Was it any coincidence that Vinnie Jones was in the dressing room the day we beat Millwall and McDermott was not around the day we beat Huddersfield? The only other game we'd won this year was at Yeovil where the wind beat everybody. Come what may, I was sure we needed three more points or I still felt I could be watching League One football again next season. Leeds ended the day in 16th spot in the table, now just eight points ahead of the final relegation position, currently filled by Millwall who had torn up the form book tonight by winning 1 – 0 at Wigan. Who said, "squeaky bum time?"

Stephen Warnock applauds us at the end of yet another fiasco

One foot on the Stairway to Heaven?

The days leading up to the Blackpool game were calm and quiet in LS11...you didn't actually believe that line did you? Of course they weren't. On Wednesday, Massimo Cellino arrived at Elland Road and had his security staff carry out a full sweep of the offices. They discovered hidden spy cameras in the board room and toilets! Quite why there were cameras in the toilets is anyone's guess; it was hardly a secret that there have been some huge cocks in charge at Elland Road recently. Cellino called the police and WYP sent in a team to investigate a possible theft of club money to install the cameras. Word would eventually come out that David Haigh had now resigned his position as MD, or was it CEO? We were never sure if he ever got to be CEO. Anyway, he was gone, but no one was sure if the finding of the hidden cameras and his resignation were connected in any way.

After a morning at ER with his finance man, Daniel Arty, arranging to pay a £500,000 PAYE bill to stave off another winding up order and then paying the balance of the players' wages, Cellino sensibly adjourned to the pub; the Old Peacock on Elland Road to be precise. He was buying drinks for fans in there and was happy to have his photo taken; photos that were soon posted all over Twitter. Later that same evening, more photos would appear of Cellino with fans, this time in the city centre.

He somehow also found time to speak with the press as well and every time he opened his mouth a richly descriptive new quote would come out. He spoke about the now infamous telephone call last Sunday saying: "I was a bit drunk and depressed, it was mean and embarrassing that he published it. But after I thought maybe it wasn't so wrong – that was me"[1.] Regarding the current status of the club, he said: "We are not sick, we are not in the hospital, we can survive. We can heal, it's a cold". He summarised his task as: "I want to transform Leeds from Highway to Hell to Stairway to Heaven".

---

1 http://www.theguardian.com/football/2014/apr/10/massimo-cellino-owner-leeds-united

He'd even tried to persuade one of the reporters to join his rock band 'Maurilios', for a forthcoming concert in Sardinia. Oh yes, a quiet week in LS11! As Cellino himself told the press this week: "You are not going to be bored with me".

Thursday saw the Football League formally but "reluctantly" clear Cellino to take up the role of Director of Leeds United, a role he was already well into by the time the FL statement hit the media. At least it was all building up to a bit of a celebration at Elland Road this weekend when Blackpool came to town. It felt like a new start for us and even Brian McDermott told us it was a, "new chapter of that book I'm going to write".

I still felt the Blackpool game was critical to our survival. Most fans were of the opinion that the run of results the bottom three teams would need to achieve to send us down was just not, well, achievable. But I wasn't sure, *always expect the unexpected*. I *was* sure that just three more points would be enough. Blackpool were on a run even worse than us, albeit not by much. The records of the two sides over the last twenty games read like a footballing horror story:

        Leeds   P20, W3, D4, L13, Pts 13
        Blackpool P20, W2, D5, L13, Pts 11

It was rumoured that Blackpool manager Barry Ferguson might be naming himself in the team to try to turn things around. Ferguson had taken temporary charge of the side when Paul Ince was sacked in January. The Blackpool Supporters Association had even sent a letter to the players demanding they up their game. In fact there was an open letter doing the rounds at Leeds too, although whereas the Blackpool letter was actually read out before training to the players, the Leeds letter became just a debating point between fans as to whether or not the Leeds players were trying or not.

I was travelling solo again today and in the Pavilion I plonked myself down at a table with the three lads from County Durham again and settled down to watch the QPR v Forest game on the big screen; the lunch time kick-off. Lee Peltier was, bizarrely, playing in midfield for Forest but to little positive effect as they'd go on to lose the game 5 – 2, further damaging their slim hopes of a play-off place this season.

One of the Durham lads was reading today's Yorkshire Evening Post and I could see the front page headline: "UNITED CALL IN POLICE OVER SPY CAMERAS; Fraud inquiry into use of club funds". At the back of the paper there were four more full pages all dedicated to telling us about Massimo Cellino; the new Messiah.

The Pavilion patrons listened as Peter Lorimer and Mick Jones joked about the cameras and then discussed the more serious issue as to whether we had enough points yet to stay up; they reckoned we did, just. I was eager to learn the line-up for today; eager to find out just who those 11 'big characters' were. Soon after 2pm, one of the Durham lads passed me his mobile showing the team:

Butland
Wootton Lees Zaliukas Pearce Warnock
Brown Tonge Murphy
Smith McCormack
Subs: Cairns, White, Pugh, Mowatt, Hunt, Stewart, Poleon

As Sam Byram and Rudy were both still injured, this was probably the team I would have picked; a glance along the names on the bench told me none of them was better than the ones in the team. Would I describe them all as 'big characters'? That's another question altogether! The side included three changes to the team that so miserably succumbed at Vicarage Road on Tuesday; out went Hunt, Poleon and Mowatt and in came Smith, Zaliukas and Murphy, the latter back after three games on the bench. The only thing that really perplexed me was how the hell are we getting away with playing Michael Brown with a huge '17' emblazoned on his back with Cellino in the stand? Kick off time today for our game, as for every other game this weekend, was seven minutes later than usual, 3:07pm. It was on 15th April, 1989, 25 years ago almost to the day, that 96 Liverpool football fans left home to go to watch an FA Cup semi-final at Hillsborough between their beloved Liverpool and Nottingham Forest. None of them would return alive. At 3:06pm, the exact time the game in 1989 was abandoned, the Leeds and Blackpool players lined up around the centre circle and a minute's silence was immaculately observed. The roar that greeted the referee's whistle at the end of the silence seemed all the louder for the contrast. 23,416 were in the ground, a decent crowd, but maybe not as many as I expected would want to greet Massimo Cellino on what was effectively his first home game as outright owner of the club. Try as I might I could not see Cellino up in the East Stand and I wondered if the maverick Italian had decided to sample the Kop instead; it was just the sort of thing he'd do. I would eventually discover he was watching from a box at one end of the East Stand. This was also the first anniversary of Brian McDermott's appointment as Leeds' manager and he seemed to be marking it with a few changes to his wardrobe. As he took his place in the technical area he was resplendent in a Leeds United tracksuit and not his usual dark blue business suit. I felt sure that must be something to do with Cellino, a symbolic gesture to try to persuade the Italian he is really a 'coach' (which is what Cellino says he wants) and not a manager. Cellino has made it abundantly clear he is the only 'manager' the club needs. After the game it was the first question Eddie Gray had for McDermott and I must admit I didn't believe McDermott when he told Eddie it was his daughter's idea; she had apparently told her Dad, "Suits are for politics". Nice try Brian, but I ain't swallowing that one. It did look far more professional to me though, sort of defined him as one of the 'team'. You would never see Stefano Domenicali in the Ferrari pit in a suit would you? Actually we wouldn't be seeing him there at all any more as he resigned this weekend, Stefano that is, not McDermott.

Leeds began the game with plenty of the ball but still looked shaky at the back to me. On one occasion Zaliukas made one of his trade-mark first time passes out to Tom Lees without really looking to see how much pressure Lees was under. Somehow Tom got himself out of trouble. There were positive signs though; in particular Luke Murphy seemed to be playing a much more attacking role, something we know he used to do all the time at Crewe. We hadn't seen it from him at Elland

Road since the opening day when he scored that winner in the dying moments against Brighton. A last ditch tackle just stopped him getting in a shot in the early moments today. In the 21st minute, after 319 minutes of football without a goal, we got the opener.

Tom Lees played his familiar diagonal ball from the right back area up to Smith. MS flicked the ball on to Ross McCormack in the inside left channel and he held it up while Murphy raced into the box. Ross then slipped the ball in behind the defence for Murphy at the back post. Initially it seemed Murphy had missed his chance as the ball appeared to be heading out of play but suddenly Luke stopped on a sixpence and shifted the ball from his right to his left foot. A 'Pool defender and Matt Gilks in the visitors' goal both bought the dummy and were now sliding past while Murphy kept his footing to sweep the ball into the net. What a relief! We hadn't scored in the last three games and we hadn't taken the lead since the Millwall home game on March 22nd. In fact, this was only the fourth time this calendar year we'd grabbed a lead; in twenty games!

The goal certainly gave Leeds a bit of a lift and Ross McCormack should probably have hit the target with a glancing header from a fabulous running cross by Wootton, who was slowly but surely acclimatising himself to the role of wing-back. Michael Tonge then hit a fierce free-kick through the Blackpool wall that Gilks did well to stop. This was much better, although I felt the OS was perhaps stretching a point to describe this phase of the game later as one of: "fantastic passing football".

The second half saw both sides go close but if anything Blackpool were now having the bulk of the possession and there was always the nagging doubt we'd get caught with one of our usual defensive calamities. In the 65th minute McDermott made his first change and judging by the reaction from the Kop it was a controversial one. Matt Smith loped off the pitch to be replaced by Noel Hunt and as the ex-Reading man sprinted on, a chorus of boos rained down from behind me. It was unfortunate; Smith has become a popular player at Leeds having scored 11 goals; Hunt runs around a lot and, if Cellino is to be believed, gets paid £1.3 million a year for doing so. It was embarrassing though and I didn't think it was right at all. We were winning the game and there was a celebratory air with Cellino sat somewhere in the ground, so there was no need for any negativity. Fortunately, it didn't seem to faze Hunt in the slightest and he immediately started to do what he does well; running all over the pitch.

Actually that isn't fair either; Hunt did win a number of headers when he arrived, something Smith hadn't done too much today. In the 73rd minute, Hunt won another header. Tom Lees launched the ball down the Leeds right wing where Hunt rose to flick a header on to Luke Murphy. The header deceived the Blackpool defence and the ball ran on to the right corner of the six-yard box, in front of the Kop. Murphy got to it and lifted it deliciously across Gilks and into the middle of the net. As Murphy danced over to milk the applause in front of the East Stand we all breathed another sigh of relief, knowing we ought now to pick up those vital three points.

There were a couple more near misses at both ends before the final whistle but it ended 2 – 0 and to all intents and purposes that was the end of the season too. We were not going down...and we had long since accepted we certainly weren't going up! Nigel and I waited for the scores from the other games but they didn't appear on the big screen so we said our farewells and I made my way back to the car.

It was FA Cup semi-final weekend, just as it was 25 years ago, although these days both games are played at Wembley. Arsenal were playing last year's winners, Wigan, who continued to pursue both FA Cup glory and promotion; I listened to the game on the drive home. Arsenal would need extra time and penalties to win through while Hull City would beat Sheffield United on Sunday in the other semi. In those crucial games at the bottom of the Championship, none of the bottom three won; Barnsley lost while Millwall and Yeovil both drew. Leeds were now ten points ahead of Millwall with four games to play, not mathematically safe, but as good as. Next week Leeds go to Oakwell; a win at Barnsley could be enough to condemn them to the drop; how satisfying that would be after the last three years of hammerings and humiliations we've suffered up there!

Leeds not exactly on fire; but lots of smoke

As I gunned the little Peugeot up the M1 for the penultimate away game of the season, at Barnsley, I confess I was feeling tired. It had been a long, difficult season, with few moments of genuine excitement and I was now looking forward to the summer holidays and a break from all things Leeds. The fact that my two lads had arrived home at 2:39am and 3:40am respectively, each climbing the stairs with all the subtlety and dexterity of a blindfolded elephant wearing clogs and cow-bells, probably didn't help either.

The more I do of these away days, the easier the logistics become; last season Mark and I found a roadside parking spot outside a Kia car salesroom on Oakwell View, which as the name suggests is just a stone's throw from the ground. I parked in the same spot this year and walked up the hill past Oakwell to the Metrodome; it was not yet noon. There were only a dozen or so folk in there initially; me, Paul and his family up from Southampton, and a handful of others. I chatted with Paul briefly before grabbing a pint. I slalomed through the Disney style 'snake' queuing system to the bar thinking it all looked a bit over the top with no one at all waiting at the time but by not long after 1pm the place was heaving. By then, not only was the 'snake' section full but the queue stretched almost across the entire room, which must be all of fifty yards or more. I was thankful I'd already had my allowance of a couple of pints as I watched folk shuffle along in the very slow moving queue. I was half watching the Leicester v QPR game being shown on a big screen at one end of the room while I chatted with Andy J and Lily and then Nigel, when he arrived. Leicester would go on to win 1 – 0 and edge ever closer to the title having already secured promotion. Andy introduced me to Paul from the Essex Whites and I also chatted with Heidi Haigh, author of the recently released book, "Follow Me and Leeds United", about being a female follower of the Whites in the turbulent days of the 1970s. At one point, while I was chatting away, I suddenly became aware of a sort of burning smell that was wafting towards me from the back of the room. I couldn't see it myself but apparently someone had decided it would be fun to let off one of those damn smoke bombs over there...inside the bloody room! I decided to escape the smoke for a few minutes and headed for the toilets at the back of the arena. The queue here was almost as long as the one for the bar and after ten minutes I'd only got just inside the toilet block door; inside it was some sight though. There was a row of hand basins along the left-hand wall and standing at the last of them was a huge bloke stood on tip-toes dangling his todger over the edge of the basin, peeing. A chant of, "He's Leeds United, he pees where he wants", spontaneously broke out with the bloke himself conducting us with his spare arm. It was another priceless image that will stay with me for years to come.

Nigel and I made our way down to the ground at about 2:30pm; it was a lovely sunny day, but strangely it was very chilly; a typical early spring day I suppose. Inside the ground the Leeds fans seemed full of the joys of spring too; at one point, in the concourse under the North Stand, a few lads managed to climb up onto the steel girders above our heads while everyone else belted out "We are Leeds" at the tops of their voices and many threw the dregs of their beer in the air for good measure! As tired as I was of this season on the pitch, I will never tire of watching the antics of our fans, despite concluding that they are all as mad as hatters!

Some 4,000 Leeds fans had made the trip to Barnsley; for once nowhere near selling out the allocation we'd been given; it was still a big percentage of the total crowd though, almost a third, that was later reported as just 15,190. That said to me that the home fans had probably already given up on the Tykes chances of hanging on to their Championship status, as Oakwell boasts a capacity of just over 23,000. I couldn't help thinking that if the roles had been reversed; Leeds fans would have packed Elland Road to the rafters to try to urge their team on. Hell, we were even climbing the rafters down in the concourse here! We pretty much still filled most of the north end of the ground today.

The team that took to the pitch with the sound of 4,141 voices belting out "We are Leeds" in their ears was not surprisingly the same one that started against Blackpool last Saturday. Indeed, the only change today was the return after injury of Rudy Austin, who took Cameron Stewart's place on the bench. I assumed that Leeds lost the toss, as the teams changed around so that Leeds kicked towards us in the first half. I do wish teams wouldn't do that but as it happens at least we got a decent view of the only goal of the game.

To be frank, this was another very disappointing game of football and as we've seen so many times this season, neither side seemed to have much grasp of the basic essential skills needed to play the beautiful game. Nigel was in his element again as he constantly complained about Leeds passing to "Mr Cellophane", his name for the apparently invisible player every pass seemed aimed at. But it was not just the passing, it was everything; the passing was poor, but the movement off the ball was also non-existent, so the bloke with the ball was seldom given an outlet even if he had the requisite skill to make the pass. On those rare occasions when a ball found the intended recipient, that player would be unable to control it and it would leak away from him. The ability of both sides to hit the target also left a lot to be desired and barn doors would be untroubled all afternoon. Both sides were as bad as each other and I was just grateful we'd already amassed enough points for it to not matter too much this season anymore. But it meant it was another poor spectacle.

The one worthy move and finish of the game came in the 16th minute and fortunately it was the team in its blue away kit, kicking towards us, that executed it. A long ball was pumped up-field from deep inside the Leeds half, up to the head of Matt Smith, about five yards outside the Barnsley area in the inside right channel. Smith's header found Ross McCormack, back to goal, on the other side of the box. Quick as a flash, McCormack flicked the ball on the volley over his head, spun round, and hit a left foot shot past the Tykes' keeper on the first bounce. It was another touch of class from the Scot; his 29th goal of the season. Leeds' fans predictably went mental, while the players celebrated on the byeline just beneath us. It wasn't long before we goaded the home fans with a few rounds of, "Barnsley's going down, you're going down, you're going, Barnsley's going down", and then on the rare occasions the home side fired a shot over or around our goal, or failed to make a telling pass, we'd remind them: "That's why you're going down, that's why you're going down". When we got bored with that we serenaded McDermott, suggesting he, "Wear the tracksuit every week", or Cellino with that badly rhyming, "Cellino-oh-oh, Cellino-oh-oh, he comes from Italy, don't pay no VAT, Cellino-oh-oh, Cellino-oh-oh". We were getting demob happy. The first half then gradually fizzled out with the only further excitement being another one of those bloody flare things that was hurled from the back of our supporters, initially landing on those at the front, while on the pitch a few tasty Michael Brown tackles got him his usual booking.

Nigel went off to the bogs at half time while Kentley and I sat and watched the on pitch entertainment which consisted of two young lads – one in a red Barnsley top and one in the blue Leeds away top – firing penalties against the Barnsley mascot, Toby the Tyke, a miserable looking dog of unknown species. Both lads were only youngsters but they both hit a mean penalty; the Leeds lad came out on top though scoring four of his five attempts. He was led back over to the Leeds end to a tremendous round of applause and a rousing "We are Leeds" that I'm sure he will remember forever.

Nigel returned just after the shoot-out finished, and he was hot and flustered, telling us: "It's bloody mayhem down there, I kid you not you can't move for folk". The game restarted and had already been underway for a good few minutes when the PA chimed out. "This is a message for the Leeds United fans still in the concourse beneath the North Stand: The game has now restarted, please return to your seats immediately, you are being recorded and the CCTV will be passed to the police". The Leeds fans response to this was pretty predictable: "We're Leeds United, we don't give a f**k"! Apparently the Leeds lads were monkeying on those girders again.

In the second half, Barnsley had more of the ball but they thankfully didn't do much with it. Time and again they worked their way into decent positions only to let fly with shots that peppered those standing at the back of the North Stand. Leeds were now a very tired outfit, with Smith and Murphy in particular looking like they were completely out of gas. On the hour, McDermott brought off Marius Zaliukas who was limping badly, and threw on Noel Hunt. There was no booing this time thankfully. McCormack switched to midfield, with Smith and Hunt up front at the head of a 4 – 4 – 2 formation, with the 5 – 3 – 2 now ditched. The fresh legs of Hunt gave Leeds a new outlet and once or twice it looked as though his pace had got him beyond the home defence only for him to fluff his lines. The lad desperately needs a goal.

Aidy White then came on for the now totally exhausted Matt Smith, with eight minutes left on the clock. Barnsley now looked to have given up the ghost and they appeared just as knackered as we did. Leeds had a spell of possession when we passed the ball back and forth along our back line and the Leeds fans chirped up that, "It's just like watching Brazil"; but believe me it wasn't; it's been a long season, forgive them!

The game ended 0 – 1 to Leeds; our first win at Oakwell since 1997 but more importantly ending that recent run of thrashings at the hands of the Tykes. It was nice to be able to honestly applaud all of our players off the pitch here for once after hurling abuse at them in the last three seasons on this ground. Nigel Gibbs and Brian McDermott were first down the tunnel that exits off the pitch below the North Stand, just to the right of where we stood. There have been rumours of late that Nigel Gibbs is to be given a more prominent role at Leeds, Massimo Cellino apparently having spoken highly of him more than once. Some had even suggested Gibbs could become chief coach ahead of McDermott. For the Blackpool game it was noticeable that McDermott stayed in the dug-out while it was Gibbs who was out in the technical area shouting instructions, further fuelling this particular rumour. As the two of them went past me today, I was struck by how it appeared to be Gibbs that was taking more notice of us than McDermott was, even giving us a powerful Leeds salute on his way past; or was that just my imagination?

I sat with Nigel for a long while as we watched the ground empty and some of the Leeds players had even returned to the pitch for their warm-down by the time we sauntered away. There was just one more away-day to go now, next Saturday at Birmingham and I just wanted to savour this one, a rare away win. As we'd told the Tykes earlier: "How sh** must you be we're winning away!"

At the end of this weekend's games, with another round of matches to come on Easter Monday/Tuesday, Leeds had 53 points and sat 16th in the table. We couldn't now be caught by any of the bottom three, Yeovil, Barnsley and Blackpool. Most teams, including Leeds, had three games to go. Ours were a home game with Forest on Monday (another live on Sky game with a 5:15pm kick-off); away at Birmingham and home to Derby on the final day. Forest and Derby still harboured hopes of a play-off spot while Birmingham were not yet safe from relegation, so all would be tough. I was concerned at how poor Leeds had played today despite getting the win, and just hoped we could find another gear before the Forest game.

Nigel Gibbs gives a very positive looking salute at Oakwell

Fiasco

I set off for Elland Road on Easter Monday at 12:15pm, it felt strange. The game against Forest was yet another Sky TV live game, this one a 5:15pm kick-off. I was half way up our road before remembering my season ticket was still on the bedside table, so I had to roll back down the slope and go and fetch it. I always try to ensure I'm at Elland Road three hours before kick-off just in case there is ever any problem on the motorway; the trip takes anywhere between 90 minutes to a couple of hours depending on traffic.

Just after junction 16 on the M6, the traffic began to slow...and then a couple of miles short of junction 17 we stopped; completely stopped. You know it's going to be a long job when blokes start to get out of their cars to nip across to the shrubbery beyond the Armco. There was soon a line of chaps stood on the hard-shoulder, backs to the road, hands hidden in front of them, steam gently rising. I switched the engine off and pressed the button to lower my window, leaning out to see if I could see anything further up the road. Nothing, just cars in three long 'snakes' going as far as the eye could see. I jumped out and took a photo of the queue and then sent it with a tweet and the hashtag "lufc", warning other Leeds fans to avoid the area if possible. Within seconds I had a tweet from the Manchester Evening News no less, asking if they could use the photo in a piece they were doing about the bank holiday traffic chaos. I tweeted them back to say they could and then began to read other tweets telling me there was a multi-car pile-up near junction 17 and it might be some time before it was cleared. The MEN tweet then appeared crediting me with the photo and then The Express and Star sent one to warn West Brom fans heading for their evening game at Man City, again using my photo! I put the phone down and gazed out of the window. On the hard shoulder I could see two magpies hopping about together; *"Well, you haven't brought me much luck"*, I thought to myself. But then I thought about forgetting my season ticket earlier and I apologised to the magpies and saluted them. I could well have been a few minutes further up the road in the middle of that pile-up...

We were stopped for about an hour in all and so I bowled into the Pavilion at around 3:30pm, still an hour and three quarters before kick-off. I arrived just as Peter Lorimer was doing his bit but I was desperate for the bog (I should have joined the lads on the hard shoulder really!) so I dashed to the toilets before grabbing a pint and sitting down with the three Durham lads who were sat at their usual table. They were eager to tell me they'd spotted my pictures in the programme again, including one of me at Wigan that Mark took. Leeds programme, Manchester Evening News, Express and Star, all in one day!

I was convinced this game with Forest would end 0 – 0. In my researches this week, I'd looked back to see when we last got three consecutive clean sheets. It was February 2013. Funnily enough, that little run also began with a 2 – 0 win over Blackpool and then we had a 1 – 0 win (Millwall) and a 0 – 0 draw with Blackburn. I thought that was uncannily similar to our current run, if we drew with Forest. I also discovered that the referee today, Iain Williamson, was also in charge for that Blackburn game! That would be spooky wouldn't it, if it was 0 – 0 today? I also factored in the two magpies for good measure and decided to risk a couple of quid on an 8/1 shot for a scoreless draw. As usual Daniel thought I was mad and he showed me the Forest team on his phone, telling me: "If we can't beat that Forest team we want shooting; it's sh***". I looked over his shoulder at the team and didn't recognise many names...except one. Matt Derbyshire was listed there. "What about Derbyshire?" I said. "He's rubbish", says Daniel. "Well he wasn't rubbish last December when he rifled a shot past Kenny to win that game at the City Ground", I countered.

For Leeds, Brian McDermott had confounded us all once again with his team selection. We guessed that Zaliukas might not be fit to play, as he'd limped out of the game on Saturday and it was no real surprise therefore that McDermott switched to 4 – 4 – 2 bringing in Rudy in his place. But why change anyone else? WHY PUT BLOODY HUNT BACK IN THE SIDE? But sure enough Hunt replaced Matt Smith. Barmy!

When I parked the car the sun was shining brightly and it felt really warm, so I decided I wouldn't need a jacket. By the time I wandered out of the Pavilion to go across to the ground it was spitting with rain and freezing! It was too late to go back to the car so I'd have to suffer! 20,517 were in Elland Road, and looking around I noticed most still had their coats on! The Leeds players might just as well have kept theirs on too...

Within 90 seconds of the start of this game we knew it was as good as over for us. It was just like being down at Bournemouth all over again; it was another complete fiasco. Forest's McLaughlin won the ball from Michael Brown out on the Forest left wing, deep in their own half. In a flash, Forest made three quick passes to open up the centre of the pitch for McLaughlin to run through. Matt Derbyshire was haring along in front of him with Tom Lees doing his 'mildly interested bystander' thing alongside him. At the perfect moment, McLaughlin slides the ball through past Lees and Derbyshire leaves our Tom for dead to side-foot the ball past Butland. It was yet another shocking example of how not to defend. For all the world it looked like Lees and Pearce still thought Zaliukas must be out there between them, so huge was the gap Derbyshire found. I sank down in my seat, distraught. I am heartily sick of us giving goals away so easily; as with Bournemouth I felt cheated; robbed not only of my two quid bet, but of an afternoon's entertainment. The whole bloody season had been one fiasco after another.

If there was any doubt this game was over after 90 seconds, there was no doubt left after 16 minutes, when Derbyshire robbed Scott Wootton 18 yards from goal to slide the ball past Butland again. I was so tempted to text Daniel just one word: "Derbyshire", maybe with a question mark for good measure.

The rest of the game was no different to most we've witnessed all season. Leeds huffed and puffed with loads of possession, but we seldom created a clear cut chance and hence were restricted to snatching half-chances which we invariably sent high or wide and never handsome. 25 shots the BBC would report we had, of which just five hit the target. Forest had only five shots all day, but all five hit their intended target. Time after time the Leeds back four would pass the ball from one to another until eventually someone would launch the ball forward looking for the head of Noel Hunt. Sometimes he would even win the header but it would never reach a Leeds player and Forest would come away with the ball. If we did try to play it on the ground, the final all-important ball would usually go astray, be intercepted, or one of our forwards would get it tangled up in his feet. This isn't enjoyment anymore. Noel Hunt looks like a player lost; a shadow of the player he once was with Reading and during the game the main debate was about why on earth McDermott had chosen him ahead of Smith again having won two games without him in the side. Jo quipped from behind me: "It used to be the 'c' word I didn't like to hear on the terraces…now it's the 'h' word I never want to hear again!" Everyone knew that on the hour mark Hunt would go off and Smith would replace him, and that is exactly what happened, once again to a huge sarcastic cheer from the Kop. But by this time it was too late; and in any case we didn't have the players on the pitch to get to the byeline to get the ball over to him. Forest were no better mind – it was clear to see why they'd just been on a run of 13 games without a win going back to mid-February before they beat Birmingham on Saturday. That referee didn't help either, at one point Smith was pulled over on the edge of the box with a Forest player clearly almost pulling the shirt off his back but the ref just waved play on. In fact the ref had a dire game and that explained to me why he'd been stuck doing Championship and League One and Two games for ten years without ever progressing to the premiership. He's cr**, that's why.

It's not the fault of the referee though that we lost this game. We are just a very poor side. Each time we win a game, we tend to forget that it's not because we've got any better overnight; it is invariably because the opposition have been dire or by some stroke of luck we've not committed Hara-Kiri in our own half. Most Leeds fans were now convinced this was the worst Leeds team to ever wear the shirt and most now agreed McDermott had not a clue what he was doing. Many even regretted the outcry made when Cellino tried to sack him way back in January. We were still 16th in the table with two games to go.

Blue Noses bloodied

After the latest fiasco against Forest on Monday, I did wonder if we might get news that Cellino had dispensed with the services of Mr McDermott. One manager that had now bitten the dust was David Moyes. In between tweeting, I'd passed the time sitting in that traffic jam on the M6 listening to the breaking news that Moyes was about to get the push from his six year contract at Old Trafford. Man U were refusing to comment, but some very experienced journalists were convinced their information was right and by Tuesday morning he'd gone; about £36 million better off for his ten month stint... The best joke I saw doing the rounds was: "David Moyes will not be out of work very long after receiving an approach from Sky TV...he's due to install his first dish on Monday."

I watched McDermott's post Forest interviews with dismay as he trotted out all the old comments about there being nothing in the game apart from two defensive lapses and how the game had been like so many since Christmas. Every second sentence was about how, "There was a lot of work to do in the summer". Most Leeds fans had decided they didn't want him doing any work over the summer, at least not for Leeds anyway. Whether Massimo Cellino wanted him was still unclear. Planned meetings between Cellino and McDermott to discuss the way forward were postponed this week with McDermott claiming he'd had no contact with the Italian. Cellino was back in the UK having flown in from Miami this week and the meetings with BM were now thought likely to take place between the Birmingham and Derby games. But another Italian, Benito Carbone, the ex-Bradford City striker, was seen at Thorp Arch on the Thursday and Friday prior to the Birmingham game. An article in the YEP suggested Cellino was lining him up to run the Leeds United academy.[1] Quite where that would leave Neil Redfearn was unclear but the YEP mischievously added:

[1] *http://www.yorkshireeveningpost.co.uk/sport/leeds-united/latest-whites-news/leeds-united-cellino-looks-set-to-hand-carbone-academy-role-1-6581643*

"Cellino is thought to hold a high opinion of the 48-year-old [Redfearn]". I wondered if Cellino was going to shuffle McDermott, Gibbs and Redfearn around a bit as another YEP article suggested that Cellino might not wish to part with the cash that would be required to pay off McDermott's contract.

That article[1], published earlier in the week, suggested that Cellino had been shocked at the scale of McDermott's salary and that he might not be keen to part with the estimated £1 million to pay off his remaining two years. The YEP also suggested that the expected major overhaul of the current playing staff would also be very costly. They estimated that at least 15 members of the current senior squad were earning £10,000 a week or more – that's more than half a million pounds a year – and the total wage bill was now over £20 million a year. The implication was that even a man of Cellino's wealth would have to consider the financial implications of his retained list very carefully.

McDermott also disclosed to the YEP that he'd been working on the next pre-season programme, albeit he said he didn't yet know where the games would take place. The YEP speculated that the main tour may well be held in Sardinia due to Cellino's connections there. I immediately started to hope that my own summer arrangements wouldn't prevent me doing Sardinia if that was indeed where they were going. I was already booked up for the Hungarian Grand Prix near Budapest for a week in July...

I took the train again for the Blues' game, a short hop from Stafford to Birmingham New Street. I was on the 10:03am Bristol Temple Meads train and predictably for a Saturday, there were plenty of football fans on it. There were several Crewe Alexandra fans going all the way to Bristol for their game against City while perhaps more surprisingly there were dozens of FC United of Manchester fans on their way to Barwell, in Leicester. FC, as their fans refer to them, would win 3 – 0 but it still left them one point shy of the Northern Premier League Champions, Chorley, and hence they now face a play-off semi-final against Ashton United on Tuesday.

[1] *http://www.yorkshireeveningpost.co.uk/sport/leeds-united/latest-whites-news/leeds-united-mac-hoping-cellino-will-stand-by-him-1-6574739*

If they were to win that and then beat either Worksop Town or Fylde on Saturday in the final they would be promoted to the Conference North where they would be in the same division as Worcester City!

I got off at Birmingham with all the FC fans who then had a twenty minute wait for their onward train to Leicester. We all wished each other well for the afternoon's games. I walked the one and a half miles or so to St Andrews and met Nigel outside the Cricketers Arms, just around the corner from the ground, in Little Green Lane. I've been to this pub on each of the last few visits to St Andrews and expected it to be open to both home and away fans as usual. But there was a problem. A notice pinned to each door proclaimed: "Home fans only". A quick tweet to the #lufc followers asked where else there was to drink in the area and the only response I got was from @LeedsMighty telling me: "its [sic] all home fans around ground today mate. Police say drink in city centre or beer in the ground". Terrific! There was nothing for it but to head back into the centre of Birmingham but it would take too long to walk back especially with Nigel in tow, so we hopped on a bus from Bordesley Circus, just at the bottom of the road.

The bus was one of those pay on entry affairs and when Nigel proffered his five pound note to the Caribbean driver he told us: "Ah dowen carreh noh change an dees buz mahn". Nigel suggested that surely he must have £1.40 he could let us have for our two £1.80 'Short Journey fares'. Caribbean Man repeated his opening gambit again but, putting the bus into gear and setting off, he added: "Do whad you wanna do mahn". So Nigel held onto his fiver and we sat down! We then understood why the driver really couldn't be arsed with us at the next stop, as he got out of the cab and off the bus to be replaced by another driver! He was obviously at the end of his shift. When the bus came to a stop at the top of Digbeth we spotted a likely looking pub called the Bull Ring Tavern and in we went. There was not a single Leeds fan in there. It's a decent enough inner city pub but the beer was lousy and there was an ominous stench in there; something on the scale midway between dog poo and body odour. We sat in a corner and I fired up Twitter again. By this time there was a tweet telling me that The Wellington in Bennetts Hill was "a great pub" that usually had 16 real ales on and another one from @royceylufc with a picture of 'The Shakespeare' although no location was given for that one. We were on the point of setting off to look for the Wellington when I decided to have a quick look at Facebook. I spotted a post on there by Mike from the Sussex Whites saying he and the Surrey Whites lads were all in the Cricketers! After confirming that they were indeed being served at the Cricketers, Nigel and I supped up and headed back to the bus stop!

It is a long story, but in essence the SAS (Surrey and Sussex) folk had seen my tweet and decided to check for themselves. Mike called in a favour from a contact he has from a previous visit to the Cricketers and a few phone calls eventually ensured a positive outcome in return for a guarantee of good behaviour by the Leeds contingent. By the time Nigel and I got back there at about 1:30pm, the party was in full swing! We stood in the sun outside the pub drinking and merry making and by the time we'd begun the short walk to the ground we had all said our farewells and wished each other a good summer. It felt very much like the end of a school year...

The stewarding and police presence at Birmingham this year was a bit heavy I thought. Nigel and I arrived just as a battalion of Roman Centurions piled off a nearby coach and we had to wait in line as each was frisked by the stewards under the watchful gaze of a secondary line of coppers in riot gear. Twice I sneaked through the first line only to be firmly asked to go back and be searched, by one of the police. Looking at the Centurion outfits, I couldn't really think of anywhere comfortable they could hide anything! After a quick paddle in the bogs, already doing a passable impression of a Roman bath that would certainly make the Centurions feel at home, Nigel and I went up the stairwell to the seats.

On reflection, I could understand the additional security today; Birmingham were in a spot of bother. A defeat to Leeds today, however unlikely that probably seemed to most Leeds fans would conceivably leave the Blues in the relegation places, depending on the other results today. They did have one game in hand over the rest, but that was against high flying Wigan, so there was no guarantee of any points from that game on Tuesday. Birmingham had not won a league game at St Andrews since October 1st last year and had only won two at home all season! Hence the natives could be a bit restless if we managed to steal three points from them today. There was also the small matter of that 4 – 0 thrashing we gave them up at Elland Road last October, probably our best performance of the season. There were not many familiar names in Lee Clark's side today, although our nemesis of days gone by, Nikola Zigic, was named to start. For Leeds, McDermott made two changes from the side that so weakly gave up the ghost against Forest; Danny Pugh returned at the back in place of the injured Stephen Warnock and Matt Smith was preferred to the 'H' word.

I guess we were all hoping for a fast entertaining game to complete our away programme for the season; hoping but not expecting. The football we've seen this season, both at home and away, has for the most part been abysmal. Abysmal in terms of its entertainment value and abysmal in terms of the paucity of skills we've seen on the pitch. The first half today was no different. In fact, in many respects it was up there with the worst. Almost three thousand Leeds fans were still having a good time mind you; we were singing our hearts out throughout but there were few moments to get the pulse even ticking over let alone racing. Birmingham had one decent chance when Tom Adeyemi ran through the Leeds defence unchallenged, but his shot did more damage to a couple of Leeds fans high up behind the visitors' goal than it did to the net. It was the signal for the Leeds fans to sing, "That's why you're going down" but there was real relief apparent too. Apart from that, the only moments that stick in my mind were when yet another yellow smoke canister was let off in the Leeds end and then when one lad began waving a six foot banana in the air. If we were all searched so thoroughly on entry today, where the hell do our lads conceal these things? Oh, and somehow the Leeds fans purloined a length of that black netting stuff that's used to cover areas of seating not in use. It stretched from the front of the stand to the back and we passed it back and forth over our heads along the full length of the Gil Merrick Stand like a very long dead snake!

The second half began with little more creativity or urgency than the first and I began to rue having bet on nil-nil for the Forest game and not this one. Even the official Leeds United website would report after the game; "The start to the second half was something of a slow burner." After 57 minutes McDermott made his first change, bringing on Alex Mowatt for Luke Murphy. Within a minute of arriving on the pitch Mowatt made his mark.

Mowatt got the ball down and sprayed a lovely ball wide to Michael Tonge, out on the Leeds left flank. Tonge wasted no time in whipping the ball across and there was big Matt Smith to nod the ball into the corner of the net. That was a special moment and Matt Smith milked the applause for all it was worth. We were still celebrating the first goal when Tom Lees stood over a free kick just inside the Birmingham half. He lofted that now familiar long diagonal ball to the edge of the Blues' area where Matt Smith out-jumped everyone to head it across goal. McCormack tried to get on the end of it but the ball broke away from him to the left corner of the six-yard box where Danny Pugh was steaming in to whack it low into the far corner of the net with his left foot almost taking McCormack's right boot with it! 2 – 0 up and half an hour to go in the sunshine! This was a great way to end our travels for the season – it was almost as if the footballing gods were just making sure we'd come back for more next season!

For a while Birmingham looked totally dispirited. Leeds on the other hand were enjoying themselves out there spraying the ball about like it was a training game. As each pass found a colleague a shout of "Olé" went up from the Leeds fans and often we managed to string 20 or more passes together. In the 78th minute we could hardly believe it as we got yet another goal. This time Michael Tonge pushed the ball through the hapless Blues' defence to find McCormack. Ross took the ball on a couple of yards before rolling a really soft pass across the edge of the six-yard box looking for Matt Smith. Paul Caddis stuck a foot out to try to beat Smith to it and the ball slid past Darren Randolph into his own net. The Leeds players looked suitably sympathetic for their hosts and hardly celebrated this one, while in the stands we all thought it must be Christmas! It is a long time since we were actually handed a goal in that manner whereas I could reel you off a number of examples where our players have made similar gifts this season.

The Blue Noses were streaming out of the ground by this time to the sound of Leeds fans chanting, "You're going down with the Barnsley" as news filtered through that Barnsley were drawing at Middlesbrough where only a win would give them any chance of avoiding the drop to League One.

Immediately after our third goal went in McDermott sent on the 'H' word to replace Matt Smith – I guess he was hoping Birmingham would now totally collapse and maybe gift a much needed goal to the 'H' word to boost his confidence. It didn't work though and in fact the next act was a piece of sloppy defending by Leeds to let Federico Macheda in between Lees and Austin at the back post from where he rifled the ball past Butland. Tom adopted the 'arse on the turf' position just to make sure we didn't get too carried away.

As the final whistle went at St Andrews, mobile phones beeped all over the place to signal that Barnsley had conceded two late goals up at the Riverside to confirm there would be no trip for us to Oakwell next season. Once again we sang, "You're going down with the Barnsley", to the few remaining Blue Noses. Yeovil had bitten the dust today too.

This had been a very satisfying 3 – 1 victory near the end of a long season; we should not forget though that a) Birmingham are a very poor side who will probably be "going down with the Barnsley" and b) despite winning three of our last four games we are also not a very good side. I hoped the powers that be at Elland Road wouldn't suddenly be thinking we had the basis of a decent side with this particular group of players. In that respect I wasn't absolutely enthralled by Brian McDermott's post-match comments which included: "The future is looking brighter as we have won three of our last four games", and, "We are now as safe as houses in this league and looking to do well next season." He also refused to be drawn on whether he would even be at the club next season. That was in the hands of our new favourite Italian.

Just a few of the gang at the Cricketers in Small Heath

One of very few pleasing sights we saw this season

Nightmare

It was not surprising that Cellino preferred to fly to Sardinia at the end of last week to watch Cagliari play Parma in a crucial Serie A game rather than be at St Andrews for the Leeds game. Cagliari would this weekend confirm their survival in Serie A for another season and in any case I fully understand that a few days in Sardinia marginally has the edge over a day in Small Heath...

On Monday 28th April, the Monday following the Birmingham game, the YEP published an article that seemed to suggest that maybe Cellino was now having second or even third thoughts about sacking McDermott. The Italian was reported to have said that the issue of Leeds United manager was the last thing on his mind at present with lots of other more pressing issues to sort out. He also denied having spoken to any other coaches. In fact, there was a tone about Cellino's words that suggested that maybe all was not yet lost for McDermott as the Italian agreed that his manager had been working in impossible conditions for most of his tenure at the club.

"Brian's a good man but they (GFH) took his soul and he's unhappy," Cellino said. "He had a dream, he had promises but then he came here and found a f****** nightmare. Because of that, I don't think he's been able to be himself. He's been someone else. He started on the wrong foot, he was told a lot of bulls**t and the best coach in the world wouldn't have done better. That is true. He was a good coach at Reading and maybe he can be a good coach here. But he isn't a manager."[1]

There was no further mention of Benito Carbone although Cellino said over the weekend that he [Carbone] would be working "for free" with the Academy to try to get more value out of it for the club; thus implying he was not convinced about all the good press that Redfearn and his troops were getting for what has often been said to be one of the best academy facilities in the country.

---

[1] http://www.yorkshireeveningpost.co.uk/sport/leeds-united/latest-whites-news/leeds-united-cellino-offers-mcdermott-new-hope-1-6583030

And so we arrived at the final game of this almost unbelievable season. A home game with Derby County that, nine months ago, we all thought might see us celebrating a return to the Premiership, or at the very least confirming a play-off place. It was not to be. Mrs W and I drove up to Leeds with no great expectations of any fireworks at this game and almost saw it as merely a bit of a pit-stop as we headed for the in-laws in Edinburgh after the game. It was there of course last June that this story really began, as I first scanned the fixture list for this 2013/2014 season.

It was typical final day weather, with a clear blue sky and bright sunshine, albeit still chilly when out of the direct sun. I had a feeling it was a mistake to leave home without the sun cream or hats though as I guessed the sun would be right in our faces for the whole game since it was a 12:15pm kick-off, as were all the final day Championship games. There were still two issues to be resolved today; who would grab the final play-off spot between Brighton and Reading? And who would join Barnsley and Yeovil in the final relegation spot? That could be any one of Millwall, Doncaster, or most likely the current incumbents, Birmingham City. Our game had nothing riding on it other than that amorphous, untouchable thing, 'pride in the shirt', and with an expectation that many of the Leeds players wouldn't be seen again, at least not in a Leeds shirt, I wondered if the game would be a quiet end of season bore. Derby were already assured of 3rd place and hence they may well be saving themselves for their play-off semi-final against either Brighton or Reading. Wigan and QPR already knew they would contest the other semi while Leicester and Burnley had long since secured automatic promotion.

The cheery face of the regular car park attendant greeted us at 9:55am and he wished us a good summer break as he stuffed my final six quid of the season into his as yet relatively empty money-bag; surprisingly he'd not had many customers so far today even though kick-off was now only a couple of hours away. Liz and Bogdan met us at the car and the four of us walked down to the Pavilion. I touched my fist against the Don's as we went past the great man's statue, thus restarting a superstition I'd abandoned for the Forest game. It hadn't worked then, so I thought I'd revert to my previous MO!

All the usual gang were in the Pavilion and at various times I bumped into Andy J, 'Welsh' Andy, Southampton Paul, The Durham Three (I must find out their names next season!), Hampshire White lady and husband (ditto on the name front!), Alan and John, Pete, John and Martin, Martin and the boys, Andrew B, uncle Tom Cobley and all. Most people I spoke to today began with the phrase, "I'm glad this season is over", or something similar in our conversation. In particular it has been the sheer lack of quality on the pitch that has worn everybody down. No one thought today would be any different and this was just a game to get over with. A few folk were looking forward to the annual Player of the Year Awards taking place this evening in the Pavilion. The main award was not of any great interest as we all knew it would be on Ross McCormack's mantle-piece come tomorrow, but those who were going were looking forward to seeing Massimo Cellino who was promised to be there doing his first public appearance in front of Leeds fans. He was also going to be 'jamming' with the Leeds band 'The Pigeon Detectives' who were booked to do a session during the evening. As everyone says, we're unlikely to get bored with Massimo!

There were no surprises when the team was announced in the Pavilion; it was exactly the same side that won so comfortably at St Andrews last Saturday vis. **Butland, Wootton, Lees, Pearce, Pugh, Murphy, Austin, Brown, Tonge, Smith and McCormack.** There were however a few less well-known names on the subs bench where Cairns, Poleon, White and Noel 'H' word were joined by Zac Thompson, Lewis Walters and Chris Dawson. Once again I couldn't see any of the latter three getting any game time unless we happened to be two-up with twenty minutes to go which I considered about as likely as Massimo Cellino being tongue-tied at the Awards do later tonight. Incidentally, Mrs W and I were not going to the Awards ceremony; I have always said I will do it the year we get promoted and not before.

I said my final farewells to those still in the Pavilion and Mrs W and I wended our way across to the stadium, once again I was conscious that I wouldn't be making this short walk for the next couple of months; it was that end of school year feeling again.

Mike, Lynn and Jo were already in their usual seats in the row behind us and Max worked his way along that row just before the game started. The girls from Leeds Uni were apparently all here again but only a couple of them were in our section as it was pretty much sold out and they couldn't get enough seats together today. I looked around the stadium and it did look pretty full in all areas apart from the East Stand Upper. The official attendance would be announced later as 29,724; a pretty good effort I thought considering there was nothing to play for and with the weather more suited to sunbathing in the back garden than Championship footie. Already the sun was burning our noses.

The players lined up around the centre circle for the traditional end of season tribute to all those connected with the club who'd lost their lives this season. The announcer also spoke of the tragic death of Ann Maguire, a Leeds school-teacher stabbed to death by one of her own pupils in class on Monday. It was usual for the end of season tribute to be a minute's applause but in recognition of the awfulness of that crime it had been changed this year to a minute's silence. On the referee's whistle, Elland Road fell silent and remained so until he blew again, one minute later. The Derby fans were also magnificent in their observance of the tribute. When that second whistle went, a huge roar rose from all sections as the game kicked-off.

The opening minutes of the game suggested that Derby would run away with an easy victory as they whipped the ball out to their left wing and swamped Wootton and Austin with pace and guile. After just seconds, or so it seemed to me, the figure of Craig Forsyth ran unchallenged through the sieve that purports to be our defence and rasped a shot that Butland did well to swat away. I looked towards the directors' box in the East Stand to see if I could catch a glimpse of Cellino to see what his reaction was to this early onslaught. I was in the process of taking a photo of the section I thought the Italian would be in when suddenly a great roar rose from the hordes of Derby fans over in the West Stand while all around me the air was blue with profanities. Derby had taken the lead.

I eventually got to see the goal online up in Edinburgh on Sunday morning. It was another shocker. Derby had a free kick midway in their own half and they just rolled it forward. They then bamboozled us with six sharp passes before the ball was clipped towards the back post where Jeff Hendrick was lurking. For some reason known only to himself, Luke Murphy was the marker in there, stood with his right arm held aloft appealing that Hendrick was offside; either that or Murphy was in urgent need of the little boys room. Hendrick swung a foot at the ball and Butland saved well from point blank range but Simon Dawkins was also on hand to scuff the ball back towards goal. It rolled ever so slowly over the line just as Tom Lees slid in to challenge and inevitably Tom would end up sat on his arse in front of goal. After the initial annoyance of giving away a soft goal yet again, the Leeds fans pretty much just got on with enjoying a day out in the sunshine. By this time I was pretending to shield the sun from my eyes with first one hand and then the other ... I was really trying to shade my nose to try to ensure I didn't arrive in Edinburgh looking like Cocco the Clown. I could see Mrs W subtly doing the same whilst peeling off layer after layer of clothes. I was getting nervous and was hoping she had a good handle on exactly how many layers she'd started with! Boy was that sun burning down on us though.

Whether it was Derby sitting back or whether Leeds finally found a missing gear I'm not sure, but gradually Leeds worked their way into the game. Our play mostly revolved around big Matt Smith winning balls in the air and then knocking them down for McCormack but everyone was doing their bit. Even Michael Brown was having a storming game despite young Will Hughes snapping at his heels every couple of minutes. Brown lashed in a long range shot that Lee Grant did well to stop. When the whistle blew for half time, it was applause that the Leeds players could hear and not boos for a change. This was a spirited performance against a very good Derby side that had now scored 84 goals in the Championship this season, the best total of any side. The question was whether we could find a way through their defence? Ross McCormack would continue to try his best as he was desperate to achieve the landmark of 30 goals in a season – something only achieved very rarely before at Leeds.

Leeds came out for the second half in positive mood and continued to take the game to Derby. Aidy White was introduced by McDermott to add some additional pace to the right wing with Luke Murphy being withdrawn. The pace of White caused Derby problems although as we've seen so often his use of the ball once he arrived in or near the opposition goal was often left wanting. In the 50th minute though, Leeds fashioned another of those rare things; a goal of beauty at Elland Road.

Jason Pearce intercepted a Derby pass just outside his own area and immediately pushed the ball short to Danny Pugh. Pugh set off at full speed and made good progress before launching the ball down the inside left channel to Ross McCormack. Ross delicately lifted the ball over a lunging challenge and then spotted Matt Smith running diagonally into the Derby area. It was confirmation that these two are now very much on the same wavelength that Smith knew exactly where Ross was going to roll the ball and as McCormack's pass was slotted inside two defenders, Smith was onto it in a flash; he took one touch and then nonchalantly clipped it left-footed over the diving Lee Grant. It was a superb goal and it also proved once and for all that Matt Smith has much more to his game than just a towering presence in the area.

With a bit more luck Leeds might have grabbed a deserved winner and McCormack might have got that 30th goal. He missed one glorious opportunity when he headed the ball straight at Grant instead of finding the corner of the net and it may well have been a case of Ross trying just too hard. But no matter, this was a pretty good performance from Leeds; too little too late of course in the context of the whole season but a worthy performance for the final game none the less.

At the final whistle, Ross once again threw his shirt into the crowd while Jack Butland went a bit further; he removed his gloves, shirt, under-shirt and then even his shorts, all of which were thrown into the Kop to huge cheers from the fans. I would reflect later that at least our final game was not pants like most of the rest have been even though we got see Butland's! We all waited while the players briefly left the pitch before returning to do their traditional lap of honour. Several had their children with them as is the custom these days. Brian McDermott and Nigel Gibbs led them around all four sides of Elland Road and as they arrived in front of the Kop that chant of, "Ooooh, Brian McDermott", could be heard coming from the back of the stand. It was being sung more as a 'thank you for trying' though than any kind of ringing endorsement of his first season in charge of the team. It remains to be seen whether he will get a second chance.

The other Championship results went up on the big screen and there were a few gasps when we eventually computed that with Birmingham getting a late, late equaliser at Bolton and Doncaster suffering a 1 – 0 defeat at Leicester, it was the Yorkshire outfit who slipped into that final relegation spot and hence out of the Championship. At the other end of the table, Brighton nicked the final play-off spot. As Mrs W and I made our way up the M1 and A1 to Scotland, we listened as Sunderland pulled off another amazing victory, this time at Old Trafford. It looked as if it would condemn Norwich City to life in the Championship next season along with Fulham and Cardiff, both of whom were now definitely relegated. It was Connor Wickham who supplied the cross from which Sunderland scored and he'd been the stand-out performer as the Black Cats had also grabbed a draw at The Etihad and wins at Stamford Bridge and at home against Cardiff in recent weeks. Wickham scored five goals in those games fully justifying Gus Poyet's decision to recall him from Leeds; he may well have been the single reason Sunderland were staying up and why I would not be going to the Stadium of Light next year!

*****

A car door slammed shut somewhere in the road outside our bedroom window and I awoke with a start. I had another one of those momentary panics as I tried to work out where I was.

As my eyes slowly cleared I could make out the outlines of furniture and the shapes of pictures on the wall. I was confused; nothing looked familiar. I'd been dreaming, or having a nightmare actually. I'd been dreaming about Leeds United; a complete season had flashed by. I'd dreamt I was in this same room in Edinburgh, lying in bed checking out the fixtures for the forthcoming season; I'd been to Stevenage for a pre-season game in which our defence was given the run around and then I'd seen more of the same as we were soundly beaten at Elland Road by an efficient German Bundesliga side. I'd dreamt about Luke Murphy scoring the winner in our first home game of the season in front of a manic Elland Road crowd and then we'd scraped through a few games by the skin of our teeth and we'd somehow got ourselves a top six spot by Christmas. I had one of those vertigo moments as I thought I was falling, falling, falling down hundreds of steep steps while seeing the lights of some far distant city...I was high up above the pitch at Newcastle. On the pitch below I could barely make out the Leeds players, they were all bent double with huge fridges strapped to their backs slowing them down while a flock of giant magpies flew past them knocking balls into our net. I dreamt we grabbed a late equaliser at the City Ground but then realised we hadn't, the game hadn't finished, the ball flashed into our net with our players all arguing with each other rather than concentrating on the player with the ball. The dream turned darker as we went to a lower league ground and seemed unable to move, unable to play, while a League Two side looking and playing like Barcelona completely destroyed us, knocking us out of the Cup. Our own fans turned on the players and hurled abuse at them – it was like being locked in a Technicolor horror movie. Hillsborough was in the news; horrible things had happened there in the past and the police were all on trial for hiding evidence and the Government was calling for another enquiry and now somehow Leeds were involved. We were playing there, at Hillsborough, and once again our players seemed to freeze on the spot; all except the usually majestic Marius Zaliukas who was running around the pitch like a six year old chasing after a huge beach ball. Sheffield Wednesday's players kept hammering the ball into our net and a huge scoreboard kept ticking over with goal after goal. Brian McDermott was urging his two new wingers to get in the game but they were both wandering around picking up daisies, making little chains. Our fans were streaming away from the ground not long after half time, tears in their eyes.

On and on we went, losing match after match and after every game our manager went on and on about having "good conversations" with his players and with one set of owners after another. It seemed all sorts of folk were turning up at Elland Road with huge suitcases full of money...only each time the cases were opened they were empty and each time anyone tried to sign the sale documents they'd burst into flames. An Italian corn farmer appeared from nowhere to offer a huge sum of money, vastly more than the club was actually worth, and our Arab owners met him on a huge rigged yacht to agree another deal. A beautiful girl was leaning on the rails of the sun deck taking 'selfie' photos on her Leeds United mobile. But no sooner had they agreed the deal than the bailiffs arrived, commandeering the yacht and demanding hundreds of thousands of euros in unpaid tax and threatening the owner with jail, saying the Italian rock star was sailing the boat illegally. At the same time Leeds were turning out for games with no shirts on their backs; the shirt sponsor was taking the club to court demanding all his money back. Still Leeds were losing game after game and then the manager was sacked and the very next game Leeds thrashed their local rivals 5 – 1 in an amazing second half in which everything Leeds tried came off. Then we found ourselves on the flooded plains of Somerset and somehow the same manager was back in the dug-out. An almighty storm got up and although Leeds weren't playing very well the wind caused the home side to blast a penalty way over the bar; it flew and flew, being blown completely out of the ground while thousands of our fans were swimming in the stand behind the goal. In the second half the incredible wind carried the ball into the home goal twice to give Leeds another unlikely win. Still the manager was having "good conversations" with his players and with the Italian who was now saying he never meant to sack him, it was all a mistake. But without the wind we began to lose games again;

even at Elland Road we were thrashed week after week. It started to look as though we'd be relegated and then the Football League refused to allow our Italian saviour to take possession of the club even though he'd already paid for it. He was now paying for everything out of his own pocket; he was paying tax bills and the players' wages, he was even laying a new Astroturf pitch himself at Thorp Arch and then he was holding rock concerts there in which he was playing guitar in one of the bands. Out of a haze of yellow smoke came the Leeds United team bus and it was the Italian who was driving; a manic figure hunched over the steering wheel shouting: "Move out of the f****** way!"

Someone then went through all the paperwork from Italy and decided that the Football League was corrupt and was not entitled to prevent the Italian from owning the club. The manager said he'd had another "good conversation" with the Italian and now all would be OK. The Italian insisted the manager ditch his usual business suit and instead wear a pink onesie in the dug-out for the next game. Coincidentally the next few games were all against teams from near the foot of the table and we managed to win some of them. We were not going down after all. There was a small dot of light shining at the far end of a long dark tunnel…it was growing larger and brighter…it was blinding me.

*****

Another car door banged shut in the road and I was suddenly wide awake again. Wow! Was that a dream, a nightmare even? I was sweating and breathless. My head slowly cleared. I was still in that same bedroom in the in-laws home in Edinburgh. I could hear Mrs W in the bathroom next door. I raised my head from the pillow and listened and could make out she was singing to herself. She was singing: "Cellino-oh-oh, Cellino-oh-oh, he comes from Italy, he pays no VAT, Cellino-oh, Cellino-oh-oh…" It all came flooding back to me. I hadn't dreamt any of it; I was merely reliving the fiasco of the season we'd just endured.

*****

Lightning Source UK Ltd.
Milton Keynes UK
UKOW04f2231160914

238711UK00016B/332/P

9 781849 144636